AFTER IRELAND

AFTER IRELAND

Writing the Nation from Beckett to the Present

DECLAN KIBERD

Harvard University Press   *Cambridge, Massachusetts 2018*

The moral right of Declan Kiberd to be identified as the author
of this work has been asserted in accordance with the
Copyright, Designs and Patents Act of 1988.

First published in the United Kingdom in 2017 by
Head of Zeus Ltd
First Floor East
5–8 Hardwick Street
London ECIR 3RG

First Harvard University Press edition, 2018
First printing

Typeset by Adrian McLaughlin

Library of Congress Cataloging-in-Publication data is available
from the Library of Congress

ISBN 978-0-674-97656-6 (cloth : alk. paper)

I ndil-chuimhne ar mo mháthair Eithne 1915–2010

Contents

Preface

*A*fter Ireland is the third volume of a trilogy that began with *Inventing Ireland* and continued with *Irish Classics*. *Inventing Ireland* had as its main focus the authors of the Irish Revival 1885–1940 (with some treatment of appropriate texts from the postlude). *Irish Classics* dealt with classic authors who wrote in both the Irish and English languages from the crisis of Gaelic Ireland in 1600, through the eighteenth and nineteenth centuries, down to the period of high modernism. *After Ireland* begins with a reading of a work from the mid-century, Beckett's *Waiting for Godot*, and brings the story up to the present moment.

It has a central contention: that the birth of the new state signalled the slow end of the national project and that this decline (always a worry, especially to writers of northern background) became conclusive in the years following the economic crash of 2008. The available forms of the state proved unable to contain or embody the very idealistic ambitions of the nation. Yet, as political hopes of sovereignty were annulled, culture became in many ways more important than ever, as a means of alerting people to the crisis and of embodying the unstilled longing for expressive freedom.

The gradual expiry of the national project has been chronicled in a range of powerful works, which address major questions: the fortunes of the native language and of religious institutions, the conflict in the north, secularization and women's rights, political and economic sovereignty. There are many fine writers who explore these themes, but I have chosen to focus on certain texts in which the issues are centrally raised. Many other works by writers treated here and by other major authors could have been included, but I hope to return to these on another occasion. Over the past two decades, students have taught me to read and re-read texts as an 'early warning system' concerning problems which became obvious in journalism of more recent times, but also as a sort of elegy for the invented Ireland of the Revivalists and Classicists.

The intention was not to rebut or withdraw the theses of the two earlier volumes, but to sharpen their analysis of culture as the site and stake of the search for expressive freedom. The national project has gone through many moments of despondency and near-death experiences, as was shown in *Irish Classics* – the Flight of the Earls in 1607, the defeat at Aughrim in 1691, the Union with Britain in 1801, the Great Hunger of the 1840s and the waves of emigration thereafter – but in the past it has always survived in new modes of self-assertion. The inventors of Revival Ireland confronted similar fears that it would disappear, under the blandishments of parliament at Westminster or in the trenches of the Somme or in the fires of civil war: yet somehow, on each occasion, a phoenix arose from the ashes.

Since independence, there have been various crises of the Free State and Republic – censorship of intellectuals, economic stagnation, further emigration and an apparent reluctance to marry among many who remained. This is not to mention the very different existential crises triggered by the Second World War, by the Troubles in the North, and by the widespread fear at the end of the century that 'the most globalized country in Europe' had lost its identity. None of the writers considered here has ever announced the final failure of the national project, but many have believed that (to borrow a phrase of Salman Rushdie) their country had been insufficiently imagined. Their writings have been often inspired by their critique of these derelictions and by their impatience with many forms of traditional nationalism. Like the texts produced by Revivalists, their work offered not only a strict diagnosis but also vital hints of a way forward. In its more familiar guises the national project might be ebbing: but the account of an ending (as was shown in *Irish Classics*) always contains within itself the narrative of a new dispensation. Emergency is not an ignoble condition: it may even be the state of mind in which every postcolonial people has to live.

I am grateful to many students and colleagues who led me through the discussions that follow, whether at University College Dublin or at the University of Notre Dame, at Sorbonne 3 or at Cambridge University: P. J. Mathews, Derek Hand, Noreen Doody, Jarlath Killeen, Wanda Balzano, Zeljka Doljanin, Stanley van der Ziel, Graham Price, Jana Fischerova, Jeff Holdridge, Malcolm Sen, Katherine O'Callaghan, Enrico Terrinoni, Chiara Lucarelli, Diana Perez Garcia, Heather Laird, Ron Callan, Brendan Kennelly, John Kerrigan, Paddy Ward, Brian Donnelly, Tony Roche, Frank McGuinness, Christopher Fox, Kevin Whelan, Barry McCrea, Jill Wharton, Dan Murphy, Guinn Batten, Oonagh Young, Christine Breen, Alan Graham, Aoife Lynch, Catherine Wilsdon, Andrea Binelli, Carle Bonafous-Murat, Fergal Casey, Bríona NicDhiarmada, Diarmuid Ó Giolláin, Mary O'Callaghan, Sarah McKibben, Brian Ó Conchubhair, Niall McArdle, Nathaniel Myers, Ailbhe Darcy, Kara Donnelly, Lindsay Haney, Ray Ryan, Rónán McDonald, David Clare, Nelson Ó Ceallaigh Ritschel, Fearghal Whelan, and John Sitter. I owe major debts to my translators Futoshi Sakauchi and Gerardo Gambolini for wonderful discussion and comradeship. My dead friends Edward Said, John McGahern and Brian Friel gave many kinds of guidance as well as inspiration.

I must thank Seán Ó Mórdha, Vivien Igoe, Edna O'Brien, Joseph O'Connor, Robert Ballagh, Richard Kearney, Lucy McDiarmid, Bernadette Comerford, Stephen Rea, Fiach Mac Conghail, Aideen Howard, Aedín Clements, Lyn Grimes, Alan Tongue, Barry McGovern, Theo Dorgan, Paula Meehan, Eiléan Ní Chuilleanáin, Harry Clifton, Gary Murphy, Gabriel Fitzmaurice and Dillon Johnston for the privilege of working with them on many projects. I am grateful to Kevin Whelan for welcoming me to O'Connell House and for making it a centre of friendship and scholarly endeavour.

This is not the first occasion on which I thank Máire Doyle for immense assistance, both scholarly and technical, in the production of a text. The kindness of Lisa Caulfield and her colleagues at University of Notre Dame has been unfailing. To Neil Belton, Ellen Parnavelas and Clémence Jacquinet at Head of Zeus, to Stephen Gilbert, and to Lindsay Waters and Joy Deng at Harvard University Press goes my appreciation for their work in taking on and much improving this text, as they did with its predecessors. My debt to Neil goes back many decades: without his encouragement and kindness, I would not have written this trilogy. Years of friendship, great fun and wise counsel mean that I should, once again, thank President Michael D. Higgins and his wife, Sabina; they will disagree with much of what follows but understand, I trust, why it is necessary to say it: 'pessimism of the intellect, optimism of the will'. I am deeply grateful to my brother Damian Kiberd for his illuminating commentaries on the Irish economy; and to my sister Marguerite Lynch for her analyses of many of the themes covered in these pages.

Most of the following chapters were written at the Tyrone Guthrie Centre in Annaghmakerrig. Its director, Robbie McDonald, and its wonderful staff have created a house conducive to creation but also to good fellowship and laughter. The late literary editor of the *Irish Times*, Caroline Walsh, kindly published my essay titled 'After Ireland' in August 2009, in the course of which many of the following arguments were rehearsed. Her death has been a great loss not only to her loving family and friends but to all literary workers in Ireland.

My wife, Beth, has been, as ever, the subtlest of all interlocutors on the matter of Ireland (and much else too). My children, Lucy, Amy and Rory, have at times rebuked me for lamenting lost worlds but they have also shown me that nothing is ever completely gone – everything is merely translated into some new form. In their lives, as in the work of the authors treated here, I have found the basis of a strange kind of hope. The lyric phase of nation-building, in which their ancestors participated so nobly, is surely over; but in the capacity of young people to offer a vision of an alternative future lies the hope of a renewed community. I have dedicated the book to the memory of their grandmother Eithne. When *Inventing Ireland* was published, she objected strenuously to the title, insisting that 'Ireland was always there'. What she might have to say about the current title can be easily imagined. But I cannot help noticing that the years of her life coincided almost exactly with the existence of a sovereign and independent nation.

DECLAN KIBERD
Clontarf, Dublin
April 2017

'. . . life has been preserved here, but at a price that is more costly than the value of life itself, because the strength for defence and survival has been borrowed from future generations, who are born in debt and weighed down by it. In that struggle what has survived is the bare instinct for survival, while life itself has lost so much that little more than its name is left. What remains standing and endures is mutilated or distorted, and what is born and comes into being is poisoned and embittered at conception. The thoughts and words of the people are never completed, because they have been cut off at their roots. . .'

IVO ANDRIĆ

We all die for Ireland in the end, whether sooner or later. I'll die myself for Ireland one of the days.

PAULA MEEHAN

1. Introduction:
After Ireland?

In 1997, it was reported that the gross domestic product in the Republic of Ireland had surpassed that of Britain. There was no rejoicing in the streets at this news, and little comment on the airwaves; the people were too busy making money and buying or selling houses.

Ten years later, the phenomenon known as the 'Celtic Tiger' was dead. After a building boom in which government had granted permission for 180,000 units, of which 100,000 remained unoccupied, the country was bankrupt. With loans from overseas banks, the Irish had merrily bought and sold real estate from and to one another.[1] Money and people had flowed into the country for a decade. As the ratio of dependents to earners dropped to an all-time low, the place had boomed: average house prices had risen in Dublin by up to 500% in the previous decade, with more than one in five workers involved in construction. Then the bubble burst. Shares in one major bank fell by a half in a single session. Under pressure from overseas financiers, the minister for finance guaranteed the bondholders and the debts incurred by a small number of Irish bankers were passed on to the people. A bondholder in New York who had failed to get his bank to buy back his bonds at 50% woke up on 30 September 2008 to the amazing news that they were again worth 100%. 'And', in the words of Michael Lewis, 'the promise sank Ireland'.[2] Future generations would have to pay off the monies owing. Young people headed for the exit ports, shaking their heads in disbelief.

The narrative of the nation had come to a juddering halt, but on this occasion the challenge to it did not come from Britain. In fact, the parliament at Westminster voted €6 billion in aid to their stricken neighbours. This immiseration of the Irish was negotiated by German and French financiers, urged on by Timothy Geithner of the United States. The debts run up by Irish financial houses were based on loans which had been given by foreign bankers themselves. The more general attempt by the leaders of the European Union to 'save the Euro' was jeopardizing the very European project itself, as Portugal, Italy, Greece and Spain were plunged into a period of austerity. In 1916, leaders of an Irish insurrection had looked to 'gallant allies in Europe'[3] for support and solace; but the new masters of Europe in Frankfurt, Paris and Brussels turned out to be strange friends indeed.

There had always been uncertainty as to how much sovereignty a small nation could enjoy in a globalizing world. Even after political independence in 1922, Ireland remained highly dependent on the neighbouring island for markets and materials, and as a source of employment. Accession to the European Economic Community in 1973 had opened a new axis to great continental cities, but it called for a surrender of much of that sovereignty so hard-won in the years leading up to 1922. Ireland might wield an influence out of all proportion to its size at the ever-expanding councils of the European Union, but that power was inevitably curtailed. When a single market was created in 1987, Irish politicians were given about £6 billion to bring voters to accept the measure, but some acerbic commentators wondered what their leaders had surrendered that could possibly be worth so much.[4] The independence project had not generated the levels of wealth expected in 1922. Writing in the wake of the Single European Act, the agronomist Raymond Crotty demonstrated that one in every two persons born in the state since independence had been compelled to emigrate.[5]

For some years in the 1990s and early 2000s, these questions had been stilled. By 2008 it was clear that the youth of Ireland (and of other peripheral countries with little economic clout but rich cultural tradition) was being 'disappeared' by unelected bureaucrats. Up to 60,000 emigrated in the following year, as the deeper underlying pattern detected by Crotty re-emerged.

Most people were astounded by the immensity of the crash when it came. Apart from a few isolated economists, nobody had predicted it or seen any sign of its coming. In the years after 2008, commentators arraigned bankers for failure, politicians for stupidity, clergy for abusing children and foreigners for taking cynical advantage of them. They insisted, in their innocence, that nobody had alerted them to the dire underlying abuses. Nobody had warned them that their very country was in danger of disappearance.

But this was not so. In every decade after independence, writers and artists had given warnings about these things. Writers in particular had suggested, even during the birth-pangs of the Free State, that the country might have been stillborn.

During Easter Week 1916 a Dublin businessman named William Beckett brought his son Samuel up the Three Rock Mountain, from which vantage point they could view the city burning below. Being a quantity surveyor by trade, Bill Beckett rubbed his hands at the prospect of lucrative business opportunities when the bombed-out central parts of Dublin would come to be rebuilt. But the ten-year-old Sam was horrified by the sight.[6]

Perhaps the sensitive boy had intuited that the birth of a nation might also seal its doom. Years later the central protagonist of his novel *Murphy* (1938) – 'the ruins of the ruins of a broth of a boy'[7] – is identified at his post-mortem by a naevus on his buttock: his birthmark becomes in effect his deathmark. The most famous Irish writer at the time of the Rising, W. B. Yeats, had sensed this too: though moved by the bravery of the rebel forces, he feared that all the cultural work of the previous decades, in establishing a national theatre and reviving a dying language, might come to nothing. All across Europe, in the years of the First World War, militarism was undoing the hopes of a generation of modern artists – and so it was in Ireland. At the mercy of the immediate moment, Yeats could not see it as part of the renaissance he had led: rather he saw it as a brutal interruption of the cultural project.

This had been the catastrophist view taken by many writers at the outbreak of the war. Writing to Howard Sturgis on 5 August 1914, Henry James had lamented: 'to have to take it all now for what the treacherous years were all the while really making for and *meaning* is too tragic for words'.[8] Five days later, in a letter to Rhoda Broughton, James wrote that they both 'should have been spared this wreck of our belief that through the long years we had seen civilisation grown and the worst become impossible'.[9]

Implicit in such lamentation was a recognition that militarism may have been an effect of, as well as an interruption to, elements of the modernist project. Yeats would surmount his shock at the arbitrary, capricious nature of the Easter Rising, reconfiguring it as part of a wider narrative of the cultural revival it had seemed to undo:

Did that play of mine send out
Certain men the English shot?[10]

His complex poem about the event, 'Easter 1916', goes well beyond any facile celebration into a mode of elegy for doomed youth, rather like the poems that mourned a brave officer cadre dying for England as it went 'over the top' in the Great War. Even though it was written a matter of weeks after the execution of the rebel leaders,

Yeats's poem would become for many one of the earliest explanations of the felt mediocrity of the post-war world.

The worship of a lost generation of geniuses became a convenient way of escaping from the disappointments of the present, especially in a land where civil war soured any possible pleasures of independence. It was the bleakness rather than the exhilaration of freedom which struck most writers in the 1920s and 1930s. The lyric phase of nation building was over. Writers, who had felt themselves key inventors of Ireland, now found themselves among its first victims, as the limitless dreams of a nation took on the rather compromised form of an inherited, shop-soiled state. No writer is ever exactly like a country's official idea of itself, so it was likely that the militarists who assumed power in uncertain circumstances in 1922 would treat free-thinking artists with suspicion. The 'literary wing of the movement' had been useful (up to a point) in mapping out ideas of independence, but now was treated, more often than not, as a damned nuisance. The sheer energy expended in dislodging the British had left little for the reimagining of Ireland by the new elites.

In 1929, the government introduced a Censorship of Publications Act under whose aegis many of the masterpieces of global modernism and of Irish writing would be banned. Unlike the top-down censorship being introduced in Soviet Russia and other autocratic states, the Irish practice was bottom-up. Less political than religiose in character, it required a citizen to file a complaint that a book was indecent, obscene or supportive of unnatural methods of contraception.[11] The earnings of Irish writers had been precarious enough, given the small size of the reading public, but censorship deprived authors of even that curtailed livelihood. Even before the 1929 act, some revival intellectuals had sensed a closing down of possibilities. Stephen MacKenna, the Gaelic League activist and translator of Plotinus, had decamped to England; the English composer Arnold Bax (who had once written folk stories under the Irish pen-name of Dermot O'Byrne) went back to his own country.

Many more artists would leave. The 1929 legislation was crucial: it was as if the nation-state was intent on self-harm, even self-mutilation. It was cutting off one of the major supply lines which had made independence possible.

If every word was once a poem before being denatured by common use, then each sentence may also be a kind of epitaph on an emotion. In an analogous way, a nation state may be an elegy for a language, a secondary institutional formation designed to fill the void left by a lost language and by the structures of feeling which disappeared along with it. The terminal decline of Ireland had begun with the Act of Union in 1801 – the clearance of cottiers, already in train, served to dismantle a carnivalesque culture, one which had been filled with diverse voices and libertarian attitudes.[12] The Great Famine of 1845–9 was the lethal blow – more lethal than any previous shock – because it revealed Gaelic Ireland for the shell it was. A people who had lost their cultural coding had few values left in whose name to combat austerity and want. They had surrendered too much, as they would again and again – they had shown too great a talent for adjustment. They had placed their faith in one economic reality (the potato) and that monoculture had failed them. Never again would they show such a trust in natural forces; never again would they feel fully at home in natural surroundings. But they would afterwards place a similarly naive trust in other entities – in 1922 the nation state, later the Catholic Church, and later still house ownership.

Many of the subsequent cruelties in Irish life have ultimate roots in the Great Famine. The abuse of children, which most often has a cyclical quality (with abusers having been abused) could go right back, at least in part, to years of privation. It may also be traceable to an enforced sexual puritanism and an exaltation of celibacy, both of which were intensified by the shock of the Famine and the elaboration of a narrow, rule-bound form of religion, which seemed an early example of a 'utopia' of bureaucracy replacing the notion of an all-watching, all-caring godhead. The casual insults inflicted upon one another by a people trapped in a subsistence economy may also arise from an acute social frustration. The extraordinary linguistic resourcefulness shown by people keen to abuse one another in their newly acquired language may have roots in the shame of its very use:

That's the idea. Let's insult one another...[13]

The rapid language-shift must have left many people marooned in a no-man's-land between codes. They spoke words in English while thinking in the cadences and syntax of a receding Irish; and many people felt, for a painful period, articulate in neither. The loss of old ways was often imaged in the person of a dumb or stuttering child, and in a perhaps linked violence against children (not just for the economic burden which they represented but for visibly bearing the stigmata of a community's painful adjustment to the future). The experience was narrated by a ruined Gaelic poet, Aindrias Mac Marcais, as far back as the 1590s:

Gan gáire fá ghníomhra leinbh;
Cosc ar cheol, glas ar Ghaeilge.

Without laughter at the antics of a child;
Music banned, Irish censored.[14]

So the culture of control and interdiction practised after 1929 in the Free State had a rather ancient lineage. And the anxieties of a society unsure about whether it even had a viable future often discharged themselves through the figure of a confused, apologetic, furtive child. If your education teaches you not to see but to look away from your setting, then your surroundings will soon begin to seem unvital and unreal. The forgetting of geography – as in the case of Beckett's tramps – soon abets the forgetting of history:

Yesterday. In my opinion... I was here... yesterday (*WG* 67)

This uncertainty in relating to an environment arose from a tragedy of land holding: those who owned the land could never fully see it, and those who could see it were never the ones who owned it.

What had once been a notable weakness in landlords of the nineteenth century now began to characterize the behaviour of the new peasant proprietors: an obsession with land ownership rather than land use. The strong farmers who dominated in the Free State had learned even before independence to imitate the less admirable features of colonialist behaviour: walking their farmlands, they looked down on landless labourers, nomads and tinkers; they adopted a monoglot philosophy of language; they practised a lazy pastoralism rather than an intensive cultivation of the land; and they repressed instinctual life. The middle-class Catholic Church which eventually replaced the old vernacular religion was really the old landlordism in drag – the presbytery was the new big house, its priest the surrogate landlord and his rule akin to the traditional *droit de seigneur* (even including the sexual abuse of the young). The crude moralism (it was hardly a theology) developed by the priesthood in the nineteenth century and after was similar to the old repression, the remedy for the recalcitrant being a sound thrashing ('spare the rod and spoil the child'). So the triumph of institutional Catholicism was in fact another delayed and occluded victory for the process of anglicization. The 'young dandies' who graduated from the national seminar at Maynooth had been taught through English and that was the language a haughty priesthood generally employed, as a way of marking self-worth.

English culture thus made some of its greatest gains just as it prepared to give Ireland up – and this was paradoxical in the sense that it was happening against a backdrop in which major attempts were being made to revive Irish and restore Gaelic culture. But even the great literary feats of the Irish Revival in English, as pioneered by Yeats and others, may be seen in retrospect as a final, long-delayed triumph of the textuality brought by the Protestant Reformation to Ireland. Sir William Wilde had argued that the best way of combating superstitions was to write them down, and this was what the revivalists did. So deeply did the new Catholicism take on a number of the contours of the Reformation faith that William Wilde, father of Oscar, could remark with some satisfaction in the later nineteenth century that the tone of the country was becoming more Protestant with every passing year.[15]

Even as the Anglo-Irish lost much of their land in a succession of agrarian reforms, the hold of anglophone culture was tightening, as a narrow, rule-bound moralism took the place of vernacular Catholicism, which had already in many places submitted to a middle-class notion of 'respectable behaviour' in the decades before and after Emancipation in 1829. That moralism sought to regulate the conduct of people's relationships with one another, whereas the old religion had emphasized their relationships with fate, destiny and the divine. Some of the more artistic souls who had grown up in this rather Victorian scheme of public moralism finally rebelled against it. W. B. Yeats once complained of the novelist George Eliot: 'If she had more religion, she would have less morals. The moral impulse and the religious destroy each other in most cases.'[16] In Yeats's ideal church there would be an altar but no pulpit. Had he lived to witness the collapse of institutional Catholicism in Ireland of the later twentieth century, he would have seen in it a predictable end to rule-bound moralism – and the hope of returning to a more visionary kind of religion.

The fitful attempts to revive Irish after the foundation of the Gaelic League in 1893 sometimes reconnected people to a more rooted set of traditions. The yearning of women for romantic love and an end to economic match-making, which colours many of the *Love Songs of Connacht* (1894), made Douglas Hyde's collection a best-seller through the years of the Irish Revival; but its tones of longing can still be heard over six decades later in another best-seller (albeit one banned for some time), *The Country Girls* (1960), by Edna O'Brien. More often than not, however, revivalists of Irish simply poured a prim Victorian moralism into Gaelic vessels. A people who in the 1830s had thought in Irish while using English words had by the 1890s learned to think in English while using Irish words. The result was what Samuel Beckett would castigate in a devastating essay of 1934 as 'the altitudinous complacency of the "Victorian Gael"'.[17]

Told in this way, the story of modern Ireland can hardly register 1922 as the moment of liberation. Nationalism (at least in twenty-six counties) did triumph over empire, but only when it seemed safe for the imperial functionaries to quit. The colony had been so comprehensively penetrated that the new rulers could be trusted to employ all the old categories upon themselves. During the civil war, Michael Collins borrowed from the British army for use against his new enemies some of those very guns which had been used to fire on him and his comrades in 1916. After the Rising, republican prisoners in English jails had with rare exceptions refused Colm Ó Gaora's offer to teach them Irish.[18] As early as 1917, Ó Gaora had deduced that, whenever these colleagues assumed power in a new state, their use of Irish would be strictly symbolic. Irish was useful, in the judgement of an emergent elite, to reinforce the claim to a separatist identity: but the arduous learning of it could be left to children. So the ritual *cúpla focal* at the start or close of a long speech in English sufficed for political leaders.

This was reflective of much else in the new state. There was no decentralization, no new capital in a renovated landscape: instead, the old imperial city just got bigger and bigger. There was no further devolution of power to local councils, as had begun in the late 1890s. The child-centred liberal education imagined by Patrick Pearse never took hold: rather, there was a mimicry of the anti-industrial ethos of British public schools, which favoured the teaching of Latin over commerce and whose SPQR mentality was now employed to buttress the spiritual empire of the Catholic Church. Its lay missionaries were often called 'legionaries' in the 1940s and 1950s. Since almost all primary schools were run by the clergy, teachers functioned in effect as the non-commissioned officers of the churches. Not without reason did Máirtín Ó Cadhain, the language activist and prose master of Irish, set his students at Trinity College Dublin a three-hour examination essay on the topic '*Sacsa nua darb ainm Éire*' (a new England called Ireland).[19]

Even the Gaeltacht areas themselves were increasingly anglicized (hardly surprising, since they were more an effect of colonialism than a response to it). People were as likely to see a bar-room television set featuring a soccer match between Manchester United and Chelsea in Casla as in Coolock. Meanwhile, Irish was being taught as if it were a dead language, imposed by whip and stick, as English had been in the nineteenth century. Like Latin, its study seemed to be dominated by strange declensions of noun, conjugations of verb and endless irregularities (the mastery of which was seen as character-forming). During the general election of 1973, when a movement for civil rights had emerged in Gaeltacht areas of west Galway, a socialist politician said in a moment of despondency: 'we think we are arguing about how to revive the language, but in truth we are having a debate about who exactly owns the corpse'.[20]

The real meaning of 1922, in the *longue durée* of history, is not national liberation but the moment of transfer from one elite to another of the responsibility for managing the slow decline of rural Ireland and the gradual demise of regional villages and towns.

2. Beckett's Inner Exile

No wonder that the boy Beckett was terrified by what he saw of the burning city of Dublin from Three Rock Mountain. He would bear the stigmata of all that history on his body and in his texts. Beckett had grown up in a home which contained neither Gaelic nor English books and so he was bound to set up shop in the void. His tramps in their dented bowler hats and shabby-genteel suits might seem like Anglo-Irish gentlemen gone to seed (for Synge had already identified the bohemian offspring of that class as a new breed of super-tramp); but they also recreated the world of *spailpín* poets in their nomadicism and desperation. The dispossessed Gaelic bards after 1600 had been like underemployed postdoctoral students today: possessed of a high self-image but scant material prospects. When Vivian Mercier told Beckett that his tramps talked as if they had PhDs, the writer shot back: 'how do you know they hadn't?'[1] They act like the ruined bards of the lost Gaelic order, whose arduous and mandarin training left them ill-equipped for a new mercantile world: 'You should have been a poet', says one; and the other, gesturing at his rags, responds 'I was once. Is it not obvious?' (*WG* 35). In the words of the despairing *spailpín* poets: 'ní hé an bochtanas is measa / ach an tarcaisne a leanann é' (it is not poverty that is the worst thing, but the insult that follows it).

More than any other modern Irish writer, Beckett registered the blasted, hollowed-out landscape of a country after holocaust and trauma. 'At the same time it (my life) is over but goes on', says Molloy, 'and is there any tense for that?'[2] Many of Beckett's jokes are epitaphs on discarded hope. They project the condition of a people who had looked backward on frustration and forward to liberation, but with no intervening period of fulfilment:

> Do you believe in the life to come?
> Mine was always that.[3]

This desolate witticism became a one-liner, painted in huge white letters on a wall in West Belfast during the 1970s: 'Is there a life before death?' All of life, in such a state of things, can seem to have been a preparation for a freedom that never eventuated.

One problem was that, through decades of ill usage, many Irish had adjusted too comprehensively to intolerable conditions. They had learned techniques for submitting to any humiliation, whether at the hands of gouging landlords or serial abusers. They had taught one another how to behave as if life were normal in a wholly abnormal situation. Beckett was both impressed and scandalized by this capacity to bear the unbearable:

> I can't go on like this.
> That's what you think. (*WG* 94)

Through his play *Happy Days*, in the course of which a woman is progressively buried in sand, neither she nor her husband attempts to tackle this situation. Passers-by accept it as unremarkable, asking only what it all means. People, the play seems to suggest, can accomodate themselves even to dire situations and not wish to live otherwise: 'all my lousy life I've crawled about in the mud. And now you talk to me about scenery!' (*WG* 94). Beckett had grown to manhood in a country whose Catholic majority accepted that life is a vale of tears and offered up their suffering to release the souls of those who burned in Purgatory.

As a young man on the Dublin art scene, Beckett was something of a loner. Among his closer friends were the painter Jack Yeats and the writer Ernie O'Malley, intellectuals whose work expressed a clear sense of frustration at the failure of the new state to deliver real freedom. Until 1922, many Irish artists had embodied in their work the ideal of a nation which as yet had no incarnation as a state. After that date they lived through the slow extinction of the national idea in a ramshackle political formation. Its problem was the same as that which would later be defined by Salman Rushdie in postcolonial India: it had been 'insufficiently imagined' by the decolonizing elites.[4] (Beckett's constant fear that he had been 'incompletely born' may have been a related worry.) The paintings of Jack Yeats or memoirs of Ernie O'Malley sometimes project the ideals of an invisible republic, still in the future, but more often an elegy for a nation stillborn. Those who had once said 'revolution or death' were now fighting the death of their revolution.

The argument had always been about sovereignty. In *aisling* or vision poems, the ruined Gaelic bards had repeated the same theme. A young man meets a withered crone on the road and she promises him the sovereignty of Ireland, if only he will submit to a few stress tests – such as sleeping with her. If he can bring himself to do this, she will become young again and walk like a queen. These poems often imagined help as coming from abroad (whether from Jacobite army, French military or American money). The source of possible redemption changed over time as the global order shifted, but the aim was to recover cultural sovereignty as a prelude to liberation.

Yet all around him the young Beckett could see how little freedom there was: so little that people lived more in the glorious past or in a distant future than in the present moment. They lacked a Protestant belief in the reality of the world, in the here and now. Years of demoralization had led them to turn away from the present and to locate their claims to land and freedom not in any document but in an oral tradition always rooted deep in the past or the future. Even newspapers seemed to be filled with accounts of old outrages or re-conquests to come. The urge was to make the unglamorous present into past or future as quickly as possible. In the words of Winnie in *Happy Days*, 'this will have been another happy day!'[5]

Beckett could sense that what was being enacted in Ireland, in the guise of the birthing of a nation, was the drama of its perpetual postponement. The question was how to end: and the search for a way of putting an end to things was what allowed the discourse of nation-building to continue. The people were seeking not an answer to the Irish Question but (in the words of one historian) 'a meaning to their question'.[6] France in the 1940s must have reminded Beckett of Ireland in the 1920s: blasted, inchoate, but with the potential to start all over again. Yet the bleakness of freedom after liberation was the abiding feeling:

> We lost our rights.
> We got rid of them. (*WG* 19)

The cords had been cut which had once bound the puppets to their masters, but there was an underlying fear that ideas of mastery could at any moment return:

> Tied to Godot? What an idea! No question of it! (*Pause*) For the moment. (*WG* 21)

On stage, the condition of freed puppets is one of dangling arms, sunken heads, sagging knees, as ape-like as any nineteenth-century caricature of a slave. But in this case it is the puppets themselves who have cut the strings that bound them to their rulers; yet the freedom they gain seems hollow. *Waiting for Godot* is in many ways a reflection on their refusal to face the consequences: their own insignificance. The widespread unemployment that affected the Irish economy in the 1920s and 1930s had added idleness to the humiliation of insignificance for many, creating a void filled with stories, jokes and minor games well familiar to Beckett long before he was counted an existentialist in Paris. It was indeed, as Oscar Wilde had predicted it would be, awfully hard work doing nothing.

Yet there was also something noble and poignant about life in such a suspended state, when old securities had been set aside and exposure to the rawness of being ensued. Beckett's sense of the absurd was developed in the Dublin of his young manhood. The fish-out-of-water state perfectly captured the attempt by a people, stunned by the departure of old rulers, to learn how to swim in a wholly new element. W. B. Yeats captured the lyric possibilities of that moment, which also held the danger of a death:

> Shakespearean fish swam the sea, far away from land;
> Romantic fish swam in nets coming to the hand;
> What are all those fish that lie gasping on the strand?[7]

The Beckett character is stranded on stage but without a definite script: so what dialogue there is must seem improvised. And while there is no supplied script, there are plenty of coercive stage directions coming from authorities elsewhere. This gives a stagey, performative quality to most actions, but also a sense of monotony and changelessness as the same old routines are repeated. A subsistence economy permits little room for the elaboration of personality: 'I might just as well have been born in his shoes, and he in mine' (*WG* 31).

The characters of Didi and Gogo seem interchangeable. At the outset of the play, Didi seems sensitive and Gogo coarse; but in the second act these roles are reversed, even as lines are swapped between them. This is a form of characterization familiar enough in Irish writing. Two flawed and incomplete characters may have the makings of a whole person, but life as created is too much for one man. This type of duo will appear in later texts by Edna O'Brien and Brian Friel. The option of emigration will press on their young protagonists as it does on Beckett's figures:

> What is there to keep us here?
> The dialogue. (*E* 58)

That dialogue is, however, subject to constant breakdown. The moment of apparent deliverance proved bitter indeed, for it was followed soon after by a global recession which emphasized the hollowness of freedom. In this, as in much else, Ireland became a test case for the world.

The tramps in *Godot* are as addicted to complaint as to suffering. If they tried to change their setting or their state, a better existence might follow, but they prefer not to. Like a couple caught in an abusive relationship or a deteriorated marriage, they are co-dependent, each abusing the other, yet looking to that other for some new response. The fear of listening to the dreams of one's partner is akin to the fear of completing a thought. 'Let them remain private', Didi says to Gogo; 'you know I can't bear that' (*WG* 16). In a climate of cultural censorship, dreams are among the most subversive and troubling of narratives, for they might express a people's fear of becoming individuals, of using thought or image as a basis for action. The heroic phase of seeking a meaning to the old question is truly over:

> VLADIMIR: Thinking is not the worst.
> ESTRAGON: Perhaps not. But at least there's that. . .
> VLADIMIR: What do you mean, at least there's that?

ESTRAGON: That much less misery.

VLADIMIR: What is terrible is to *have* thought. (*WG* 64)

– because owning a thought creates the fear of experiencing and acting on it.

Apart from the work of a limited number of intellectuals, Ireland in the later 1920s and 1930s ignored the work of thought and feared confrontation with the self. Beckett remarked in a 1934 essay that most of the country's poets found that in self-perception there was 'no theme'.[8] (By analogy, over a decade later, Alain Robbe-Grillet would write of Godot as 'the man who keeps thought enslaved'.[9]) Although written in France over a decade later as a response to the Second World War, *Waiting for Godot* was also a warning to Ireland, in the tradition of James Joyce's coded attacks on the censorship in *Finnegans Wake*:

Yes, and now I remember, yesterday evening we spent blathering about nothing in particular. That's been going on now for half a century. (*WG* 66)

Beckett saw to it that the play was put on in Dublin, where half a century earlier audiences had watched, at the end of Synge's *The Well of the Saints*, two tramps shuffle off a stage in hopes of a freedom in which they did not really believe. Now, however, *they do not move*, but remain stuck fast at the crossroads, at the point of a perpetually postponed decision.

The fear of thought-in-action was not peculiar to Irish intellectuals. *Godot* also rebukes those who would offer, instead of direct action, a pretty speech. In an earlier draft of the play the author had referred to two characters, Bim and Bom, as 'Stalinist comedians';[10] and it is hard not to think of these as exemplars of Left Bank intellectuals, staging plays for audiences that included Nazi officers, while Beckett fled those same officers for his life.

The tramps opt for inaction: 'Don't let's do anything. It's safer' (*WG* 18). What can be read as a critique of Irish neutrality may also be a comment on writers of commitment. As Søren Kierkegaard had written: 'there are two ways – one is to suffer; the other is to become a professor of the fact that someone else has suffered'.[11]

The tramps choose life rather than death, so that they can, as mere survivors, avoid the unknown. As survivalists it is better that they do not even remember the ideals which once actuated them:

> VLADIMIR: What was it you wanted to know?
> ESTRAGON: I've forgotten.

The forces which allow a person to overlook the present pain of a passing beggar are manifold – the notion that God will reward the sufferer in the next life or that charitable gestures are inappropriate from one who looks to a future socialist state. Although Beckett inherited an urgently Protestant sense of the need to act positively in this world, he could not long be a believer in faith without good works. That was the besetting vice of all extreme sects, whether Christian or socialist: but for him all those 'isms' were 'wasms'. The word *Godot* was suggested by the French for 'boot', *godillot*; and whenever Godot seems about to appear the boots start to tighten on Estragon: but that is the perennial flaw of humans, to blame on their boots (or God) the flaws of their feet (or themselves). On this kind of evasiveness, the physicist Albert Einstein had a most penetrating statement:

> . . . if something did not fit, he would not seek to ignore or escape it – he would not wait for the Messiah, the world revolution, the universal reign of peace and justice to dissolve the difficulty. If the shoe does not fit, it is no use saying that time and wear will make it less uncomfortable or that the shape of the foot should be altered or that the pain is an illusion. . . There was only

one world, the world of human experience; it alone was real. Beyond it there was mystery – the fact that the universe was comprehensible was the greatest of mysteries; yet no theory was valid which ignored any part of human experience, in which he included imaginative insight, arrived at by paths often far from conscious.[12]

The problem with all available theories was that they were based on an absolute rhetorical account of the world, which could never explain all that was resistant to the hopeful schematizations of persons or to transformation by the imagination. As Clov observes to Hamm in *Endgame*: 'I use the words you gave me. If they don't mean anything any more teach me others. Or let me be silent' (*E* 32). Beckett had made the transition to writing in French in order to break out of the Anglo-Irish paradigm: asked whether his move from Ireland meant that he could now be taken as an English author, he said '*au contraire*'. He may have shifted to French in order to submit himself to the experience of language change undergone by so many Irish in the nineteenth century, and to have re-processed early experiences in a second language allowed him to filter out some too pressing memories of his earlier years in Ireland: it was a means through which he would 'forget' much of the past. By embracing French, he could change languages but never countries. Donning the mask of a French author, he was free to explore his own nation's experience as he never could have done in either English or Irish.

The problem was how to finish things off. 'It's time it ended', says Hamm early in *Endgame*, 'and yet I hesitate to end' (*E* 12). The sort of stasis which Beckett knew well as a member of the chess club in Sackville Street, Dublin, was a fair symbolization of the state of the country. The endgame happens when there are no longer enough pieces to mount an attack on the king, but the monarch himself is resourceless too. Beckett (in a rare moment of explanation) told the actor who first played the part of Hamm: 'A good player would have given up long ago. He is only trying to delay the inevitable end. Each of his gestures is one of the last useless moves which put off the end'.[13] Yet the complaints voiced in Dublin may have been no different from the disenchantment expressed after the First World War, as when T. S. Eliot asserted that *The Waste Land*, far from expressing the disillusion of a generation, simply exposed their 'illusion of being disillusioned'.[14] In *Godot*, as in the Gaelic *aisling*, the predicted messenger never comes: but in *Endgame* the unexpected figure (a boy) appears but is not recognized as a deliverer.

A people numbed-up by suffering may no longer notice every salient detail:

HAMM: Nature has forgotten us.
CLOV: There's no more nature.
HAMM: No more nature! You exaggerate.
CLOV: In the vicinity. (*E* 11)

Even the eyes of a healthy person see only what they are trained to see. People began to register fogs in London after Impressionists began to paint them. But a sensibility forged in 'mud' may not be best fitted to appreciate 'scenery'. Hamm sometimes expresses hope of better landscapes but only when the co-dependent Clov has ceased to believe in them. Hamm defers the end with painkillers, stories and small routines: but what he fears as much as an impending end is the awful silence in which each character might have to confront himself. Everything depends, as always in Beckett, on the sort of silence one keeps: but for those who fear an ending, the hum is better than silence.

The shape of *Endgame* may be different from *Godot*, but the conclusions to which both plays come are similar. There can be no rhetorical substitute for compassionate action: 'All those I might have helped. Helped! Saved. Saved! The place was crawling with them.' And then, to the audience: 'Get out of here and love one another. Lick your neighbour as yourself!' (*E* 68). Yet no sooner is the message of tender care voiced than it is undercut by the licking jest. This is in the tradition of a people who, as Sean O'Casey said, treat a joke as a serious thing and a serious thing as a joke.

If the trivial comedy is for serious people, every serious point must be made to appear trivial. Embarrassed by his own intermittent shows of emotion, Hamm must annul them with the epitaph of a joke. The problem in the end is that Clov can never know when Hamm is joking and when he is in earnest, as each epitaph overrides the life that gave rise to it. His desperate need to keep establishing a context is another element which prevents him from looking within his personality, but so also does his addiction to acting a part rather than articulating a self. J. W. von Goethe might have fore-diagnosed his condition, for he was the writer who could forgive the faults of men in actors but not the faults of actors in men.[15]

A Neutral Ireland?

Ireland remained neutral throughout the Second World War. After the convulsions of its own war and civil war, it was still rebuilding slowly. At the outset of international hostilities, some nationalists supported the Axis powers, on the extremely dubious principle that they might assist in recovering the six lost counties. Most people had some sympathy with the British, especially after major cities of the United Kingdom (with many Irish resident there) were bombed. A slogan did the rounds: 'we're neutral – but who are we neutral against?' British soldiers who stumbled across the border were quietly repatriated. German aviators who crash-landed in Ireland were detained (not to their total chagrin) in fairly relaxed internment camps (with weekend release for men to attend dances with local women). Members of the Irish Republican Army were interned in more severe conditions at the Curragh, because of a fear that some might prejudice neutrality by seeking a military alliance with Hitler. During the fierce debates that often raged among Curragh internees, it was said that opinion invariably split three ways – between pro-Germans, pro-British and Brendan Behan.

Cut off from the world, Ireland grew more introverted. But the continuing availability of good meat, pure butter and healthy vegetables made a city like Dublin a place of some attraction for British intellectuals, in flight from the more strict rationing in their own country. The city became a kind of displaced bohemia, where bottle parties were held by experimental dancers such as Erina Brady or visiting poets such as John Betjeman. Snooping on these dens of iniquity kept the Special Branch of the police busy once the last of the republican militants had been locked away.

Samuel Beckett had left in 1939, telling his mother that he preferred to live in a France at war than an Ireland at peace. He deplored the affectation of neutrality. For most Irish citizens, especially in the early years of the war, that neutrality was proof of a sovereignty hard won, after the anti-conscription success of Sinn Féin at the polls in 1918 and the subsequent securing of independence. But a suspicion persisted that neutrality, far from being a positive policy, might become indistinguishable from indifference. The prevailing introversion was not all bad: it did give rise to honest soul-searching, especially in a journal such as *The Bell*, established by Seán O'Faoláin in 1940. But the poet Louis MacNeice expressed reservations felt by many when he mocked the very notion of self-sufficiency implied in the words 'sinn féin' and in a state seeking to provide all of its own food:

> Ourselves alone! Let the round tower stand aloof
> In a world of bursting mortar...[1]

In France, Beckett again and again risked his life as he assisted Jewish friends to escape from the Nazis in Paris: eventually he had to flee the city himself. After the war, this ascetic and fastidious man was appalled at the way in which his relations in Dublin gorged on vast amounts of food, while those who had stood against fascism on the continent still went hungry. It is possible that the character Pozzo, with his complacent blindness and luxurious food, might be read as a negative representation of Irish neutralism in the

Second World War, with Lucky embodying the hunger-wracked, devastated French population after the cessation of hostilities. The tramps, Didi and Gogo, may epitomize Beckett himself, as a volunteer at an Irish Red Cross depot in the ruined city of Saint Lô, seeking to understand the meaning of it all.

In a subsequent talk for Radio Éireann rebuking Irish neutrality, Beckett wrote with rare directness about his time at Saint Lô. He lamented the sense of disconnection between the Irish officers and the people they were treating: 'their way of being was not our way, and our way of being was not their way'. The extreme difference in recent national experience made it impossible for one group to understand or be understood by the other. Yet Beckett had no doubt that the very basis of the human condition was being rethought and remade at Saint Lô: 'the whole enterprise turned from the beginning on the establishing of a relation in the light of which the therapeutic faded to the merest of pretexts'; he felt that the Irish volunteers in France were the real exponents of the old national genius for building something good amid the ruins of a community. The nurses, doctors and relief-workers 'got at least as good as they gave. . . got what they could hardly give, a vision and a sense of a time-honoured conception of humanity in ruins, and perhaps even an inkling of the terms in which our condition is to be thought again'.[2] France, *après la guerre*, might contain secret messages for a secret Ireland yet to be constructed. The talk was carefully typed in double space and the words carefully chosen – but the broadcast itself was never made. Only in 1983 did a zealous researcher at the station exhume the typescript.

3. 'Gaeldom is Over':
The Bell

The editor boasted that *The Bell* was 'the only magazine in the world printed on lavatory paper with ink made of soot',[1] but that was the inevitable fate of a monthly Irish journal of art and ideas founded in 1940. Its glory days under the guiding hand of Sean O'Faoláin were the war years of paper shortages and curtailed newsprint. It was a tribute to O'Faoláin's visionary zeal that even after he resigned from the editorial chair in 1946 *The Bell* lasted, with some breaks in transmission, until 1954.

O'Faoláin was a man of letters, excelling at writing in many genres, whether novel, short story, biography, historical narrative or essay. He devoted much energy, which might otherwise have gone into creating more novels, to editing *The Bell*. Some might have seen in this yet another case of a good writer fallen among controversialists, what W. B. Yeats had warned against as the chief temptation of the artist, 'creation without toil'.[2] But O'Faoláin had his reasons, chief among them the banning by the Free State government of hundreds of works of literature, some penned by himself and his friends. Among other functions, *The Bell* bravely fought that censorship with reasoned critique and constant reminders of how ludicrous it must seem to overseas commentators.[3]

In his young manhood, O'Faoláin had been a volunteer in the fight for Irish freedom. Having said 'revolution or death' in 1921, he was by 1940 confronted by the death of the revolution. Éamon de Valera (of whom he had written a hopeful, admiring biography in the 1930s) now wore a top hat to attend the Royal Dublin Horse Show and was turning the country into a conservative, theocratic state. *The Bell*'s call was for a completion, not a liquidation, of the anticolonial revolution: the use of tillage to replace livestock (beloved of profiteering ranchers); the reconfiguration of cities and towns along civic rather than colonial lines (challenging Dublin-centric versions of national life); and the further redistribution of land among rural smallholders after the expropriation of the Anglo-Irish ascendancy.

Kelly Matthews (in her history of the journal) shows that the magazine's circulation started at 5,000 and steadied out at 3,000 (about 1,000 of which went overseas). It is hard for readers now to understand the sense of excitement which attended the arrival of each monthly issue in a rural parish, as copies were passed from librarian to schoolteacher, from the more liberal sort of priest to the more intellectual type of landless labourer. The Censorship Acts, which had been implemented by the government in 1929, were a snooper's charter, an example of cultural democracy grown manic. If any citizen objected to a book, he or she simply referred it to the Censorship Board with the accompanying complaint (indecent or obscene). As discussed earlier, in totalitarian societies such as Soviet Russia or Nazi Germany, the censorship by 1940 was top-down, but in Ireland it was really bottom-up. O'Faoláin tried to develop a more sophisticated literary sensibility among the community and to expose the ill effects of rampant self-censorship, all the more lethal in a country whose pose of wartime neutrality entailed a heavy curtailment of news from overseas sources.

He could do this because he was one of the 'risen people' himself, the son of humble parents in Cork, and therefore not perceived as greatly 'above' the people to whom he addressed his journal.

The newly literate masses, as Jonathan Rose has shown in *The Intellectual Life of the British Working Classes*,[4] were no great lovers of experimental modernism; and neither was O'Faoláin. He admired Flaubert, Balzac and the realist novelists of nineteenth-century France, and sought to emulate their representational accuracy in his magazine as well as his art. After the turbo-charged poetics of Yeats and the vertiginous prose of Joyce in the period of national revival, it was time, he contended, for the realists to take stock and to give an honest accounting of just how far actual Ireland fell short of its founders' dreams. Matthews rather strangely attributes O'Faoláin's scepticism concerning modernism to the fact that 'it was still a new phenomenon in the early 1940s',[5] but the truth is that the emerging Irish writers of that time had had quite enough of it. The expressive achievement was intimidating more than enabling. One poet compared Yeats to a massive tree, whose roots sucked all life to themselves even as its branches blocked out all light.[6] Joyce was seen as a great artist but an unusable model, of interest more to American professors than to Irish realists. (Matthews is wrong, however, to say that the sale of *Ulysses* was banned in Ireland: no case was pressed because none of the snoopers felt able to offer a sufficiently confident interpretation of the book to mount one.) *The Bell* set its face against modernism, which it saw as a thing of the past, coincident with the early, lyric phase of Irish nationalism and revivalism: but it attempted nonetheless to engage with modernity, with the messy democratic polity and 'the filthy modern tide'[7] so castigated by Yeats. In this it was wholly successful. Its essays covered everything from poetry (it introduced Patrick Kavanagh and John Hewitt to a wider audience) to basket-weaving, from amateur drama to the making of hats. Contributions came from every class: readers learned of a day in the life of a single mother, a slum family, a country doctor, a steeplejack, a prisoner who did penal servitude. There were crisp, lucid articles on 'Irish fisheries', 'street rhymes' and the Irish Grand National horse race at Fairyhouse.

Such essays owed something to the fashion for Mass Observation among British writers of the 1930s, but they were often more subtly novelistic in their psychological analysis, constituting a study of mentalities of a kind which would be developed with even greater rigour by Pierre Nora in his *lieux de mémoire* commentaries on the culture of modern France. It was these articles that proved the major selling point of *The Bell* and made it popular not just in Dublin but right across the countryside. Why should this have been so? Although Ireland was independent, it was still not unified in any cultural sense: the people of its regions remained strange, even mysterious, to one another. John McGahern, who was born in 1935, once told me that if, as a boy, he cycled ten miles away from his native parish in Co. Leitrim, he found himself in a foreign land, where the people's clothes, their flower arrangements and ways of walking or talking all seemed utterly different from the life he knew. In theory, Ireland (or most of it) had been unified by a triumphant nationalism and by the usual effects of railways and printing presses, but in fact the people still needed to hear and get to know the full range of voices in a genuinely national debate. Once again, O'Faoláin was completing a job left undone by the Free State's founders and left undone afterwards by its radio service. Even in 1940, many people did not own wireless receivers; whole communities would gather around a single radio to hear a football match.

Perhaps this helps to explain why O'Faoláin was rather dismissive of the use of radio by artists and intellectuals. True, its pay cheques provided what some of them laughingly called 'indoor relief', but he felt that the half-hour broadcast of short stories had done nothing for the genre, introducing only 'a fake air of intimacy' which licensed 'the button-holing technique of the Club Bore'.[8] This was a none-too-concealed jibe at his fellow Corkman and friend Frank O'Connor, who loved to deploy the techniques of oral tale-tellers ('Be the hokies, there was a strange man coming down the road...') in his stories, written and oral, and who would defiantly codify some of these techniques in his study of the form, *The Lonely Voice*, over two decades later.

Nevertheless, O'Faoláin in *The Bell* was doing what radio should by 1940 have done – articulating Ireland to itself and to significant numbers of its people (and their well-wishers) overseas. The tattered condition of most surviving copies suggests widespread use. Like all gifted editors, O'Faoláin was something of a monomaniac. He encouraged young authors with the utmost generosity of spirit and, unlike some editors of literary journals, he paid his contributors promptly and well: but this did not prevent him from issuing correctives to them in public print rather than in private conversation. *The Bell* was to have a consciously 'improving' function and so its editor disdained private channels of admonition in favour of 'advice given on the printed page with the whole of Ireland looking on'.[9] Some of the more intrepid younger authors occasionally snapped back, if only to prove that they could bite the hand that fed them. Rashly but gallantly, O'Faoláin commissioned two as yet unknown critics, Vivian Mercier and Conor Cruise O'Brien, to write essays on the fourth estate in Ireland, not excluding one on *The Bell* itself. Mercier might have been young but he was not easily frightened:

> For Sean O'Faoláin is not just a figurehead – he is the magazine, as you find out after, or before, you have written one article for it. He writes his own Editorial, all 3000 words of it; he usually has another piece – a lecture, short story or what not – under his own name; he writes the little blurbs in italics which appear at the head of most *Bell* contributions; and, if I am not careful, he will write most of this article too.[10]

O'Brien went even further, offering parodies of *Bell*-type articles in a 1945 issue: 'Crubeens v. Boxty: A Symposium'. Under cover of a pseudonym (necessary for a civil servant in those days), he gave the magazine's readers a rather sour image of themselves in 1946: 'In its caution, its realism, its profound but ambivalent nationalism, its seizures of stodginess and its bad paper, it reflects the class who write it and read it – teachers, librarians, junior civil servants, the lettered section of the Irish petty bourgeoisie'.[11] It was, in fact, far more audacious and witty than that. It is a measure of O'Faoláin's liberalism that he printed such condescending *haut-en-bas* piffle from a man who would in later years aim his sarcasms at far worthier targets and whose marvellous prose style was honed in such early work for the journal.

The Bell took its name from *Kolokol*, a magazine edited by Alexander Herzen in the 1850s and 1860s. Herzen used it to ventilate the debate between Slavophile lovers of Mother Russia and Westernizers who turned to the more 'advanced' countries of Europe for models. O'Faoláin was a great Europeanizer, one who hoped that Ireland might one day be a little more like the great republic across the Channel. He was French in his love of good food, in his determination to study the fashion system (his wife Eileen wrote an essay on hats) and in his barefaced cheek in persuading two of his mistresses (Honor Tracy and Elizabeth Bowen) to write for the journal. Apart from the nod to Herzen, the titular 'bell' may also have been faintly parodic of those church-oriented magazines which circulated in even greater numbers throughout Ireland in the 1930s and 1940s. The anticlerical tones of a secularizing French intelligentsia informed much O'Faoláin commentary: he once called the Irish, 'a nation of apple-lickers' and, when asked to explain, said breezily 'people who, if tempted in the Garden of Eden, would have licked rather than bitten the apple'.[12]

In that cautious land, many feared to be European lest the huckster across the street call them English.[13] The value of *The Bell*'s Francophilia was its challenge to compatriots to stop explaining everything by reference to an Anglo-Irish axis. At the outset, O'Faoláin intended to reverse the flow of usual analysis by advertising a special 'English Issue', in which a mainly Irish writing team would study the people who for centuries had purported to study them. 'It is essential for the mental health of Ireland that we should as quickly as possible get to the stage where we do not give a damn about Britain',[14] he snorted. This was bracing stuff, but wartime restrictions meant that the issue never got published. Instead, *The Bell* had to content itself with special 'Ulster Numbers' devoted to the nature and effects of the partition of the island. In this, at least, O'Faoláin showed that he was capable of an ambivalence similar to that displayed by his hero turned villain, de Valera. In his Constitution of 1937, de Valera had renewed the time-honoured claim to the six northern counties but had also managed, by a typical casuistry, to give a first formal recognition to the actually existing Northern Ireland by including the phrase 'pending the reintegration of the national territory'. Although his Constitution would be denounced as obnoxiously predatory by later critics of nationalism, at the time of its enactment it evoked little complaint, except among northern nationalists, who knew from its wording that their goose was cooked.[15] O'Faoláin, like de Valera, urged people to think of themselves as Irish rather than Catholic or Protestant, but his Ulster Numbers in their very title duplicated the realism of the Constitution in accepting partition as a fact. Indeed, those issues reinforced a grudging acceptance of the northern difference, Matthews contends,[16] by demonstrating just how distinct, a couple of decades after the settlement of 1921, the states of Ireland had grown.

Of course, north and south had been different – as different as east and west – long before 1921. The leader of Irish nationalism at Westminster in the late nineteenth century, Charles Stewart Parnell, had warned his people that they must resign themselves to the cursed versatility of the Celt. O'Faoláin took this literally. He published an article by an anonymous 'Ulster Protestant' (actually the broadcaster and poet W. R. Rodgers), warning that the average unionist farmer really did believe that, if Britain were to sanction the formation of an all-Ireland government, his land would 'be taken away from him and given to a Catholic neighbour':[17] but he also included articles by republican authors who believed that Northern Ireland had already become 'a totalitarian state'.[18] Confronted by such polarized politics, it says a lot for the pluralism of *The Bell* that its most distinguished poetry editor, the Belfast classicist and son of the manse Louis MacNeice, was recruited to the post through the offices of a former IRA gunman, Ernie O'Malley. If only Ireland could always have been like that!

There were limits to O'Faoláin's tolerance. Today, younger scholars might accuse him of being Eurocentric, of romanticizing a Europe that perhaps does not deserve, and maybe never did deserve, such unqualified tenderness. Matthews is right to say that his deep respect for European realism left him rather baffled by modernist art. In her book, *The Bell* is depicted as a thoroughly postcolonial project in its themes (which it surely was), but such a description could hardly be applied to O'Faoláin's own techniques as novelist or storyteller. Like the novels of certain of his French contemporaries, O'Faoláin's are often radical in content but old-fashioned in narrative form. For O'Faoláin, to be modern was to be European – it did not strike him that Ireland, before its accession to the European Economic Community, might have been an example of an alternative modernity. If he had made a deeper study of Joyce, he might have found his own path to the postcolonial modernism which cheerfully acknowledged the Dubliner as one of its founding fathers. As matters stood, Europe and verisimilar realism were the *ne plus ultra* of his ideals for an Irish polity and for Irish letters. And it was hardly his fault that the leaders of Ireland in the later decades of membership of the European Union produced in the Celtic Tiger not so much an imitation of Europe as its caricature.

There were good reasons for all this. Even in 1940, the Irish bourgeoisie had not been fully formed. As a novelist, O'Faoláin fretted about what he called 'the problem of adequacy', of a country which still lacked many of those middle-class institutions and protocols off which the novel as a form feeds.[19] In some desperation, he often recurred to the question put by Henry James about post-independence America: 'How can you write a novel of manners about a society that has none?'[20] When O'Faoláin wrote novels, he found that he had to invent whole elements of a middle-class world in the very act of reporting it, or else there might be no story at all. The novel presupposes a made society, but Ireland in 1940 was still a society in the making. This explains an uncertainty of tone that may sometimes be found in the narratives of O'Faoláin, leaving him a better short story writer than novelist: but it also accounts for a final (and wonderful) peculiarity of *The Bell*. Many of its essays turn out, on inspection, to concern themselves with the question of how to become a better bourgeois in an Ireland which has seen a rather vulgar arriviste middle class take sudden control. O'Faoláin worries about how to be 'elegant', in phrasing, in decor, in craft. He wants people to make their rooms tasteful and beautiful. He feels that the natives, now that they own the environment, should care more lovingly for it. While insisting that culture is ordinary, he extends this idea to the suggestion that the production of a perfect furrow in a ploughing field might be an artistic achievement.

It is a beautiful and brilliant programme, even if it carries echoes of Sir Roger de Coverley (who would not scruple to lecture rising poets on the ways of elegance, either). The essays in *The Bell* are in some ways (for understandable reasons) a throwback to the world of the periodical essayists of England in the eighteenth century, the world of Joseph Addison and Richard Steele (whose texts are often recommended to *Bell* readers). They tell those readers many things they want to learn: how to find a post for your son in the office of a solicitor or of a country vet; how to buy better hats and wear them in style; how to keep a cleaner house. They provide the compost (as Addison and Steele did for England) that underlies the emerging form of the social novel, that thick description out of which the form can spring – because they make real those materials from which a novel of manners can come.

O'Faoláin was one of the very few intellectuals who had a palpable effect on society, but his pluralist Ireland only came into being decades after he had planted the seeds (and he lived to take pleasure in the changes). That Ireland may be found in the Programmes for Economic Expansion of the 1950s and 1960s, when de Valera's pastoral made way for the white heat of free trade; in the early years of RTÉ television, which developed the nation's conversation with itself along lines that he had so intrepidly mapped out; and in the critique of narrow-gauge identity politics which emerged against the backdrop of the Northern Ireland Troubles.

It is the misfortune of original minds to seem less and less remarkable in proportion to their success in changing public opinion. O'Faoláin's star waned in recent decades, because his realism began to seem tepid and wan at a time of dazzling experiment in post-colonial cultures. But he was, despite his formal conservatism, a postcolonial intellectual par excellence, who said in 1943 'Gaeldom is over. . . let Ireland begin' but feared that what emerged from the Irish revolution was not so much a society as a middle-class putsch.[21] The insurgents of Easter Week were rebels who knew what they were against (an empire) but needed also to be revolutionaries, with a clear sense of the society they wished to create.

O'Faoláin's sense of anticlimax chimed with the sense of uncertainty among intellectuals after independence. But Gaeldom was not quite over yet. Four years after his utterance, Gaeldom discovered what seemed to have eluded him: a way of being Irish and modernist at one and the same time.

4. A Talking Corpse?
Sáirséal agus Dill

When Seán and Brighid Ó hÉigeartaigh founded the company of Sáirséal agus Dill in 1947, writing in Irish seemed weak indeed. A state founded in 1922 had, by its standardizing of Gaeltacht idiom and by its pursuit of moral rectitude in texts, wrung much of the life out of a language it claimed to revere. The policy of imposing Irish as a compulsory subject of study in schools had led many children to experience the language as a threat rather than a gift.[1] There can have been few more counterproductive examples of affirmative action in the twentieth century. If a student failed Irish, he or she could be deemed to have failed the entire state exam; and many plum positions in the new state's apparatus were unobtainable without a pass in Irish. On the other hand, if students sat an algebra test in Irish (i.e., using Gaelic rather than Roman letters), they could get a ten per cent bonus. Not even an Einstein could have defeated some Irish-speaking geniuses in a state physics exam. Such inducements characterized the land that, in the words of the satirical magazine *Dublin Opinion*, 'lost the leprechaun but found the pot of gold'.[2]

The texts studied in Irish classes reflected a narrow nationalist ideology. If Soviet leaders at much the same time were destroying graphic art in Russia with injunctions to provide 'Girl Meets Tractor' posters, writers of Irish produced what Máirtín Ó Cadhain would later deride as texts fit mainly for a readership of credulous schoolchildren and pre-Vatican Two nuns.[3] This was all part of a wider censoriousness. The banning of literary masterpieces in English was so comprehensive that Flann O'Brien came up with a mischievous scheme: if every volume suppressed in English were to be instantly translated and made available solely in Irish, this would provide the ultimate incentive for citizens finally to learn their native language.

By the 1940s, much of the early fire had gone out of the language revival movement. A free state invented by artists and intellectuals had become a tedious theocratic bureaucracy, censoring its best minds and exporting many of its finest graduates. They left not necessarily in search of work, but because the life available at home seemed boring and mediocre.[4] In a famous speech he made at a debating society in Trinity College Dublin, Seán Ó hÉigeartaigh pleaded with classmates to stay in Ireland and stage a rearguard action. Yet many who heard his eloquence – such as the Yeats scholars A. N. Jeffares and Peter Allt – felt obliged to go.

Ó hÉigeartaigh kept his word. With a bequest of £300 from an aunt, he began to publish the work of a new generation of experimental poets: Máirtín Ó Direáin, Seán Ó Ríordáin, Máire Mhac an tSaoi. He insisted on attractive, up-to-date formats, with covers specially commissioned from artists such as Anne Yeats and Charles Lamb. He had an eye for as yet unproven talent. One of the funniest chapters in the history of the publishing house – crafted with devotion by his children Cian Ó hÉigeartaigh and Aoileann Nic Gearailt – recounts his months of 'foreplay' with the young Brendan Behan, whose visits to the Aran Islands (to improve the Dubliner's creative but wayward Irish) the publisher generously bankrolled. The stern but kindly patron received regular letters from a priest-spy on the islands, explaining that much of the money was being spent in the local bar (admittedly a good place in which to learn certain forms of Irish) or even more extensively on prolonged travels to the English-speaking mainland. In fact, Behan appears to have treated Aran as a sort of police station at which he had to register from time to time in order to prove his fidelity as a true Gael. Nothing came of this poignant courtship – *An Ghiall/ The Hostage* were still years ahead – but one is left with a profound admiration for a private publisher who constantly put himself and his wife out of pocket in the attempt to promote fine writing.[5]

Throughout the two decades of his efforts, Ó hÉigeartaigh held a senior post as a civil servant in the Department of Finance, helping to negotiate Irish entry to the European Economic Community. It was as if T. S. Eliot had taken on the directorship of Faber & Faber while continuing to hold ever more senior positions in Lloyds Bank – a punishing regimen. Ó hÉigeartaigh cycled home from work every day, retreated to the garden outhouses at six o'clock and began his second job – nothing less than the attempt to reconfigure a national culture in a minority language. A scientist by training, he was a true Renaissance man. He introduced new modes of printing to Irish, with some pagination fonts based on French models he had come to admire on his trips as a civil servant (the layout of Françoise Sagan's novel *Bonjour Tristesse* being one of these). He published academic textbooks on Latin and French, and on European as well as Irish history – and these doubtless served many students well as they went in search of the extra percentage points. But he also commissioned original, path-breaking studies of great figures from the Irish past (Robert Emmet, O'Donovan Rossa, Dr Patrick Dinneen, Arthur Griffith) and he did so without fear or favour in a land still nervous after a lethal civil war and nervous also about 'unfinished business' in the northern counties. Sometimes, the books published annoyed the state authorities because of the politics of their subjects; at other times, it was the willingness of freethinking authors to criticize bishops that offended official Ireland. Máirtín Ó Cadhain, of course, offended under all categories, being a socialist, a republican and a militant language rights activist; but the publisher, as the son of the agnostic republican P. S. O'Hegarty, never for a moment blinked. The company did receive grants for its work, but these were grudgingly given by a bureaucratic elite and were never enough. Máirtín Ó Cadhain once told his students in Trinity College Dublin that, but for Seán Ó hÉigeartaigh, he would have lost the will to write fiction after the 1940s. Ó hÉigeartaigh was one of those who persuaded the authorities at Trinity to appoint Ó Cadhain as a lecturer in Irish, one of the bravest appointments that that often endearingly eccentric college has ever made. Ó Cadhain had as qualifications only a primary teacher's diploma, a long stint of internment as an IRA activist and – of course – the authorship of *Cré na Cille* (*Graveyard Clay*, 1949), the greatest novel in the language.

The sheer quality of all this production meant that ambitious young writers in the 1950s and 1960s bypassed state houses and sent their work to Sáirséal agus Dill: Seán Ó Tuama, Diarmaid Ó Suilleabhain and many more. Ó hÉigeartaigh seems to have based much of his programme and design values on those of the Yeats family at the Cuala and Dun Emer presses (and his sister Gráinne, a famous harpist, married the poet W. B.'s son Michael). But the deeper and more contemporary analogy, I think, is with Faber & Faber (who were in a sense the real opposition). In an era when Faber's distinguished back catalogue was augmented by the young Heaney and McGahern (and thereafter by dozens more Irish writers of English), Ó hÉigeartaigh offered the very best to that small but significant audience which now existed for quality writing in Irish. The volumes were good value but never cheap. They were read with pleasure by everyone into whose hands they came (and some sold quite well over extended periods in print). It seems likely that the very smallness of the select intellectual audience permitted much of the formal experimentation with language and styles; there emerged, therefore, a literature of existential alienation in what was already an alienated literature. Texts such as *An Uain*

Bheo by Ó Súilleabháin or *An tSraith Ar Lár* by Ó Cadhain bear that verdict out. Some years afterward in Paris, Gilles Deleuze and Félix Guattari would write that nothing in modern literature was important except the 'minor'.[6] Those who work in 'major' world languages are constrained by many things: the calcifying power of custom, the coercion of market forces, the fickleness of popular opinion, and the slow emasculation of an idiom used mainly for internet babble and airport bookings. Seán Ó hÉigeartaigh seems to have instinctively understood all this: that literary breakthroughs are more likely to happen in a discourse the wider world is not anxiously weighing and watching. After all, when James Joyce created his own radical innovations on the outer edges of European literature, he was not yet 'James Joyce'.

The story of Sáirséal agus Dill is very well documented, thanks to Cian Ó hÉigeartaigh and Aoileann Nic Gearailt. Their history of the enterprise must be one of the most detailed books ever written about the development of a small modernist press. It is surely the most generously documented, with remarkable reproductions of accounts, advertisements and gloriously feisty letters in which cranky geniuses berate the publishers for literary offences (almost all imagined rather than real). There are also letters from the publishers to tardy authors or foot-dragging officials, usually civil but with an occasional note of *saeva indignatio* which Jonathan Swift would have loved. Swift lived in a time when English was being codified and standardized as a literary language, as was Irish in the decades of Sáirséal agus Dill. The Ó hÉigeartaighs held a precarious balance above grossness and below refinement, recognizing that there must always be a tension between the language of literature and the demotic of the streets. The official history of the publishing house contains many word lists made by Brighid Bean Uí Éigeartaigh. In the end, this remarkable woman may have done more than any government agent to produce a literary standard that was not deadened by unnecessary caution but instead supple and vital in its nuances.

The company had a further flowering in the years after 1969, thanks to support from that most raffish and undecodable of all Irish politicians, Charles Haughey. In the years of his decline, Haughey invariably refused interviews to national radio but would emerge suddenly on Radió na Gaeltachta to enunciate a major policy. In his pomp, he was a bruiser and lover of fine wine. On 14 May 1969, when Brighid Uí Éigeartaigh went to petition him, he had an especially bad hangover and realized that he had at last met his match. He gave the money she requested and the company had a brilliant diminuendo, until ill health compelled Brighid to close it in 1981. In its later years, it sold between 20,000 and 30,000 volumes. That might not seem a lot: but it is worth recalling that when the Gaelic League was founded in 1893, there were only six books in print in the Irish language. Now, hundreds are produced each year, some of the best by Cló Iar-Chonnacht, which has taken over the Sáirséal agus Dill copyrights and has done full justice to its founders. Near the close of their history of the firm, the offspring of the Ó hÉigeartaighs pose a question: was it all worth it? Any lover of modern Irish literature will answer that of course it was – but will also understand why the question had to be asked.

Seán Ó hÉigeartaigh died of a massive heart attack in 1967, aged only fifty. At his funeral his wife placed copies of the books alongside him in his grave. It was in its way a salute to the man who had brought the talking corpses of Ó Cadhain's *Cré na Cille* to the world: but it was a richly ambiguous gesture, as if the widow wished for one desperate moment to bury along with her beloved husband those very books which had shortened his life. She did persist, however, and government subventions flowed more freely for a while, perhaps augmented by a guilt felt by official Ireland. Ó Cadhain had often complained that the Irish knew how to deal with a person's death – it was life that they found difficult and tricky. He used to joke that there was something irretrievably respectable about the national dead – as if a tidied corpse achieved that which was withheld from it in life, a place among the revered middle classes. He wrote *Cré na Cille* to mock such thinking. Its power to disturb all official codes has not abated, and the many ill-fated attempts to get it into English are a high absurdist story in themselves.

Ó Cadhain himself seemed unconcerned about the recurrent attempts by Seán Ó hÉigeartaigh to commission a viable version in English. It was difficult to strike on a form of Hiberno-English that answered to the various tonalities of the original text. If other modernists sought to cope with the language of exhaustion, Ó Cadhain had to find in himself a response to the apparent exhaustion of a language. His base-language was that of his native townland, An Cnocán Glas, but he also revived words from Old Irish, borrowed others from Scots Gaelic, or simply invented words of his own. For many decades, purists held that such a book could not be translated into English at all. The shifts of register from portentous to demotic seemed beyond rendition. At one point, however, a sample translation entered in an open competition by a young woman from Co. Leitrim was so good that Ó hÉigeartaigh sent her a contract in 1961, only to receive an apologetic letter from her mother explaining that her daughter had now entered a convent and could not undertake the work. It seemed as if the higher powers had declared *Cré na Cille* untranslatable.[7]

Ó Cadhain found it strange to write in a language which he feared might be dead before he was.[8] He set *Cré na Cille* in a Gaeltacht cemetery. In each of its ten 'interludes' a new body from the village above is interred, bearing news and gossip to the truculent corpses below. In Ireland, as W. B. Yeats once mischievously observed, the dead may not even know that they are dead, but go on talking anyway. So the central character, Caitríona Pháidín, bemoans her cheapskate burial and dreams of reinterment in a better-class grave; and all of the corpses discuss the sex lives of those below and above. Even a French aviator, who died after crash landing nearby, adds his own complaint in the style of a Parisian existentialist:

'Ils m'ennuient. On espère toujours trouver la paix dans le mort, mais le tombe ne semble pas encore être le mort. On ne trouve ici, en tout cas, que de l'ennui'.[9] Or, as Samuel Beckett, in Paris during the winter of 1948–9, was writing about the dead: 'To have lived is not enough for them. They have to talk about it'.[10]

Many centuries earlier, *The Book of Common Prayer* had stated that the living could not talk directly to the dead in the funeral ceremony.[11] The dead could only be talked about, because they were beyond human contact. Much Irish writing after the Reformation seems like a sustained flouting of that ban on communication between living and dead. In plays from Boucicault to Behan, a dead body arises and orates. Yeats awards some of his best lines to those who speak from beyond the grave. Joyce bases his last work on the ballad of Finnegan, who rebukes the revellers at his own wake. The poet Nuala Ní Dhomhnaill has described Gaelic modernism itself as 'the corpse which sits up and speaks'.[12]

Ó Cadhain's novel is a central document in this tradition. Written in the golden age of the radio play, it is filled with contesting voices, each with its own tag line. And the graveyard's tutelary spirit, Stoc na Cille (the Trumpet of the Graveyard), speaks in a portentous tone which is mocked by the demotic of the buried villagers, who quarrel over the number of priests or cars at one another's funerals. Conversations are endlessly repeated, but there can be no developmental plot and, strangely, no sense of a hereafter, for the time is 'eternity'. Lives are over and yet they inexplicably continue; and there can be no fitting tense for that magic realist world of undevelopment (later captured by Gabriel García Márquez).

Parts of *Cré na Cille* were serialized in the *Irish Press* newspaper in 1948; and they brought fame to the author. People, spotting him on his way to a football match at Croke Park, would say, 'There goes Cré na Cille'. He was the greatest master of Irish-language prose for three centuries. He had lost his job as a primary schoolteacher because of his membership of the Irish Republican Army; and was interned during the Second World War by a government fearful that a pro-German wing of the IRA might jeopardize Irish neutrality. So the author (a committed anti-fascist himself) had a good opportunity in the Curragh Camp to listen to officially 'dead souls' in daily conversation. By setting his dialogues among the bodies in a graveyard, he may have been voicing his despair about the very idea of language revival.

The setting may have a further meaning. The author was looking to a future when his book, like certain Latin classics, would live on after its own language had fallen out of daily use. He may even have imagined a time when literature itself would be erased as a cultural institution, if not those voices which enabled it. Yet he must also have sensed, from the many near-death experiences in Irish culture, that a tradition often lives most potently in the lament for its passing. The very energy with which each death is announced in *Cré na Cille* seems to deny the possibility that the native language could finally die. And, despite Ó Cadhain's fears, it still survives, albeit precariously, as a community language. The dead bodies remain as truculent as ever.

5. A Parrot in Ringsend: Máire Mhac an tSaoi

B orn in 1922, and so the same age as the state, which she served well for a time as diplomat, Máire Mhac an tSaoi has never confused that state with the nation, whose traditions, oral and written, she has upheld.[1] She is one of those writers who has let the literary tradition speak through her and trusted her individuality to look after itself. Oscar Wilde once joked that man is least himself when he talks with his own face but if you give him a mask, he'll tell the truth.[2] In her case, that mask was Gaelic tradition. She wrote in both English and Irish over the years, but her English had a stiffness and correctness which never manifested in Irish. There is something of the Victorian classroom about her autobiography, *The Same Age as the State*, whereas her Irish writing has a freshness and candour before and beyond gentility. Synge once observed that the problem with the English language was that you could never swear in it without vulgarity, but that Irish had a clarity which made any statement in it seem concise and classical. He pointed out that the word 'shift', which sparked off a riot at the performance of his *The Playboy of the Western World*, was used as 'léine' without difficulty in Irish.[3] Mhac an tSaoi shared Synge's dread of vulgarity, and included as examples of the vulgar those metrical clichés and obvious rhythms to be found in school anthologies read by her generation, most of whose members would go on to equate such effects with 'poetry'.[4]

Hers is a double language: the spoken Irish of Corcha Dhuibhne learned in childhood but also the written Irish of such master lyricists as Piaras Feirtéar. In rare moments of uncertainty, her lyrics can oscillate between slack speech and poised formality; but most often she gets the balance exactly right, in a language above grossness and below gentility, where exactitude is possible. She understands that there is a necessary tension between the language of the streets and the language of poetry. If they move too far apart, the result is a precious, factitious world of unreality; but if they are aligned too closely, the lines that ensue can be banal and lacking in intensity.

Gaelic poetry had been composed almost exclusively by men – and that was true also of the poetry of sexual passion. There had been spectacular exceptions, of course, such as *Caoineadh Airt Uí Laoghaire: The Lament for Art O'Leary* by Eibhlín Dhubh Ní Chonaill. But usually women were the objects rather than the makers of lyrics of passion. What makes Mhac an tSaoi's work radical is an unabashed exploration of what poets of the *dánta grá* knew well: chancy, risky love, most often unrequited or fatally out of synchrony. The obsession with the love object is so all-consuming as to verge at times on hatred or resentment. It is a dependency so absolute as to show scant curiosity about the psychology of the unresponding man, or indeed about what may be the blocking factor in their relationship.

Desire is sinful (according to the dictates of church and community) but ever increasing. It goes beyond intellectual analysis into zones of pure emotion. The problems to which it gives rise are insoluble, but their very insolubility proves unacceptable.[5] The writer shares with such immediately contemporary prose authors as Françoise Sagan and Edna O'Brien a hurt sense of ill-use at the hands of men, but retains a margin of pride and dignity. The only hope of soothing such pain is to describe it very well.

It need not have been so. In early poems Mhac an tSaoi wrote what may be the most beautiful account of a teenage summer romance in Irish. Part of its charm is a sweet acceptance that 'Jack' knows little or nothing of her feelings:

Strapaire fionn sé troithe ar airde,
Mac feirmeora ó iarthar tíre
Ná cuimhneoidh feasta go rabhas-sa oíche
Ar urlár suimint' aige ag rince.

Ach ní dhearúdfad a ghéaga im thimpeall,
A gháire ciúin ná a chaint shibhialta –
Ina léine bhán, is a ghruaig nuachíortha
Buí fén lampa ar bheagán íle. . .

Fagfaidh a athair talamh ina dhiaidh aige,
Pósfaidh bean agus tógfaidh síolbhach,
Ach mar chonacthas domsa é arís ní chífear,
Beagbheann ar chách ób' gheal lem chroí é.

Barr dá réir go raibh air choice!
Rath is séan san áit ina mbíonn sé
Mar atá tréitheach do dté críoch air –
Dob é an samhradh seo mo rogha 'pháirtí é. (APM 48)[6]

A fine fair-headed six-foot fellow,
A farmer's son from the country westward,
On hard cement we danced together
A night in the future he'll not remember.

But I won't forget how his arms embraced me,
His quiet smile, civil conversation –
In his clean white shirt, his neat combed hair –
Yellow in the lamplight as the oil ran lower.

He'll get the land his father leaves him,
Marry and raise a houseful of children
But no-one will see the man I danced with –
What did I care who saw my fancy?

All that is best in the world I wish him,
Blessings on every place that holds him,
Every promise fulfilled in living –
My chosen partner for all this summer.[7]

His unawareness enhances the sweetness of the moment. That he should be quite unaware of his charm adds all the more to it. Already, however, there is an ominous sense that the woman who knows more than the man will, in her sense of a past and future pressing in upon this golden moment, suffer much more. The most popular collection during the Irish Revival had been *Amhráin Ghrá Chúige Chonnacht: The Love Songs of Connacht*, published by Douglas Hyde in 1894. Some of those songs were cries of frustrated love by young women unable (often for economic reasons) to marry the man they loved. Mary Colum thought that book quite incendiary in its critique of Victorian values, especially a poem like 'A Ógánaigh an Chúil Cheangailte: Ringleted Youth of My Love'. Mhac an tSaoi reworked that tradition in describing how a young woman might feel tortured at the passing by of a youth whom she could never have:

Is a chaológánaigh, do réifeadh dom fáil scartha leat –
Cleamhnas dom do dhéanfadh mo mhuintir i bhfad as so;
Salmaireacht na cléire, sacraimint na heaglaise,
Do thabharfaidís chun céille mé – dá mb'fhéidir liom tú dhearmad.
(APM 72)

And o slender young man, I'd be all right if we parted –
My people would arrange a match somewhere far away;

The chanting of the clergy, the church's great sacrament
Would bring me to my wits again – if I could forget your face.
(*APM* 73)[8]

The romantic young woman would prefer not to re-enact the tradition: but half-suspects that her attempt will serve only to deepen its hold. It is a woman's right to refuse, and also to refuse a refusal!

'Ní bhearrfad m'ingne'
Adúirt sí siúd
Is do thug cúl don saol
De dheascaibh an aonlae sin –
Lena cré
Ní mhaífinnse
Ná mo leithéidse, gaol –
Cíoram mo cheann
Is cuirim dath fém bhéal. (*APM* 46)

'I will not pare my nails,'
She said
And turned her back on the world
For the sake of that solitary day – .
With her breed
Neither I nor my likes
Would claim affinity –
I comb my hair
And colour my lips.' (*APM* 47)[9]

Some central 'sorrows of storytelling', narrated by women, concern the plight of a trapped female, who may affect a free choice only to be told by a scolding king: 'Tá do chleamhnas déanta, a Ghráinne' (Your match is made, Gráinne). There is no safety to be found even in acceptance of such a fate. The poet can sympathize with Gráinne, aching at the mercy of the moment, even as the teller of the tale is doomed to take the longer view:

> *Cárbh fhios di siúd cad a bhí roimpi*
> *Nuair a d'umhlaigh sí dá thoil go dílis?*
> *Mearbhall grá agus seachrán oíche*
> *Agus éad ban Éireann go lá na scríbe.* (*APM* 68)

> As she bowed to his will, did she realise
> What would follow after:
> Blinding love, ceaseless wandering,
> The eternal envy of the women of Ireland? (*APM* 69)[10]

The woman who yields to passion may endure the eventual hatred of those who chose not to yield.

But young men, especially those of humbler origin, need also to make much of time: in the longer run, their attractions also will fade, and no woman look twice at them. There is a strange atavism in certain poems of this author, a remorseless sense of all body clocks ticking. It is difficult at times to know whether the blind spots of a male courtly love tradition are being sardonically inverted at the expense of men or merely being replicated. In 'Cad Is Bean?' (What is Woman?) the demonization of woman, propounded by many misogynistic scribes of holy Ireland, is unqualified; and then taken to a level of denunciation that is perhaps unprecedented:

> *Mar tá sí gan chéim chumais*
> *Ach i mbun millte,*
> *Nimh léi gach fiúntas dearbh*
> *Phréamhaigh sa tsaoirse.* (*APM* 84)

> Accomplished at nothing
> But sheer destruction

She despises all virtue
Rooted in freedom. (*APM* 85)[11]

What if a man of the mid-twentieth century had written such lines? The sheer conviction of the rhythms and the fact of female authorship might make a reader wonder whether this is a wily diagnosis of self-loathing brought on by a sexist culture – or just a refusal of sorority. Mhac an tSaoi's is indeed a voice without restraint but nothing like the voice of a conventional feminist. Rather her female personae are figures who seized what freedom they could, taking it as a personal right rather than a communal objective.[12]

It was the sequence *Ceathrúintí Mháire Ní Ógáin (Mary Hogan's Quatrains)* which won her lasting fame. It is worth remarking that such a work, if published in English in a magazine and book of the mid-1950s, might well have been banned. Synge had joked that you could sometimes get away with freedoms in Irish that would not have been tolerated in English.[13] The seven-part sequence was to be first published in separate units (possibly for reasons of discretion, but perhaps also in hopes of having some improving effect in the relationship described). 'Máire Ní Ógáin' was a time-honoured name for a foolish woman in Gaelic tradition: and the sequence is a lover's complaint, written in the first person, but also a fierce self-denunciation, even a kind of self-harming in the mode of Deirdre of the ancient legend, who threatened to destroy her own beauty rather than submit to a loathsome lover.

The ferocity and extremism of mood is a consequence of the speaker's lack of freedom. Even in 'Cad Is Bean?' there was an attempt to explain the destructive urge as the hitting-out of a trapped person. Part of the entrapment here is an inability to live happily in the present: the speaker is always taking long views, looking forward or looking back. The golden moments, for whose sake the illicit love was maintained, are literally indescribable: they remain unrendered. Nor is there any complex evocation of the beloved. The ideal man, it is implied, would be one who showed a tender sensitivity towards the restrictions of the woman's predicament; but there is no such figure in the poem. Rather there is an unrequiting lover, told to say yay or nay, but who has already been renounced, not just as an occasion of sin but as a hopeless case.

For this is a poem that feasts on abstinence and negation. In an interview given in 2000 the poet named 'refusal' as her central narrative.[14] That statement linked her to the aesthetic of Samuel Beckett, who made failure his mode and who was tempted into silence. Even more clearly it linked her to another major Gaelic poet of the twentieth century, whose quatrains of poetry in bardic mode became sumptuous with refusals and denials:

> *Fornocht do chonnac thú,*
> *A áille na háille,*
> *is do dhallas mo shúil*
> *ar eagla go stánfainn*

> Naked I saw thee,
> O beauty of beauty,
> And I blinded my eyes
> For fear I should fail[15]

Mhac an tSaoi, whose sex life was more unbuttoned than that of Pearse, nevertheless always expressed a deep admiration for the way in which he inspired her own rhetoric of renunciation:

> *A fhir dár fhulaingeas grá fé rún*
> *Feasta fógraím an clabhsúr:*
> *Dóthanach den damhsa táim,*
> *Leor mo bhabhta mar bhantráill. (APM 76)*

Man, for whom I suffered love
In secret, I now call a halt.
I'll no longer dance in step.
Far too long I've been enthralled. (*APM* 77)[16]

The poem opens with an image of entrapment, and a prayer to be freed from the 'net'. Yet the more the speaker struggles to free herself of the net, the more caught up in it she becomes. She knows that to continue the affair means that she cannot take communion at Mass; but then she hopes, when restored to a life of piety, to pray for both lovers. In the meantime, the memory of their bliss will help her to break free: a dubious proposition, which casts some uncertainty over the speaker's hopes to break the 'bond'.

And a bond it surely is. The second section opens with a repetition of phrases ('beagbheann'; uncaring – 'neamhshuim'; indifference), designed to demonstrate her indifference to damnation by clergy or public opinion. The phrases have the opposite effect in their thumping repetition, showing that the speaker cares far too much. Worse still, the image of sexual passion evoked is hardly anything other than a physical version of the current blockage:

Beagbheann ar chros na sagart,
Ar gach ní ach bheith sínte
Idir tú agus falla. (*APM* 88)

I care little for priests' prohibitions,
For anything save to lie stretched
Between you and the wall. (*APM* 89)[17]

'Sínte' is a verb often used of a corpse ('stretched'). If this is the consoling deposit of memory, it is also an image of her impasse. She heightens its negativity by next speaking of 'faobhar na leapan' (the sharpness of the bed, apparently like that of a knife). This was endured as a searing experience for the space of a year, but is recalled as no pleasure: merely a mechanical repetition of flesh-on-flesh, for the sake of the original pledge.

The sequence passes through an astounding range of moods: from repentance, through wistfulness, tenderness, betrayal, regret, down to a childlike jealousy. That image of a bitter, vengeful child morphs into that of frustrated lover and blocked mother: as if all the frustrations of womanhood, the pain of birth and stillbirth, of postnatal depression and exhausted mothering, are somehow brought to a focus in the negligent lover:

> Tá naí an éada ag deol mo chíchse,
> Is mé ag tál air de ló is d'oíche. . . (APM 90)

> The child of jealousy is sucking my breast,
> While I curse it day and night. . . (APM 91)[18]

But the plea for renewed copulation is expressed in a language of animality so abject as to constitute a prior interdiction of the proposal:

> Ar láir dhea-tharraic ná déan éigean
> Is díolfaidh sí an comhar leat ina séasúr féinig. (APM 92)

> Do not force a willing mare,
> And she will recompense you in her own season. (APM 93)[19]

It is as if the wan hope of love has been replaced by a need for the sort of decent treatment given to useful beasts of burden. The poem ends in the same confusion with which it began: seeking repentance as prelude to a repetition of the forbidden love. As it moves to a conclusion, its phrases become short, almost catatonic. There is no calm of mind. Only a kind of exhaustion supervenes, sufficient to bring silence.

Out of such emotional destitution is crafted a major poem, which does not simply report feelings but seems to invent them. In a work of deep experience, there are no redundant adjectives: just a directness of statement, which captures mental confusion but with an absolute clarity. Mhac an tSaoi has the courage to use poetry to deal with what perplexes and tortures her, with what lies beyond the comfort of an analysis. The sequence thus becomes not only an account of her inner conflict but the very form of it. The writer's alertness to the feeling of each passing moment means that it becomes something of an adventure to explore her sensibility through the local alertness of her writing.

This story of a relationship with an unsatisfactory, only intermittent lover may, for all its negations, serve as a positive account of the poet's own relationship to tradition. That tradition enabled the very utterance which it would also, in the fullness of time, imperil. In her later years of writing, the writer found that the rich language of Corcha Dhuibhne, with which she had kept faith, had all but disappeared. As she remarked in 1988, 'it is too late for me to look for another habitat. It used to be said that the last native speaker of Cornish was a parrot and that he lived in Ringsend. I am that parrot.'[20]

6. Growing Up Absurd: Edna O'Brien and *The Country Girls*

I rish writers born in later decades of the nineteenth century often equated their childhood with that of the nation, before the fall into political violence and civil strife. In their autobiographies a boy or girl began as a subject in a colony, clashed with overweening authority, and ended life as a free citizen of an independent land. A nonentity to begin with, the protagonist blossomed into a person. In these accounts, childhood was often described as a privileged zone, populated by colourful characters and doting relations.

Edna O'Brien, however, was born in 1930 at Tuamgraney, Co. Clare, into a new state still soured by the aftermath of a bitter civil war. The 'nationalism of mourning', sketched by Beckett,[1] is carried further in her writing. For her there would be no idyll of a national childhood. The girls and young women of her novels are worldly wise and sardonic from the outset, in ways their predecessors never dared to be. In *The Country Girls*, her first novel, childhood ends abruptly with the death by drowning of a beloved mother.[2] The brutal husband left by the dead woman is a hopeless, heedless alcoholic, his inadequacy as a parent being a clear sign of a society unsure of its direction. This is a censorious world of adults who often behave like children and of children compelled at a ridiculously early age to take on the responsibilities of adults. Until his death, Caithleen Brady has lived in daily fear of her father's beatings. Her childhood is a prolonged period of worry as to whether he will complete the ruin of the family estate begun when the Black and Tans burned the ancestral home. The theme of failed fatherhood, which so dominated the writings of Joyce, here takes on an even sharper terror, when a young woman is the victim.

The book was banned by the state censors. In a country which piously urged young women to treat their father as a kind of god, it was subversive to depict scenes of parental violence as routine. In the United States of the 1880s, Mark Twain had been similarly castigated for his presentation of the drunken 'Pap' in *The Adventures of Huckleberry Finn*, but O'Brien added further layers of complication by being a woman. The new Ireland was described by Seán O'Faoláin as a nation of apple-lickers: people who if tempted in the Garden of Eden would have licked rather than bitten the apple. Young people emigrated in droves, not (as once) in flight from a hated British law, but because the life offered to them seemed boring and mediocre. In this new scheme of things, young women were not encouraged to write books in which they divulged their innermost thoughts and sexual desires. The secret life of the more freewheeling young people was known to some: but such knowledge was to be maintained at the level of local gossip, and certainly not to be published for the condescending amusement of the outside world.

To write in that charged context was an act of rebellion, a satanic pact which might place the writer outside the community forever. The first-person narration of *The Country Girls* means that nothing will be hidden: the reader will know exactly how Caithleen processes everything, and also those things she hides from herself. Although the state authorities effected the bans on literature, the real source of repression was the Catholic Church: for, as O'Brien explained, 'the Russian censorship has always been political, and the Irish has always been religious'.[3] The Russian curtailments were imposed from above by the political elite; whereas the Irish ones arose from below, once a citizen had made a 'convincing' case. One effect was to infantilize much of the adult population, who were in effect treated as being incapable of mature judgement.

In *The Country Girls*, the children are old beyond their years, taking on worries about heedless parents, even as many adults appear immature. None of the adult males appears to have transacted or worked through a real childhood, and they remain as a result forever childish. Even Mr Gentleman, the middle-aged Lothario, in his sexual overtures to Caithleen sounds more like a boy than a man: 'show me your naked body' (*CG* 103). Her instinctual honesty appeals to a grown man who feels like a misfit: but such men are portrayed here as developing a rather unhealthy interest in the image of the child. Jack Holland places his hand on Mrs Brady's knee and keeps it there, in full view of her daughter Caithleen; and the mother, like many docile women of the time, accepts this without a word of rebuke, despite the bad example it gives to her daughter. There are times, as in this scene, when the daughter seems more like a protective chaperone, a partner to her mother, than her child; and one, moreover, who shares her sense of ill-use at the hands of men.

The Irish had long viewed childhood as a holy state, a zone for the protection of spiritual values often put in jeopardy by the world. Unless the faithful became as little children, they would not enter the kingdom of heaven. The need for such a comforting illusion grew all the greater in the messy years after political independence, but O'Brien effectively questioned it. In *The Country Girls* her account of a raffle during the interval in the performance of a play stresses how even the prizewinners were so timid as to be ashamed to collect their winnings. She is even more corrosive, however, about the use of children to draw the winning tickets, 'as they were supposed to be honest' (*CG* 46).

'Supposed to be honest': it is a telling phrase, and hardly accidental that it is used in a theatrical context. For Caithleen is a sort of Irish Lolita, destined to be at once infantilized and sexualized. The child as an actor of innocence is a postmodern type: one who gives adults the pleasure of fiction but also frees them of the guilt of seeming to believe in it. Mr Gentleman's infatuation with Caithleen means that everything she does is seductively inscribed in quotation marks. This gives to the child an air of insouciance, just out of reach of the adult in a zone of pleasure and dread. Children are double performers, by virtue of the roles they play *and* by virtue of the very fact of being children. They love to impersonate the sort of innocent souls they are supposed to be, but with a *gaucherie* that can be knowing, which will allow them to manipulate adults who are not even aware this is going on.

By the 1930s, the intensification of the family as the locus for all Irish destinies had become extreme. The family was the very basis of the nation as defined in the 1937 Constitution, passed into law under the guiding hand of Éamon de Valera. This was perhaps an inevitable after-effect of the colonial period, during which the family had become the largest social institution with which many people could identify. Yet the fetishising of the family, even after independence, meant that it became an alternative to the very idea of the social, which it was supposed to serve. Under pressure of such absolute, idealizing expectations – not to mention constant migrations – many families cracked and many childhoods were disrupted.

The child had been an endlessly poignant image in the writings of Patrick Pearse: his poems and plays emphasize the redemptive strangeness of a child bearing to fallen adults messages from a purer world.[4] Hence also the desire of de Valera to write into the statute book an ideal version of the family which he had never himself known in his insecure, earlier years (when he was raised by an aunt). Yet O'Brien challenges these understandings. Her book consistently questions the notion that childhood exists as a state of unspoilt nature outside the culture in which it is produced. There is no *cordon sanitaire* around Caithleen Brady's home, which exactly reflects all the corruptions of the outside world. She is not innocent to begin with, merely inexperienced: and her desire is to gain experience as fast as possible.

Writers such as Pearse had indulged the hope that children might preserve for grown-ups a set of values which stood in danger of collapse, and by a kind of ventriloquist's trick they caused children in their texts to provide such reassurance. But by casting her tale in the first person singular, O'Brien, like Twain before her, tried to counter this projection of adult desire upon the image of the child. In the process she managed to question all the older colonial stereotypes of a childlike Hibernian peasantry. She showed a darker truth: that the childish adults and careworn kids of her story are caught in cycles of cruel repetition. Parents, incapable of self-appraisal, feel quite free to criticize their own inadequacies as recreated in their children, who reciprocate by being hypercritical of all forms of authority. As a child, Caithleen owns a toy tea set, but she seldom plays with it lest it break. The fitments of her mother's home are all either broken or out of use.

This is not to say that *The Country Girls* lacks freshness or charm: in fact it oozes with both. The prose is direct, seemingly guileless but often subtle in effect. Short, honest sentences imply a great deal more than they bother to say. For O'Brien grace is a movement engaged in with the least necessary effort.[5] That notion of style as thrift is an aesthetic preached by Mrs Brady from the start. Although her daughter owns a good pair of slippers, they are kept out of commission and used only on special occasions, such as visits by relations. The house is already a kind of postcolonial museum. Objects in daily use are soon broken and seldom if ever fixed. In the local sweetshop the blinds are kept down at all times, lest the sun's rays damage jams or confectionery; and children sneak-read magazines because they have no money to buy them.

The independent Irish, having missed out on the heroic phase of the bourgeoisie, when strong industries were founded and quality goods produced, know only how to consume – and theirs is largely the practice of a consumerism without goods.[6]

What is depicted in this world of Co. Clare in the 1950s is not so much a functioning economy as its caricature. For months, mother and daughter wait fruitlessly for a man to come to fix the toilet, much as they wait fearfully for the nightly return of the man who is the house's head. The hired hand, Hickey, is owed a lot of back-money and must therefore be allowed to give away the occasional pullet to Mrs O'Shea, his favourite barmaid at the local hotel. The O'Sheas are themselves owed even more money by Caithleen's father, who always puts bills behind the crockery and forgets them: and the result is that ten of the O'Sheas' cows have grazing on the Brady lands for life. The style in which such adjustments are described is both innocently direct and sardonically observant. The child, who is not allowed to wear her own slippers very often, cannot help noticing what happens to those worn by Mrs O'Shea every day: 'Her bedroom slippers looked as if the greyhounds had chewed them. More than likely they had. The hotel was occupied chiefly by greyhounds' (*CG* 18).

All this talk of slippers evokes the story of Cinderella, of which *The Country Girls* is to be a modern version. The young girl's first love is Hickey; and so Mrs O'Shea, with those damaged slippers, becomes her unlovely rival. (Slippers were, of course, a rare commodity in rural Clare, where some children still went barefoot, as did many tellers of the original fairy tale). Hickey is poor, friendly, unaffected: 'thinking is pure cod' (*CG* 10), he tells Caithleen. The 400 acres of the farm are falling into ruin, despite his hard work, because of the father's neglect; and even Hickey, for all his reliability, brings out her fear of being abandoned.

Each night she listens closely for him to come home. The impression is of an entire community whose women's main function is to wait for men to return. But Hickey is a less than polished swain. On each nightly return, before going to bed, he pees into a peach tin and pours the contents out of his window, imperiling the life of the shrubs beneath. Caithleen's only real solace is her mother, who tries to make the ruined house into the semblance of a home by the subtle placement of lampshades and fire screens. She is the sort of instinctive sage who 'knew things before you told her' (*CG* 10), rather like the narrator Caithleen, who seems to intuit things before they are fully understood. But this second sight leaves both mother and daughter knowing far too much, bearing too great a burden of consciousness. Mrs Brady's escape from a dire marriage leads only to her early death – whether in the company of a lover (as suggested by gossips) or on a solo defection remains unclear. What is made painfully obvious is that mothers who abandon their task as carers may be punishable by death.

Caithleen, so afraid in the dark that she leaves her bed six or seven times each night to say aspirations (religiose practice overlapping with obsessive-compulsive disorder), has one great fear: that her mother might die while she is at school. Mrs Brady is admired also by all the local men. One shopkeeper, Jack Holland, completes the Cinderella motif by conflating it with the Cathleen Ni Houlihan paradigm, when he tells Caithleen that her mother has 'the ways and walk of a queen' (*CG* 17). This feeds a pet revivalist theory of his: 'You know how many Irish people are royalty and unaware of it. There are kings and queens walking the roads of Ireland, riding bicycles' (*CG* 16). Perhaps Caithleen is such an inheritor, the awkward but gifted one who will someday come into her own. As in most fairy tales, the central characters here are women, but it is the infantile men who believe in the ideology of the fairy story – it is one of them who suspects she may be of the blue blood.

The fairy tale element is compounded by the second love of Caithleen's life, Mr Gentleman, 'a beautiful man who lived in the white house on the hill' (*CG* 15). This was not his real name, which is never given, because he exists less as reality than as the site of Caithleen's desires. (Some readers believe that he is based on Sean MacBride, son of Maud Gonne and former IRA chief – in keeping with O'Brien's frequent tendency to be star-struck by strong republican men). Mr Gentleman remains a rather shadowy figure through *The Country Girls*, his grey hair, satin waistcoats and slightly French intonation ('as if there was a damson stone in his throat' (*CG* 16)), holding out to Caithleen not just the promise of romance but a stylish surrogate for her own inadequate father. He appears to embody all the worldly experience she lacks but deeply wishes she had. For the true subject of *The Country Girls* is parental rather than sexual love. Caithleen and her friend Baba will be propositioned by much older, inappropriate men, or else seek them out, as if forever in search of a father substitute. And each father in the book is utterly dissatisfied with his biological child. Each child is potentially well cast, but for a role with a father not their own.

In her last days at primary school, Caithleen notices how the poorer girls are given all the dirty, menial jobs. She is above such things, but only by virtue of her cleverness, which has helped her win a scholarship to a convent school. Her mother wanted her to know that convent life, perhaps because of her own frustrating experience with men. The local village, like one of Synge's dystopian townlands, offered the girls only older men or foolish youths: but the cycle of repetition is remorseless. Whether in convent school or later in city life, the two girls find it almost impossible to meet and engage with boys or young men of their own age.

Baba is also to attend the convent school, but as a fee-payer. She sends Caithleen a note which insists 'it's nicer when you pay'. Its postscript will be repeated throughout the novel: 'You're a right looking eejit' (*CG* 21). Baba is extrovert, headstrong and confident, whereas Caithleen is thoughtful, hesitant, troubled. If Baba seeks sex, Caithleen wants romance.[7] Together, the duo might have the makings of a whole person. They are a pseudo-couple in the great Irish tradition of Wilde's Jack and Algy, Joyce's Shem and Shaun, Beckett's Didi and Gogo, but with this difference – they are a female rather than a male duo. That repression which once led to male splitting into the Double seems at last to have overtaken women as well.

At the primary school the teacher, Miss Moriarty, had looked perpetually cross, her eyes locked into a frown brought on by reading too much. Caithleen, her star pupil, will run similar risks, but O'Brien guards against an over-literary prose by regular use of colloquialisms ('twas'). Baba wears a white cardigan draped over her shoulders with unfilled sleeves, rather in the manner of a cloak worn by one of Cinderella's sisters. Careless of the good opinion of others, when offered a box of biscuits in Caithleen's home, she takes all the chocolate-covered ones. Her mother, Martha, is beautiful but cold. She beats the family servant and hides choice cuts of food from her husband, with whom she lives on terms of barely suppressed rage. As manipulative as her daughter, she seeks only two things in life: drink and the admiration of men. Yet, such is the complication of O'Brien's narration, that she also emerges as another possible Cinderella, a lost and neglected princess. When her husband, Mr Brennan, ill-fed and ulcerous, gently chides her ('Better look up how to cook peas, Mammy'), this is a reference to that scene in many versions of the legend when Cinderella is told to sift the peas from the cinders into which they have fallen.[8] Yet the class hatred that smoulders beneath the surface of the Brennans' marriage erupts under such provocation: 'I was eating peas when his thick lump of a mother was feeding them nettle-tops. Jesus'. (*CG* 40). The relationship shows Caithleen that the agendas of sex and romance will not be easily reconciled. In that narrow world, a woman's fulfilment as a sexual being may involve her annihilation as a person – or vice versa.

It is telling that in both the Brady and the Brennan households, the mother is the decisive influence in determining the fate of her daughter, for good or for ill. Caithleen's mother is indulgent, but to the point of folly. When she goes to sleep alongside her daughter, she notices a half-chewed sweet stuck in the child's mouth; but, rather than remove it, she remains watching over her charge – tender, protective, sacrificing her own rest, but in a deeply silly fashion. This is hardly practical parenting. And the mother never devises a way to protect the daughter from the father's repeated brutality.

Caithleen had always feared losing her mother to illness, but not to accident. The mother leaves the loveless, violent marriage, taking her rosary beads from the nail above the dresser: 'She was gone. Really gone' (*CG* 31). If the writers of pre-independent Ireland had often featured Ireland as mother, post-independent Ireland would frequently be haunted by the figure of the missing or lost mother – as if the desired being were not really there: just a vacuum where a parent might have been. Martha Brennan passes her revulsion against her husband onto her children (not that Caithleen agrees, for Mr Brennan is the father she would have liked to have had). Mrs Brennan, addicted to male endorsement of her beauty, is less the mother than the sister type. There are no good marriages in this book: people will do whatever they can get away with.

Mrs Brady's escapade ends in her drowning in a nearby lake; and Caithleen is left at the mercy of Baba, decamping to her house and sleeping with her in one of her nightdresses. The earliest versions of the Cinderella legend involved such a moment: in the words of Marina Warner, 'the good mother often dies at the beginning of the story.'[9] Stories like *The Winter's Tale*, which chronicle a good mother's return, have never been as popular as those in which she is replaced by a tyrant. That monster's role is discharged here by various women, from Martha Brennan to the mother superior of the convent, who prolong the humiliation of this Cinderella. In most modern versions 'the absent mother no longer returns',[10] but in *The Country Girls*, Caithleen, who has lamented the lack of a grave on which she might lay flowers, actually fears that her mother might come back: 'What is it about death that we cannot bear to have someone who is dead come back to us? I wanted Mama more than anything in the world and yet if the door had opened and she had entered, I would have screamed' (*CG* 53). Lacking a marked grave, the mother is more dead than anyone she had ever heard of.

Baba jokes that Mama might return to pass on to her all her wonderful jewellery; but to Caithleen the loss is like the loss of a lover, whom she had wooed away from her brutal father's side:

> I could see Mama on the pillow beside him. Reluctant and frightened as if something terrible were being done to her. She used to sleep with me as often as she could and only went across to his room when he made her. He wore no pyjamas in bed, and I was ashamed even to think of it. (*CG* 58–9)

Her own developing relationship with Mr Gentleman is different, compounded of high courtesy and mutual consideration. On an expedition to Limerick to buy her secondary school uniform, Caithleen has lunch with the great man, whose cheese smelt like socks but who confessed that she was 'the sweetest thing that ever happened to me' (*CG* 65). She has worn lipstick, but he prefers her to go without it.

The religious strain inherited by Caithleen from her mother makes her a kind of mystic. By installing Mr Gentleman as a corrected version of the father, she may have confused God with a mere man. The man she wants does not exist in any human form. She believes so deeply in the ideals of Christian tradition as to immobilize herself in the world, leaving Baba to make all the running and all the practical interventions. Caithleen, who sought an over-abstracted image of her own mother, makes the same error with Mr Gentleman: and, unless she breaks out of this cycle, risks repeating the same mistake.

At the convent school, everything is forbiddingly clean and tidy: 'Dirt can be consoling and friendly in a strange place, I thought' (*CG* 74). Just as Cinderella hugged the ashes so that she might stay close to her lost mother, so does Caithleen seek to embrace the dirt of death; and she is rewarded for that steadfastness by many images. As the girls sing a hymn, 'Mother, Mother, I Am Coming', she recalls the day on which they both watched a skylark carry specks of sheep's wool from a wire fence to make a homely nest. In a school regime where each girl begins by crying for her mother, that is a comfort far greater than is to be had from any of the pseudo-mothers among the nuns. Confronted by their resolute anonymity, Caithleen wonders, 'if I could ever get to know them from their backs' (*CG* 81). The nuns open and read Caithleen's letters from Hickey and from her father, who tells of how he (like the last of Maria Edgeworth's Rackrents) was happy to move into the gate lodge now that the big house is too large for his purposes.

School discipline offers no escape from the Cinderella role, however. Having come first in examinations (for which the prize was a statue of St Jude, patron saint of hopeless causes), Caithleen knows the stress of having to maintain that position by endless work. Befriended by a charismatic older girl named Cynthia, she learns to live without Baba (who implores her to cut out the new friend). Her Catholic faith is rule-bound rather than visionary – and so her nights are tortured by the fear that sins committed by her mother after her last confessions, such as a failure to return excess change in the grocer's shop, may be exposing her to the fires of perpetual punishment. Where Joyce's hero Stephen had gone in terror of eternal pain for himself, Caithleen dreads it for her mother.

The comic potential of convent school life is emphasized – everything from tossing bad, inedible meat into a nearby lake on a Sunday walk to the contortionist's art of undressing in dormitories under cover of a dressing gown. A talk on sex education by a priest prompts the nuns to ask Caithleen to hang a notice outside: 'Do Not Enter – Lecture On Here'. However, she places it (whether by accident or design is unclear) on the nuns' lavatory. The girls suspect the nuns of sleeping in their own coffins. When Baba and Caithleen circulate a note offering a graphic description of what Father Tom may be doing to Sister Mary (who has a permanently ecstatic expression), they are summarily expelled. 'Poor Caithleen', laments Mr Brennan after their return, 'you've always been Baba's tool' (*CG* 118). In saying as much, he may also have been thinking of himself as the tool of his wife: it is clear that Mama and Caithleen were just the sort of wife and daughter he would like to have had. 'If one could only choose one's children' (*CG* 118), he sighs. The fact that one cannot is what leaves Caithleen's own father being told by her that she hates him.

In many versions of the Cinderella tale, 'a persecuted heroine must flee home in order to escape a parental oppressor';[11] but before she leaves, the bad father must be punished. The unhappy daughter seeks a better parent, on the Nietzschean principle that if you have not had a good father, you should go out and invent one. So the thwarted love for Mr Brennan must be transferred to Mr Gentleman. Such a trajectory had always characterized the fairy tale as deeply subversive of patriarchal values.

Caithleen has little room for manoeuvre. Already another problematic older man, Jack Holland, has set his cap at her and only the presence of Mr Gentleman allows her to extricate herself from his clutches. As she prepares to leave the village, she studies some grunting pigs as they stick their snouts through creels from which they can never hope to flee. She isn't one bit sorry to quit the place: 'there seemed to be fewer geraniums in the upstairs windows than there had been when I was a child' (*CG* 130). The west of Ireland is dying on its feet. For all its brio, *The Country Girls* is part of that long tradition of Irish writing which conveys the sense of an ending, as 'the last of' the rural valleys is denuded of its young.

Urbanization affords only temporary distraction from all this woe: but by contrast with the west, Dublin is a true 'fairyland' (the word being used in this quite un-Yeatsian fashion to celebrate its flashing neon lights). 'I loved it', Caithleen wickedly adds, 'more than I had ever loved a summer's day in a hayfield' (*CG* 141). This is a Cathleen Ni Houlihan who gladly gives up her green fields, for which she does not care all that much. As she and Baba trail through the city streets, they marvel at passing women with large, painted eyes, who seem to search the night for something poignant. To Caithleen such women appear beautiful in their stylized grace: to Baba, however, they seem like 'something dug up'. The implied comparison to those nuns who may sleep in their coffins is no accident, for the whores in their underwear may have more in common with the holy nuns than anyone might suspect. Baba senses the potential of life in a modern city: 'I'm going to blow up this town' (*CG* 141). The avowal is somewhat undercut by the fact that she can dramatize that aspiration with nothing more portentous than a brown-paper chip bag, which she inflates and then bursts. In *The Country Girls* emotions can at times float free of their human exponents, as if in excess of the available roles, for nothing in the actual Ireland is commensurate with these young girl's youthful yearnings.

Living in defiant style, the country girls confront the Irish capital. People there are not quite as nice as their rural counterparts. Established in lodgings, the girls are amused by a foreign gentleman who sits at table 'holding an egg in his lap as if he weren't supposed to be eating it' (*CG* 133). At once, Baba starts to play the lady of the manor: 'Oh lady supreme, will you pass me the cream?' – and then, turning to the gent, now hidden behind his newspaper, she says 'you bald-headed scutter, will you pass me the butter?' (*CG* 134). A hand comes out from behind the paper and slowly pushes the dish to the mortified girls.

They adopt black underwear, which is racy, and Caithleen even favours black stockings, which are literary, though one cannot help also taking them as a sign of her unconscious mourning for her dead mother. She is by now writing verse, but Baba scoffs that she has encountered superior samples in mawkish mortuary cards. She has also encountered the writings of the city's greatest chronicler, James Joyce; but Baba finds all talk of this writer tedious: 'Will you for Chrissake stop asking fellas if they read James Joyce's *Dubliners*? They're not interested. They're out for the night. Eat and drink all you can and leave James Joyce to blow his own trumpet' (*CG* 159).

Yet *Dubliners* holds the key to the meaning of the girls' experiences. They have a long-planned assignation with two wealthy, older men; but the encounter is terrifying and banal by turns, and quite devoid of any satisfactory climax – these men cannot satisfy desire and one actually falls asleep. The 'Two Gallants' with whom the girls have a date are just ageing idiots. Baba ends up succumbing to tuberculosis and having to give up her nightclub life for a sanatorium. Caithleen is rescued from the frightening encounter by Mr Gentleman, who sweeps her away to safety in his car. She feels herself safe in his loving presence, as if someone were tickling her stomach from the inside, which is to say as if he were already inside her. But he never does this, failing to materialize for the promised date on which they were to fly away to Vienna for a consummation of their love. He exists only in his need for an idea of her and in her need for an idea of him: but 'no one would ever really belong to him. He was too detached' (*CG* 178). In the end, Dublin lives up to the reputation given it by Joyce as the centre of paralysis, the site of arrested impulses, summed up in a terse telegram: 'Everything gone wrong. Threats from your father. My wife has another nervous breakdown. Regret enforced silence. Must not see you' (*CG* 187).

Caithleen's condition recalls that of the character Eveline in Joyce's *Dubliners*: a moment of glamour has been held out before the protagonist, only to be taken away, as the futility of all attempts at escape is revealed to the victim. But this Eveline *would* have gone with her man, had he dared make the trip. If this had been a novel by Balzac or Stendhal, it might have ended with the protagonist from the provinces looking across the rooftops of the capital and asserting a sense of centrality and triumph: but that is not how things work out here. Dublin is just a fake Vienna and Mr Gentleman a pseudo-continental. If this had even been a true story of Cinderella, it might have climaxed with the heroine's triumph over adversity and her sinking into the arms of a princely youth: but it is not really that either. The dress with which Caithleen is supplied to go to the ball with Mr Gentleman is borrowed from her fat landlady Joanna. In storage since the older woman's wedding, it smells of mothballs and camphor, though it might have been the fashion in Mr Gentleman's distant youth. At any rate, Caithleen never gets to wear it and she returns limply to her bedsit world.

There she has already experienced something like a Joycean epiphany. At breakfast one day she has noted the date on the newspaper, 15 May:

> There on the very first page under the anniversaries was a memorium for my mother. Four years. Four short years and I had forgotten the date of her death; at least I had overlooked it! I felt that wherever she was she had stopped loving me, and I went out of the room crying. It was worse to think that he had remembered. (*CG* 181)

This ending is neither Balzac nor Cinderella but pure Joyce: and the entire novel might be re-read in that light. *Dubliners*, O'Brien has gratefully written, 'was the first time in my whole life that I happened on something in a book that was exactly like my own life. I had always been a stranger from what had been my life up to then.'[12] What had marked Caithleen off from Baba all along was her ability to find moments of beauty even in humble people (like Hickey) or settings like the fields around the farmhouse.

Even deeper than that, however, was her capacity to transcend the maternal tie, a capacity shared with Joyce, of whom O'Brien has written:

> There is one thing in Joyce's life which defies belief. Never in all the years since her death did he allude to his mother. It is hard to think that she who had such a vast influence on him was not mentioned in any of his letters home and not referred to after his father's death or his daughter's breakdown. It is a fierce and determined repudiation. Her death he had described as 'a wound on the brain'.[13]

At the time of the death, Joyce showed no grief: but later, after the fierce repudiation, his mother returned as persecutor.

The Country Girls displays a similar ambivalence towards a beloved mother. The wicked stepmothers (the nuns) and stepsister (Baba) soak up all the anger and bile, preserving below the level of consciousness the image of the perfected Mama. Joyce had in *Ulysses* called a mother's love the only true thing in life: yet he had also caused Stephen to accuse his mother of being a ghoul and chewer of corpses: 'No, mother. Let me be. Let me live!'[14] So it is in *The Country Girls*, where Caithleen fears being haunted by the spirit of the being she has most greatly loved. Of such an ambivalence Bruno Bettelheim remarked:

> So the typical fairy tale splitting of the mother into a good (usually dead) mother and an evil step-mother serves the child well. It is not only a means of preserving an internal all-good mother when the real mother is not all-good, but it also permits anger at this 'bad' step-mother without endangering the goodwill of the true mother who is viewed as a different person... The fantasy of the wicked stepmother not only preserves the good mother intact; it also prevents having to feel guilty about one's angry

thoughts and wishes about her – a guilt which would seriously interfere with the good relation to Mother.[15]

Why does Caithleen forget the anniversary of her mother's death? Perhaps she felt unconscious resentment at a perfect Mama for abandoning her at all. Away from the adults known through childhood, the girls felt no need to refer back to the parental base, or to analyse their experiences through the theories of their religious or educational formation. Until the identity building of an adolescent is complete, it may be difficult for the person to make a direct confrontation with the past that is to be mourned. Freed of the pressure of suffocating parents, the teenager is often distracted by investigating other ways of being or of becoming adult.

Caithleen was the sort of child who over-identified with her perfect mother, the very separateness of whose existence she may not have recognized in her early years. She confused dependence on another with her own omnipotence. The later, pained discovery that sources of gratification lie outside this sacred relationship could have led to the restoration of the fantasy of the all-powerful perfect mother. Caithleen's inability to mourn arises from an intense rage against a lost love object, preventing most recollections of her mother being processed as happy experience or savoured as memory. Melanie Klein once wrote that an early feeling of overpowering rage against a mother may make it hard for a child to synthesize good and bad.[16] Hence Bettelheim's analysis of fairy tales as examples of 'splitting' between a good and bad mother, because children are often afraid to admit that they harbour negative feelings towards those whom they love.

The Country Girls is a novel about mourning the modern inability to mourn. The bright lights of the big city distract Caithleen from working through her grief about her mother: in such a setting, there can be few, if any, communal expressions of sadness: 'Weep and you weep alone' (*CG* 39), as the mother had taught. The newspaper memorial reminds her that at some point her father had in fact loved her mother and entertained his own high hopes for the relationship. But the daughter is in flight from his subsequent derelictions. Tired being an adult child responsible for feckless adults, she finds in Dublin the chance to explore that childish irresponsible element of herself, which she had never fully had the luxury of knowing. But the old cares erupt again when she is stopped short by the notice in the paper.

Edna O'Brien's 1999 study of Joyce might indeed be read as a marginal set of commentaries, offered four decades later, on themes and issues raised by *The Country Girls*. The fear of loss felt from the beginning by Caithleen is projected onto Joyce's mother in the work of critical study: 'But already from the mother he so loved he was distancing himself. When making his confirmation at Clongowes and being allowed to choose a saint's name he chose Aloysius, the saint who, in imitation of Pascal, would not allow his mother to embrace him because he feared contact with women.'[17]

O'Brien's interpretation of May Joyce's letters to her dissident son in Paris portrays them not as long-distance attempts to enforce parental control as much as pleas for some sort of spiritual companionship. Her son behaves as if he were an only child rather than the first of many; and she never questions his lofty arrogance, seeking only to shield him and to ensure his success. O'Brien, who regards the protection of the young as an ethical imperative, would well understand such motives. The spiritual longing she attributes to May Joyce and Caithleen Brady was also something Joyce himself felt. Although his brother Stanislaus sourly commented that 'if James longed to copulate with a soul, he ought to get himself born anywhere other than Ireland',[18] W. B. Yeats expressed the same underlying idea somewhat differently when he remarked that the tragedy of sexual intercourse is the perpetual virginity of the soul.[19] O'Brien has said that 'it is only with our bodies that we ever really forgive one another: the mind pretends to forgive, but it harbours and remembers in moments of blackness'.[20]

By blending elements of the story of Cinderella with the defeated epiphany of Joyce, O'Brien created her own form of anti-magic realism. That combination allowed her to offer a radical challenge to both the validity of feminine romance and to the masculine tradition of the *Bildungsroman*. Too many critics of O'Brien have noted only the romantic magazine element: but it is the combination of this with Joycean realism which is so subversive. If Joyce felt that no psychological development was possible for young men in the society depicted in *Dubliners*, O'Brien addresses the same problem for young Irishwomen.

The disappearance of children and childhood is usually linked, as Shakespeare intuited, to the disappearance of adults; and, in their place in our postmodern world, comes a sequence of eternal adolescents, forever repeating the songs of their youth, the 'positively final performance' of a rock star now old enough to draw a pension. Once adolescence is identified as a category of intensified life, it tends to expand both forward and backward, thereby reinforcing the paradigm of a child-adult and the adult-child. Franco Moretti has said that in the formless world of permanent adolescence, an endless experimentation with roles means that people 'lose their youth without ever becoming adults'.[21] In his study of the male *Bildungsroman*, *A Way in the World*, Moretti remarks that the European novel of the nineteenth century offered eternal role play rather than a preparation for adult stabilization – 'except in England', he added, 'where novels were still fairy tale in structure, more emphasising childhood than adolescence, as they defend stability rather than privilege the revolutionary strains and claims of adolescence.'[22]

While that is certainly true of the fairy tale element in *Great Expectations* or even *Pride and Prejudice*, it could never be said of *The Country Girls*. In the arms of Mr Gentleman, Caithleen almost repeats the cycle of her mother's foolishness and despair, but she is in the end saved from all that by the failure of the fairy tale structure. From that defeat, she learns something worth knowing. She was repressed in early years by an apparently perfect mother, whose marriage was not really a good model of adult sexuality. Hence she represses the memory of her in the years following her death, much as Joyce repressed the memory of his mother, who also had appeared more in the guise of spiritual companion than exemplary parent. What Joyce remarked of his own family might equally have been said by Caithleen of hers: 'My mother was slowly killed, I think, by my father's ill-treatment, by years of trouble, and by my cynical frankness of conduct.'[23] Looking at his mother's body in a coffin, Joyce said that he saw a victim and that he cursed the system that made her a victim.

Edna O'Brien has reserved particular praise for the quality of Joyce's letters to his partner Nora Barnacle, which deal with 'her own sexual prowess, no small thing for a convent girl from Galway and a radical thing in defiance of that male illusion whereby women were expected to maintain a mystique and conceal their deepest sexual impulses'.[24] O'Brien's commentary on this insists that sexuality and maternity are not contradictory, but also explores the possibility that sexual and personal fulfilment may be irreconcilable in a pornographic culture which often sees a woman's involvement in sexual activity as conditional upon her erasure as an individual.[25] What attracted Joyce to Nora Barnacle may have been what interested Caithleen in Mr Gentleman: 'a hazy and sensual disposition'[26] which might be remoulded upon lines best pleasing to the remoulder. Bringing such awesome and discrepant expectations to relationships, such persons were bound for disappointment.

The Country Girls does not just rewrite the Cinderella story and *Dubliners*. It also rejigs, at certain moments, *Castle Rackrent*. The once proud estate is run at the end not by its owner but by a more astute hired hand. The drink-addled owner is glad to abandon the pretence of presiding over a mansion and relieved to live instead in a gate lodge. He remains untransformed and unfulfilled, in contrast to his daughter, whose maturation is possible precisely because her romantic wishes have not been achieved. She experiences instead the full meaning of her own aborted epiphany.

The romance of a young woman and a middle-aged man was, of course, a hangover from the nineteenth century. In its classic pedagogic novels, such as *Pride and Prejudice* or *Jane Eyre*, a man well versed in the ways of the world explained them to a clever woman who was much younger. But that tradition judders to a halt here and is exposed as null and void. O'Brien's work is utterly contemporary and part of an international trend. As a coming-of-age story of confused teenagers, it might be read alongside *The Catcher in the Rye*; but it arises more directly from the world of frustrated female *Bildung* in which the plots of *Lolita* and *Bonjour Tristesse* were still possible, as the old pedagogic novels fell to pieces.

7. Frank O'Connor: A Mammy's Boy

It was said of the great nineteenth-century Irish poet James Clarence Mangan that he had two personalities, one well known to the muses and the other to the secret police.[1] The same was true of Frank O'Connor, artist and storyteller, who had once been Michael O'Donovan, Gaelic revivalist and republican revolutionary.

Autobiographies, when written by such people, can pose an obvious problem – are they to record the life of the active person (*bios* meaning body) or should they explore the growth of the mind (*auto* meaning self)? Some settle for the practical option and recapture a life of camaraderie, ambushes and political action, leading to frustration on the part of their readers, who feel that more might have been said of their authors' inner development. Most forms of autobiography tend to privilege the *bios* at the expense of the *auto*, because the interior life of people (once so strictly policed by priests in the darkness of a confession box) is regarded as too risky for public ventilation.[2] Hence the complaint of Stephen Spender that so many modern autobiographies 'write the life of someone by himself and not the life of someone by his two selves'.[3]

In *An Only Child* and *My Father's Son* there is no such split, for the simple reason that O'Connor's autobiography in Ireland becomes effectively the autobiography *of* Ireland. Born in 1903, O'Connor was perfectly positioned to record the years of cultural renaissance and state formation. The paradigm which he established in these books has now become familiar: the writer is born in a colonial setting, whose poverty is mitigated by an eloquent cast of dotty grandmothers, boozy fathers, suffering mothers and wild rebels, before a spell in the nationalist movement gives way to life as a citizen of a newly independent state, confronted by the bleakness of a freedom which nobody quite knows how to use. Again and again, O'Connor alerts us to the connection between self and world: 'A revolution had begun in Ireland, but it was nothing to the revolution that had begun in me'[4] or 'the Irish nation and myself were both engaged in an elaborate process of improvisation' (*OC* 129).

A reader might be unnerved by the casual ease with which O'Connor substitutes himself for his country, but it is a technique made possible by the moment through which he lived and by the way in which public events swamped his personal life. It may also owe something to his reading of the classic literature of revolutionary America, for his project is rather like that of Walt Whitman's poetic epic of the United States:

One's self I sing, a simple, separate person,
Yet utter the word Democratic, the word En-Masse.[5]

O'Connor was teaching on US campuses in the 1950s when he composed much of this memoir and its implied address is to an American reader – on the opening page a half-crown is explained as sixty cents – who will understand the manoeuvre.

O'Connor had intended to call the first volume 'Mother's Boy', but an editor at Knopf warned him that this might suggest that he was a sissy. 'That's precisely what I was', he laughed, before obediently changing the title.[6] His narrative, however, remained unchanged in its portrayal of how a melancholy, dirty, drunken father and a buoyant, beautiful and purposeful mother struggled for possession of his soul.

The father belongs to the British Army but, beyond that soldierly loyalty, is indifferent to politics. He comes most fully alive as the drummer in a local nationalist band. The rivalries of the two local bands split the community down the middle but seem rooted more in personalities than politics – a lethal but unnecessary division which seems to anticipate the civil war with which the book ends. The travails of the orphaned mother in early life are rendered so intensely as to seem even more real than O'Connor's own early experiences. It is as if, through constant telling and hearing, they have been made his own. When she is left in an orphanage by her mother and told they 'have no home now' (*OC* 44), it is as if the plight of Ireland under foreign usurpation has been laid bare.

'Mother' herself emerges as a great, large-hearted character, insisting that the refusal of people to attend the funeral of a local Protestant is neither a proper Catholic nor a proper Irish response. She also shows a notable independence of mind even in old age, suppressing her own portrait by the painter George Russell on the grounds that it made her 'look like a poisoner' (*OC* 41) or amazing her son when he brings her to the Alps by saying 'there should be great drying up here' (*OC* 68).

Perhaps the greatest gift she passed on was a respect for imagination and a love of books. The only child is solitary and so he sees things more vividly than other children. He consorts less with them than with adults and is less likely to develop a crush on a local girl than on some older man, who may become for him the sort of authority figure his father has so manifestly failed to be. But, most of all, he feels vibrant as he reads books and boys' weeklies.

Long before O'Connor risked martyrdom for the Irish Republic, he had become in effect a martyr to *The Gem*, *The Magnet* and the popular stories of English public schools. Another title briefly considered for his opening volume was 'Invisible Presences', meaning those honourable schoolboys who know how to take a punishment without complaint and how they must never betray a friend to the authorities. This code was far removed from the behaviour of boys in the backstreets of Cork. So a split emerged between the child's reading and his world. His fantasies were, however, seldom checked by close involvement with other children and so he was always 'half in and half out of the world of reality, like Moses descending the mountain or a dreamer waking' (*OC* 93). As in so many of O'Connor's finest stories, the narrative here is constantly moving toward a moment when some illusion is stripped away and the dreamer faces reality. The anticipation of fulfilment, especially in the long lead up to the Christian feast, is far more moving than the fulfilment of the anticipation – a baby Jesus left in his crib without any seasonal present, just like the bereft boy.

But the rhythm of this autobiography is never depressive: no sooner does one door close than another is opened. The budding atheist has his spirits restored by the first in a series of charismatic mentors, the primary schoolteacher, writer and sage Daniel Corkery. This tiny, forceful man walks into a classroom and writes 'Muscail do mhisneach, a Bhanba' on the blackboard, without explaining that it is the opening line of a famous seventeenth-century Gaelic poem, 'Awaken your courage, Ireland' (*OC* 103). Soon Corkery is using the set texts of the colonial curriculum, like weapons captured from the British enemy, to promote rebellion.

For a boy who honoured the public school codes, this was a moment of supreme challenge. The 'Invisible Presences' – Harry Wharton and the chums of Greyfriars – must now look upon the Cork youth as a 'traitor' and he for his part could only regret just how much they 'had taken me in' (*OC* 111). It was a discovery rather like that of James Joyce's Stephen Dedalus that the words *home*, *Christ*, *ale* and *master* sound very differently on an Englishman's lips and on his own, because 'his language, so familiar and so foreign, will always be for me an acquired speech. I have not made or accepted its words. My voice holds them at bay'.[7] Daniel Corkery, perhaps recalling classroom experiences with the young Michael O'Donovan, had complained in a famous passage that the colonial education set up a dispute in children between intellect and emotion, between their reading and their world; so that under its deforming effect their own immediate surroundings begin to seem unvital, second-rate, derivative. It was a problem that would be reported from many another setting later in the twentieth century, whether in a poem by Derek Walcott about growing up in St Lucia or an essay by V. S. Naipaul about reading the English literary canon in Trinidad.[8]

Under Corkery's guidance, the young student began to read instead about the boy-deeds of Cuchulain, the ancient Celtic hero: yet he could not help feeling an ongoing sense of indebtedness to the English codes he was now rejecting: 'If I had to reply that I was different, it was because of what they and theirs had done to make me so' (*OC* 114). Lady Gregory's own book *Cuchulain of Muirthemne* had been a bestseller among English schoolboys in the previous decade and not without reason, for the warrior's combination of pagan energy and Christ-like suffering made him an early version of the muscular Christian, which is to say a sort of public schoolboy in the disguise of Gaelic hero.

The English substratum in the mind of Irish nationalism remains an Invisible Presence to the end, even after the experience of war and civil war has chastened the author. Patrick Pearse, leader of the Easter Rising of 1916, is but another prisoner of the schoolboy's chivalric code who 'woke up too late' and really 'didn't want to die' (*OC* 177). The main literary influences on the republican prisoners during the civil war were Shelley and Meredith, with their romantic cult of self-sacrifice and of 'dying for its own sweet sake' (*OC* 176). O'Connor's own war was more like a search for literary material than a searing ideological crusade. When he steals the cap of a dead boy, it is like a scene once read about in Tolstoy. When he falls in love with an Irish-speaking girl in a safe house, he has 'no notion of how to make love to her, because she appeared to me through a veil of characters from books I had read' (*OC* 161).

The horrors of that civil conflict soon become real enough, in the image of a battered youth or in the burning of a widow's home: 'this was all our romanticism came to' (*OC* 169). Ever alert to ironies, O'Connor notes again and again the remarkable number of romantic Englishmen who attach themselves to the cause of Gaelic revivalism or of the Irish Republic. Although never quite saying so, he seems to worry that the whole national renaissance may have been itself an aftershock of English Romanticism, or as the poet Patrick Kavanagh dubbed it, 'a thoroughgoing English-bred lie'.[9] O'Connor's suggestion that there might be an unhealthy intersection between revolutionary politics and the Romantic literary vision has had a major influence on subsequent critiques of Irish nationalism by Conor Cruise O'Brien,[10] just as his narrative of struggle out of childhood poverty may be seen to provide a model for a more recent bestseller, *Angela's Ashes* by Frank McCourt.

In the end, however, O'Connor recognizes that his own 'make-believe' education succeeded just as well as the 'improvised' government set up by the rebels. In both cases the virtual became real. But his deeper interest is to tell the story of how Michael O'Donovan became Frank O'Connor. Rather in the manner of the clearly autobiographical story 'First Confession', the tone veers between the chatty and the magisterial, as the innocent young fantasist is recalled by the rather sardonic adult he has become. O'Connor loved to hear and to tell short stories and there are many embedded in both of these volumes. They carry the timbre of his speaking voice. Just as his own father loved to read snippets aloud from a newspaper, adding vast layers of commentary in order to raise the printed word to a more intensely oral type of experience, so does O'Connor infuse his stories with the rhythms and inflections of his own voice. He favoured the short story form because it allowed for poetic effects and a climactic epiphany: and his marvellous study of that genre, *The Lonely Voice*, mimics in its very title *An Only Child*. His theory in that study was that the short story was the appropriate form for the lives of the Os and the Macs, the 'submerged population groups' of insurrectionary Ireland, who went on to invent a free and independent state.[11]

There is also a suggestion in the title that its author remained only a child. He would certainly have questioned the widespread notion that 'innocence' is something lost in a careless half-hour at the age of seventeen or eighteen. For O'Connor, people either were or were not innocent to begin with, and most remained as they began to the very end of their days. He himself was innocent in the root-Latin meaning of that word: *in-nocentes*, open to injury, open to the hurts of a full life. The imagination he compared to a refrigerator, whose contents even after decades could emerge intact, older in years if not in experience. Sometimes, this can seem a little ludicrous, as when the young librarian catches George Russell saying in the 1920s what Joyce had him saying in the *Ulysses* of 1904 ('The only question about a work of art is out of how deep a life does it spring' (*MFS* 212)). Sometimes, it can be touching, as when the adult mask of Lennox Robinson slips to reveal the joking boy beneath. And on occasions it can be quite heroic, as when W. B. Yeats tells him 'all the things I wanted to do when I was eighteen I am doing now that I am an old man' (*MFS* 339).

If O'Connor had a model in shaping this account, it must have been Yeats's own *Autobiographies*. Throughout he uses Yeatsian signature words (such as 'phantasmagoria'), rhythms and ideas. Painfully shy in youth, both men learn how to project a personality through a phantasmagoria that will somehow protect their inner-most privacies. Although O'Connor tells us a lot about the growth of his mind, he remains remarkably reticent about love affairs and personal life. Perhaps he was merely illustrating the truth of his wisecrack that 'an Irishman's private life begins in Holyhead' by showing that in a book set only in Ireland there will be no personal details at all. In this discretion too he followed the example of his master. Yeats in his memoir uses other, older men in order to explore his own emergent self: and so it is here. Each of O'Connor's mentors holds out a possible identity to the youth, but one that seems finally botched or incomplete. Daniel Corkery is the provincial intellectual, art lover and critic, whose charismatic teaching lapses finally into dogma, placing nation before art. Osborn Bergin is the gifted scholar and inspirational Gaelic revivalist who succumbs to pedantry in the end, pointing out the grammatical mistakes on funeral inscriptions. George Russell is the sage and small-town visionary who enables the young but fails to measure up to his own contemporaries. Richard Hayes is the social snob who worked selflessly to save the lives of the poor, but was overtaken by vanity and intrigue. Only Yeats emerges in something like unqualified glory, as a man who could make his own inner contradictions work for him, and so become the great poet of the age who recognized nevertheless that the future of Irish literature lay in realist prose. It is a striking fact that O'Connor's autobiography ends with Yeats's death.

Secularization

It was often said that Ireland had too much Christianity and not enough religion. The observation was first made by Jonathan Swift, but it became apt in a new way in the second half of the nineteenth century, when popular devotions began to be replaced by a more rational, middle-class theology. The old practices of vernacular Catholicism may have verged on superstition but they gave people a sense of connection with a world beyond. Those practices which supplanted them seemed little more than a set of rules designed not to facilitate encounters with the numinous, but simply to regulate the ways in which people dealt with one another.

At times, customs became almost mathematical – three Hail Marys said at the right time would help you pass an examination; attendance at Mass on nine successive first Fridays would release a suffering soul from Purgatory; and so on. Those who took the communion wafer without fasting from the previous midnight were guilty of a serious sin. Seen in retrospect, this kind of rule-bound church was not a haven of old-time religion but the sign of a very modern phenomenon: a secularized bureaucracy which compensated for its lack of trust in a transcendent God by devising a strict rule for every conceivable occasion. In that sense, the world of daily communicants and fiery preachers mocked by James Joyce was arguably an example of the first wave of secularization in Ireland. So lacking was it in visionary content that, when its moment of crisis came, it would collapse like a house of cards.

The second phase of secularization began in the 1960s, as holidays abroad and television programmes at home aroused longings for material comfort and sexual fulfilment. While religious practice was not immediately affected, the vocations of young men and women to a life of holiness certainly were. The papal prohibition on contraception made it difficult for younger priests to hold to the old line, as did the insistence on clerical celibacy in a world increasingly sexualized. After 1967, the number of youths entering seminaries dropped sharply; and by the early 1970s many priests and nuns had decided to relinquish their religious vows. Mass attendance, especially among the young, fell away; and the authority of the clergy was more and more thrown into question. In the earlier decades of the twentieth century, newspapers routinely printed the pastoral letters sent out by bishops every year; now they were more likely to publish articles challenging the teaching on contraception and divorce. The strict censorship of literature by the state was relaxed after 1968; and in the electronic media, the opinions of non-Catholic church leaders, as well as the ideas of atheists and agnostics, received a more sympathetic hearing.

The effects of the Second Vatican Council, which had been called by the liberal Pope John XXIII in 1961, were already palpable within the Catholic community when John Montague wrote a poem about young people making love at a Fleadh Cheoil in Mullingar, as the pope lay slowly dying in June 1963:

> In the early morning the lovers
> Lay on both sides of the canal
> Listening on Sony transistors
> To the agony of Pope John.

Yet it didn't seem strange or blasphemous,
This ground bass of death and
Resurrection, as we strolled along:
Puritan Ireland's dead and gone,
A myth of O'Connor and O'Faoláin.

The dying pope believed that his vision of *ecclesia semper corrigenda* (an ever-reforming church) was a return to his vision of a pilgrim people. The Mass sung in the vernacular had its attractions, whether in the pulsating rhythms of the African Missa Luba or in the plaintive chants of the Ó Riada version sung by the choir of Cúil Aodha. John had believed that if the worker-priests of Italy could be proletarianized, the laity might become priestly. Lay ministers of the eucharist duly followed and the novelist Eilís Dillon worked with other artists commissioned to draw up a liturgy whose cadences might compete with the stately idiom of the King James Bible. The 'priesthood of the laity' was welcomed by many clerics who were visibly tiring of the burden of carrying so much spiritual baggage for an entire community. They felt that all too often they were expected to enact a sanctity which many members of that community were suspiciously anxious to suppress in themselves.

Yet somehow the potential of that moment was lost. In all probability the Council had been convened by Pope John to arrest trends of secularization that had been obvious in most other European countries for some time. As sexuality became for many young people an experience embodying ecstatic impulses once discharged by religion, more and more Catholics jumped ship. Conservative Catholics saw this as a necessary cleansing and felt that radical priests were trimmers who had no legitimate place in a church which based its rituals on immutable truths. But the loss of liberals led to a dire constriction of debate. Some of the Vatican Council's central protagonists, not least Joseph Ratzinger (the future Pope Benedict), repented of their youthful radicalism.

Under the media superstar Pope John Paul II the socialist element in 'liberation theology' was marginalized; yet the Holy Father himself created a dirigiste bureaucracy which was remarkably similar in some of its structuring to those Stalinist regimes he genuinely abhorred and worked so effectively to bring down.

The Catholic Church's control of schools and hospitals, though challenged, was maintained through these changes, although fewer and fewer religious could be found to staff these institutions. Those priests and nuns who remained in their posts, influenced in many cases by the ideas of liberation theology brought back to Ireland by missionaries in Africa and Latin America, began to question whether they should be educating the children of the middle class rather than working among the poor. Even as liberal editorialists complained monotonously about a state which still deferred out-wardly to Catholic values, the remaining clergy began to ask whether a still fragile and impoverished state had made wily use of the church to create a rudimentary welfare system in schooling and health which could not otherwise have been afforded.

By the late 1970s, the condition of the Catholic Church had become so vulnerable that an unprecedented event occurred: a pope visited the island. Millions turned out to pay homage to the charismatic John Paul in 1979, but what at the time seemed like an affirmation of old Catholic Ireland turned out to be its wake. One year later, a radical priest and literary critic, Peter Connolly, predicted on RTÉ radio that religion would die in the next fifteen years in Ireland; and that it would disappear so fast that few people would even realize at the time what exactly was happening. The Sacred Heart lamps in most kitchens had made way for television sets; and, although a time would come when younger writers would find in such images of Catholic kitsch a mode of ironic resistance to the global consumerism of MTV, that time was still far in the future. It would come only at the start of the twenty-first century and then only among a small minority of writers.

8. Richard Power and
The Hungry Grass

E veryone's life is a ruin among whose debris an artist may be able
to deduce what that person might have been. That injunction
pressed heavily on Irish people in the aftermath of the Great
Hunger of the 1840s. According to folk tradition, whoever walks on
the grass where a Famine victim fell dead risks a similar affliction:
hence the 'hungry grass' of the book's title.[1] Perhaps it is a fear
of seeming famished which causes Father Tom Conroy to refuse
offers of food at various moments. But the novel also engages with
a wider sense of emotional and cultural starvation: of the tragedy
that is underdevelopment and of the underdevelopment that is
tragedy. Every so often the celibate Father Conroy imagines scenes
of conjugal love, not as a grand passion but in terms of the kind of
warm fire which seems to be missing from his own life. Of course,
he curbs these reveries for the sake of his vocation. The hungry grass
could never be ploughed by farmers who feared infection from it;
and the parish priest of Kilbride confronts a related problem, in
that he is expected to supply the spiritual nourishment his flock
needs. But there is nobody to nourish him.

At its publication in 1969 it was acclaimed for the way it broke
free of saccharine depictions of the Irish priest, that 'soggarth

aroon' beloved of nineteenth-century novelists and twentieth-century Hollywood movies.[2] The priest who is its central character is sardonic, even to the point of being caustic about those trendy clerics of the 1960s who call for a revival of rural Ireland. In his world (just before the changes unleashed by the Second Vatican Council), the Mass is still said in Latin, a language whose aphorisms are often quoted with urbane approval by Tom Conroy. His Catholicism is as much rule-bound as it is visionary. For example, he suffers from 'scruples', not just about wet dreams but about being late with his daily reading of the Holy Office.[3]

Father Conroy's initial vocation seems to have been dutiful rather than Damascene. He simply took the place of his brother, who had suddenly abandoned the seminary, as if he were a volunteer soldier substituting for an army deserter. Never sure as to exactly why he joined, he lives an inner life too deep ever to risk vulgar self-definition. He is the sort of man who would have understood the Ulster poet John Hewitt's answer to the question 'what is the religion of all sensible men?' – 'they are far too sensible to define it'.[4]

Father Conroy outrages colleagues who realize that he has not troubled to compose a last will and testament, as if such things were a matter of the sordid letter rather than the inner spirit. Yet his negligence also bespeaks the crisis of a rural Ireland with little sense of its own future. More than once in the narrative, as his powers wane, he finds himself expected to deliver a homily for which he has not prepared, as if in his ideal church the altar would take strong precedence over the pulpit. He is shrewd enough to intuit that the moral and religious impulse may destroy one another in the end. Hence his indifference to his curate's social programmes and to his uncle's partisan campaigns, for as a man of God he must seek the spiritual rather than a political kingdom.

The disinclination to write a will suggests an inner suspicion that the Catholic Church will not be central to shaping the Irish future. Ten years after *The Hungry Grass* was published, Pope

John Paul II visited Ireland, the first pontiff ever to do so. On the surface of things, that visit seemed an example of the Church Triumphant, with more than a million people attending each Mass he celebrated; but, deeper down, his coming registered an immense crisis. Ever since 1967 there had been a sharp decline in vocations to the priesthood and the official teaching on contraception was widely disregarded. An urbanizing laity was more likely to practice an à la carte Catholicism, or none at all.[5]

Read against this wider perspective, *The Hungry Grass* might be taken as an elegy for a doomed way of life and for a priesthood which did little or nothing to arrest its own decline. As a young priest during the war of national liberation, Tom Conroy acquires a reputation for favouring socialism and is transferred by a nervous bishop to a poor, out-of-the-way parish. Even after this punishment, which he humbly accepts, Father Conroy continues to harbour sympathy for dissidents, silently endorsing the actions of a poor boy who stole the silver of another priest in order to give himself a start in life. He notes with dry asperity the emergence of a new kind of party hack in politics after independence: a coalition of large farmers, publicans and ward heelers sailing, like new recruits to a pirate ship, under a flag of convenient pietistic nationalism. Landless labourers, once welcomed without stint at the food table of families for which they worked, are now made to eat at a separate bench as members of a lower order, and the cost of that food deducted from their wages. Father Conroy is not in the end a social radical but all around him he notes the hidden injuries of snobbery and respectability destroying the new state.[6]

The old Latin rituals persist and the priest says Mass at an altar facing a crucifix, but already – before the shift in furniture ordained by the Vatican Council – Tom Conroy has a tendency to confront that final puzzle: his own congregation. Its members may take him for granted, as he sometimes does them. 'What do ye want a church at all for?' (*HG* 169) is a question which may trouble him even as he puts it to his people. He is alert to the absurdities of a subsistence economy which calls men in their forties and fifties 'boys' simply because they are still waiting to inherit their families' land. He can mock the obsessive-compulsive religiosity of elderly men, while recognizing that many old men he encounters may be versions of himself as he prepares to die. His inadequate speeches are increasingly followed by a clued-in, turbo-charged alternative, tossed off with fluent insincerity by one of the men of the new order. In that ambiguous context there is a certain nobility to be found in his refusal to pontificate or to state what he does not truly feel. This priest is too honest for self-assertion.

The rising cadre of switched-on priests speak the same language as soap advertisers on television; however, Tom Conroy is something of a latitudinarian on postmodern culture and, while not deigning to purchase a TV set, he likes occasionally to eavesdrop on the absurdities of some of its programmes. He seems to sense, however, that most of the Father Trendies will not be long in the priesthood. And he can sense the deadlock in a society most of whose youth were compelled to emigrate to a life of hard labour in Britain, while large farmers tighten their hold on the land.[7] Between the year of independence in 1922 and 1969, one in every two people born in the country left it. That missing middle generation, which might have refereed the conflict between tradition and modernity, thus achieving an intelligent balance, has gone forever. As Antonio Gramsci remarked of the rural communities in southern Italy, also devastated by emigration, the haemorrhage of a middle generation caused the old to elaborate fantasies of a reactionary conservatism and the young to submit to a heedless, depthless consumerism.[8]

A certain kind of priest might once have filled the vacuum left by that lost generation with an alternative kind of leadership but Father Conroy cannot do so. He ministers in the years after ordination to the migrant community in England, fretting ever afterward about the fate of his brother Owen, who died in his twenties, leaving two young sons whose names the man of God never knows.

That deficit of knowledge hints at a certain coldness in his character, perhaps even some incapacity for primary experience in the living stream of persons. 'A true priest is never loved', wrote Georges Bernanos (cited here *HG* 19). However, the quality of this priest's solitude, though at times almost chilling, can bring out a loving tenderness in others. His loneliness is so deep and invincible as to cause many people to offer him banknotes which he neither needs nor desires. He stores the money up over a lifetime, intending to give it to some worthy recipient but never quite managing to do so. It is as if, like an overripe potato, it is forever sprouting pointless and uncontrollable shoots.

If banknotes represent a form of human labour that has never been materialized, they may be a fair image of their owner's condition: alienated from his original home at Rosnagree, to which he hopes one day to return. He is haunted by letters sent decades earlier by another priest of the family from a mission to South America. If such writing is a metaphor for going into exile, then exile is the condition of much of Richard Power's writing, which in *Úll I mBarr Ghéagáin* (*Apple on the Treetop* 1959) and *The Land of Youth* (1964) had taken estrangement for theme. Even the language in which the characters achieve expression in this book seems like an estranged form of Irish ('and she munching slowly as she read' (*HG* 58)), of a people still half-thinking in Irish while using English words. The dialogues driving this novel are richly flavoured, the Synge-song of a kind which – like the community itself – is still hanging onto old ways but near to the moment of its erasure. The younger priests do not speak in such phrases, although the narrative itself often does, as if in tacit endorsement of jeopardized tradition. The lines of farewell in which the 'last of the bards', Aogán Ó Rathaille, spoke about going into the clay which held his pre-Christian ancestors seem to spread like a dye across the final pages.

The novel began with Father Conroy's death and the revelation that neither his brother nor his sister managed to attend his funeral. This foreknowledge adds a poignancy to accounts of his fumbling encounters with members of his family in the ensuing narrative, while also raising a question as to whether some emotional blockage was a strong element of the family inheritance. There is something rather withheld about Tom Conroy's very presence in the most central of the novel's scenes. However, against that must be set his capacity for unexpected moments of passing grace: 'he'd see a pain inside you' (*HG* 22). This is what makes him a vessel of God, yet that very empathy is disabled by a self-protective irony with which he deflects deep feeling at just those moments when it may become both lucid and intolerable. The loneliness endured by Father Conroy is that of a man who knows more than it is decent to know about the lives of his community. That community finds him essential to its self-definition but displays remarkably little interest in his priesthood: he is simply part of the givenness of things. He must embody a holiness which ordinary parishioners cannot afford to admit in themselves but also a clarity of vision found more often in artists.

Richard Power's portrait is of a good man blocked by the very culture which makes him possible and disabled by that very sensitivity which makes him such an honest minister. James Joyce had once written of the priesthood whose vague acts pleased his protagonist by reason of their semblance of reality and at the same time their distance from it.[9] If Joyce anticipated John McGahern in offering compelling portraits of the artist as frustrated priest, Power has offered something which is even more unusual – a depiction of the priest as a type of the 'removed' artist.

The money saved and never used becomes a symbol of a life lived at a remove from the wellsprings of emotion, a life often fearful of committing itself to the here and now. For the Famine had not only destroyed people's trust in nature but also left them fearful of living with full relish in the present moment. Such an incapacity for primary experience was frequently notable in people of high intelligence, who might have what Flann O'Brien once mordantly called 'a memory and no experience to account for it'.[10] The fear of submitting to the sacrament of the present moment became also a fear of the future, causing terrible, shoddy compromises (such as panicky marriages based on convenience rather than on true feeling). To people of Power's generation, the whole of life could seem like a preparation for something that never finally happened. For stay-at-home peasants, the saving of money in a stocking was one way of evading experience in the here and now; for richer people, that might involve the adoption of a profession which proofed them against real adventure. And the priesthood, as George Bernard Shaw said more than once, was like all professions: a conspiracy against the laity.[11]

It took its harshest toll not on that laity but, as Power shows, upon the priests themselves. Tom Conroy remains at all times stoic and unsentimental: unlike the sugary padres of preceding popular novels, he knows it would be sentimental to invest his own life or world with more significance than God would give them. Some readers have found the novel's diminuendo a little less compelling than the passages at its centre,[12] but that surely is exactly as it should be: the kind of *dénouement* in which people are dismayed not only by fate but saddened by the fact that they are saddened so little. For this really is a story of emotional underdevelopment, in which the worst must ultimately return to laughter. There is no other position possible for those who believe in God than to find the antics of mankind hilariously funny and touching, 'as if bubbles of pure laughter were trying to break through' (*HG* 13).

Patrick Kavanagh once said that tragedy is underdeveloped comedy, comedy not fully born. Behind its sombre moments and chilly witticisms, *The Hungry Grass* is a supremely divine comedy: God's laughter at the shattering of a world. In the end that world proves too strong for one mortal man to sustain and so he must feel himself set free of life rather than deprived of it.

Emigration

Ever since the Famine, the Irish have emigrated in great numbers. Many left from economic necessity in the first instance, but later, people went simply to be with friends in New York or London. The tradition had become self-sustaining. By the mid-twentieth century, the young were leaving because their lives at home seemed boring and mediocre. In fact the few periods of social progress occurred when emigration briefly stopped and the young who stayed fought social stasis. In the 1880s a global economic downturn prevented migration and one consequence was the land agitation of the last decades of the nineteenth century; during the First World War, international travel was hazardous and many young people got caught up in the 1916 Rising; and one consequence of the prosperous periods of the 1960s and Tiger years of the Noughties was that stay-at-homes initiated social reform.

Between the foundation of the Free State in 1922 and the year 1982, however, one in every two people born in Ireland left the country. By doing so many (though by no means all) ensured a better life, both for themselves and for those who remained. If all who had left had stayed on, Ireland might have been even more impoverished than it was and Britain (in particular) would have been deprived of many bricklayers, nurses and teachers. In *The Best Are Leaving* (2016), her study of emigration and post-war Irish culture, Clair Wills finds in the stories of migration of the 1950s and 1960s certain recurring themes: an anxiety about moral decay amid the growing consumerism of 'pagan England' and a worry about the tendency among Irish males to drink hard and fight often.

Emigration to Britain had a 'performative' element, with the coming and going of people being assessed by a stay-at-home audience caught between guilt and judgmentalism. Major concern was voiced about under-educated, gullible youth who went straight from rural communities to the fleshpots of Brixton or Coventry. It seems that migrants from Dublin had already been despaired of as hopeless cases (money-grabbing, spineless, unreliable). For those seeking proof of the corrupting effects of urbanization on innocent youth from rustic places, Edna O'Brien's *The Country Girls* had become exhibit A. The revivalist notion of the city as inherently un-Irish still held sway; and a character in a play by John B. Keane could casually refer to a townie as 'a pervert from a built-up area'. The experience of migrants in the United States was different, if only because the distances involved were so much greater and it was harder for the Catholic Church to send 'emigration priests' like Eamonn Casey to tend to the faithful, while checking on the faithlessness of their cousins up the road in a clearing hostel.

The literature of emigration inevitably offers a lament for a lost sense of community: but those migrants who made it into evening classes were soon reading similar elegies by British authors: for example, Richard Hoggart's *The Uses of Literacy*, with its nostalgia for the world of his grandmother in which he had once felt so secure. In plays like Tom Murphy's *A Whistle in the Dark*, an obsession with cultural declinism exists alongside a sense of wounded masculinity (hence the recurrent brawling which earned for some the name 'fighting Irish').

Among the Irish in Britain, women were more likely to integrate quickly into the host community, through contacts at local churches or schools, whereas men continued often to cleave to their Irish sub-group of fellow workers. The many navvies who never married faced an unenviable fate, working often 'on the lump' without official documentation, losing one community without ever quite gaining another. By the 1960s, their plight would become a key subject for worried sociologists. In the United States, with its openness (in those days) to rapid assimilation of immigrants, men quickly integrated too. But one irony characterized the behaviour of most Irish exiles: they continued to uphold, and even to sentimentalize, the culture responsible for their plight. Not all did, however. The young writer John McGahern overheard a navvy on a building site responding to news of a flood in his native village: 'may it fucken drown them'.

There was a ridiculous imputation of guilt surrounding those who 'deserted' the native land in its hour of need, an attitude of priggish essentialism which went back as far as Maud Gonne. She was typical of purist nationalists in dubbing emigrants 'apostates' (as someone with close-up knowledge of poverty in the west of Ireland, she should have known better). Of course, this kind of thinking was a classic projection of an even deeper survivor guilt felt among those who remained in Ireland. The subsequent frustration of the independence project was registered less in votes by young people on election day than in the practice by youth of voting with its feet (many who went to Britain and the United States helped to build up the Labour and Democratic parties).

The 'great silence' that enveloped commentary on the Irish language often characterized discussion of the emigrant experience too. Though they had long constituted the largest migrant group in Britain and the US, the exiles were seriously under-studied and under-recorded in literature, with the consequence that they sometimes seem to have become invisible and inaudible to themselves. Wills argues that creative writers often recycled old tropes, not mainly to feed prejudices in the old country so much as to please an international readership, which had already decided what Irishness might be.

Ireland in the 1950s and 1960s had a small enough population – about the same size as that of Greater Birmingham in central England. Many of that city's products took it as axiomatic that they might have to leave in order to find work or a partner or a less restricted life. Few would have shed tears over it and fewer still would have sentimentalized either those who went or those who remained. There was something plaintive about so many Irish figurations of emigration, perhaps because so much of it was forced against the wishes of a home-loving people. But equally there were (and still are) many who enjoyed better wages abroad, especially in a globalizing world which allowed ever more frequent returns for a holiday at home.

Was it really the best who left? Many exiles stormed the citadels of academia and the arts, of media organizations and building companies: they went because their genius was such that the home country could never fully contain them. On the debit side, many were poor and could not rise above a life of binge drinking and casual labour. In that sense, emigration had something in common with colonialism (while being an ultimate effect of capitalist colonialist policy). It removed from the homeland some of its most energetic, as well as some of its least endowed, people. In Britain and the US they were all expected – as were the British out in the colonies – to impersonate just the kind of average home type they manifestly could not or would not be.

9. Emigration Once Again: Friel's *Philadelphia*

A concern about fathers and the adequacy of fathers is a sign of a community that fears it may have lost its bearings.

One of the great clichés of modern Irish culture has been the over-intense, clutching relationship between mother and son and, like all clichés, it has an irresistible attraction for the second-rate writer or dramatist, just as it casts its phoney spell over the second-rate mother and the second-rate son. From Barry Fitzgerald's tear-in-the-shamrock Irish son in Hollywood to Patrick Pearse's excruciating poem to his mother, this hoary old stereotype has run the gamut of emotions from A to B, and always as low-budget melodrama. 'There are some things that no man should do for his country', wrote the wise old Fenian John O'Leary, 'and one of them is to weep in public'[1] – but Irish sons and mothers always do.

'My only son was shot in Dublin', sings the rebel's mother – and the greatest pleasure the condemned Pearse can know is to anticipate and share vicariously in the exquisite pain of his mother when her two sons have finally been assassinated by firing squad:

I do not grudge them: Lord, I do not grudge

My two strong sons who have gone out, they and a few,
To break their strength in bloody protest for a glorious thing.[2]

If Pearse had written a poem in his own voice with a title like 'A Soldier's Farewell' he might have seemed a more orthodox exponent of prison literature, but in choosing to speak in his mother's voice, he seems to be hoping to borrow from her searing experience an authenticity he has never found in his own, not even as the leader of one of the most romantic rebellions in history. The mother's love is all-enveloping; and even the middle-aged revolutionary cannot deny the superiority of its emotional force even to the Rising he has just led. He cannot deny it because the mother's love feeds his egotism even as it robs him of his self, gratifies his vanity even as it drains him of all hope of constructing a personality of his own.

Almost thirty years later, when Patrick Kavanagh writes *The Great Hunger*, melodrama and heroics have given way to quiet desperation, but the same cloying relationship with an aged mother stunts Patrick Maguire's hopes for growth:

No crash, No drama.
That was how his life happened.
No mad horses galloping in the sky,
But the weak, washy way of true tragedy,
A sick horse nosing around the meadow for a clean place to die.[3]

The reasons for this widespread disease have little enough to do with the Catholic Church. They stem, rather, from the habit of late marriage forced on reluctant men and women by conservative fathers who would not retire before death, or by mothers who would not allow their farmer sons to bring a young wife into the house to challenge their emotional hegemony. In this gerontocracy, late marriage or permanent bachelorhood became a habit even when it was no longer an economic necessity, with the dire results that all Irishwomen know. 'Adolescence' became a highly flexible concept for the Irish male – lasting in some cases into deep middle-age, as one TD proved in the Dáil when he referred to 'boys' of forty-five and forty-six still waiting to inherit land. In a country which denied youth the pleasures of a short, sharp, subversive adolescence, ageing men go out for 'a night on the tear with the lads' in a fatuously nostalgic attempt to recover an adolescence they never really experienced. It was a stroke of genius which caused the producer of a recent Abbey version of *Philadelphia, Here I Come!* to depict 'the lads' who drink and play football with Gar as ranging in age from seventeen to close on forty-five. When the teenager of the trio is asked by Gar why he doesn't go with him to America, he replies: 'Only that the mammy planted sycamore trees last year, and she says I can't go till they're tall enough to shelter the house.' Gar responds, 'You're stuck for another couple of days then.'[4]

The comedy and the ludicrous absurdities to which such mother love would give rise were deftly depicted by Lennox Robinson in his slight but very accurate play *The Whiteheaded Boy*, but it was left to Patrick Kavanagh to count the bitter cost of it:

Maguire was faithful to death:
He stayed with his mother till she died
At the age of ninety-one.
She stayed too long,
Wife and mother in one.
When she died
The knuckle-bones were cutting the skin of her son's backside.
And he was sixty-five.
O he loved his mother
Above all others.
O he loved his ploughs
And he loved his cows
And his happiest dream

Was to clean his arse
With perennial grass
On the bank of some summer stream;
To smoke his pipe
In a sheltered gripe
In the middle of July –
His face in a mist
And two stones in his fist
And an impotent worm on his thigh.[5]

The exhausted thigh and its drooping worm contrast utterly with the sinewy thighs celebrated by Yeats as the sign of a heightened sexuality.

Clichés have a habit of petrifying around unexamined assumptions and so it was with the mother/son syndrome which became a classic theme in Irish literature, more often presented than analysed. Neither Pearse nor Kavanagh could see the underlying truth that the intensity of the mother/son relationship in Ireland implied something very suspicious and worrying about the Irish male, as husband and as father. Women sought from their sons an emotional fulfilment denied them by their men, and that suggests that their husbands had failed as lovers; but (and this is what is so remarkable) they could not have achieved such dominance over their sons if their husbands had not also abdicated from the role of father. The space vacated by the incompetent or ineffectual father was eagerly seized and occupied by the all-powerful Irish mother, who became not just wife and mother, but surrogate father as well. The first-rate writers of Ireland, the Joyces, Synges and O'Caseys, therefore side-stepped the cliché and resolved to examine the deeper underlying problem of the inadequate Irish father. It is remarkable that Synge and Joyce both depict motherless sons in their masterpieces (*The Playboy of the Western World* and *Ulysses*), the better to dramatize the real roots of the problem in the Irish male as inadequate father. This is the tradition taken up by Brian Friel in *Philadelphia, Here I Come!*.

Friel's play is an account of what happens to a village when even the Shawn Keoghs decide to emigrate. Unlike their predecessors, they emigrate not because they are wanted by the corrupt British law or oppressed by poverty; as Frank O'Connor observed, the emigrants of the 1940s, 1950s and 1960s left not because the land was poor and they oppressed, but simply because the life offered them there was tedious beyond belief.

This drama is a most complex and complete analysis of emotional inarticulacy in a father–son relationship, dealing with the plight of a twenty-five-year-old rural Irish bachelor on the eve of emigration from the general store run by his widowed and elderly father. By the simple device of using two actors to record both public statements and private musings of Gar O'Donnell, Friel manages to show how poignantly little is said in a culture where so much is deeply felt. This is due to the fact, so often found in Irish males, that Gar's verbal fluency is far in excess of his emotional maturity. But the fluency is entirely internal, and never serves its true purpose, either in forming adult relations with girls or in speaking honestly with a father who, in turn, is himself unable to articulate heartfelt emotions.

The theme of the play is non-communication between father and son – but that is simply a symptom of each man's failure to open the lines of communication to his own deeper self, of each man's failure to achieve a full integration of his own personality.

The opening stage directions explain it all – how Private Gar is invisible to everybody and how nobody, not even Public Gar, sees him or looks at him, because 'one cannot look at one's alter ego' (*PHIC* 12). This is *the* problem – that most of Gar's untapped potential is repressed in order that he can function as a public young man in Ballybeg. Hence, the rich fluency of his private thoughts finds no outlet in his public role in village life. And although he is the only character on stage represented by an alter ego, it is clear that this fractured and fragmented sense of self afflicts all the inhabitants of the village. The twenty-five-year-old Gar is still an adolescent in the deepest sense, experimenting with multiple roles: master conductor, champion footballer, lethal lady killer, etc. This uncertainty is repeated in the behaviour of others, for example Kate Doogan, who cannot decide between marriage to Gar or to Dr King. Friel delights in sporting with multiple names for his characters to capture this splitmindedness, so Gar never knows whether to call his sweetheart Kate, or Katie or Kathy.

This uncertainty about one's true identity is not cured by the expedient of education but, rather, is reinforced by it. Gar's Aunt Lizzy returns from the United States as a performing Elise, more as a sign of personal insecurity than as a show of confidence. No sooner does she start to act the role of a sophisticated Americanized Elise than the housekeeper Madge counters with an equivalent ploy and refers with exquisite formality to Gar as 'Gareth'. When the maudlin and very drunk Lizzy includes her own name in the roll call of her dead departed sisters, her husband reminds her 'Honey, you're Lizzy' and 'you're not dead' (*PHIC* 61); but in a deeper sense Lizzy is dead, murdered by Elise, just as the histrionic melodramatic self in all these characters usurps the tenuously real self that has scarcely begun to exist. When the emigrants pose as Elise and the stay-at-homes start making formal statements to Gareth, each group is acting a role for the other, and thus confessing that they are not truly at home with themselves. Moreover, this equation between both groups proves that you cannot leave your insecurities behind you in Ireland. In the deepest sense of all, nobody ever really emigrates: they simply take their native mental landscape with them where they go. Lizzie's pastor in America is a Father O'Flaherty who spouts the same anti-ecumenical trash that she would have heard anyway in Ballybeg. The only real American in the group, Ben Burton, speaks the blunt truth when he says 'It's just another place to live, Elise. Ireland – America – what's the difference?' (*PHIC* 62) There is no difference – and no real communication in either place.

Most of Lizzy's talk is maudlin, meandering soliloquy, and even her soliloquies are often derailed by her own incoherence and drunkenness. Gar may never have passed First Arts, but he has acquired just enough education to wince at his aunt's atrocious grammar and syntax: 'your Uncle Con and me have finalised all the plans', 'our apartment is located in a pretty nice locality' (*PHIC* 55). He is shrewd enough to sense that he may simply be the latest male target of his aunt's monstrous egotism, that she who was thwarted in her desire for a child may stifle him with oppressive mothering and 'tuck you into your air-conditioned cot every night' (*PHIC* 65). It is important to emphasize Gar's parody of his aunt's Americanese, because too many critics have hastily assumed that Gar has been seduced by the lure of Broadway, and that, like certain bad country-and-western singers in Ireland, his sense of self is so tenuous that he yearns to overlay it with an American accent and a transatlantic style. But nothing could be further from the truth. It is true that the radio and the records in Gar's room add to his restlessness and to the cultural gap between himself and his father. They make him aware of a sophisticated alternative world; but his final attitude to the facile patter of the DJ is the same as his attitude to the constipated repetitions and silences of Ballybeg – it is one of parody. Gar is, like most Irish young people, caught between both worlds, yet feels fully at home in neither. In a world which offers such false alternatives, people will speak either too little or too much.

Nor do the young people of Ballybeg find any consolation in the mute language of the body. Gar plays freely with the ageing housekeeper Madge, mischievously grabbing her and dancing her across the kitchen floor – but he flinches from the overtures of young girls like Kate, and is positively disquieted by the constant physical touching of his aunt Lizzy. To a great extent it is Gar's own fault that there is no communication with his father, for in the macho culture of Ballybeg, all men and even some women must suppress traces of tenderness and emotion. So Madge, who has prepared all Gar's clothes for his departure, says 'Your tea's on the table – but that's a matter of total indifference to me' (*PHIC* 20). Yet no sooner has she repressed her own tenderness than she enters a plea on behalf of someone else's. Just because Gar's father doesn't say much doesn't mean that he hasn't feelings like the rest of us, says Madge, recalling that 'he said nothing either when your mother died'. But Gar says 'to hell with him. . . I'm damned if I'm going to speak to him first' (*PHIC* 20). So when his father arrives, Gar assumes a gruffness of manner which is his characteristic way of coping with the old man.

If S.B. postpones the moment of communication with his endless silences, Gar postpones it with his facile hip-talk – the manic patter of the disc jockey who knows that words are important for what they conceal, not what they reveal, and that to talk glibly is at least to defer the real moment of self-confrontation. So Private Gar says to Public: 'An' you jist keep a talkin' to you'self all the time, Mistah, 'cos once you stop a talkin' to you'self ah reckon then you just begin to think kinda crazy things' (*PHIC* 26). But of course, Private is being sarcastic, for like a lover across the dance floor, he yearns for the moment when Public will find the courage to confront him. On other occasions, Private tries shock tactics, as when he mocks Public's egg deals as a poor entrepreneur's basis for a marriage to Kate Doogan – and puts the boot in by saying 'O my God, how you stick yourself I'll never know!' (*PHIC* 28). Gar lacks the confidence to win Kate, because he is still treated as a boy. His skilful private parodies of Senator Doogan and all the others prove that he does not lack the necessary linguistic flair to overcome them all. He can play every part on that stage except his own; his problem is to find a social context for this gift in Ballybeg, but he cannot. Private says far too much to compensate for the fact that Public says far too little, and so he flees from the Doogan residence.

He lacks the mature confidence which would turn his linguistic gift to use. The casual obscenities of his conversation are a sign that he is still an emotional adolescent, a big awkward boy who was bathed every Saturday night by Madge until he was fourteen. Gar has no privacy in such a narrow world, and the intensity of feeling which results from his narrowness simply complicates his emotions, making it harder than ever to leave, even as it makes it more necessary to do so. 'No obscenities, Father dear; the child is only twenty-five' (*PHIC* 39), says Gar sitting to table with the father who is the real cause of his failure with Kate Doogan by his refusal to give Gar a fair share in the shop. 'Maybe he'll die tonight of galloping consumption!' (*PHIC* 29), muses his son, in the honourable tradition of Christy Mahon.

Perhaps because Gar never had a real mother, he seems to reincarnate elements of the absent female's sensitivity in himself – just like Christy Mahon with his small delicate feet and his nuances of emotion. Sometimes Private plays the role of female in his American fantasies, as Public asks: 'Mind if I walk you past the incinerator to the elevator? You're welcome, slick operator' (*PHIC* 36). It is this sensitive private voice which accuses his father of callousness in evading the life of emotion; Gar is leaving, he says, not because he is paid less than Madge, but because '*we embarrass one another*. If one of us were to say "You're looking tired" or "That's a bad cough you have", the other would fall over backways with embarrassment' (*PHIC* 40). Now, before going, Gar pleads privately for one unpredictable remark, so that on the plane he will at least have some doubts. But none is forthcoming – just the usual repetitions of a bored paterfamilias. As we will later see, his failure is not a lack of emotion but a defeat of language.

Master Boyle, the drunken schoolmaster and failed poet, then arrives, as if to supply Gar with more reasons for departure to America: 'I gather it's a vast restless place that doesn't give a curse about the past; and that's the way things should be. Impermanence, anonymity – it offers great attractions' (*PHIC* 44). What is interesting about that speech is the way in which Gar himself recycles it almost word for word in his subsequent and final encounter with Kate Doogan. Under the pressure of intense emotion, he can give no better reason for his leaving than a rehashed version of Boyle's clichés: 'Impermanence-anonymity – that's what I'm looking for; a vast restless place that doesn't give a damn about the past' (*PHIC* 81). It is clear that Gar is still unable to think clearly for himself, and moreover it is clear that the young rebel who mocked his father for predictable repetitions is just as prone to them himself.

Boyle represents for Gar a possible version of himself and what will happen to him, if he stays in Ballybeg; for Boyle hit the drink and self-pity after being rejected by a beautiful woman, Gar's own mother. 'You might have been my father' (*PHIC* 46), muses Private, trifling with the possibility of Boyle as a surrogate father, whose sensitivity and poetry would supply the image of true authority lacking in old S. B. But Boyle will never play Bloom to Gar's Stephen. He is an abject failure, borrowing drink money from an emigrating youth: talking too much, as he admits, yet never keeping to his point; pretending he has a prestigious job lined up in Boston and then lamenting that Gar will forget to write to him after the first or second year. Even the old men in this place are dreaming of America – land of jobs, or if not jobs, of magazines that may at least publish their poetic dreams. Yet the gift of the old master's book of poems prompts Gar to doubt the wisdom of leaving, and so he employs the public idiom of a song, 'Philadelphia, Here I Come', to suppress the more authentic, less articulate private voice that raises such doubts. Language again is enlisted to conceal or suppress authentic feeling; this is the meaning of Gar's repeated quotation from Burke's essay 'It is now sixteen or seventeen years since I saw the Queen of France' (*PHIC* 51 etc.). This is used by Gar in much the same way as Stephen Dedalus uses the learned Anglo-Saxon phrase 'agenbite of inwit' as a method of nervously papering over a crack in the emotions associated with his dead mother. A little learning is a dangerous thing when it can block a man's access to his own emotions. In a play about memory and the distortions of memory, this repeated paragraph from a famous Leaving Certificate prose essay suggests the inadequacies of an educational system that teaches young people how to memorize purple passages, but not how to use literature as an element of their daily vision. Language in such a system becomes autonomous, something into which Gar can retreat like his upstairs room, an escape from life rather than an honest commentary on it. Constrained by his obsession with incorrect grammar, his rote-learning of purple passages and his fastidious distaste for repetition ('located in a nice locality'), Gar is a perfect product of a pedantic system whose maturity of language is useless because it has been purchased at the cost of a permanent atrophy of the emotions.

As in Synge's *Playboy of the Western World*, the young men of Ballybeg seek an outlet for their inarticulate emotions and frustrated sexuality in games of violence and grotesque farce, venting their spleen in violent language and the prospect of sinking their studs into a rival football team. Like old S. B., like most of the village, they refuse to admit that Gar is leaving and use a crude language to defeat the silences in which this painful fact might come to light. But, as Friel says in a stage direction, there is something false about their bluster - and that falseness is pierced by the intermittent silences that fall like cadences between them. As in Beckett's plays, 'to defeat [these silences] someone always introduces a fresh theme' (*PHIC* 71). In the end, the gang leader Ned has no words to express his desolation at Gar's loss, and can only fling his belt awkwardly across the room to Gar, a gruff gift 'if any of them Yankee scuts try to beat you up', 'I meant to buy you something good, but the aul fella didn't sell the calf to the jobbers last Friday... and he could have, the stupid bastard, such a bloody stupid bastard of an aul fella' (*PHIC* 76). So we get the sense that the war of son against father is being waged in every home in the parish. As Ned slowly fumes and rages, before leaving to gawk at English girls through hedges, his second lieutenant Tom realizes that this is his cue to mythologize him: 'The blood's up... Oh, by God, when he goes on like that, the... the blood's up all right' (*PHIC* 76). Tom and Joe thus live their lives vicariously through Ned, just as Madge lives vicariously through her grandnieces and grandnephews, just as Lizzy would like to live vicariously through Gar. Nobody from Ballybeg can live for themselves, because nobody in Ballybeg has constructed an integral self worth living for. Without a full self, each person is a hollow performer of roles rather than an exponent of true emotion. Lizzy acts sophisticated for Madge, so Madge acts formal for Lizzy. The boys, it transpires, never wanted to visit Gar at all, but were bribed by Madge into a performance of leavetaking with the promise of drink – and the cult of drink and easy girls is their biggest role of all. Moreover, all roles are finally punctured: the boys are exposed as frauds despite Madge's attempt to cast them in the role of true friends just as poor Madge discovers that the Mulhern baby was not named Madge but Brigid. No good deed goes unpunished in Ballybeg.

It is part of this play's immense subtlety that, towards the end, it becomes clear that Gar Private may as easily stand for the unspoken thoughts of the father as for those of the son. 'My God, have I been unfair to you?', muses Private of his father. 'Is it possible that you have hoarded in the back of that mind of yours' (*PHIC* 89), that is, is it possible that you too have a private dimension which is lost on me? In particular, Gar wonders if his father recalls the great happiness known by both boy and man as they fished in a boat on a local lake: 'there was this great happiness, this great joy', recalls Private, 'although nothing was being said' (*PHIC* 89–90). Again, true emotion between Irish males occurs only in moments of shared silence, never of speech. 'It wasn't that we were talking or anything' (*PHIC* 105), he will say to his father, as if talking spelled the end of sincerity. But when Gar summons the courage to voice the recollection to his father, the old man remembers it very differently, if he remembers it at all. Memory turns out to be the greatest liar, the greatest distorter, as Gar himself suspected when in private he had considered how he would be highly selective in recalling only the golden moments with the boys: 'Just the memory of it – that's all you have now – just the memory; and even now, even so soon, it is being distilled of all its coarseness; and what's left is going to be precious, precious gold' (*PHIC* 79). If the Irish educational system purported to train the young in the art of accurate memory, it has been less than successful. America cares nothing for the past; Ireland cares so much that she has to convert history into science fiction, recasting the past in terms of some ideal golden future.

The church is the one institution which conceivably might open the lines of communication between past and present, between the generations; but it does not – the canon merely joins Screwballs in his safe repetitions. Gar Private echoes Joyce in his denunciation of a priesthood which has long settled for a practical power rather than true spiritual authority. What he accuses the church of is a failure of language:

> There's an affinity between Screwballs and me that no one, literally no one could understand – except you, Canon, because you're warm and kind and soft and sympathetic – all things to all men – because you could translate all this loneliness, this groping, this dreadful bloody buffoonery into Christian terms that will make life bearable for us all. And yet you don't say a word. Why, Canon? Why, arid Canon? Isn't this your job? – to translate? Why don't you speak, then? Prudence, arid Canon? Prudence be damned! Christianity isn't prudent – it's insane! Or maybe this just happens to be one of your bad nights. (*PHIC* 96)

It is fitting that a play about non-communication should find its climax not in words alone, but in the music of Mendelssohn which flows from Gar's security shelter. Gar Private knows that there is only himself and his father, that each is all the other has, and yet they cannot even look at one another. As he listens to the non-linguistic climax of the music, his feelings break through the bonds of inarticulation and he voices his protest at Screwballs and the Canon who cannot even hear his music: 'To hell with all strong silent men!' (*PHIC* 98). Still waters run deep, but Gar Private fears they may have run out.

Yet the tragic paradox is that Gar Public has already become a strong silent man himself. Throughout the play he has displayed many such traits: promising to Kate that he would beat the tar out of his sons; relying on Madge to pack his clothes and butter his bread; roaring for Madge when the bread runs out, etc., etc. In the final scene, when he and his sleepless father come down the stairs and meet awkwardly in the kitchen, Gar proves as inarticulate as his father and this time it is he who is guilty of the very repetitions for which he denounced old Screwballs:

> s. b.: It's hard to sleep sometimes...
> PUBLIC: It is, aye... sometimes...
> s. b.: There's tea in the pot.
> PUBLIC: Aye?
> s. b.: If it's a headache you have. (*PHIC* 101)

In the end, Gar Public turns out to be just like old S. B. – reticent, guarded and inarticulate, yet on a deeper level tender and emotional. As with Old Mahon and Christy, those who seemed to be opposites turn out to be doubles. (A similar pairing occurs in *Riders to the Sea*, when the young girl Nora, who had denounced old Maurya's repetitions, inadvertently ends up repeating them herself under pressure of a heartfelt emotion.) As Madge says with clear-sighted prophecy: 'When [Gar] is the age the boss is now, he'll turn out just the same. And although I won't be here to see it, you'll find he's learned nothin' in-between times' (*PHIC* 109). Gar is like his father even in the tricks memory plays on him, for Madge cannot match S. B.'s recollection of Gar in a sailor suit. The two men fumble in that final scene towards an awareness that they have these things in common, but even this new half-solidarity cannot be admitted in words. So when Madge breezes in and asks 'Were you and the boss chatting there?' (*PHIC* 109), Gar abruptly avoids the emotion and changes the subject: 'When's the christening?' (*PHIC* 109).

What makes Gar's plight tragic is not so much this inarticulacy as his failure to allow for a similar emotional complexity in his father, a failure to realize in full the implications of what he briefly suspected – that Gar Private represents the hidden, undiscovered private self of his father, and that all the words uttered by Private on Gar's behalf might just as easily have been uttered on behalf of the father. To have felt that silent moment of solidarity in the kitchen should have been enough for Gar, but it was not, because of his excessive belief in redemption through language. That belief is typical of the attempt by postcolonial peoples to build a world elsewhere – the phrase is, of course, Richard Poirier's – in the domain of style and language; and this attempt is doomed to fail, since it is based on the crazy notion that language can do your living for you. 'It wasn't that we were talking or anything' (*PHIC* 105), says Gar, who by the end of the play should know better than to equate an emotion with its expression. If a feeling isn't uttered, Gar won't believe it exists, and so he cannot appreciate that his father may have his own Private Gar, his own antiself or Mask.

Language, therefore, is what comes between Gar and the fresh-ness of experience; and he knows this, admitting that the present moment is being transformed before it is even experienced, so that, before life is possessed and fully lived, it is changed into a mode of remembrance (like Synge's Old Maurya looking forward to the long nights after Samhain, or Beckett's Winnie saying 'this will have been a happy day'). With memory itself so gapped and unreliable, these characters can have no clear sense of who or what they are. Gar has to 'construct' his mother from the shreds of reminiscence shared with him by Madge the housekeeper. And because his history is gapped and broken, his tale cannot be told to a conclusion... any more than can his father's. If old S. B. had expressed himself more fully, then so would the son, but as things stand, the defects of one are recreated in the other. S. B. probably acts callously towards Gar because he cannot bear to see what he was once like himself. Gar must therefore become, in a sense, his own parent ('You'd need to be careful out there, boy' (*PHIC* 88)), but the parent he is becoming is almost an exact replica of S. B. (he'll never marry... bachelor's written all over him... or else when he's old, maybe forty-three, he'll fall madly in love with a nineteen-year-old). This may, indeed, be another reason why Gar Public cannot bear to look straight at Gar Private, because to do that would be to look into the heart of his own father – and that is something few sons ever have the courage to do.

Gar Public's fear of Gar Private offers a variation on the contrast which dominated Joyce's *Ulysses*, between the richness of a man's interior life and the poverty of its social occasions. There is one major difference, however: no longer is the interior monologue a source of consolation for defeats in the external world, as it was so often for Mr Bloom. Now it is almost always a liability. As a boy, Gar seems to have stood up for himself and to have had, in consequence, a fuller relationship with S. B. It was only when Gar grew more like S. B. that the latter began to reject him. Unable to voice his resentment against this process, Gar split in two, with Private henceforth voicing his withheld feelings. The older and the more like S. B. that Gar becomes, the more power is given over to Private to attack both. Gar Private contains Gar Public, by not allowing him to feel. He holds Public back with his crippling scrutinies. Public would relax more easily, if he had the courage to tell Private to shut up. It becomes clear that Private, in control, does not want Public to have an open relation with S. B. because if that happened, Private would lose most of his power. By this reading, therefore, Private has stymied Gar's engagement to Kate and literally driven him from home; and he will go, as Private needs him to, without breaking the pattern of silence. When Public needs emotional support, Private is not always available, but when it comes to criticism which can undermine Public's confidence, Private is always around.

Of course, S. B. has been less than helpful; as he ruefully admits, he is too old to be Gar's father, more like his grandfather really. But he has long since abandoned the struggle for selfhood. His self-relegation to the domestic periphery is typical of a whole generation of Irish fathers, whose plight has been poignantly assessed by Nancy Scheper-Hughes in a study of mental illness in rural Ireland entitled *Saints, Sinners and Schizophrenics*. Scheper-Hughes describes one rural household where the husband sat apart from the animated conversation of mother and children, was never introduced to visitors and newcomers, and was often belittled for his careless dress or deportment[6] – like S. B.'s performances with the false teeth. Divested of authority, without education or affluence, that generation of rural fathers could provide no adequate image of authority for their sons. Yet as Hugh Brody showed in *Inishkillane: Change and Decline in the West of Ireland*, the sons privately sniggered at the crudeness and lack of sophistication of their fathers while publicly continuing to submit to the most patriarchal regime in Europe.[7] It was inevitable that Private Gar and Public Gar would be the offspring of such a lunatic culture.

Northern Troubles

Riots had been a feature of life in Belfast in 1920. A unionist state of six northern counties was part of the settlement of 1921 and it offered, in the words of Lord Brookeborough, 'a Protestant parliament for a Protestant people'. Discrimination in the awarding of jobs and houses kept Catholics aware of their status as second-class citizens. Unlike the Gardaí Síochána in the Free State, the Royal Ulster Constabulary carried arms and administered beatings to nationalists, among whom high rates of unemployment were endemic.

Few southern nationalists or people living in Britain seemed over-concerned, although in 1936 the British Council for Civil Liberties complained that unionists 'under the shadow of the British constitution have been allowed to create a permanent machine of dictatorship'. It was indeed strange that a Britain which would soon lead the war against fascism and found a welfare state nevertheless maintained a one-party state on its doorstep. The 1937 Irish Constitution, while claiming the whole island, afforded the first formal recognition of partition by a Dublin government in excluding the six northern counties from de facto jurisdiction, 'pending the reintegration of the national territory'. Acerbic nationalists correctly deduced from this that they were of marginal interest to southern politicians.

The lip service paid to Irish unity had even less conviction than that paid to the Irish language. Young men who joined the Irish Republican Army during the Second World War (on the basis that England's difficulty was Ireland's opportunity) were interned and some few even executed for their actions. A military campaign by republican activists along the border in the 1950s and 1960s was ineffectual. The official army of the Irish state won plaudits through the 1960s as peacekeepers for the United Nations in such trouble spots as the Congo and Cyprus, as they would later do in the Middle East. The tradition of neutrality was helping to raise Ireland's profile internationally, as the non-aligned nations gained in moral authority. In the mid-1960s the Taoiseach Seán Lemass paid a courtesy call on the Prime Minister of Northern Ireland in Belfast. It seemed that the troubles of the past might be over, but one third of registered unionists pronounced themselves opposed to further contacts.

Marches for civil rights were batoned off the streets in 1968 and in 1969 the British Army arrived on the streets of Northern Ireland, intended to protect Catholic enclaves from attack by armed loyalist groups. Soon, however, it became itself a target for a reinvigorated IRA, which also bombed property and killed civilians. Internment without trial in 1971 merely drove more young men and women into republican militancy, as did the shooting dead of thirteen unarmed civil rights marchers on 'Bloody Sunday' in January 1972. Later that year the IRA killed eleven civilians with bombs on 'Bloody Friday'.

The Republic's economy had flourished through the later 1960s, a decade in which the standard of living actually doubled. In the early 1970s, its people voted to enter the European Economic Community, removed a reference to the special position of the Catholic Church from the constitution, and generally began to think of itself as sophisticated, modern and open-minded. Many citizens were baffled by a northern community whose members seemed to live more in the aftermath of the 1690s than of the 1960s.

In 1974, a power-sharing executive, consisting of politicians from the Unionist Party and from the Social Democratic and Labour Party, was brought down by a loyalist workers' strike, which the British Labour government failed to arrest. In that same year over thirty people were killed in the Republic by bombs planted by the Ulster Volunteer Force (with alleged collusion from British security forces). It was becoming clear that a balance of terror was about as much as any side in the conflict could hope to achieve.

10. Seamus Heaney: The Death of Ritual and the Ritual of Death

'Wherever there is Ireland, there is the family', wrote G. K. Chesterton, 'and it counts for a great deal.'[1] The south Derry farm on which Seamus Heaney grew to young manhood offered a wholly secure world, in which everyone knew their place and in which every tree or flower had a meaning in the scheme of things:

> The landscape was sacramental, a system of signs that called automatically upon systems of thinking and feeling...There, if you like, was the foundation for a marvellous or magical view of the world, a foundation that sustained a diminished structure of lore and superstition and half-pagan, half-Christian thought and practice. Much of the flora of the place had a religious force, especially if we think of the root of the word 'religious' in religare, to bind fast. The single thorn-tree bound us to a notion of the potent world of the fairies – and when the Blessed Virgin appeared in a thorn bush in Ardboe, a few miles up the country, the fairy-tree took on a new set of subliminal attributes.[2]

In May, buttercups flowered and the pagan goddess gave way to altars dedicated to the Virgin Mary. Members of the community 'genuflected a million times, blessed ourselves a million times, never felt ourselves alone in the universe for a second'.[3]

Such a sense of security was rooted also in the life of an extended family. The intensity of religious ritual and of family living among rural Catholics in Northern Ireland was, to some degree, attributable to the fact that there was no larger social institution with which they might identify. The law, the army, the civil service, even local government itself, were all the preserve of the unionist majority, a group never slow to proclaim its superiority from the rooftops. Against that backdrop, the family was a haven, but a haven in a heartless world.

The poetry of Heaney has much to say of that childhood and of its subsequent loss. Early lyrics in *Death of a Naturalist* (1966) record the decision of a bright young scholarship boy to 'dig' with his pen rather than his father's spade, to record farm life and rural crafts before they die away. Many modern poets return to scenes of childhood in their fifties or sixties: but Heaney was writing with tenderness, exactitude and lyricism about that lost world in his early twenties. The eruption of political violence in Northern Ireland after 1969 complicated this task but never wholly distracted the writer from it; and the recapturing of childhood scenes took on a new urgency in *The Spirit Level* (1996), following the ceasefire by the Irish Republican Army. While other Irish writers of the 1990s offered bitter exposés of alcoholic fathers and abusive clerics, Heaney wrote moving lyrics in memory of parents, uncles and aunts, as well as celebrations of a brother who still farmed the land. The farm had seemed to the younger writer to have been filled with a poetry not yet conscious of itself as such: and, even when reviewed by the sadder, older man, it was still capable of transforming people from prisoners of the dire political experience to possessors of it.

Like Mark Twain, Heaney looked back upon his childhood as upon a zone of radical innocence before a fall into civil strife.

He understood that every child, in its phases of growth, relives the fundamental experiences of the human race. There is a distinctly evolutionary quality to many memories – of unwanted pups being drowned, of tadpoles taking the shape of complex life, of traditions passing from generation to generation. Inevitably, the adult poet will find in some childhood memories elements of that fear and loathing which led him, in some distress, to evoke them. The Wordsworth of *The Prelude* will be his guide through such moments, for he also had tried to bring the world of boyhood into alignment with that of the man he had become: 'He feels like a traitor among those he knows and loves. To be true to one part of himself, he must betray the other part. The inner state of man is thus shaken and the shock waves in the consciousness reflect the upheavals in the surrounding world.'[4] This conflict has been experienced by many poets in the aftermath of a failed revolution. John Milton was the first to attempt at the level of poetic practice a transformation no longer possible in his society, an effort that would be repeated by Blake and by Wordsworth. Each had supported a revolution in its early stages, only to be disillusioned by the cruelty later unleashed.

Born in 1939, Heaney was a beneficiary of the 1947 Education Act, like so many other supporters of the civil rights marches in Northern Ireland of the 1960s; and his subsequent experience of the 'People's Park' movement in Berkeley, California, taught him that even his poetry could be 'a mode of resistance'.[5] By 1970 the uglier side of American radicalism had begun to manifest itself in shootings and bombings. 'In contrast to the revolutionary language of America,' he wrote somewhat naively in December of that year, 'the revolutionary voice of Ireland still keeps a civil tongue in its head.'[6] Within a short time, however, the brutality of the IRA and of British securicrats changed all that. If there was to be a revolution, it would have to happen – like Milton's, Blake's and Wordsworth's – inside the head.

The polarities of the conflict had by then become clear to the young man in coded but troubling ways. While he was reading the writings of the anticlerical Joyce at college, he might also find himself driving his mother to attend May devotions in the local church. He might confess to sins of impurity, yet find himself studying the novels of D. H. Lawrence. He had to relocate his Pioneer Total Abstinence medal inside his lapel before attending sherry parties at university. One effect of the divided society was to give a defiantly conservative cast to northern Catholicism. It is most unlikely that a southern student moving, say, between a Wicklow farm and Trinity College Dublin would have felt so acutely the sort of strain recalled by Heaney:

> As a northerner, my sense of religion and my sense of race or nationality or politics were inextricably twined together. If you have ever walked through a Belfast street on Ash Wednesday, your forehead badged with the mortal dust, you will know how this sense of caste is enforced by the sectarian circumstances. If you have ever blessed yourself in a city bus (or, more piercingly, not blessed yourself for fear of being noticed) you will know it too.[7]

Over the years, that religious practice was eroded, partly due to 'problems with some central mysteries',[8] but the poet also recognized that the cultural conflict between Catholic ritual and secular art might be more apparent than real. Insofar as it was real, it had value as one source of poetry, but what was at stake was a crisis in the very status of ritual itself. By the mid-1970s, as political scientists pronounced Northern Ireland 'a problem without a solution',[9] some of the better-publicized explanations of the Troubles began to wear a little thin. The socialist analysis, which cast the problem in terms of the economic oppression of a minority by a majority, lost traction as the memories of the student radicalism of the previous decade faded. The purely political accounts did not seem to explain the appalling intensity of feeling on all sides. The official churches had repeatedly condemned the gunmen, to no palpable effect. Against that bleak backdrop, people began to look to the poet for the sort of vatic wisdom once expected of the *fili*. For some years, Heaney had been compelled to make statements in prose as to why he was making none in poetry. Then, in 1975, he published *North*, a work of epic scope which seeks, like Milton, Blake and Wordsworth, to solve an irreconcilable conflict by outgrowing it, by developing a 'new level of consciousness'.[10]

Previous volumes of his had contained the usual accumulations of poems over a three- or four-year period. *North* was shaped, however, around a set of linked themes. Throughout the volume, central, if never directly expressed, was a diagnosis so surprising that it was not noticed by those commentators calling for a solution: to the effect that the death of rituals in modern life had led to rituals of death. Marxists might complain that such analysis attempts to solve at the level of ritual problems which can only be treated in the body politic. But it was his application of the methods of comparative anthropology that permitted Heaney to take the longer view; this 'solved' the question not so much by changing it as by extending it right back in time. He excavated the meaning of the present not by going back twenty years but 2,000.

The poet suggested that to understand the strange clash, the 1600s were scarcely more helpful than the morning newspapers: better to re-read Tacitus. The mythical was reasserting itself in a world stripped of useful ritual. Such an analysis shocked left-wing nationalists, able to quote hard-and-fast statistics of discrimination on housing and jobs. To them it seemed like a culturalist over-interpretation rather than a true account of the psychology of the killers, most of whom were lapsed members of their respective Christian churches. But Heaney could see that those who thought of themselves as having stripped away all pointless rituals were submitting, unconsciously, to a repetition of some of the oldest rituals of all. Such a diagnosis had much appeal for anti-materialist intellectuals, since it secured their role in any ensuing debate – and in any possible solution. Many overseas intellectuals found Ireland fascinating, because (in the words of Bernard Shaw) the laws of economics seemed to stop at Holyhead (the embarkation point for the sea journey to the island).[11]

In *North*, a line of anthropological writing about Ireland that began with Edmund Spenser and continued through Swift comes full circle. Such a writing asked (in Spenser's case) where the ferocity of rebels came from and (in Swift's) what the cruelty of the official response told the planters about themselves. The main focus in *North*, however, is on the sufferings and sins of those on the nationalist side. Whether through courtesy or a decent reticence in the face of the unknown, the poet has surprisingly little to say about the unionists.

It begins with a domestic scene: the poet's aunt Mary baking in the farm kitchen, a gesture of creativity in a broken, breaking world. Yet a companion piece, 'The Seed Cutters', suggests a violence even in domestic ritual. The aunt dusts the floor with a goose's wing and the cutters bisect every root. Like those seeds split in half, *North* is divided into two parts. The first is mythical and ancient-seeming, concerned with the meaning of bodies dug out of old bogs. The second is documentary and apparently contemporary, about the challenges that current affairs pose for language. Splitting might seem a fitting response to a divided society, but the artist's real concern is to align mythical and mundane, a technique derived from Joyce's *Ulysses*. In that book a Homeric grid was brought down on the characters from above, its arbitrariness being part of its point, a contraption which in its attempt to impose order on the chaos of modernity might seem more real than the experiences on which it was being imposed. Heaney's bog myth is, by comparison, overt and earned and slowly evolved in response to the pressure of experience.

The woods had once marked the frontier between native and planter, and so became an image of the unconscious, as in American culture. But now they were gone, and so the earth itself became a symbol of a world once populous and noisy, to be contemplated by the silent poet-archaeologist, striking in and down.[12] These zones would, like the American frontier, be a place where the theory of original innocence and the facts of human corruption are confronted. The pioneers celebrated in Heaney's bog poems, unlike the Americans, were less interested in subduing the land than in studying it; they were interested in learning from it rather than measuring it out. Unlike the American frontier, the bogs could never disappear. Far from being erased by an encroaching civilization, they were augmented by each development. Ever since the time of Spenser, the Irish had been depicted as bogmen, dwelling in softlands and luring imperial soldiers clothed in heavy armour into such terrain. For centuries 'bogman' had been a term of racist abuse, but it was now occupied by Heaney as a term of defiance, complication and resistance not just to colonialism but to the effects of time itself. The man had been taken out of the bog but he had no desire to let the bog be taken out of the man. For the bog preserves not only bodies and objects but also consciousness.

A strong suggestion all through *North* is that the dead themselves may not recognize that they are dead but think of themselves as translated into a new dimension. The emphasis, however, is steadfastly on the community which unites at a wake rather than on the departed: hence the rather stately, dignified diction. The grave honour done to the dead at wakes attended by the teenage boy contrasts utterly with the randomness of contemporary slaughter in the north:

I shouldered a kind of manhood
Stepping in to lift the coffins
of dead relations.
They had been laid out. . .[13]

For a young man in an unjust state there will always be a question as to where 'manhood' is to be found. This will be exacerbated if he chooses a career as a writer, since (in the words of an Italian proverb) words are feminine, deeds masculine. Heaney's own frequent characterization of unionists as masculine and the colonized Catholics as feminine suggests that a degree of sexual anxiety attended a literary career in a place where Protestant schools took pride in their profile in the sciences (leaving Catholic ones to stake claims in arts). Hence the occasional assertions by Heaney of a masculinity which the very act of becoming a writer may have thrown into question.[14] Newsreel footage through the 1970s featured teenage boys (less likely than older men to be arrested) shouldering the coffins of dead IRA comrades; and he knew that many nationalist males, emasculated by decades of unemployment, were turning to the IRA to assert a jeopardized virility. Writing, however, was Heaney's alternative to violence, his way of taking power.

Nothing in Heaney's world seems as remote as the recent past: and his language deliberately distances funerals of corpses with 'dough-white hands' and 'igloo brows' until they seem like glaciers moving into prehistory. The long-familiar is presented as the ever-distant:

Now as news comes in
of each neighbourly murder
we pine for ceremony,
customary rhythms... (*N* 16)

The problem is acute. Between the 1950s and 1970s the world around the Derry farm has been disenchanted and its ceremonial elements all but lost; and this has happened all over Europe – Bologna has its car bombs as well as Belfast. What little ritual remains has been stripped down to the level of routine. Even the flag-draped, glove-topped coffins at IRA funerals – so patently modelled on those of the British army – are a belated attempt to restore that sense of ceremonial dignity lacking in the lives of those who are mourned. Deprived of ritual, people had grown disillusioned with political leaders, whom nevertheless they accused of acting false roles all the time. Northern Ireland, far from being aberrational, simply poses an intense version of the common problem.

So the poet proposes a healing ritual, a funeral to end all other funerals, a pilgrimage of forgiveness in which past grudges will be buried in the Neolithic chamber of Newgrange. Standing by the Boyne, a river sacred in memory to loyalists whose ancestors triumphed there in 1690, it will now provide a locale which transcends such divisive moments with an appeal to a shared pre-history. The great house of the Celtic dead is also the vault into which the sun shines every winter solstice, on 21 December, the shortest day of the year. The old imagery of loyalist marching or of nationalist martyrs will be subsumed into a pilgrimage affirming a common life. The appeal made to a pre-Christian, pagan bedrock of values by W. B. Yeats is now amplified by Heaney, who emulates his predecessor by using painfully paradoxical phrases ('neighbourly murder'), in order to show that sacrifice is not at all remote in a community at war with itself. In doing this, Heaney also follows in the tracks of Synge, who went to Aran in the poet's account 'to put on the armour of an authentic pre-Christian vision which was a salvation from the fallen world of Unionism and Nationalism, Catholicism and Protestantism, Anglo and Irish, Celtic and Saxon – all those bedevilling abstractions and circumstances'[15] The objective embodiment of a subjective consciousness which Synge found among the stones of Aran was discovered by Heaney amid the boulders of Newgrange:

Now I would restore

the great chambers of Boyne,
prepare a sepulchre

under the cup-marked stones.
Out of side-streets and bye-roads

purring family cars
nose into line.
The whole country tunes
to the muffled drumming

of ten thousand engines.
Somnambulist women,
left behind, move
through emptied kitchens

imagining our slow triumph
towards the mounds.
Quiet as a serpent
in its grassy boulevard

the procession drags its tail
out of the Gap of the North
as its head already enters
the megalithic doorway. (*N* 16–17)

The resolution is merely imagined, but the search is for a ceremony equal to the suffering of 'each blinded home' (blinded by grief, even more than prejudice, with its curtains down). The image is of the old *péist* of Gaelic mythology, one serpent not yet banished by St Patrick from the nearby hill of Slane; and the vaguely threatening animal recalls Yeats's own rough beast slouching to a holy place as another ceremony of innocence is annulled.

But Heaney knows that he can never be a Yeats. Facing the collapse of ceremony, Yeats called for its renewal, but went further and created in *A Vision* an entire philosophical and religious system that would give it a claim on people's attention. It is possible, of course, to laugh at this as the 'southern Californian element' in Yeats,[16] but at least it offered a positive theory of the world and not just a diagnosis of its limitations. Heaney, born over seven decades later (in fact in the year of Yeats's death), is too honest to simulate belief when he feels none and so he is at the mercy of the finality of early death. The act of terrorism takes away the only life many members of the community believe that they will ever have. There is here no Yeatsian faith that can look through death, but rather the funeral offers a way of controlling grief until it is slowly purged in this life.

The model for such renewal is Gunnar of *Njal's Saga*: a warrior who managed to smile and sing of ancient heroes in his burial vault, even as his own killing went unavenged. If the first part of 'Funeral Rites' made the familiar farm world seem remote, this third and final section makes that ancient saga world seem familiar. The restoration of a true sense of community demands fortitude and forgiveness, as well as the dismantling of current names (always insisted on by recent winners) down to their source meanings ('Strang and Carling fjords'). Gunnar is himself literally re-membered, a warrior whose body did not rot. So he is transformed into a sort of saint, who learned how to praise the world as he found it:

Men said that he was chanting
verses about honour
and that four lights burned

in corners of the chamber:
which opened then, as he turned
with a joyful face
to look at the moon. (*N* 18)

Despite his sweetness of temper, the old warrior sickness (chanting verses about honour) asserts itself, but on this occasion is cured by the four votive lights that turn the verses into a prayer to the moon, symbol of love and beauty. The corpse which sings is an ancient motif, from Gaelic lore to the poetry of Blake, but rarely has it such poignant force.

'Viking Dublin: Trial Pieces' considers objects taken from the bog and displayed in the National Museum in Dublin, itself a Viking settlement. On the bones of dead people artists doodled, in search of a convincing line (much like the poet himself, who wonders whether a child attempted to trace on one just the sort of longship out of which the relics came). The longship drawn by the ancient child 'enters my longhand' in an act which is at once repetition and translation of the original impulse into a new element. The subtle calligraphy has to be 'magnified on display', like the poet's tabulating, noun-centered art; and he is amazed that it is on the jaws and ribs of the dead that images of vibrant life, 'foliage, bestiaries', are inscribed (*N* 22). The process is both reassuring and barbarous (rather like the cuff-links made of 'genuine human molars' worn by a businessman in *The Great Gatsby*).

Thoughts of Scandinavian founders lead to that Denmark which produced not only the bog-preserved corpses, on which many poems here focus, but also the tale of Hamlet, the intellectual unfitted for a bloody act in the rotten state. The implication seems unavoidable:

> I follow into the mud.
> I am Hamlet the Dane,
> skull-handler, parablist,
> smeller of rot
>
> in the state, infused
> with its poisons,
> pinioned by ghosts
> and affections,

murders and pieties,
coming to consciousness
by jumping in graves,
dithering, blathering. (*N* 23)

Yeats, in 'Meditations in Time of Civil War', had turned upon the stairs of his tower to ask whether he could have proved his worth in a direct action 'that all others understand or share'. By the end he had settled for 'the half-read wisdom of daemonic images'.[17] So does Heaney. By his day Percy Shelley's definition of the poet as unacknowledged legislator of the world had been reversed in a famous quip by W. H. Auden that 'such a description better fits the secret police'.[18] *North* will record injunctions by admirers to 'be the poet of your people', but when the Royal Ulster Constabulary fire at his former schoolmates in Derry in 1969, Heaney will find himself suffering 'only the bullying sun of Madrid' outside the Prado, which houses Goya's painting of a revolution bringing forth monsters (*N* 69).

Hamlet is a figure in whom many Irish writers have seen a version of themselves. Yeats's Hamlet was a deployer of masks, feigning madness; Joyce's a man intent on becoming his own father; and Heaney's a man who stands in graves, dithering and blathering. There is more than barren self-accusation or self-justification at work: for Hamlet, like Heaney, expended his greatest energy in trying to realize the state of being dead. His jump into Ophelia's grave is a logical part of that investigation. The analogy is quite pressing: a man in his thirties who, after a protracted education, is about to come into his proper inheritance but then is confronted by a ghost and must thereafter defer that moment when he would have become his destined self. The role of people's avenger is one to which Heaney is ill-suited by temperament, and so he becomes instead a troubled soliloquist, obsessed with ritual, role-play and acting. Hamlet coaches Polonius and the players in the actor's art;

he tells the queen to assume those virtues which she does not have; he punctures the facile disguises of others; and he develops a boundless gift for mimicry, until in the end he can play virtually every part except his own. When he appears among the graves in Act V of the play, following a period of withdrawal (much like Heaney's move from Belfast to Wicklow in the 1970s), he is a sort of revenant, back from the death intended for him, but expected to simplify himself for the sake of a revenge tragedy. Heaney, of course, will deviate from the ur-plot as Shakespeare's hero could not do: and he will seek instead a line of escape in the figure of Sweeney, the visionary man-bird who fled the field of battle to live among the trees. For he knows just how little words of his can do but how vitally important it is that they do it: soothe a community's pain by describing it so well. In doing as much and as little, he may raise the consciousness of some people to a level of understanding at which the currently irreconcilable positions seem ill-conceived, even meaningless. If you cannot solve a question, that may be because of the silliness in which its terms are put: and your words can at least discredit those terms.

There is no pretence of superiority or objectivity. If there is poison in the state, the poet also is 'infused' with it. He knows that his is a carrion art. The word 'blathering' is borrowed from Synge, who never forgot the bones beneath the skin and who insisted that 'before verse can be human again it must learn to be brutal'.[19] Living in the gate lodge of the Synge family estate in Glanmore must have reminded Heaney of that duty to record the violence at the heart of man's sense of beauty. One section, indeed, ends with a quotation from Synge's *Playboy of the Western World* – 'did you ever hear tell of the skulls they have in the city of Dublin?' Synge often reminded himself, as he held the actress Molly Allgood in his arms, that one day she would be whitened bone: he was as excited as Webster by thoughts of 'the skull beneath the skinne'.[20] In 'Bone Dreams', however, the gesture goes beyond mere frisson to a slow, steady consideration of such ossification:

Come back past
philosophy and kennings,
re-enter memory
where the bone's lair

is a love-nest
in the grass.
I hold my lady's head
like a crystal

and ossify myself
by gazing: I am screes
on her escarpments,
a chalk giant

carved upon her downs.
Soon my hands, on the sunken
fosse of her spine
move towards the passes. (*N* 29)

The word 'ossify' suggests drunkenness as well as a measurement
of bones; and the hint of necrophilia is deliberate, for the poet
knows that the pornographic imagination may in extremity seek
the ultimate fulfilment in death. Synge had said that all poetry,
though a tender flower, has strong roots among clay and worms.[21]
The necrophilia is invoked here in the attempt to achieve a fuller
understanding of tradition, for the bog preserves not just bodies
but consciousness; it is not only a graveyard but a house of love:

And we end up
cradling each other
between the hips
of an earthwork. (*N* 29)

Many of these themes achieve a most complex articulation in 'Bog Queen'. Up until this moment in his bog poems, Heaney had been willing the dead bodies to speak, and now at last one does. Unlike Tollund Man and Grauballe Man, this one is feminine, dug out of an Irish rather than a Danish bog:

> I lay waiting
> between turf-face and demesne wall,
> between heathery levels
> and glass-toothed stone. (*N* 32)

Caught between the native boglands and the compounds of the Ascendancy, this queen bore the cultural history of the island on the shorthand of her body.

The opening line will be repeated, as if to echo the old republican motto (*éireoimíd arís*: 'we will rise again'), but also as an emblem of that condition known by the destitute tramps of Samuel Beckett – 'My body was braille/for the creeping influences' (*N* 32) – because the bog has preserved not only her body but her consciousness. Every level of earth has a particular history, translated into the facts of a geography; and, like all who make the desperate bargain to live in a culture, she has been preserved by the sheer weight of that earth which also suffocated her:

> the illiterate roots
>
> pondered and died
> in the cavings
> of stomach and socket.
> I lay waiting
>
> On the gravel bottom
> My brain darkening. . . (*N* 32)

She is assimilated back into nature from culture, yet some recessed part of her causes her to resist and persist; as in the case of Beckett's protagonists, the more her body fades, the more defiantly active is the mind which records that fading. Here is an inversion of the sky-woman or *spéirbhean* of Gaelic tradition, now found not on high but deep in the earth, as a reminder of how a tradition will always be reborn in the lament for its disappearance. The dead, though forgotten, are never truly gone; and since they do not recognize death, they must be just wintering out:

> My skull hibernated
> in the wet nest of my hair,
>
> which they robbed.
> I was barbered
> and stripped
> by a turfcutter's spade,
>
> who veiled me again
> and packed coomb softly
> between the stone jambs
> at my head and at my feet. (*N* 33)

Literally, the kind turf-cutter (who accidentally dug her out) re-membered her, reassembling her bones in proper order before the discreet 'veiling'. This was the very moment for which, all along, she had been waiting, that instant when she would re-enter human minds and come forth as a challenge.

The facts, however, record otherwise: that when she was dug out on Lord Moira's estate in 1781, her body was not accorded the dignity deserved by such patient, prayerful waiting. The cutter was given cash and Lady Moira plundered the corpse, which might better have been respectfully restored to its resting-place:

Till a peer's wife bribed him.
The plait of my hair,
a slimy birth-cord
of bog, had been cut

and I rose from the dark,
hacked bone, skull-wave,
frayed stitches, tufts,
small gleams on the bank. (*N* 34)

The grave decorum of the earlier stanzas is turbo-charged at the close: and some readers hear in its defiant rhythms an echo of Sylvia Plath's 'Lady Lazarus': the rocking, metronomic movement of a reborn woman, back from the dead, protesting the insult to a body reduced to mere exhibit. Deeper still is the sense of the anonymity of pain, as suffering erases all trace of the individual, while past wars are waged in new ways in the present. Even the dead, as Walter Benjamin warned, may not be safe from an enemy who wins.[22]

Yet, by contrast with some earlier bog poems, there are no suggestions here that a pornographic imagination might find its ultimate satisfaction in the extinction of the other party. Nor does the Bog Queen resemble Plath in experiencing her own slow-motion disintegration as the ultimate aesthetic experience. There is no sense of the vengefulness to be found in Plath's closure:

Out of the ash
I rise with my red hair
And I eat men like air.[23]

Rather, what is asserted, more in the rhythms than in the statement ('I rose') is a dignified margin of possible hope. This Cathleen Ni Houlihan is not the 'bitch' with a 'surly gob' lamented by Sean

O'Casey,[24] but a figure of perfect poise and patience. The greater the humiliation of her body, the surer her mind's recovery from it. Although she feels violated by the planter's wife, even in this abjection she finds a sweet vindication of all her waiting, sure in the knowledge that she would rise. Her plight may be similar to that of the later Plath, but her thought is closer to the later Yeats:

A brief parting from those dear
Is the worst man has to fear.
Though grave-digger's toil is long,
Sharp their spades, their muscles strong,
They but thrust their buried men
Back in the human mind again.[25]

A good lesson also carries warnings, as do these lyrics. The figures of Bog Queen and others are made available for contemplation by their status as prized exhibits in museums, but the very principle of museumization is discredited in the poetic enactment. Denying the Bog Queen's fixity as an exhibit, Heaney prefers to return her to a world of process and transformation. The imagining of the fuller details of her story is a refusal to connive in the common curatorial desire to present everything old as an artwork. That curatorial effect is usually achieved by removing objects or human remains from their proper contexts: estrangement and defamiliarization seem to confer on them the arbitrary qualities of a modern work of art. The danger here is that a discourse of connoisseurship (such as Lady Moira's) will take the place of the turf-cutter's honest workings. The impulse to adore may carry an undertow of prurient curiosity and titillation (as Heaney had conceded in 'Punishment', by dubbing himself an 'artful voyeur').[26] There is indeed something savage at the heart of some acts of apparent veneration. Better by far to return such objects to the bog which will preserve them more fully than any museum. The primary forces of nature in Ireland seemed to conspire in such a natural process, providing the wood for making works of art and the rains which dissolve them. As Chinua Achebe has observed of somewhat similar issues in Africa: 'When the product is preserved or venerated, the impulse to repeat the process is compromised.'[27]

The 'melancholy of the collector' is a phenomenon well known among both modernists and Irish revivalists. Collection is one way to bolster and ratify a self felt to be in jeopardy, and that self may respond with demonstrations of its power to tabulate 'numbered bones'. But that is a one-way transaction, affording the dead no chance to answer back. In *North*, that unilinear anthropology is disrupted by a poet who warns repeatedly against fetishism and who refuses to possess objects, which seem instead to possess him. The personation of the dead in the politics of Northern Ireland had always been legendary and continued so into the years covered by *North*. After a narrow victory by a very few votes in the 1969 election in Belfast, the socialist MP Gerry Fitt received a telegram: 'Congratulations Gerry. Can only quote Pearse: the fools, the fools, the fools – they have left us our Fenian dead.'[28]

The anthropologist in Heaney sees the crisis in cultural rather than economic terms, as the vestige of an ancient battle between devotees of a goddess and a god. Protestantism is male, imperial, English; Catholicism is female, nationalist, Irish. Some might consider the division vulgar for such a subtle poet, but it was hardly of his making. 'I think that the Hail Mary is more of a poem than the Our Father', he told an interviewer: 'Our Father is between chaps, but there's something faintly amorous about the Hail Mary.'[29] In a benchmark lecture written during the work on *North*, Heaney offered the Royal Society of Literature a completely cultural explanation of the northern wars:

There is an indigenous territorial numen, a tutelar of the whole island, call her Mother Ireland, Cathleen ni Houlihan, the poor

old woman, the Shan Van Vocht, whatever; and her sovereignty
has been temporarily usurped or infringed by a new male cult
whose founding fathers were Cromwell, William of Orange or
Edward Carson, and whose godhead is incarnate in a Rex or
Caesar resident in a palace in London. What we have is the
tail-end of struggle in a province between territorial piety and
imperial power.[30]

So in poems he explores analogies between the male victim of an
ancient fertility rite and those modern youths who sacrifice lives
to appease Mother Ireland – or between a sacrificed Scandinavian
woman and the tarring and feathering of a woman who mixed with
British soldiers. The typology, however, is never quite as pat as that
makes it seem: the deeper analogy in 'Punishment', for instance, is
with the poet who pursues his own instinctual desires above and
beyond the code of his tribe. The poems summon up feeling for the
ancient victims, which flows like a tributary back into the flood of
emotion felt for current sufferers.

If present horrors seem too much and journalism inadequate,
then one way of realizing current atrocity is through ancient
experience, to measure what Helen Vendler has tellingly called 'the
insult of the actual'.[31] That technique may (again) owe something
to Synge, who wrote that the profoundest moments in poetry are
achieved when the dreamer is reaching out to reality. Each lyric here
protects itself from sounding too pleased with its own conclusions
by raising the essential criticisms of the code to which it adheres.
Lest ancient image seem beguiling, the poet weighs it against

> the actual weight
> of each hooded victim,
> slashed and dumped. (*N* 36)

Yet, along with the ethical need to make an inventory of the present is a desire to remember the future: as the ancient victims seem to us, so shall we seem to people 2,000 years from now.

'*Tout comprendre, c'est tout pardonner*'? Not quite. The risk is that culturalist explanations might seem to absolve murderous activities; and even one of Heaney's staunchest admirers was worried that the method might accord 'sectarian killing in Ulster a historical respectability which it is not usually given in day-to-day journalism'.[32] It is a measure of how dreadfully the IRA campaign and British army response impinged on even the most intrepid minds that such speculations could even be entertained.[33] For many decades, what had been lacking from most Irish cultural debate was the sort of comparative dimension that Heaney applied. A revivalist myth of national exceptionalism had left generations of political scientists, folklorists and literary critics indifferent to (or unaware of) analogies with the outside world. In later decades, Heaney would multiply the comparisons, with eastern Europe, rural England, St Lucia, as part of his 'nostalgia for world culture'; and others like Brian Friel would do the same. It would, however, be difficult to overstate its liberating effect on young Irish readers in 1975, exhausted by the conflict yet anxious to make sense of it in terms of a wider Europe suffering its share of car bombs, street disturbances and police atrocity. The method was not wholly new, since Joyce had used Homer to suggest a mythic parallel. What was new was that a sponsor of such an analysis might be accused of conniving with the very chaos his myth sought to bring to order and control. It may seem banal to repeat the point: *North*, in seeking to understand sacrificial myth, does not propose its re-enactment. Heaney's implicit allegation against the killers is that they have degraded sacred ritual to the level of a killing routine and so done the work of the colonizers in further disenchanting the land.

Heaney's focus may be on his own side, but he is hardly a doctrinal adherent. Its codes shaped him but he in turn reshaped them:

I grew out of all this
like a weeping willow
inclined to
the appetites of gravity. (*N* 43)

If Catholics over time had tended to impatriate through memories of history (all those lost battles, rebel songs and so on), Protestants in search of their Irish identity had found it most often in geography (landscape, the lore of place). The bog poems, however, offer a point at which history and geography meet. The attainment of a higher level of consciousness, beyond the terms of current conflict, is to be found at the lowest levels of the earth.

The final poem of Part One might easily but glibly be read as a celebration of Hercules' holding aloft of the body of Antaeus, a way of preparing for the more discursive, willed and pragmatic poems of Part Two. Heaney had long contended that there were two kinds of poems: the one given and received by sheer instinct, and the sort knowingly shaped by force of will. Antaeus, with his feeling for the artesian wells beneath, is a sponsor of the first kind; and Hercules, impelled by an urge to order and control, seems to phase in the second. The poet had been wary of becoming excessively self-analytical, lest the element of risk and surprise which bless any creative process be lost, as will exceeded imagination: 'A poem always has elements of accident about it, which can be made the subject of inquest afterwards, but there is always a risk in conducting your own inquest: you might begin to believe the coroner in yourself rather than put your trust in the man in you who is capable of accident.'[34] There has been a tendency to see the sections in *North* as replicating that dualism; but the structuring is not so straightforward. The first section will, of course, expose the shallowness of many journalistic clichés about the conflict in the second section, yet many of those clichés will repeat earlier points. The very looseness of some of the poems in the follow-up section suggests an ease, an instinctual element in the writing, whereas Part One, though filled with depth and suggestion, is arguably the most knowingly assembled of all of Heaney's poetic sequences.

Part Two is less dense and difficult. Much of it is slack and conversational in the ad-lib manner favoured by Patrick Kavanagh. Confronted by journalists seeking views on 'the Irish thing' (a phrase Kavanagh often used to disparage Yeats and the Revivalists), the poet considers the various languages by which people evade a full awareness of current atrocities. Journalists with their talk of 'polarization' and 'long-standing hate' may be no worse than cautious neighbours:

'Oh, it's disgraceful, surely, I agree',
'Where's it going to end?' 'It's getting worse'.
'They're murderers'. 'Internment, understandably. . .'
The voice of sanity is getting hoarse. (*N* 58)

Against these clichés, heartfelt but threadbare, must be pitted the unanswerable facts: 'Men die at hand. In blasted street and home / The gelignite's a common sound-effect. . .' (*N* 58), and the poet seeks the 'right line' to expose the bigotry beneath sham platitudes.

The impulse here is Orwellian in the good sense: based on the conviction that an inadequate language reflects a prior corruption in politics, which can only feed off it. The 'famous Northern reticence' may be just an excuse for refusing to referee between two sides, one of which may actually be worse than the other:

Of the 'wee six' I sing
Where to be saved, you only must save face
And whatever you say, you say nothing. (*N* 59)

The childhood idyll is now thrown into question, with memories of a 'land of password, handgrip, wink and nod', by which names and addresses reveal sectarian affiliations. In 'The Ministry of Fear' Heaney recalls his early experiments as a secondary school poet with Seamus Deane, his friend at St Columb's College:

> I tried to write about the sycamores
> And invented a South Derry rhyme
> With 'hushed' and 'bulled' full rhymes for 'pushed' and 'pulled'.
> Those hobnailed boots from beyond the mountain
> Were walking, by God, all over the fine
> Lawns of elocution. (*N* 63–4)

The same sense of being invaders of an 'English' space might be felt in later years at a police roadblock, where the very name 'Seamus' was enough to prompt the constable to read the letters sent by his poetic collaborator:

> Ulster was British, but with no rights on
> The English lyric: all around us, though
> We hadn't named it, the ministry of fear. (*N* 65)

The poetic problem mirrored the wider social one: somehow the rights of British freemen to jobs, housing and 'one man, one vote' had not been extended to nationalists. 'A Constable Calls' honestly locates this troubled recognition back in the beloved farmhouse in which Heaney's Aunt Mary did the baking in the opening poem: but now it is darkened in memory by the presence of a policeman, suspicious that the tillage returns might be incomplete. Only as the constable cycles away does the full menace of state power become apparent: 'And the bicycle ticked, ticked, ticked' (*N* 65).

Yet that experience, which left Heaney the poet of two traditions, was what would in time bring him global fame as a representative instance of the postcolonial poet. It would explain and enrich his collaboration with Derek Walcott, a native of St Lucia, who would write in similar vein: 'Mongrel as I am, something prickles in me when I see the word ASHANTI as with the word WARWICKSHIRE, both separately indicating my grandfather's roots, both baptizing this neither proud nor ashamed bastard, this hybrid, this West Indian.'[35] The double structure of Walcott's *The Arkansas Testament*, dedicated to Heaney, with its division between Here and Elsewhere, is a homage to *North*:[36] and so also is its determination to embrace the language of Shakespeare, Wordsworth and Auden as of right:

> In the rivulet's gravel
> light gutturals begin,
> in the valley, a mongrel,
> a black vowel barking (*AT* 21)

'Even the most imposed-upon colonial', Heaney would say years later in one of his Oxford Lectures on poetry, 'will discern in the clear element of Herbert's 'The Pulley' a true paradigm of the shape of things',[37] and his nostalgia for world culture will lead him to imagine a free space 'where one will never have to think twice about the cultural and linguistic expression of one's own world on its own since nobody else's terms will be imposed as normative or official'.[38]

The affinities between Heaney and Walcott are a useful reminder that theirs is a vernacular modernism, quite different from that of a Proust or an Eliot writing at the metropolitan centre; and that what looks like pastoralism or archaism in their works is usually framed by some more radical, modern consciousness. 'Act of Union' by Heaney is not just a traditional Gaelic attempt to imagine the Anglo-Irish relation in terms of a marriage which has come under dire strain: it is also an account of a New Age father apprehensively watching over the birth of a child who will bring unprecedented challenges into the world.

The closing poem of *North*, 'Exposure', places the book's two modes, the mythical and the documentary, into a dynamic equilibrium. Written in his new exile in Co. Wicklow, it shows a poet surrounded by woods into which Irish rebels traditionally retreated for cover until the next fight. He has made a separate peace, like previous exiles, through literary history from Ovid ('weighing / my responsible tristia') to Mandelstam ('an inner exile') (*N* 73). The old temptation to be the people's hero has been passed up: but the writer is not wholly satisfied with his Yeatsian choice, fearing that he may have missed a potentially defining moment. The title is ironic, for the poet, having fled from the northern violence, must expose himself to a different set of dangers, the quarrel with himself. He had followed the example of the mad king Sweeney in seeking an exposure to nature, away from the noise of battle, a line of flight made possible to those who abandon the territorial imperative and take to the air:

> I am neither internee nor informer;
> An inner émigré, grown long long-haired
> And thoughtful; a wood-kerne
>
> Escaped from the massacre,
> Taking protective colouring
> From bole and bark, feeling
> Every wind that blows;
>
> Who, blowing up these sparks
> For their meagre heat, have missed
> The once-in-a-lifetime portent,
> The comet's pulsing rose. (*N* 73)

Edmund Spenser had described the wood-kernes as emerging from the trees, famine-stricken, on hands and knees, 'like anatomies of death, they spake like ghosts crying out of their graves'.[39] But, akin to the Bog Queen and to Yeats's buried men, they had already found in poetry a force 'analogous to the immunity system of the human body', and so, like all of them, the speaker, denied illumination but expecting the aurora borealis, can lie patiently, waiting for his next moment to arrive, ensuring that there will be a life before death.

Europeanization

In the early years of the twentieth century, the playwright John Millington Synge had written caustically of certain Irish nationalists who feared to be Europeans lest the huckster across the street call them English. Yet it was in Paris that Synge had his fateful first meeting with W. B. Yeats, who advised him to write about the Aran Islands. The book that ensued was full of European comparisons, notably between Irish and continental folk tales; but it also treated the island community as a version of the anarchist commune, not unlike the one established at Montmartre in 1870–1. It was in Paris, also, that Synge argued aesthetics with the young James Joyce and politics with the militant republican Maud Gonne. That city was not just 'the capital of the nineteenth century' (in the words of Walter Benjamin), but also the crucible in which many elements of the Irish Revival were tested. The scholarly writings of Henri d'Arbois de Jubainville on the Irish heroic cycle were translated for use by a rising generation of Irish artists and activists, some of whom wrote essays reminding readers that the fame of Ireland had once extended across the educational centres of early Christian Europe, which had looked to its north-western outpost as 'the isle of saints and scholars'.

In some respects, the nationalist outpourings of writers of English in the mid-nineteenth century had represented an interruption of this more expansive and less introverted tradition. The earls and clerics who fled the onslaught of occupying armies in 1607 had fanned out across the cities of Europe, in which their men of learning were as likely to write poems and tracts in Irish as in Latin or Spanish. Catholic universities such as Louvain and Salamanca maintained strong intellectual ties with Ireland. The leaders of the defeated Jacobite armies at Aughrim in 1691, and subsequently at Limerick, became the famous 'wild geese' who enlisted with honour in the armies of Catholic Europe. The young James Joyce felt himself an upholder of that tradition when first he arrived as an exile in Paris in 1902.

These historical connections were often invoked in the early 1970s, as the country faced a referendum on the possibility of joining the European Economic Community. Some radicals feared that joining would compromise Irish sovereignty for the sake of a merely economic arrangement. Others pointed to a strong element of Catholic social thinking in much EEC legislation. The British (Ireland's largest market) seemed about to join anyway; and membership of the wider community would open newer markets to Irish exporters.

It was also hoped that a wider European perspective might help to bring the antagonists in Northern Ireland to a sensible compromise. The religious wars of the 1600s were long forgotten on the continent. The EEC, itself founded in 1957 as an attempt to make an economic peace between belligerents of the much more recent world war, was intended to bring an affluence to impoverished regions that would help to dissolve old resentments. Educators on both sides of the border hoped that, with the softening of cultural differences, it might be possible to offer integrated courses in Irish Studies, outlining how deep and comprehensive were past interactions between the cultures of Irish and English languages.

A playwright such as Brian Friel, in retelling the story of the Sons of Usna, sought to excavate a common Scottish and Irish substratum in the ancient story, even as his fellow dramatist Tom Murphy explored the deeper meanings of the Anglo-Irish relationship.

11. The Art of Science: Banville's *Doctor Copernicus*

John Banville has always been wary of attempts to fit his work into any Irish literary tradition. He has preferred to consider the artist as a humble egomaniac, manufacturing a purely personal world out of the fragments of European culture. Yet he has also run the risk of becoming famous for his reticence about the cults that can surround famous novelists. Banville was born in Wexford on the Feast of the Immaculate Conception in 1945, and attended the Christian Brothers' school and St Peter's College there. Once, when asked how he had managed, in his trilogy of novels on Renaissance scientists, to document the late medieval world in such convincing detail, he laughed and said: 'That was easy. I grew up in Wexford in the 1950s.'[1] In the 1960s he worked as a clerk for Aer Lingus and the British Post Office; and through the 1970s and early 1980s he was a subeditor of the *Irish Press*, before becoming literary editor of the *Irish Times*.

Banville's novels are a strange blend of the playful and the poetic. All point to the difficulty of recapturing past moments. *Birchwood* is a hilarious send-up of the Big House novel, complete with brooding unhappy father, put-upon mother, an artistic son and a sinister granny who dies by an act of spontaneous combustion. In his science trilogy, which concerns Copernicus, Kepler and Newton, Banville explores the nature of creative genius, imparting a sense of adventure to the life of the mind, as the old world of witches and spells turns into the modern era of scientists and doubt. The third of the trilogy was to have been about Newton, but became instead a short narrative on the plight of a scholar who found it quite impossible to write about Newton. He had sought peace and quiet in a rented cottage on the fringe of a decaying Anglo-Irish estate but, rather like the scientists who sought to flee a disorderly world, found himself embroiled instead in the chaos of everyday lives – the lives of the occupants of the Big House on the estate.

Despite his interest in history and science, Banville has often insisted that he is neither a historical novelist nor a science writer but rather a man who knows how to mock his own obsessions and especially his obsession with the form of the novel itself. Like Schiller, he implies that man is most human when he plays. His books are full of puns and ludic routines, because their author, like his own exemplars, Borges and Nabokov, wishes above all to entertain.[2] Some commentators have found his sustained intellectual concerns and beautiful style too dauntingly self-conscious, as if the writer were compensating with a vengeance for the university education he lacked. But that is to miss a key element in his work. While Banville is deeply moved by the sufferings endured by his scholars in pursuit of truth, or at least in pursuit of a zone of order apart from the turbulent world, he is also ready to see the comical side of their pain. So he debunks the self-importance of intellectuals who, while they explore the starry heavens, are nevertheless afflicted by such banal and earthbound discomforts as constipation and winter draughts. Like Beckett, this writer knows that nothing is funnier than unhappiness.

To say that Banville is an aesthete is to recognize that sound and shape may be more vital to his art than sense and meaning. Form is certainly anterior to theme. 'In fiction, the thing said must always be subordinate to the way of saying',[3] he wrote in 1977, and over the following decade that view did not change. In this period, he often had resort to the word 'redemptive', used alongside the word 'style'. For him, a serviceable style would redeem the fallen material it embodied; redeeming it not by any perfect fusion with the material but precisely because it was imposed and extraneous.[4]

This has left Banville opposed in these years[5] to the Joyce who allowed the many styles of *Ulysses* to evolve from their multiple subjects in ways the contemporary writer finds drearily schematic: he has cited the 'Oxen of the Sun' section as notably offensive in this regard. He has voiced reservations about Joyce's claim that the ordinary is the proper domain of the artist since the extraordinary can safely be left to journalists (among whom Banville has spent much of his working life). His own art insists that the actual is fundamentally extraordinary. To prove the point, he carried for many years in his wallet a clipping from the *Evening Press* of the 1970s about an old woman on Dublin's North Strand who really did self-ignite: and this in answer to those who scoffed at the incredibility of the feat of spontaneous combustion in *Birchwood*. The literalist account of the facts is something he finds stranger than any fiction. His art is committed to an exploration of the relation between the quotidian and the miraculous, between the tedious afflictions of ordinary life and the soaring imagination of genius, between the world of scientific fact and the zones of artistic value. These he investigates not as categories of opposition but as modes of interdependence. The ordinary is extraordinary (Joyce's thesis) only because the extraordinary is quotidian (Banville's first law).

Banville has expressed a deep admiration for Samuel Beckett, who cheerfully conceded the extraneousness of style when he compared it to a bow tie worn over a throat cancer. For both, it is the shape of a sentence or a work which counts. Insofar as it makes a limited kind of sense to locate Banville within an Irish tradition, he might be considered to exist on a line which moves via Beckett back through Yeats to Wilde – a set of writers for whom style, despite its extraneousness, is everything. Banville began his novel *Kepler* with a shape rather than an idea, or, more accurately, with a shape as an idea. There were to be five sections, with the number of chapters in each corresponding to the number of sides on each of five polygons, and all chapters of equal length in each section. Time in each narrative unit was to double back to its start at the end, not tracing a perfect circle but an ellipsis, as in planetary motion.[6] Doubtless, many who enjoyed *Kepler* did so without knowing this, as most early readers of *Ulysses* were unaware of the Homeric analogy, but for Banville the scaffolding was essential. Without it he might not have written the book at all. It was this realization that led him to claim that content is no more than an aspect of form.[7]

Wilde wrote that in matters of grave importance, style rather than sincerity was the important thing, and Yeats, perhaps developing that idea in *A Vision*, called his system 'stylistic arrangements of experience'.[8] Both men saw style as sustaining a possibly feasible fiction, a working arrangement by which other suppositions become tenable. Like Yeats, Banville is haunted by the notion of civilization as manifest illusion, and by the suggestion that genius is nothing other than the capacity to break up the life-lie which characterizes an epoch or a civilization. Those who do this can do so by virtue of the fact that they are offering a new and more serviceable fiction in its place. They are the makers and unmakers of supreme fictions, just as a major artist is one who in creating a new form in literature necessarily helps to break up another. These ideas were brilliantly summed up in Yeats's autobiography:

> All civilisation is held together by the suggestions of an invisible hypnotist, by artificially created illusions. The knowledge of reality is always in some measure a secret knowledge – it is a kind of death.[9]

Yeats was convinced that every culture has a dual impetus. On the one hand, its sponsors tend to consolidate the feasible fiction and when a culture blossoms its artists are the hypnotists who reassure their people with illusions of a durable beauty. On the other hand, it just as surely contains the seeds of its own destruction, when some probing or artistic spirit summons the courage to go beneath the veneer of things, shattering their provisional style of coherence and offering instead a stylistic derangement of experience. Yeats was sure that modern man lived at a time of the shattering of such illusions and he wrote in 'Meru':

> Civilisation is hooped together, brought
> Under a rule, under the semblance of peace
> By manifold illusion; but man's life is thought,
> And he, despite his terror, cannot cease
> Ravening through century after century,
> Ravening, raging and uprooting that he may come
> Into the desolation of reality.[10]

For Banville, such a time of change was the late medieval world, which provides him with a correlative to his own. His interest in magic is at least as strong as his interest in Renaissance science, because both worked hand in glove to overthrow the feudal hierarchies of the medieval world. The prejudice which holds science and magic to be opposites is of a relatively recent vintage, as Synge discovered on the Aran Islands. Renaissance scientists, however, were often mentioned in the same breath as alchemists (indeed some were alchemists). Both groups were viewed by the church authorities as subversive and sinister, threats to the God-ordained feudal order, since each suggested that mankind (and not God) had the making and remaking of human conditions.[11] In *Doctor Copernicus* it is hardly surprising that the subject should win an even greater reputation throughout Catholic Ermland for his healing potions than for his science.

If all scientific cosmologies and all physicists' codes are precarious and provisional arrangements, this makes them like Banville's notion of literary tradition: strictly temporary arrangements, subject to endless modification on a principle of general relativity. That in turn is reminiscent of Banville's view of the single paragraph in his writing as a fragile construct whose beauty can be deliberately jeopardized by some risky effect, like the violent introduction of a four-letter obscenity into an otherwise reticent passage. These effects abound. They are indulged partly in an attempt by the writer to see whether he can get away with them, and also to establish whether the edifice of rigorous order constructed by his style will crumble or hold in face of the assault. In Beckett's prose trilogy, words like 'fuck' and 'cunt' also asserted themselves at the most unexpected moment in the middle of pellucidly beautiful paragraphs. Those who employ such devices expose themselves to the charge of a showy, self-congratulatory experimentalism: but the method is perfectly defensible as part of Banville's investigation into the way the mythical construct of a genius is constantly colliding with the lumber of the matter-of-fact. These worlds, far from being opposed, are themselves revealed as one. Every four-letter word was, after all, once a poem so expressive in its initial effect that it was robbed of that pristine beauty by overuse.

That unity in diversity is the central intuition of *Doctor Copernicus*: the proposition that the genius of science and the genius of art are finally of one and the same kind. Astronomy, which once linked heaven and earth, may now link art and science.[12] Banville himself, as an artist, supplies his book with many cross-references, quotations from James Joyce or Wallace Stevens, as well as a working bibliography attached to the end, listing debts to such scholars as Frances Yates and Arthur Koestler. This scientific and scholarly methodology comes the more remarkably in a work of almost pure fiction, given that so little at the level of indisputable fact is known about Copernicus. This allows that the scientist Copernicus can be treated as if he were an artist – that word was indeed used to describe him, perhaps disparagingly, in a contemporary report.

The initial discovery concerning the location of the earth is seen as an artistic leap of faith, based more on instinct than on evidence, which would take many years of scientific hackwork to verify. If Banville the artist may claim something of the rigour of the scientist, in the figure of Copernicus he celebrates the artistry of all scientific thinkers:

> Before, he had naturally assumed that the new methods and procedures must be devised first, that they would be the tools with which to build the theory; that, of course, was to miss the essential point, namely, that the birth of the new science must be preceded by a radical act of creation.[13]

At such a juncture, a merely scientific approach would prove a major impediment to the kind of inductive artistic thinking which alone guarantees a real breakthrough. Progress, as so often, can be made only through an act of apparently diabolical disobedience of all known laws:

> No sooner had he realised the absolute necessity for a creative leap than his instincts without his knowing had thrown up their defences against such a scandalous notion, thrusting him back into the closed system of worn-out orthodoxies. There, like a blind fool, he had sought to arrive at a new destination by travelling the old routes, had thought to create an original theory by means of conventional calculations. (*DC* 85)

Now Copernicus resolves to make his risky claim about the centrality of the sun in an immensely expanded universe:

> Of course. The verification of the theory, he knew, would take

weeks, months, years perhaps to complete, but that was nothing, that was mere hackwork. What mattered was not the propositions, but the combining of them: the act of creation. (*DC* 85)

It is central to Banville's acute comic awareness of the absurdity of great ones in their moments of triumph, and of the provisional nature of the triumphs they secure, that Copernicus, in his visionary ecstasy, should stare exultantly at the sun, that centre of the new cosmology, only to find that clouds have gathered once again and it cannot be seen. The actual world, it is hinted, will forever be stronger than the most intrepid system building.

This understanding of the given universe as a flawed medium through which to intuit divine harmonies becomes a central focus of the novel, as well as the underlying explanation of Banville's obsession with style. If he inherits romantic notions of the imagination as the divine spark which remains in the human personality, he is also possessed of the darker modern awareness that language itself is tainted and alienated.[14] From the very outset, the narrative returns again and again to one question: how to find the word to express the thing? The debt to Joyce's *Portrait* is clear:

– Tree. That was its name. And also: the linden. They were nice words. He had known them a long time before he knew what they meant. They did not mean themselves, they were nothing in themselves, they meant the dancing singing thing outside. (*DC* 3)

A little later, the child worries that there might be a difference between reality and his interpretation of it:

Everything had a name, but although every name was nothing without the thing named, the thing cared nothing for its name, had no need of a name, and was itself only. (*DC* 3)

The defiant refusal of things to submit fully to human schematization is what fascinates Banville, whether that schematization takes the form of literature or of science. Yet humanity must persist with the illusion that such a schematization has been workably achieved, and then maintain that illusion unquestioningly within the received domain of language. Even God's hold on illusions may loosen, as when he drops the mother of Nicholas out of his embrace into the still truth of death. The information that his mother was now in heaven, although her dead body was laid out in front of him, raises again for Nicholas the question of a split between value and fact, between a representation of a person and what he calls her 'corpse', a mere thing. Likewise, he soon learns that coins are a mere picture of the value inherent when a gentleman gives his word, another precarious fiction. In the manner of Joyce's Stephen Dedalus at Clongowes, Nicholas discovers that language is at best a slippery medium – Copernicus is apparently a noble name, yet it comes from the Polish word *coper*, meaning horseradish.

The philosopher Jacques Derrida has written of 'the barbarism of a name', regretting its vulgar attempt to label a self or a thing which is in perpetual flux. So the child Nicholas soon senses that to his uncle Lucas he is not a person but an idea called vaguely Child, Nephew, responsibility. Nicholas himself begins to put words in framing devices, the better to register their absurdity, engaging (as the narrative says) 'in what they called play for an hour' (*DC* 17). Yet all the time he dreams of healing the split between name and thing, between his exalted and his base self: and the unlocking agent of that redemption will be not so much an idea as a style, a new way of seeing or intuiting the universal harmonies. Hence the recurrence through the book of his *doppelgänger* brother, the haunting, syphilitic Andreas, a permanent reminder of the recalcitrant realities of that messy world above which Nicholas wishes to soar, a filthy manifestation of all that must be ignored or passed over in his brother's version of harmony. Andreas is the voice of that actuality which refuses to conform to any given theory; and his brother envies, yet fears, his immersion in the immediate flow of life.

Banville himself has a literary brother who writes criticism for newspapers and who is himself so addicted to the notion of internal splitting that he publishes sometimes under a half-pseudonym, Vincent (his real forename) Lawrence. In most of the novels of John Banville there is some version of the double – sometimes one dies young and the other is forever haunted by his sense of himself as a mere fraction wishing to regain his standing as an integer. Here, however, Copernicus is guilty of suppressing the knowledge of his brother, only to have it erupt at the end, like the return of the repressed, as Andreas brutally lists all the thingness of things in a world Nicholas has spurned so as to achieve his scholarly vision. Andreas is the author's reminder that piercingly original insights into one aspect of reality are achieved usually at the cost of remaining blind to all of its other aspects.

In the great final scene of the book, Andreas says, 'Why, simple brother, we ARE the truth...this world and ourselves' (*DC* 239). In saying that, he is merely repeating the early lesson taught by Canon Wodka at the start, when he told the young Nicholas that 'the world is *here*, that it exists, that it is inexplicable' (*DC* 23) and that all theories, however persuasive and beautiful, are just names, but 'the world itself is a thing'. Ordinary mortals make an easy, thoughtless leap from the recommended name to a given thing and soon lose their sense of wonder at the actual, learning to talk with unquestioning confidence. Copernicus, as his teachers uneasily sense, wishes to move in reverse, making a difficult, self-questioning transition from the world of things back to a new, unfamiliar naming. He is aware from the beginning that this attempt – although it may achieve a fuller explanation of the universe than any previous description – is doomed to futility:

Yet the world was more, and less, than the fires and ice of lofty speculation. It was also his life and the lives of others, brief, pain-laden, irredeemably shabby. Between the two spheres of thought and action he could discern no workable connection. In this he was out of step with the age, which told him heaven and earth in his own self were conjoined. The notion was not seriously to be entertained, however stoutly he might defend it out of loyalty to the humanist cause... If such harmony had ever existed, he feared deep down, deep beyond admitting, that it was not to be regained. (*DC* 27)

In other words, Copernicus has made the leap from medievalism not to Renaissance humanism, but beyond it, to postmodernism, a world where all attempts at harmony are made in the foreknowledge that to be an artist is to fail, and in the premonition that every raid on the articulate will be 'a new kind of failure, with shabby equipment always deteriorating'.[15]

Copernicus also discovers that every other scientist is a secret, if unwitting, postmodernist. The mathematicians know that Ptolemy's theory is gravely wrong but have too deep an investment in it to concede as much. Professor Brudzewski devises a workable theory grounded in Ptolemy's errors, yet accounting superficially for the observed motions of the planets. This is called *saving the phenomena.* For Banville, the working hypothesis of the Renaissance scientist is but a version of Wallace Stevens's idea of a supreme fiction; by which the poet meant a comprehensive and consoling fabrication of the world created by men for men, out of sheer desperation after the disappearance of God. Whereas older fictions were unquestioned, and therefore in the deepest sense myths, *modern* versions will be self-avowedly false, provisional, but intermittently workable. The principle governing Copernican science will be the same principle that rules Flann O'Brien's postmodern fiction *At Swim-Two-Birds*: 'A satisfactory novel should be a self-evident sham to which the reader could regulate at will the degree of his credulity'.[16] Thus Banville's own book.

Precisely because the known facts about the life of Copernicus are scant, this narrative (which is insistently subtitled *A Novel* by John Banville) can be both contemporary and historical, using his fertile imagination while balancing its products on a historical framework, incorporating many contemporary literary devices but retaining a period flavour. This, in turn, permits Banville to remind his readers by artistic means of something he has also said in a discussion with Francis Stuart: 'Fact is not truth. People think that when they're getting fact they get the absolute unadorned truth. But fact of itself is nothing, it doesn't exist. Since I started writing novels based on historical fact, I've realized that the past doesn't exist in terms of fact. It only exists in terms of the way we look at it.'[17] This is to say that the contents of any historical record are always largely determined by the constraints of the narrative form in which it is encased.[18] Every historian, like every scientist, whether they admit it or not, must conduct their work under the disciplines of art. Form and style truly are powerful and extraneous forces which may redeem material by saving the phenomena for the contemporary mind: and they are pervasive, anterior, primary. In the end they are all we have with which to grasp at a world, and all that remains after that world starts to dissolve. As Joseph McMinn has suggested, Banville knows that history becomes fiction and that every fiction has a history, but his real interest is in the relation between both processes.[19]

In the earlier novel *Birchwood*, Banville chronicled the decline of an Anglo-Irish Big House in a spoof of the Gothic mode, a spoof driven by the recognition that you cannot write any historical account without adapting the facts to the demands of literary form, which are as distorting and as exclusive as any other kind of convention-based art. And in *The Newton Letter* he would write of the poise of the Anglo-Irish in terms which suggested that their training was but a preparation for this moment when there was nothing left to them but style, a style of endurance which allowed the manner to remain intact long after the matter had snapped. Hence the consistency of Banville's books, the sense that he is forever rewriting one narrative, about the impossibility of any master narrative.

At the centre of each of his narratives is the perception that men like Copernicus and Kepler, for all their zeal to reform science, were far more committed to creating elegant models than to telling the truth. Far from being an indictment of their dishonesty, this is seen as a sign of their genius. Being a postmodern artist, Banville shares the Copernican conviction that truth does not exist in any comprehensible or explicable mode. It may, in Yeatsian terms, be embodied by Andreas, but it can never be actually told by Nicholas. 'There are only workable versions of truth which we contract to believe in',[20] Banville has remarked: and because man, even scientific man, is an aesthetic creature, he invariably chooses the most elegant. Einstein, for instance, claimed that for his theory of relativity he might have chosen any of ten possible models. However, he was attracted to the most beautiful.[21]

Crucial to Einsteinian physics was a principle of high irony: the notion that with every structuralization of chaos, chaos itself increases, because each new structure gives rise to new reactions. Even entropy can, in this molecular system, lead to distropy. That is, of course, the reason why people like Copernicus and Kepler are chaotic in the impression they create and in the lives they lead. They talk of bowel movements one moment and stellar movements the next, and that becomes an infectious style of juxtaposition, leaking into the Banvillean narrative and causing him to write fluently one minute and jaggedly the next. Nor is this mere mimicry by Banville of his subjects. Rather is it his way of reminding his readers that style and form come between the person and any reality depicted, and that they determine just how much of that reality a person may be permitted to see.

The world of Banville is a place of chaos, subject to intermittent structuralizations, performed by those souls audacious enough to insist that it is not enough to save the phenomena. It is also necessary to explain them, a hopeless task yet one that great souls can never shirk. So, rejecting a system in which all must be taken on God-given faith, Copernicus instead tries to place man at the centre of things as the perceiving subject, who must bring all theories into harmony with what he sees, rather than, as the old-fashioned inquisitors do, see only those things which ratify a prior theory. In the beginning was the word, the name that was God: but if God is gone then the word is wrong. So, instead of jumping from a name to a thing, the empiricist Copernicus will try to jump from a thing to a name. To that extent, at least, he is a kindred of Andreas, who insists that everything begins with this world.

The problem is obvious: how to begin with the world, since it only exists in our perception of it? When Copernicus returns to his old haunt of Frauenburg, he feels that the city is different, while knowing that the real change is less in the city than in himself. As the novel proceeds, he becomes more and more troublesomely aware of his perceptual limits as a constraint upon all that he sees. In his desire to know the desolation of reality, he constantly comes up against other people's limits and their willingness to settle for soothing fictions. What he says of other people may also be true of the world – they are not known, merely invented. His aim at the start is to break that closed system of self-deceit, so that it can transcend itself and its concerns and 'become an instrument for verifying the real rather than merely postulating the possible' (*DC* 83).

In that sense, Copernicus is like Marx or Freud or Loyola: he becomes the creator of a new discourse, which will give rise to many other discourses, and so the patenter of a new world.[22] The severance of traditional ties that follows robs him of his security and of his nationality too, as the designation Pole or Prussian or whatever becomes meaningless. Behind the mask of Ermlander, 'he was that which no name or nation could claim. He was Doctor Copernicus' (*DC* 94). In short, he becomes the consummate Banvillean artist, for whom tradition is not a *datum* of tribe or nation, but a purely individual reinvention of all that has gone before.

This involves less a denial of identity than its expansion – Banville's self-conception as a European rather than an Irish artist. For him most Irish novel writing falls within an outmoded tradition of literary nationalism, which regards the world as a given and Irish tradition as a stable element in that handover.[23] His hope is not to write from within that secure culture, but to take up a position above and beyond it, describing and analysing all those forces which have made the very phrases 'Irish tradition' or 'Polish tradition' problematic. For him, as for all radical thinkers, Bohemia is the native country, the one place where men are free to be artists and to improvise their own patterns of meaning out of the shreds of all national cultures as they disintegrate.

To such a point has Copernicus come when, in a central scene, he confesses to his pox-ridden brother that 'the world is absurd' (*DC* 103). Andreas is delighted and agrees to haunt him no more, secure in the belief that his wantonness was the appropriate response to such a dreadful, chaotic place. Against such a backdrop, people will believe anything they want to believe. Copernicus is dismayed to find out just how great is the reputation for miraculous cures won throughout Ermland by his outlandish potions, which he privately admits to be fake. In this uneasy guise, of course, he anticipates a remarkable recurrence of the figure of the faith healer in contemporary Irish writing, from Friel's Frank Hardy through Tom Murphy's JPW King, all of them indicative of a view of the artist as a conman who knows that he is fraudulent but persists in offering his sustenance to a credulous population despite that knowledge.

The space in Copernicus's world once occupied by God has been replaced by nothing – literally, by a void – and so, with the maker of the ultimate fiction absconded, all secondary fictions become self-enclosed. If the world is not in fact an imitation of a more perfect one, then art and science can no longer be renditions of the world, becoming instead just stylistic arrangements, patterns of internal coherence which make no serious attempt to enter into a contest with reality. What is possible is only the private perception of a hermetically sealed artist: and every scientific theory is at once as self-sufficient and as rigorously beautiful as a work of symbolist art: 'He had believed it possible to say the truth; now he saw that all that could be said was the saying. His book was not about the world, but about itself. . .' (*DC* 116).

Moreover, like a piece of symbolist art, that work was useless in direct proportion to its beauty. Its arrangements might amuse the mind while steadfastly refusing to teach men and women how to live. This was what Canon Wodka had warned. Indeed, the book repeats exactly his earlier words, quoting itself as if to dramatize such barren but intriguing self-referentiality: 'Beware these enigmas, my young friend. They exercise the mind, but they cannot teach us how to live' (*DC* 21).

Once Copernicus reaches this stage, the void at the centre of his cosmos seems merely a version of the vacancy at the core of himself. His performance of rituals is aloof, perfunctory, as if 'all was hollow save for one thin taut cord of steely inexpressible anguish stretching across the nothingness' (*DC* 132). Yet it endears him for the first time, perhaps, to rulers like Albrecht, master of the Teutonic Knights, who must daily turn in such performances in order to keep the credulous masses secure. 'You and I', says Albrecht, quoting Wallace Stevens, who will be born four centuries after him, 'we are lords of the earth, the great ones, the major men, the makers of supreme fictions' (*DC* 136). Even the powerful knight attempts, in his way, to unite the real and imaginary.

And this is the main thesis of *Doctor Copernicus: A Novel* by John Banville. Whereas in traditional God-fearing society, religion offered a consoling life-lie and fiction was just a parable of right morality, now in the postmodern world, constructed on a void, fiction is a grim necessity. If God really has gone, the only trace of a divine spark remaining may be found in the human imagination, which becomes, despite its reduced state, even more valuable than ever. The more the novel is a self-evident sham, the more often a fiction breaks the mimetic illusion to admit that it is only fiction, the deeper and more desperate the need for such a work becomes.

It is at this stage that Banville's strategy as a novelist becomes clear. He is, on the one hand, opposed to mere realism of the kind practised in the nineteenth-century novel: and he is equally opposed to the sort of fabulism found in some postmodern narratives. However, he is committed to a fusion of both methods within a single work. His critical articles in the years surrounding the writing of *Doctor Copernicus* call for the Victorian novel minus its clutter and didacticism but retaining its commitment to the banalities of the everyday world, and for the postmodern narrative which vigilantly interrogates the conditions of its own possibility.[24] The resultant blend of the mythical and mundane may have more in common with, say, the methods of Seamus Heaney in *North*, published also in the mid-1970s, or with the both/and aesthetic of Friel and Tom Murphy, than its analysts would care to concede.

This attempted fusion of realism and fabulism is Banville's version of the project of Copernicus to align things and names. According to Banville, a fact out of context, a decapitated fact unredeemed by its place in an aesthetic scheme, is simply dead; equally a pattern of beauty without a factual component is also deadly.[25] The *nouveau roman* of Alain Robbe-Grillet is factually saturated but deficient in wholeness, because it excludes ideas.[26] Unfortunately, many contemporary novels of ideas achieve their effect by discounting any trace of the factual: and this is a pity to an artist who finds the factual extraordinary.

His ideal novel is, therefore, inclusive and also self-sufficient, a pure form of modern art which contains itself adequately within its own limits. Such a literature, being purely itself and at the same time offering commentary on itself, combines the classical ideal of self-containment with the romantic drive for self-awareness. In that process, although it makes no claims to reflect reality as a photograph would, the novel does something far more difficult. It shows people how to grapple with reality for themselves. Quite literally, it teaches them how to read, providing not experience but the knowledge of how it is perceived.[27]

In a sly parody of Shelley, Banville once wrote that novelists are the unacknowledged historians of the world.[28] Which is to say that they take the facts of history for subject matter, and then supply the fiction which alone can bring those facts to life. In *Doctor Copernicus*, the writer evokes not just the historical setting. He also vivifies it with an overlaid modern consciousness, as when Albrecht quotes a modernist American poet. It is not the history that is important so much as the way it is seen and told. Hence, the third section is narrated through the consciousness of Rheticus, a student of Copernicus who provides many alternative versions of the story, calling Nicholas's beloved a *focaria* and bitch. He juxtaposes his own style against his master's, realizing that style is all that now stands between them. Rheticus discovers that the emptiness at the core of the Copernican system is a reflection of the appalling cynicism of the man himself; yet he is just as cynical, disbelieving the theory but hoping to climb to fame on the coat-tails of its maker. Rheticus – a telling name in a book held together simply by the concept of style – finds that there is no centre to Copernicus's world, not even the sun. In withholding that information, Copernicus behaves, in his judgement, more like a magical alchemist than a true exponent of modern science.

Rheticus becomes what the youthful Nicholas once was: a mocker of those, like the Roman priests, who transform the horror of the time into empty ritual, dressing up in outlandish clothes in order to sustain their silly fictions. He confronts his hero, only to find that Copernicus, despairing of truth, no longer even believes or disbelieves his own theory. His master has turned into a Wildean artist. 'All that mattered to him was the saying', he mimics, 'not what was said' (*DC* 176). To him Copernicus now seems no better than papist fiction-mongers: 'Words were the empty rituals with which he held the world at bay. Copernicus did not believe in the truth' (*DC* 176). So he would not publish his distressing announcement that the earth was not at the centre of the universe: instead, he proposed to destroy it. And why? Because of his jaded awareness that even his theory, superior to its predecessors, is nonetheless only an exalted naming, a sort of dream. Even if the earth were to be banished from the core, the stars would still shine in their places, the grass would still be green, and the thingness of things would remain unviolated by that knowledge.

There was another reason for Copernicus's reticence. Luther, who had already stripped away many outmoded beliefs, had offered no equal fiction to take their place, and because of his failure to understand man's deep necessity for ritual, all of Europe had been plunged into turmoil with peasants' uprisings. Copernicus fears that his work will further erode all authority. He is yet another conflicted dissident, like Banville himself, so unnerved by the freedoms he has taken as to feel the pressing need to retreat into a traditional style. Historians of science aver that Copernicus's very thesis projected that inner ambivalence, 'being at once ancient and modern, conservative and radical'.[29] The undertow of conservatism in a radical thinker is obvious also in the fact that a man so anxious to change the common understanding of the cosmos was also willing 'to deny the existence of a comparable change in his own society'.[30]

For Copernicus, as for Banville, the danger in stripping away illusions lies in the possibility that people will be gulled into taking what is uncovered as the truth. But truth is something which Copernicus knows to be unreachable. He becomes in the book, therefore, not just the one who takes a step beyond the Renaissance into modernity – that, after all, was Luther, with his this-worldly notion of man as the measure of all things – but rather the one whose theory carries him straight to postmodernity, since at the centre of his world is not even the sun but a heavy emptiness. Copernicus emerges as the first truly deconstructive critic, since his *Book of Revolutions* is described as 'an engine which destroys itself' (*DC* 217), a theory which is no sooner enunciated than it annuls itself, by admitting its own redundancy. More amazing still, according to Rheticus, the theory was not even Copernicus's own.

When, in the final, fourth section, Andreas makes his last visitation, he accuses his brother of having foolishly sought only to know the heavenly harmonies, when he should also have been seeking to reconcile them with the messy nature of life on earth. This fatal division in Copernicus was acidly noted by Rheticus too, in the telltale fact that his master could have lived so long with Anna Schillings and yet never discussed his ideas with her, conveying to his partner the impression that he was just a magician and faith healer.

As a postmodern novelist, Banville has, therefore, a lot in common with his own Copernicus. His book, like the *Book of Revolutions*, is not something that explains everything: it tries not to mean but to be. And, once Rheticus is let loose in the penultimate section to accuse his master of being a dishonest plagiarist, it becomes a machine of self-destruction. The hyper style of Rheticus amounts to an equal and opposite annulment of the classical forms used until that point to evoke Copernicus.

However, there is one vital sense in which this novel is wholly un-Copernican. Unlike its subject, it attempts at all times to maintain a scrupulous balance between the exalted and the quotidian, the artistic and the chaotic. In its final intimation that Andreas is not a brother but an aspect of Copernicus himself, seeking integration and wholeness, it manages to suggest that at least within the limits of art intimations of such harmony may be glimpsed. The earth may not be the centre of the universe, but it seems to be the centre of all that man can know: and in living on the earth a person can embody the force of life without ever quite understanding it. Such knowledge is not of this world and can be found only, with the absconded God, outside of life altogether, in the heavenly music of the eighth sphere.

The disenchantment of the medieval world, as the old certainties exploded, had many analogies in Ireland after the Second World War. *Doctor Copernicus* is a book about the non-publication of a book in a climate of fear and self-censorship. Its subject fears the people and their disapproval even more than he fears castigation by intellectuals. Banville's own shyness about writing direct auto-biography is reflected in Copernicus's anxiety not to reveal himself. Copernicus half suspects that once he completes the work of art, his fate will be that of a pure aesthete – the work will flower and he die. The progress of a great scientist, no less than that of an artist, is a continual self-extinction.[31]

Even the conflict between a Catholic and Protestant mindset in the late-medieval world allows Banville a way of exploring at a safe remove the sectarian conflict of the 1960s and 1970s in the north of Ireland.[32] The theme is the same as that analysed by Seamus Heaney in *North*: how the stripping away of ancient rituals has inflamed many people, leading to rituals of death, as some are seized by the illusion that some new 'truth' can be found in their place.

Urban Ireland was still producing pastoral in the 1970s. Indeed, even as the census of 1971 revealed that more people now lived in cities and towns than in the countryside, the lure of pastoral for many grew stronger still. Heaney's early evocations of life on a farm spoke to as many as Kavanagh's had done in the previous generation. However, Banville's displacement of an almost unspeakable slaughter in urban centres such as Belfast and Derry onto a medieval rural world is accompanied by his pursuit of autobiography through distant surrogates. Because so little is known about Copernicus, the empty spaces in his story allow this most self-effacing of writers to express more than usual about himself. The mask of late-medieval Europe permits him to tell some home truths about Ireland (the censorious Canon Wodka recalling the more repressive Christian Brothers at the school in Wexford), but all done at a remove which will not imperil his style. The centre of Europe in the wars of the sixteenth century may have too many tell-tale analogies with 1970s Ireland: as a pilot airily observed while holding his plane over Belfast airport, 'we are now approaching Aldergrove: please put your watches back three hundred years'.

This is science fiction, but of a kind located in the past rather than the future. It is also a form of Gothic, its mad scientists and warring overlords based on a repression of the fears generated by the Troubles. By the time Banville was working on his book, political scientists feared that there was no answer to the Northern Ireland question,[33] and so people turned in their bafflement to artists for a *meaning* to the question. This left many of them feeling as fraudulent as did Copernicus at certain moments of vulnerability, but, coded into Banville's book, as into slightly later works by Brian Friel and Tom Murphy, is the notion of the artist as a necessary healer, whose cures are based on faith rather than fraud.

Many other debates of the 1970s reverberate through Banville's book. Its scepticism about establishing an authoritative record reflects the questioning in university history departments about the accuracy of the nationalist story fed to children for fifty years after independence; but the bright hope of the 'revisionists' that they were replacing this with an accurate account (based on the experiences of women, the poor, the ruined aristocrats et cetera) is given no sanction by Banville. He considers that mistake to be at least as old as the Reformation: the foolish conviction that, as a document-driven culture displaces an oral one, what emerges will be unvarnished truth. It will just be another version, for the problems which dog science are the same as those which taint history writing. As Banville produced his book, Hayden White was demonstrating to his fellow historians that every narrative of the past is written at the mercy of the literary form in which it is encased, whether *jeremiad*, *Bildung*, *nouveau roman* or tale of people's liberation.[34] In every case, the aesthetic – in the sense of the most elegant working model – trumps the actual narrative of the past as surely as it also determines the claims made by science. Banville had never been an admirer of the old national liberation story, but he was far too canny a thinker to sanction the revisionist belief that the 'new history of Ireland' was likely to be objective truth. The coincidence of a new revisionist history with the spread of early years of free secondary education for all meant that his warning was all the more tonic, although he could scarcely have been pleased by the way in which the spread of that education in a more practical mode eventually absolved most students of the duty to engage with history at all.

In Northern Ireland there had been a rather different educational debate, in the course of which, along unfailingly Manichean lines, Protestant schools claimed to excel in the sciences, even as Catholic schools produced students successful in the arts. There was, for once, some statistical basis to the sectarian claim; and it was rooted in the distrust of science by the Catholic hierarchy. The implication of priests and nuns was that scientists were too often atheists or agnostics; and that a little of that type of thing went quite far enough. The ensuing stereotyping was quite extreme and it was based on a foolish antithesis between sciences and arts which Banville's book tried to challenge.

While these debates simmered away in schools, the question of Europe dominated in politics. After Ireland was admitted to the European Economic Community in 1973, many hoped that that wider sphere of political action would reduce the appeal of sectarian politics in the north, revealing it at last, even to combatants, as an after-effect of the Thirty Years' War rather than a debate still meaningful in Strasbourg or Wittenberg. The two Johns, Banville and McGahern, abided the question. 'I am trying to open a window on Europe', said Banville in a sly parody of Russia's Peter the Great. 'Yes, and I suppose you think', sniffed McGahern in reply, 'that I am trying to shut it tight'.[35]

Banville tried to make his stories of European scope, while McGahern chose rather to find the universal in the local. Between them they taught younger artists how to think globally, but act locally. Many of McGahern's deeper inspirational sources were in fact European[36] – Tolstoy, Flaubert, Proust, Camus – just as many of Banville's deeper themes were invincibly Irish. If anything, McGahern's resolution to take Leitrim as a test case of the modern world proved even more in keeping with the spirit of the age, for the 1970s and 1980s saw the emergence of local radio and local publishers, as well as of vibrant theatres in each of the regions, as a counter-response not only to the massification of the European union but also to the casual slaughter by some of those agitated about the national question.

As if to suggest that all humanist notions of progress are illusory, *Doctor Copernicus* returns at the end to the linden tree described at the start. Each individual section also returns to some of the words with which it started. Time is circular. Banville had written in *Birchwood* about the Great Famine, an event which would challenge anyone's belief in improvement over time. Yet, for all its postmodernism, *Doctor Copernicus* expresses a more old-fashioned modernist longing for wholeness and for a notion of 'how to live'. The younger Copernicus is incapable of admitting error, yet he wants to regain a felt relationship with the world. The flawed Canon Wodka warns him to beware of enigmas which tease the mind but do not teach a person how to act. The earlier Copernicus was incapable of compassion for his brother Andreas's bodily afflictions; by the end, he has renounced his own vanity and reconciled with his brother. He has abandoned all those universal ambitions with which he started out. The two men – as so often in previous works of Irish literature – have between them the makings of a whole person. Yet they can offer no hope or help to the starving poor. They might have been the very ones to develop new forms in which to record the human predicament, but even that opportunity has passed them by.

The reason is that memory deceives and language imprisons everyone in a personal narrative. Past moments coexist with present ones in a manner that allows only briefly shared interpretations. In *Birchwood*, Banville had written that 'all movement is composed of an infinity of minute stillnesses'.[37] The implication was that narrative was an arbitrary assemblage of static scenes and exemplary moments, ripped out of chronology and experienced most often by people undergoing traumatic flashbacks. No wonder that the book's late-medieval European nobles can quote Wallace Stevens. Poets really are the unacknowledged legislators, just as aesthetic form drives everything from scientific revolutions to historical documentary.

The brutal realities of politics are among those forces which prevent Copernicus from publishing his radical theory, but his scruples are ultimately more personal: the fear that everything in his system, as in his world, lacks a centre. Is he scientist or charlatan? Pole or Prussian? Can any centre in a Europe of wounded peripheries 'hold'? Copernicus's followers, who crave publication, would say that a new account, however flawed, allows people to 'fail better'; and that even a flawed account can in time become the basis of further progress. But Copernicus, towards the end, believes that science can only define the limits to knowledge, not the possibilities of increasing it. The vanity of many radical workers in the field is that they now think science can do the work once properly undertaken only by philosophers: the attempt to know God through creation. Finding he cannot gain this knowledge, Copernicus fears that God has abandoned him.

Yet his desire would reassert itself in all the great phases of scientific research, as in the physics of the modern period, or in the palaeontology of Teilhard de Chardin, who saw in the unconscious of earth the buried life of an entire people's hymn to the universe.[38] Copernicus finally turns inward, finding the given world enough – perhaps even more than he can bear. Like the modernist poets who are forever being quoted here, he knows that he must fabricate his own tradition and construct something on which to rejoice. The scientist and artist are engaged in playful hypotheses. It may be easier to lie beautifully about distant constellations than about the earth on which politicians and historians solely focus. Yet the new lie, in questioning the centrality of an earth over which they all fight so much, may cause the worst violence of all. Copernicus is truly a Tory anarchist, who rejects the brutal everyday world of religious war – but also the brutalizing effects of his own fastidious thought: 'He believed in action, in the absolute necessity for action. Yet action horrified him, tending as it did inevitably to become violence' (*DC* 38).

It is a line which reflects Banville's own life as a subeditor on the *Irish Press* through the first half of the 1970s, constantly processing stories of ghoulish murder, torture and mayhem, enacted just seventy miles from his desk. Even as he tried to maintain a fragile belief in the claims of art, all around him were others, savage and sadistic, seeking some kind of release in the fatal lure of action. A man such as Copernicus who had enough violence in him to break up an entire planetary system might feel that he had captured far more of the spirit of the age than he wished.

12. The Double Vision of Michael Hartnett

Yeats once said that every Irish writer has a choice: either to express the country or to exploit it.[1] An artist could either express the people to themselves with honesty and flair – a frequently thankless task – or exploit their antics for the amused condescension of an overseas audience in England and North America, who might reward the performance with money and acclaim. For some writers, this has become a choice between writing in Irish or in English. The tell-tale instance is Brendan Behan, whose sensitive analysis of Anglo-Irish relations in *An Ghiall* was converted on the London stage into a raucous stage-Irish romp, with fashionable references to homosexuality, the Profumo scandal and the starlet Jayne Mansfield.

However, the question may be more complex than that. *The Hostage* may be less a misrepresentation of *An Ghiall* than a wholly different text, one of the earliest examples in British theatre of 'the Empire Writes Back'.[2] If Shaw's *John Bull's Other Island* held different meanings in Dublin and London, Behan was probably taking that contrast onto a new plane when he reworked *An Ghiall* for a London audience. By creating two texts where there might only have been one, he was also offering a subtle critique of notions of authorship, authority and indeed of singular identity itself. He was, after all, the artist who in a poem saluting Oscar Wilde praised him for having things 'both ways'.[3]

It may well be wrong to say that a writer chooses to produce a text in a given language, when often it is a case of a language choosing a given writer. We tend to think of most writers as exponents of a single language, but this is often nothing like the full story. The poet John Milton wrote in Latin and Italian before finally coming to the realization that the great epic of his people should be written in their very own vernacular, English. It took the young writer quite a few years to work this out. His Latin and Italian productions are rather stilted by comparison with his English poems, but many survive. In much the same period, Dáibhí Ó Bruadair wrote accomplished poems in English, all of which have unfortunately been lost: and this despite the fact that most of his Gaelic poems survive (more are attributed to him than to any other poet in the Irish language). In a somewhat later period, Eoghan Rua Ó Súilleabháin wrote ballads in English, such as 'Rodney's Glory', which celebrates a British naval victory in the Caribbean, while also penning Gaelic lyrics during sojourns in London.

Many more poets have been bilingual, or even trilingual, than we have been led to believe. After all, Seán Ó Ríordáin began his career writing sprung rhythms in English after the style of Hopkins, before settling to a lifetime of writing in Irish. And this is true not only of poets. Pádraic Ó Conaire wrote his first short stories in English under the influence of Dickens and the Russians, before a fateful meeting with William Ryan, who urged him to try his hand at Irish. He did so and the result was *An Cheád Chloch*, a book which so inspired the young Seosamh Mac Grianna that he abandoned his romantic lyrics and stories in English and turned henceforth to his native language for self-expression:

Nuair a léigh mé an leabhar seo stad mé ag cur focal Béarla le ceol m'aigne. Bhí blas ar an leabhar agam mar bheadh blas ar fhíon ag an té nach raibh a fhios aige go dtí sin go raibh ar an saol ach uisce. Chreid mé go mb'fhéidir litríocht uasal fhiliúnta a scríobh i nGaeilge.

When I read this book, I stopped putting the music of my mind into words in English. This book was to me like the taste of wine to a man who until that moment had only known water. I believed that it was possible to write a noble, poetic literature in Irish.[4] (Present author's translation)

In each of these cases, a particular language chose an author through whom to realize its innate genius. It is, however, safe to assume that, unlike Behan or Flann O'Brien, men like Ó Conaire or Mac Grianna did not write especially well in English. Otherwise, more of their work might have survived. One author who did write well in both Irish and English was Patrick Pearse. Poems such as 'The Fool' or 'Fornocht Do Chonnac Thú' will live as long as there are readers in Ireland. Yet Pearse was himself the deviser of a foolish division between the languages, based on a youthfully dogmatic notion that the very idea of an Irish national literature in English was untenable. While still only a teenager, he wrote an irate letter to the editor of *An Claidheamh Soluis*, suggesting that Yeats had no right to call his theatrical company Irish:

If we once admit the Irish-literature-is-English idea, then the language movement is a mistake. Mr Yeats' precious 'Irish' Literary theatre may, if it develops, give the Gaelic League more trouble than the Atkinson-Mahaffy combination (of Trinity College). Let us strangle it at its birth. Against Mr Yeats personally we have nothing to object. He is a mere English poet of the third or fourth rank, and as such he is harmless.

But when he attempts to run an 'Irish' Literary Theatre, it is time for him to be crushed.[5]

This became not only a core policy of the Gaelic League but, later, of the independent state, which promoted an artificial division between writers of Irish and English in the nation's classrooms. The theory was that Irish people would finally all make the perilous but necessary crossing back to the native language and that anything in English was foreign, derivative, second best. In the early transitional period after the Revival, it was felt that translations from Irish to English had some validity, if only as cribs to help learners master the native language: but eventually they would be quite unnecessary, once the language had been fully revived.

This led to some rather extreme statements, as late as 1941, by people like Daniel Corkery: 'The English language, great as it is, can no more throw up an Irish literature than it can an Indian literature. Neither can the Irish nation have its say in both Irish and English.'[6] The fact that Corkery's own grasp of Irish was weak, and that his repute as a master of English extended to London and New York, did not blunt his ardour in expounding his extreme theory. Yet it was he also who in his literary criticism ignored the foolish academic division between Irish and English and went on to write brilliant commentaries contrasting the Nativity Odes of Aodh Mac Aingil and John Milton or the homely lyrics of a Robbie Burns and an Eoghan Rua Ó Súilleabháin.

The case of Michael Hartnett may be the most interesting of all. In 1975 Hartnett produced a poem called 'A Farewell to English' in which he seemed to bid a last goodbye to the making of poetry in that language. This was not, therefore, to be a case like that of Behan or even Liam O'Flaherty, writers who worked on an alternating current between English and Irish. It was intended to be a complete self-transformation. The language in which Hartnett made his farewell was unambiguous, trenchant, even sneering towards those

Anglo-Irish poets who had included shards of Gaelic tradition in their work – and the major culprit named and shamed was W. B. Yeats. Austin Clarke had complained that Yeats was like a great chestnut tree which, though grand and beautiful, blocked the light which might have nourished those trees and flowers which tried to grow up after him. A poet like Patrick Kavanagh, lacking Irish, could only wrestle with the anxiety of Yeats's influence in a put-down sonnet which ended by castigating the 'cautious' bard 'sheltered by the dim Victorian muses'.[7]

Hartnett's move to Irish makes sense, as a way for the gifted young poet to fight free of the Yeatsian legacy, and there is a palpable sense of relief in the lines through which he casts off those chains. The lines also read like a rewrite of Kavanagh's insult about college learning and the 'breed of fakes' – and Kavanagh was timid enough in the end to remove that sonnet from his *Collected Poems* – but Hartnett, more intrepid, gives the attack on Yeats a central billing in his farewell poem:

> Chef Yeats, that master of the use of herbs
> could raise mere stew to a glorious height,
> pinch of saga, soupçon of philosophy,
> carefully stirred in to get the flavour right,
> and cook a poem around the basic verbs.
> Our commis-chefs attend and learn the trade,
> bemoan the scraps of Gaelic that they know:
> add to a simple Anglo-Irish stock
> Cuchulain's marrow-bones to marinate,
> a dash of Ó Rathaille simmered slow,
> a glass of university hic-haec-hoc;
> sniff and stand back and proudly offer you
> the celebrated Anglo-Irish stew.[8]

– and in the process of compounding the original insult, Kavanagh's sonnet has been shorn of one line. Well might the happy desecrator go on to say, 'The act of poetry is a rebel act'.

Deeper than these negations, however, is a positive sense of restoration – a sense that the act of 'restoration' initiated by Irish independence in 1922 has been incomplete, that (as Sean O'Casey predicted) the fight for Irish had been reduced to 'a fight for collars and ties'.[9] Too many revivalists had settled for the respectable life of the *Gaeilgeoir oifigiúil* lampooned already by Myles na gCopaleen, Behan and Máirtín Ó Direáin. The latter exposed the gap between Pearse's rebels and their successors in the Department of Education:

> *Sinne a n-oidhrí*
> *Beidh cuimhneach orainn*
> *Faoi ualach deannaigh*
> *Inár ndiaidh in oifig stáit.*[10]

> We are their inheritors
> And will be remembered
> Under a load of dust
> Left after us in a State Office

In *Mo Bhealach Féin*, Seosamh Mac Grianna had denounced the settled complacency of a new state class, for whom bureaucracy had replaced insurrectionism. Hartnett lines up with these accusers, suggesting that the real meaning of the revolution has been stolen from its children, people like himself and his friend Brendan Kennelly:

> So we queued up at the Castle
> in nineteen-twenty-two
> to make our Gaelic
> or our Irish dream come true.
> We could have had from that start

made certain of our fate
but we chose to learn the noble art
of writing forms in triplicate.
With big wide eyes
and childish smiles
quivering on our lips
we entered the Irish paradise
of files and paper-clips. (*HCP* 144)

Not that Hartnett favoured insurrectionism. Far from extolling the ancient fight in the bloody 1970s, as the northern body count rose ever higher, he substituted for it something more radical – the thing fought for. This was not the tokenistic few words of Irish intoned by leaders as 'the memory of a mother-rape they will / not face' but the authentic Gaelic world and mindset, 'our final sign that / we are human, therefore not a herd' (*HCP* 146). The last lines combine the same pride and sense of vulnerability to be found in such ruined bards as Aogán Ó Rathaille:

But I will not see
great men go down
who walked in rags
from town to town
finding English a necessary sin,
the perfect language to sell pigs in.

I have made my choice
and leave with little weeping:
I have come with meagre voice
to court the language of my people. (*HCP* 147)

– but there is also the humility of the lover who knows that his marriage proposal may be rejected. This is a powerful poetic sequence, built around a structure far more extensive than the shorter lyrics for which by 1975 Hartnett had won a deserved reputation as one of the finest love poets in the contemporary English language. The sequence runs through an awesome range of emotional registers, from tenderness to wry mockery, from satire to self-deflation, from anxious love making to bestial contempt, but done with such amazing grace as to throw into question the very plausibility of the farewell being announced. In these lines, the English language which the poet denies throbs with an astonishing vitality. In some ways, this is reminiscent of Samuel Beckett's 'I can't go on, I'll go on'; in other ways, of John Montague's epic sequence of 1972 *The Rough Field*, which also agonized in English over the sapping effects of the death of Irish on the people; but most of all it recalls great poems written by the ruined *filí* after the Elizabethan conquest. Some of these lyrics bade farewell to the making of poetry in Irish, but in lines of such pulsating beauty as to throw the reality of the underlying thesis into question. In the eyes of such bards, for whom the writing of poetry was under ban (an offence possibly punishable by death), the act of poetry really was a rebel act:

Ní snithe snátha an fheasa,
ní leanta craobha coibhneasa,
greas duan ní déanta d'fhighe,
luach dréachta ní dlighfidhe.[11]

The threads of learning are not to be woven;
the genealogies are not to be traced;
the patterns of a poem are not to be created;
it is not lawful to write verse.

The lines breach the very ban they report. The more dead Fear Flatha Ó Gnímh proclaims the Gaelic tradition, the more he seems to infuse it with his own vitality: and the effect is to make his very destitution seem sumptuous.

So it is for Hartnett in English. As the wily Jacques Derrida once warned us: 'one should never pass over in silence the language in which the question of the language is raised'.[12] Even Hartnett's dismissal of the easy applause and cheap triumphs possible if he were to continue in English seems a reprise of the famous lament of Eochaidh Ó hEodhusa:

Do thréig sind sreatha caola
foirceadal bhfaobhrach ffrithir
ar shórt gnáthach gréas robhog
is mó as a moltar sinde.[13]

I have abandoned the sharp
and refined compositions,
for a more facile and commonplace art,
which brings me greater praise.

Ó hEodhusa was bemoaning the replacement of learned patrons by the humiliation of market forces – 'the perfect language to sell pigs in'.

It would be tempting, with all of Hartnett's references to rebel acts against English commercialism, to read into his sequence a willed 'return to the source', a search for origins and an embrace of his own people after a youthful apprenticeship in Dublin, London and Spain. The fuller, expanded version of *A Farewell to English* appeared in 1978, as if to confirm that the long goodbye was getting even longer; but 1978 was also the year in which the leading Kenyan writer Ngugi Wa Thiong'o, on finding himself jailed without trial, announced that henceforth he would write in Gikuyu rather than English, so that his compatriots might fully understand his work. So well did he succeed in this that his next novel was read aloud in bars and restaurants. His critical book *Decolonising the Mind: The Politics of Language in African Literature* opens with a sentence that seems pure Michael Hartnett: 'This book is my farewell to English as a vehicle for any of my writings. From now on it is Gikuyu and Kiswahili all the way.'[14] Ngugi's subsequent analysis is like a rewrite of Daniel Corkery's strictures in the opening chapter of his book *Synge and Anglo-Irish Literature* (1931). He asks whether it is not a dreadful betrayal for a man to abandon his mother tongue and learn someone else's. Ngugi recalls how his own colonial school created in his personality a conflict between his education and his cultural inheritance. He remembered with pain how fellow students were punished if caught speaking Gikuyu rather than English:

> A button was initially given to one pupil who was supposed to hand it over to whoever was caught speaking his mother tongue. Whoever had the button at the end of the day would sing who had given it to him and the ensuing process would bring out all the culprits of the day. Thus children were turned into witch-hunters and in the process were taught the lucrative value of being a traitor to one's immediate community.[15]

As a poet, Michael Hartnett himself always laid primary emphasis on emotion and stressed the limited importance of learned allusions as compared with the pressure of the felt experience. He saw that the flaw of most contemporary poetry was that it was too obviously destined for the classroom and the college seminar. He shared Ngugi's sense that there must be something wrong with a learning which became for an African child a cerebral activity rather than an emotional experience:

> The language of an African child's education was foreign. The language of the books he read was foreign. The language of his conceptualization was foreign. Thought, in him, took the visible

form of a foreign language. He was being made to stand outside himself and look at himself.[16]

Education, far from imbuing students with confidence in their capacities, all too often made African students feel only their inadequacies.

Ngugi shares Hartnett's view that the native elites which emerge in the struggle against colonialism will often turn to native traditions, but only in a shallow, opportunistic way which allows them to mark themselves off from the occupying power. The literature of national revival in Africa, he avers, 'drew its stamina and even its form from the peasantry: their proverbs, fables, stories, riddles and wise sayings'.[17] This sounds like Hartnett on Yeats. 'Later', adds Ngugi of the post-independence phase, 'when the comprador section assumed political ascendancy and strengthened rather than weakened the economic links with imperialism in what was clearly a neocolonial arrangement, this literature became more and more critical, cynical, disillusioned, bitter and denunciatory in tone.'[18] That sounds like the voices of O'Connor and O'Faoláin – and of Behan, Flann O'Brien and those other anatomists of the betrayed revolutionary hope.

Although these complaints about the 'swindle' of independence were valid, says Ngugi, and though appeals were made for redress, as in the poems of Hartnett to the peasantry and to the urban working class, 'this search was still conducted within the confines of the languages of Europe'. Yet the literature so created was filled with agonizing over the crises of identity among the independent people, a crisis which to Ngugi seemed only soluble by a return to the people's language. The literature produced in English or French or other imperial languages seemed not really indigenous, but a subcategory of the art of the old conquering nation. Ngugi's conclusion was stark: in such a setting 'a writer who tries to communicate the message of revolutionary unity and hope in the language of the people becomes a subversive character'.[19]

This would certainly be a handy thumbnail sketch of Máirtín Ó Cadhain – but does it fully cover the case of Hartnett? Is this why he called the act of poetry a rebel act? While there are many elements of Ngugi's analysis which help us to understand Hartnett a little better, there are also fundamental differences. Although Hartnett was a keen analyst of political forces, he was not an activist. Indeed, because Irish independence came four decades before African, he was a lot more sardonic in his comments on activists and seemed to suggest that the IRA might be just a latter-day version of the postcolonial swindle. His ballad 'Who Killed Bobby Sands?' was so trenchant in its denunciations of all concerned that the *Irish Times* (which often ran articles by him) felt unable to print it in the charged emotional climate of the hunger strikes; but there is evidence to suggest that Hartnett, like his friend Nuala Ní Dhomhnaill, was keen to delink the Irish language from narrow-gauge nationalism and especially from a nationalism that used Irish for its own purposes. Such reservations had been voiced by some far-seeing *Gaeilgeoirí*, even before the achievement of independence, as Colm Ó Gaora testifies in his marvellous autobiography *Mise*.[20]

For all his instinctive socialism and talk of rebellion, Hartnett was more a personal than a political writer, in search of a self which could not easily be located and found in any language. His situation was even more complex than that of Ngugi. Irish might be his native language but it was certainly not his mother tongue, as Gikuyu was for the Kenyan. He grew up not in the Gaeltacht so much as in its penumbra, in Newcastle West where his grandmother was a living connection with the lost Gaelic tradition, and where people still spoke of the seventeenth-century poet Dáibhí Ó Bruadair as one of their own. But it was a hyphenated world, neither fully Gaelic nor fully anglicized, a fact later symbolized by the reconfiguration of the name Harnett into Hartnett with a 't' – as if to restore one of the lost letters of the Gaelic Ó hAirtnéide, but not the whole lot.

One of the clear implications in many of his most moving poems is that a willed return to the source of meaning, though desirable, is often difficult and may be doomed to frustration, for even the culture to which a man thinks he is returning may itself prove to be as spiritually hyphenated as the returner:

'A Visit to Croom, 1745'

The thatch dripped soot,
the sun was silver
because the sky
from ruts of mud to high blaze
was water.
Whitewashed walls were silver,
limeflakes opened like scissored pages
nesting moss and golds of straw
and russet pools of soot;
windows small as rat holes
shone like frost-filled hoofprints,
the door was charted
by the tracery of vermin.
Five Gaelic faces stopped their talk,
turned from the red of fire
into a cloud of rush-light fumes,
scraped their pewter mugs
across the board and talked about the king.
I had walked a long time
in the mud to hear
an avalanche of turf fall down,
fourteen miles in straw-roped overcoat
passing for Irish all along the road,
now to hear a Gaelic court
talk broken English of an English king.

It was a long way
to come for nothing. (*HCP* 140)

A further irony of Hartnett's career is that, like so many other Irish
people of his generation, he reconnected more successfully with the
ancestral culture in a period of early exile than he had ever done in
his formative years of education at home. In the early weeks of 1965,
while visiting the library in High Street, Kensington, in London,
he came across a copy of Gerald Murphy's book *Early Irish Lyrics*.
He was entranced by the exactitude of the poets' language, its
capacity to give the image received without fussy mediation: but he
was also frustrated by what he saw as Murphy's poor versions, which
did not really capture the beauty of the originals. He concluded
that a translator must be a poet, but one who loves the original
poem even more than the poem he is making of it.

What fascinated Hartnett was the very act of translation, of
carrying something over from one code to another. His true reality
was not that of a man securely established in Irish or in English,
but that of a nomad forever crossing between the two. This may
be why he preferred the *breac-Ghaeltacht* to the real thing, and
why he often found as he wrote in one language that words from
the other were constantly insinuating themselves. In that sense
he was perhaps the embodied answer to a question first posed by
J. M. Synge in a private notebook kept on the Aran Islands in
1901: 'has any bilingual writer ever been great in style, crois pas?'[21]
Even the opening pages of *A Farewell to English* contained a whole
spray of Gaelic words – *mánla, séimh, dubhfholtach* – which, though
clichés in the *dánta grá*, proved that each could be resuscitated in
the new English context, and thereby revivified. It was as good a
demonstration as any of Ralph Waldo Emerson's truism that every
word was once a poem.[22]

Hartnett's wife, like Yeats's, was an Englishwoman, and this
added further layers of complication to the attempted farewell,

not least by encouraging him to equate the English tradition with a symbolic feminine figure. Yeats himself had come to the same conclusion – that even though he wished to be counted one with Davis, Mangan, Ferguson, he also owed his soul to Shakespeare, Spenser and William Morris, because all that he loved (including a wife) had come to him through English. 'My love tortures me with hatred',[23] Yeats marvelled, 'and my hatred with love.' In 'Dán do Rosemary' Hartnett explored the positive possibilities of a similar ambivalence:

> *Thréig mé an Béarla*
> *ach leatsa níor thug mé cúl:*
> *caithfidh mé mo cheird*
> *a ghearradh as coill úr:*
> *mar tá mo gharrán Béarla*
> *crann-nochta seasc:*
> *ach tá súil agam go bhfuil*
> *lá do shonais ag teacht.*
> *Cuirfidh mé síoda do mhianta ort lá.*
> *Aimseoimid beirt ár Meiriceá.*

> I abandoned English
> but never you:
> I have to hone my craft
> in a wood that's new;
> for my English grave
> is naked, barren:
> but I hope your day
> of happiness is coming.
> You'll have the silk of your heart one day.
> We'll find us both our America.[24]

That the option for writing in Irish should eventuate in a line which echoes John Donne ('O my America, my new found land') is a perfect illustration of the constraints on the poet.

In his public justification of the move to Irish, Hartnett wrote a fascinating essay in the *Irish Times* of August 1975. This seemed to echo Behan's notion of a return to a language more exact, muscular and supple than a jaded, cliché-ridden English: 'My going into Gaelic simplified things for me and gave me answers which may be naive, but at least give me somewhere to stand.'[25] The phrase 'going into' is telltale, suggestive less of homecoming than of a deeper, if voluntary, exile. For Hartnett poetry must always remain estranged, isolated, even alien. He knew that the best poems are those which, however often they are read, never quite lose their quality of strangeness. For that very reason, he went on in the essay to admit that the 'somewhere' on which he might stand could still be a quaking sod:

> There are Gaelic poets and Anglo-Irish poets. To qualify for either epithet they must live in or have lived in this country and their poetic sensibilities must be moulded by its countryside, its people, its history and literature both Gaelic and Anglo-Irish. The sonnet and *rannaíocht mhór* must be their common property. Both must know as much about Liam Rua Mac Coitir as they do about John Todhunter. The only difference between them should be their language.[26]

This is an honest admission that even those who write in Irish will be, in the deepest sense, Anglo-Irish poets, hyphenated by their debts to John Donne as well as to the *spéirbhean* figure, as Hartnett was in the poem just discussed. No wonder that that other great Anglo-Irish *Gaeilgeoir*, Seán Ó Ríordáin, could refer to Irish as *A Theanga Seo, Leath Liom* (English, O Language Half Mine) or salute the fairy folk at the foot of the garden as *Gan Béarla acu ná Gaeilge* (without English, or Irish).

This is why all poets are – because they must be – translators. Every poem in any language is, as Plato and Aristotle taught, an imitation, a version of the world, which is itself only a copy, itself only a translation. Ever since our mortal ancestors offended the gods and built the Tower of Babel too high, we have been cursed by a diversity of languages. Only the poets and translators seek to repair the damage and to return us to the original language, the pure note sounded only in the music of the spheres. The poet, in purifying a given tongue, does this. So also does the translator, who seeks to find in the common thread linking two languages a means of retracing a way to the common source. This is the real explanation of the differences, as well as similarities, between 'Cúlú Íde' and 'The Retreat of Ita Cagney'. To most people with a reasonable knowledge of Irish, they seem like two different and powerful poems on the theme of a woman who chooses to turn her back on respectable society and bear a child out of wedlock – as different indeed as *An Ghiall* was from *The Hostage*. Over a decade after the composition of the work, Hartnett explained the bilingual weave out of which it came in an interview with Dennis O'Driscoll:

> I would sit down and write a few lines of the poem unthinkingly. I'd come back to it and see it was half in English and half in Irish or a mixture. Both languages became so intermeshed. One is not a translation of the other. They are two versions of the one poem; but what the original language is, I don't know.[27]

The original language might well be the perfect language before the fall of Babel's Tower; and the original poem, of which they are both really translations, existed deep in the recesses of Hartnett's head – in that lost language.[28] My contention is, therefore, that in his return to the ancestral voices locked away in Irish, Hartnett was repeating that search conducted by all true poets for the lost source-language of poetry.

Every poet senses that all official languages are already dead languages. That was why Hartnett said farewell to English, while knowing that Irish was itself dead already too. As he wrote himself in 'Death of an Irishwoman', 'I loved her from the day she died'. Likewise with English – no sooner did Hartnett write it off than he felt all over again its awesome power, for it had become again truly strange to him, as all poetic languages must. A similar thing happened to Beckett. He turned to French early, *'parce que c'est plus facile d'écrire sans style'*, but also because he could use it with all the steely precision of a second-language learner to whom it would seem very strange. Yet when in old age he had gained almost total mastery as one of France's revered authors, he suddenly reverted to English, much as Hartnett would eventually do in *Inchicore Haiku*.

All of this shows that Hartnett was at his most creative in the open spaces between languages. There is a beautiful poem of his called 'Impasse', which exactly renders the teasing excitement of that threshold condition, as well as the frustration. The poem's title sums up the overall sense:

> The students crowd the bar.
> In the immense silence of their foreign talk
> an occasional noun
> flashes across the backdrop of my mind
> like a falling star.
> I watch them eat *éclairs*,
> secure in their own linguistic shells.
> (I have poems at hand:
> it's words I cannot find.)
>
> I cannot explain my unease even in my own tongue:
> perhaps it's best explained by my ignorance of theirs.
> I can see the poem plain:

it's the words I cannot hear,
as my tongue-tied muses and myself
dumbly regard a poem that waits
for a language to bring it home
to some understanding ear. (*HCP* 194)

It is not the least achievement of this poem in English that it reads like a careful translation. Hartnett always liked his languages foreign, and non-respectable. 'The Retreat of Ita Cagney' was in fact a metaphor for the poet's own return to West Limerick and to the Irish language, she sadly observed, was no longer used as a careerist tool by the emergent bourgeoisie but slowly being disposed of by the new elites as an anachronism and an embarrassment.

That disposal was, of course, a repeat of something that had happened before in the 1600s, as a new middle class rapidly anglicized itself for the sake of profit and material comfort. Hence Hartnett's identification with poets like Pádraigín Haicéad, Aogán Ó Rathaille and, most of all, Dáibhí Ó Bruadair. They also lived through a great cultural crisis and tried to chronicle its phases without sentimentality or flinching. They also were proof positive that some elements of a culture will always survive its general eclipse. Though Ó Bruadair ended his days as a labourer in the fields, his poems lived on after him, as rebukes to the fake aristocracy which had taken the place of the real noblemen of Gaelic Ireland. Surrounded by the new elites of land speculators and supermarket owners, Hartnett had no difficulty in spotting the analogies. Even Ó Bruadair's pose as a broken dandy is repeated in Hartnett's pained awareness of the strict redundancy of his elegance in a despised and ebbing language. By becoming a scathing critic of the times, each poet became his age's honest chronicler.

There is a sense in which, when he discovered the author Ó Bruadair 'outside' himself, Hartnett was at last enabled to unleash the artist 'within'. If he found it difficult to speak in a wholly convinced and convincing voice in either Irish or English – and he told us in both languages that he did – there is about his translations the authentic force of the man himself speaking in all his own urgency:

> All the same it would make you laugh
> instead of the dances and games of the past
> not a tittle is raised abroad in this land –
> we ourselves have buried the summer at last.

> The once-proud men of this land have swapped
> giving for gaining, culture for crap:
> no tunes on the pipes, no music on harps –
> we ourselves have buried the summer at last.[29]

Hartnett felt that a race which runs in fear of its own traditions will not survive for long: and in this poem he found an early example of 'the minds of Irish country people today who maintain that the summers are bad because there is no longer any respect for old ways'[30].

Ó Bruadair was a poet of the European baroque, who saw nature in decay and lamented the death of the old gods (*'chuireamar féin an samhradh i gcill'*), whose passing would make way for a new religion of mortified flesh. That religion saw catastrophe as inevitable, even character-forming – hence Ó Bruadair's keynote image of *'long-bhriseadh'* or 'shipwreck'. Hartnett's translations capture the Gaelic poet's melancholy sense that nature is dead and that all objects have been hollowed out, no longer possessed of value, only a market price:

> O pity the man who won't spend his days
> securing his goods before going astray:
> I have anguish at home when the dawn turns red
> and no one believes I have sense in my head.[31]

The broken shards and shells of tradition are all that remain to a poet, who builds his works as ruins from the very outset and who almost yearns to see the ravages of time reduce his texts to even greater fragmentation.

In Hartnett's analysis, Gaelic culture died with Ó Bruadair, even though the language lived on, much utilized by songsters bereft of real sensibility. His translations were written to prove that poetry need not get lost in the carry-over, and many of them appear to provide examples of 'added value'. What Hartnett writes at the start of his introduction to his versions of Ó Bruadair – that his subject could be funny, obscene, anguished, bitter and dignified – was also true of himself. His genius for translation went far deeper than one for turning the words of one language into another. It involved a capacity to project a lost culture, and the very act of losing it, in English.

In that strict fashion Hartnett was himself 'a character in search of an author'; and his translation no mere mimicry but an electric connection of one artist with another. 'Nor must we forget', writes Renato Poggioli, 'that such a quest or pursuit may intermittently attract the original writer also, when he too must search for the author in himself'.[32] Many of Hartnett's versions of Haicéad, Ó Bruadair or even Ó Rathaille seem to exceed at certain moments the achievement of their originals, in the way that much fine writing can surpass the usual potentials of its own language. This shows, once again, how every work reaches out to a universal language, and that the more completely translated a work is, the more fully may it seem to perfect its destined, inherent form. After all, the earliest translators of sacred scripture hoped to exceed their originals, to use them literally as pre-texts for even greater inspirations in their own languages. Hartnett released qualities of humour, wit and self-mockery which often lay only latent but not fully articulated in the original poems. The ultimate irony is that the results of Hartnett's complex manoeuvre represent an augmentation of writing in the English language, for as Walter Benjamin wrote:

It is the task of the translator to release in his own language that pure language which is under the spell of another, to liberate the language which is imprisoned in a work in his recreation of that work. For the sake of pure language, he breaks through decayed barriers of his own language.[33]

And this is the savage paradox: that ultimately in his versions of Gaelic baroque Hartnett was pursuing further potentials of his own English, but in an act of remembering, of putting together lost and unused elements of a predecessor culture.

All progress in life depends on some form of translation. Even the child in learning how to speak uses known words in the attempt to master and become familiar with unknown ones. This is one of art's ultimate challenges – how to ravish the ineffable in a language dense with precedents. Like most true artists including Beckett and O'Flaherty, Hartnett found in the end that he was also compelled to translate himself, to turn his own Irish poems back into English, as if to show that none of his texts or languages could claim official status. He repeatedly challenged and disproved the illusion that one can produce original work only in one's mother tongue, as surely as had Joseph Conrad and Vladimir Nabokov before him. And his writing, like theirs, comes under the sign of Babel.

That biblical myth told of how God the Father, who alone was the origin of a perfect, universal language, was driven by an Ó Bruadair-style anger to punish the Semite imperialists who built their tower 'as high as heaven'. Their punishment was the proliferation of mother tongues. The story is a warning against all who would try to make their language compulsory. Only James Joyce in *Finnegans Wake* had been able to take the analysis even further than Hartnett, for in that book he found an absolute idiolect which conflated many languages. However, if we want one of the fullest artistic accounts of the search for that idiolect, it is to multilingual poets such as Pessoa and Hartnett that we must turn.

Hartnett was the greatest translator of Irish-language poetry in the second half of the twentieth century: but, being that, he was also his country's most underrated poet. He left major poems in both languages, but also the certainty that there can be no final farewell to English.

13. Brian Friel's *Faith Healer*

Faith Healer (1980), by Brian Friel, may well be the finest play to come out of Ireland since J. M. Synge's *Playboy of the Western World*. It is also, without a doubt, one of the most derivative works of art to be produced in Ireland in the twentieth century – and this gives rise to a question. How can a play which is indebted so heavily to a number of previous works be nevertheless a work of profound and scintillating originality? And how can a play consisting of four separate monologues by characters who never openly confront each other be a fully dramatic work, in any real sense of that word?

We should first consider Friel's debts. *Faith Healer* might be called an intergeneric work where the forms of novel and drama meet, for it is a kind of dramatized novel. The idea of four contradictory monologues may have come to Friel from a reading of William Faulkner's most famous novel *The Sound and the Fury* (1929). The method is identical, even down to the detail of having one of the monologues narrated by a witness of unstable mind, in Faulkner the lunatic Benjy, in Friel the shattered and suicidal Grace Hardy. This attempt to take an outstanding device of the modern novel and redeploy it in the dramatic form is a characteristic modernist strategy, for modernism loves to mix genres – one thinks of Eliot's fusion of drama and poetry, Joyce's use of drama in the middle of *Ulysses* (1922), Flann O'Brien's crazy blend of cowboy tale and Celtic lore in *At Swim-Two-Birds* (1929). Although Faulkner's novel and Friel's play both challenge the audience to judge for itself the inconsistencies between the various monologues, there is one crucial difference. The novel can be reread; the play cannot be rerun to some point of contention. To that extent, the dramatic form is even more baffling and unsettling in its effect on its audience.

Friel's other debt is even more striking. *Faith Healer* is clearly a remoulding of the legend of Deirdre of the Sorrows, a tale which has been dramatized by many leading Irish writers from George Russell to W. B. Yeats, from J. M. Synge to James Stephens. The idea of a well-brought-up girl, destined for a noble calling in the north of Ireland, but spirited away to Scotland by an attractive but feckless man, to the great dismay of an elderly guardian – that, in a nutshell, is the plot of both Friel's and Synge's plays. In Scotland, the lovers live well enough for many years, supported by their manager, Teddy, who discharges the same role in *Faith Healer* as that played by Naisi's brothers, Ainnle and Ardan, in Synge's play. Ultimately, however, their nomadic and rootless life is felt to be increasingly hollow and stressful. With some foreboding, they decide to return to Ireland, but in their nervousness and apprehensiveness, each lover attributes the decision to the other. Their worst fears are realized on arrival in Ireland. As Francis Hardy says: 'there was no sense of homecoming',[1] or as Synge's Naisi says, looking at the shabby rooms and open grave, which the king offers by way of greeting: 'And that'll be our home in Emain.'[2] Earlier, he gloomily remarks that 'it's little we want with state or rich rooms or curtains, when we're used to the ferns only, and cold streams and they making a stir'[3] – a sentence which could just as aptly describe the raw, open-air life of Francis, Grace and Teddy camping out by the fields and streams of Scotland.

One of the great themes of Synge's play and of the original

Gaelic legend is Deirdre's love of place. Before her final departure from Scotland, she lists the names of all the abandoned places with tender care. So it is with her laments for Glen Ruadh, Glen Laid, the Woods of Cuan and so on. In one of his less well-known essays on 'The People of the Glens', Synge had remarked on the 'curiously melodious names' to be found in Wicklow-Aughavanna, Glenmalure, Annamoe[4] – and he built lilting lists of the names into his Wicklow plays. Friel self-consciously builds on the ancient Gaelic tradition in those passages where Francis and Grace recite the Scottish place names, as the Faith Healer says, 'just for the mesmerism, the sedation, of the incantation' (*FH* 11). This is an ancient Gaelic device redeployed by Seamus Heaney, for example in poems such as 'The Tollund Man':

> Something of his sad freedom
> As he rode the tumbril
> Should come to me, driving,
> Saying the names

> Tollund, Grauballe, Nebelgard,
> Watching the pointing hands
> Of country people,
> Not knowing their tongue.[5]

What is revealing in Friel's play, however, is the fact that Grace fouls up the order of her husband's incantation. She omits his third line from the list and, at the end of her monologue, is so distraught that she cannot get beyond the opening lines:

> Aberarder, Kinlochbervie,
> Aberayron, Kinlochbervie,
> Invergordon, Kinlochbervie. . . in Sutherland, in
> the north of Scotland. . . (*FH* 127)

She trails off helplessly, and this linguistic failure is the sure sign of her imminent collapse.

In *Faith Healer*, as in the Deirdre legend, the lovers return to Ireland with the premonition that it will be a return to disaster and even death for the hero. And this is what happens. Only at the very end does Friel depart radically from Synge's plot. Whereas Synge's Deirdre dies soon after Naisi in the romantic medieval versions, Friel follows the more hard-edged Old Irish rendition by having her live on for a year in misery, before her eventual suicide.

Wherein, it might therefore be asked, does the originality of *Faith Healer* lie? One could answer by saying that the notion of the artist as inspired conman is one of Friel's innermost themes and that all those debts to previous works and authors raise the whole question of the artist as conman in our minds. So the play turns out to be about itself, since it, like its central character, veers between conmanship and brilliant innovation. The artist is like the Faith Healer, a man who never knows for certain whether he has been successful in bringing off an effect, a broker in risk who must stand before the audience nightly with no assurance that his magic will rub off on others yet again. Moreover, like the Faith Healer, the artist knows that if he gives free rein to his own self-doubts, the gift may desert him. Too anxious a self-scrutiny may kill the very gift the analysis is supposed to illuminate. This is a truth even more obvious to the manager, Teddy, than it is to the healer himself. In his contrast between two performing dogs, Teddy illustrates for us the sense in which the artist has to be a conman; one dog, sensitive and resourceful, could switch on the fire, pull the curtains and leave the master's slippers by the chair, but in front of an audience she went to pieces. The other dog hadn't the brains to learn his own name, but could perform to perfection on the bagpipes for any given audience. Teddy also cites the case of the brainless Miss Mulatto, who could talk to 120 pigeons in different languages, yet never know how she did it – she just made sounds. This leads Teddy to conclude that artists must not only have talent and ambition, but that they must also have no critical self-consciousness about their gift:

> They know they have something fantastic, sure, they're not that stupid. But what it is they have, how they do it, how it works, what that sensational talent is, what it all means – believe me, they don't know and they don't care and even if they did care they haven't the brains to analyse it. (*FH* 29)

So the first audience the artist must con is himself. He must still those impulses to self-doubt and self-questioning which erupt in him from time to time. 'Francis Hardy, Faith Healer, One Night Only' (*FH* 11), says the tattered poster. Hardy knows that that 'one night only' suggests the touch of the charlatan, the poseur who will not stay around to face the consequences of his own claims or the critical response to his performance. At times, he sees himself possessed of an awesome gift; on other occasions, a mere trickster – but there were moments, he still insists, when the gift *did* work.

When Francis Hardy talks about his gift, he sounds remarkably like Seamus Heaney discussing his involvement with poetry. 'How did I get involved? As a young man I chanced to flirt with it and it possessed me. No, no, no, no, no – that's rhetoric' (*FH* 12). This seems close to Heaney's quotation, that a young man dabbles in verses and finds they are his life – a remark that becomes even more interesting when Heaney himself points out that it was Patrick Kavanagh who originally made it.[6] Francis Hardy claims, more humbly, that he did it because he found that he *could* do it. Heaney's account of poetry as a gift for divination is very close indeed to Francis Hardy's view of his gift. According to Heaney, divining is a talent for being in touch with what is there, hidden but real – 'a gift for mediating between the latent resource and the community that wants it current and released'.[7] The water diviner resembles the poet in his function of making contact with what lies hidden. To an artist like Friel that contact may be made with further possibilities lying dormant in previous works of literature such as the Deirdre legend; but if he becomes too self-conscious about those debts, he will never create anything original, because he will have no basis on which to build. So he must ruthlessly and mindlessly assimilate whatever resources from the past may be turned to use. Heaney compares this mindless wisdom to that of a somnambulist and sees one of the great pleasures of poetry in that somnambulist process of search and surrender, like the water diviner who moves forward with eyes closed, following only the hint and tug of the wooden stick. A process as unselfconscious as this is an exercise in high risk, but to become self-analytical would be the greatest risk of all.

The artist can seldom, if ever, be his own critic. 'A poem always has elements of accident about it, which can be made the subject of inquest afterwards', commented Heaney in a radio talk, 'but there is always a risk in conducting your own inquest. You might begin to believe the coroner in yourself, rather than put your trust in the man in you who is capable of accident'.[8] It is precisely that ailment which afflicts the Faith Healer in his final days, as he comes to believe even more in the coroner of certainties than in the creator of risks. His first monologue is far too self-analytical for his own good as an artist:

> Was it all chance? – or skill? – or illusion? – or delusion? Precisely what power did I possess? Could I summon it? When and how? Was I its servant? Did it reside in my ability to invest someone with faith in me or did I evoke from him a healing faith in himself? Could my healing be effected without faith? But faith in what? – in me? – in the possibility? – faith in faith? And is the power diminishing? You're beginning to masquerade, aren't you? You're becoming a husk, aren't you? (*FH* 13)

By Hardy's second soliloquy we realize that he is in fact speaking from the dead – a device appropriate enough for a man who is indeed his own coroner. Moreover, it is clear that he has returned to Ireland and to Donegal deliberately to seek out this death, because he can no longer bear the high risk tensions of life as an artist, the uncertainty of a life spent hovering between mastery and humiliation, the uncertainty which is the true source of his mastery just as it is the inevitable prelude to his failure.

Hardy steps before us out of the darkness and into a ray of light at the beginning of the play, and recedes into the black at the end. This light/dark strategy is identical to that employed by Beckett in many dramas. Beckett explains it as a metaphysics of risk:

> If life and death did not present themselves to us, there would be no inscrutability. If there were only darkness, all would be clear. It is because there is not only darkness but also light that our situation becomes inexplicable. Take Augustine's doctrine of grace given and grace withheld. . . in the classical drama, such problems do not arise. The destiny of Racine's *Phèdre* is sealed from the beginning: she will proceed into the dark. As she goes, she herself will be illuminated. At the beginning of the play she has partial illumination and at the end she has complete illumination, but there has been no question but that she moves towards the dark. That is the play. Within this notion, clarity is possible, but for us who are neither Greek nor Jansenist there is no such clarity. The question would also be removed if we believed in the contrary – total salvation. But where we have both dark and light we also have the inexplicable. The key word in my plays is 'perhaps'.[9]

Beckett's plays are poignant satires on those still foolish enough to seek for signs and certainties – on critics – and a celebration of the random and chancy – of artists. Friel takes up where Beckett leaves off and in *Faith Healer* he depicts that lust for certainty as the last infirmity of the bourgeois mind.

This is pictured most satirically in Grace's account of the fearful symmetry of her family home, with its Japanese gardens, straight avenues and ordered poplars. This haven of order she abandons for a life of risk which will lead finally to her self-destruction. Her sedate solicitor father is merely an extreme example of that rage for order which dominates most of the characters in the play. The patients who come to Hardy's performances come in search of certainty even more than a cure. In a perverse kind of way, they come to be cured of uncertainty even more than to be cured of disease. Francis Hardy understands this well:

> [B]y coming to me they exposed, publicly acknowledged, their desperation. And even though they told themselves they were here because of the remote possibility of a cure, they knew in their hearts they had come not to be cured but for the confirmation that they were incurable; not in hope but for the elimination of hope; for the removal of that final, impossible change – that's why they came – to seal their anguish, for the content of a finality.
>
> And they knew that I knew. And so they defied me to endow them with hopelessness. But I couldn't do even that for them. . . Because, occasionally, just occasionally, the miracle would happen. (*FH* 15)

In the end, the healer felt that it would have been a kindness not to go near them, not to unsettle them with hope. Yet he knows, too, that it is the function of art to terrify and unsettle a community, to insult even more than to flatter it, to be unlike its idea of itself. The community may hate the artist for the cruel and sharp light he throws on reality, but it knows also that his is a necessary insult, a necessary evil. The healer recalls evenings when he could sense that there were hundreds of people holding their breath in the locality, 'waiting in the half-light'. They were people poised between the certainty of darkness and the certainty of light, anxiously waiting to see what would happen to those audacious enough to attend the healer's meeting, intrepid legates on behalf of those too timid to look into the artist's face and handiwork. 'And sometimes I got the impression, too, that if we hadn't come to them, they would have sought us out' (*FH* 15). So the community assaults and finally slays the artist, whose ministry it nevertheless finds essential to its well-being.

The healer can sense the poignancy of those people's search for certainty, precisely because he can feel that yearning so deeply in himself. If safe, settled folk can feel that need, then how much more will he whose life is lived on a knife edge of risk and somnambulist groping. At the end, the broker in risk runs out of courage and decides to cash his chips in return for a racing certainty. So, in his last days, as his conman's courage dissolves, he lacerates himself with self-doubt and deliberately seeks out a spectacular failure that will kindly put an end to his own slender surviving hope. What he has tried and failed to do for others, he hopes now to achieve for himself – the elimination of hope. As he walks towards the drunken men in the bleak morning light, he knows that nothing will happen except his own death and finds a strange consolation in that knowledge:

> And as I moved across that yard towards them and offered myself to them, then for the first time I had a simple and genuine sense of homecoming. Then for the first time there was no atrophying terror, and the maddening questions were silent.
> At long last I was renouncing chance. (*FH* 44)

But for the artist that is the only mortal sin, and Hardy must ultimately be judged as an artist, for that is the only word his wife can find to describe her dead lover to the doctor:

'He was an artist', I said – quickly, casually – but with complete conviction – just the way he might have said it. Wasn't that curious? Because the thought had never occurred to me before. And then because I said it and the doctor wrote it down I knew it was true. (*FH* 22)

The thought strikes her almost by accident. Unlike her husband, who turns out in the end to be just like her orderly father, she has the courage to submit herself to chance. For her the accidental betokens a higher truth, for which she will die, rather than return to the world of bourgeois certainties which drove her mother mad. In the final scenario of his career, Hardy renounced change – and, in doing so, he degraded himself from the status of artist to that of mere performer. The artist always keeps his eye remorselessly on his subject, whereas the performer is always watching his audience. The artist risks the displeasure of his audience as he maintains a congenial relationship with his subject, whereas the performer risks the betrayal of his subject as he seeks a congenial relationship with his audience.

All through his career, up until this final night, Francis Hardy has been an artist, humble in the service of that mystery which has chosen to reveal itself through him, humble even to the point of believing that the world of family happiness and personal fulfilment is well lost for art. At the outset, he was so incorruptible that he resisted all the efforts of his manager to degrade his healing artistry to the level of mere performance, and so he resisted the use of background music. He scrupulously avoided stagey or theatrical effects, as on the night when in serene silence he cured ten in the village of Llanbethian. The garish Teddy is still amazed to recall that 'there was no shouting or cheering or dancing with joy' and 'hardly a word was spoken' (*FH* 32). He admires the professionalism of a healer to whom the only final reality was his work. But, as his confidence waned, Hardy began to rely on the fake support of background music and surrendered to the view of himself as a mere performer. On his last night, the erstwhile professional declines into an amateur magician and prostitutes his art in a cheap publicity stunt. Seeing the bent finger of a Donegal farmer, he feels certain that he can cure it and so he seeks his own fate. Up to now, the audience, great or small, has gathered around him, but now he goes in search of the audience's approval and esteem. He seeks the certainty of public acclaim and sees the corruption of his art into a gaudy ad-man's dream. Up to now, he had wisely allowed his gift to possess him, but now he falsely tries to possess his gift. It is, of course, unnecessary to elaborate on the appropriateness of Friel's attack on art as mere entertainment in what is his most complex and underrated play.

If Friel had chosen to leave things at that, this would be a deft and subtle play about art and artistic illusion, but he extends these perceptions brilliantly to show how they apply also in life. If excessive self-scrutiny can destroy an artist, the playwright shows that it can also destroy anyone. The most moving element of the play is the strange, inconclusive but very deep relationship between Francis Hardy and his wife. It is a coupling that is full of cruelty – his cruelty to her in the momentous labour of childbirth; her vicious mockery of him when his charisma fails; their joint harshness to Teddy whom they abandon for days on end; their neglect of parents whom they have left behind in Ireland. It is a relationship which, like most deep loves, has awkward zones of emptiness and inscrutability where little is shared or understood. In a perverse way, Grace resented Hardy his moments of mastery, when he would stand (she says) 'looking past you out of his completion, out of that private power, out of that certainty that was available only to him. God, how I resented that privacy... And then, for him, I didn't exist... But before a performance this exclusion – no, it wasn't an exclusion, it was an evasion – this evasion was absolute: he obliterated me' (*FH* 20).

It is, nevertheless, a relationship as beautiful as it is baffling, full in some respects, empty in others, but, above all, clumsy and inconsistent. When it is good it is good by accident, but when the intention to make it good is too overt, then it inevitably fails. Francis and Grace are aware of the rich potential of their love, but as often as not they are baffled when a tender impulse is misconstrued. Like the artist's attitude to his secret art, theirs is a relationship of fluctuations, which neither can hope fully to control; and Friel seems to be hinting that all good couplings must stay that way. If they become self-analytical in the attempt to remove imperfections or uncertainties, then they may also remove that element of risk which is the ultimate sign of love. To love someone is to risk hurting or even losing that person, but if such risks are not run, there can be no real relationship, no sense of something freely given despite its potential cost. In general, it seems to be true that most people only begin to analyse relationships when they start to go wrong – the glossy magazines are filled with news of famous couples splitting up just two months after they had analysed and explained their happiness to some nosey reporter. In its handling of this theme, *Faith Healer* is remarkably similar to *Philadelphia, Here I Come!*, which showed how a young man's conscious attempt to clarify his bond with his father failed.

Both dramas make great play with the distortion of memory, the most obvious being that nobody in *Faith Healer* can summon the courage to describe the murder in Ballybeg, just as nobody in *Philadelphia* could accurately recall the momentous events of the past or face the fact that Gar is about to emigrate. Both plays focus on the importance of names as a sign of that distorted memory – Francis Hardy, F. H., Faith Healer, if you are a believer in fate. To name something is to exercise a power over it, much as Hardy intones the list of those small village communities over which he has exercised his power. He remembers them clearly, but not the surnames or place names of his own wife's origin: 'Grace Dodsworth

from Scarborough – or was it Knaresborough? I don't remember'
(*FH* 14), as if to suggest my earlier point that *this* is one relationship
he can never hope to control completely.

As if to confirm this loss of control, the healer's second
soliloquy becomes stuck in a groove with the endless repetition of
Kinlochbervie, the place in Scotland where Grace bore, and lost,
their baby. That emotional scar is too deep to allow him to continue
the recital. If by naming something we show our power over it, by
misnaming it we may be showing its power over us. Grace thinks
at first that Hardy constantly changed her surname in order to
humiliate her, that he called her mistress instead of wife to upset
her, that he said she was from Yorkshire or Kerry or London or
Scarborough instead of Ulster to deprive her of an identity. But
he told the theatre audience that he *honestly* could not remember
where she came from. Because he is a lifelong healer of audiences,
one assumes that it is part of his nature to be more honest with
large audiences than with private individuals – his distrust of
phoney background music testifies to that. The real reason why he
unknowingly represses or distorts the details of Grace's background
is that he feels a deep guilt over the suffering he has inflicted on
her and her parents. He tries to displace or remould an emotion,
the better to cope with it; and so he never once mentions the loss
of the baby in Kinlochbervie, or his own callous behaviour there,
but simply pretends that Kinlochbervie was the place in which
he happened to be when news of his mother's death arrived. By
remoulding an emotion that might otherwise control him, he can
begin to control it, and this is why Grace rightly calls him an artist,
with a compulsion to adjust and refashion everything around him.
She denounces him for this gift and bluntly opines that she would
have been far happier if he had never had this capacity to remould
twisted fingers or unsatisfactory lives. She sees that those he cured
were not real to him as persons but as fictions, extensions of himself
that came into being only because of him.

Nevertheless, by the end of her soliloquy, Grace is pleading to be reinstated as one of Hardy's fictions. Recognizing that she needs Hardy in order to sustain her own illusion of being, she concedes that the distortions of the artist, however frustrating on a superficial level, are in the deepest sense necessary. By naming him 'an artist', she establishes him as such, thereby reshaping and remoulding his character from quack-doctor to master artist – she engages in the very process for which she had earlier denounced him. Implicit in this is Wittgenstein's idea that the limits of my language are the limits of my world; that a thing only begins to exist when it is named. Of course, we cannot be sure of all the facts in Grace's own testimony, for her sentences are fragmented and she is verging on nervous breakdown. She is quite wrong to say that in his artist's egotism Hardy saw all successful cures as fictions that worked – extensions of himself – and forgot the failures.

He was, in fact, haunted by his failures with clients even more than he was haunted by his failures in life. He could breathe life into others, but not into his own child, and so he suppressed all memory of the dead child and deliberately recast his own autobiography in more flattering terms. Thus, Grace's sufferings when her father fails to recognize his returned vagabond daughter are recast in the myth as Hardy's own pain at not being recognized by his father, because this makes him feel better, more sinned against than sinning. By reshaping past events into a less accusing pattern, Hardy can save himself for his art, that art which has been the cause of sufferings in others which he must pretend to have been his own. This is yet another version of history as science fiction, of past events being remodelled in terms of a utopian future. Hence, Teddy is probably right to assert that Hardy, in his weird private way, almost certainly felt and understood the plight of the grimy stillborn infant whose tragedy he had caused but refused to witness.

Teddy's soliloquy initially promises to clarify some of the discrepancies between earlier accounts, if only because he is an apparent outsider to the relationship, an objective professional manager. 'Personally, in the privacy of your heart, you may love them or you may hate them', he says, 'but that has nothing to do with it. Your client has his job to do. You have your job to do' (*FH* 30). Moreover, Francis Hardy has already hinted at unsuspected depths in Teddy, a man who was outwardly a romantic optimist but may secretly have been more realistic about their prospects. Sure enough, at the start of his talk, he does clarify one problem, as to who exactly chose the theme music. Grace chose a song which was a hit when she married Francis, but the couple soon forgot that and blamed Teddy's twisted mind for the selection. Thus they too create those necessary fictions which allow them to survive with a modicum of self-respect.

On a more serious level, it emerges from Teddy's account that Grace has also been lying to herself about the stillborn child, pretending that it was Francis who said the prayers and raised the cross, when in fact it was Teddy who did those things. Teddy remembers the village in question as sparkling and sunny; Grace recalls it as rainy and dull. Teddy is sure that the cross is long since gone; Grace that it must still be there. In the end, it is not even safe to assume that Teddy can be trusted as an objective professional witness; for it transpires that he has been secretly in love with Grace all along. This was something Hardy, with his second sight, knew; and the healer may even have sought his own death so that Grace would be free to join herself to a man of compassion who could return her love.

Although a mere manager, Teddy shows a subtle awareness of the power of illusion, of the capacity of words and names to confer a sense of reality, and of the way in which this gift seemed to pass from Hardy to his clients in those successful moments of healing. So, in the Welsh village where all ten supplicants were cured, an old farmer could say: 'Mr. Hardy, as long as men live in Glamorganshire, you'll be remembered here'. 'And whatever way he said Glamorganshire', recalls Teddy, 'it sounded like the whole world' (*FH* 32). Teddy knows, however, that that power to maintain a successful illusion is jeopardized by Hardy's self-analytical brain, his self-questioning, his mockery of himself as a mere 'performer'. Soon, Teddy sees, he will come to believe even more in his own mockery than in his own performance. He could have been a great artist but he had too many brains, analytical brains which allowed him to see that everybody else is a con man and an illusionist too. Hardy's anger at the allegations made by Grace's father does not last, for 'I had some envy of the man who could use the word "chicanery" with such confidence' (*FH* 41). Even the recognition that professional lawyers are also illusionists, employing the paraphernalia of gowns, wigs and a secret jargon, does not save the healer from himself. Hardy, the greatest liar in the play, is also an honest man.

The healer keeps the inaccurate newspaper report of his feats not so much for reassurance as for self-identification: 'it identified me, even though it got my name wrong' (*FH* 40). The namer of things needs someone to name him; and the distorter of names and histories yearns for someone to distort his own. Like Grace, like Beckett's clowns, he too needs someone to give him the illusion that he exists. It is brutally appropriate that, in a drama which has made such play with true and false names, Hardy in the end should not even know the names of two of the men who come to kill him, thereby continuing the assault on his identity begun in the botched newspaper report. As the men advance menacingly on him, he begins to feel that they also are fictions, illusions without physical reality, and that each man present exists only in his need for others. He senses that they need the tale of his death in order to satisfy their rage against a life which has so cruelly maimed their friend.

Faith Healer is an eloquent apology for the distortions of memory, for it argues that every man must be an artist and illusionist, that every person must recast memories into a pattern that is gratifying enough to allow them to live with themselves. As a consummate artist, Friel implicates himself in the process, for that is precisely what he has done in his play to the Deirdre legend – remoulded it subtly in accordance with his current artistic needs. There is a theory propounded by Harold Bloom in *The Anxiety of Influence* which suggests that every major artist is a kind of Francis Hardy. Bloom's strong artist creatively misreads a work of past art in order to clear a little imaginative space for himself.[10] Like Hardy, such an artist cannot afford to be a critic seeking the absolute truth, but must follow the accidents of impulse, creatively distorting an available myth in order to express something of himself – otherwise, he will be smothered by the influences of the past. The artist thus has a vested interest in misunderstanding and distorting a received text, for if he ever fully understands his model, then he will be overwhelmed by it and become a derivative writer, much as Arnold in 'The Scholar-Gipsy' failed to do more than rewrite some of the better-known lines of Keats. The strong artist imperfectly assimilates past models and is therefore not overwhelmed, but saved, by his mistake. Like Blake, he goes wrong in order to go right. So Joyce in *Ulysses* can rewrite *The Odyssey*, but in the process remould it to his modern purposes, inflating the Telemachus father/son theme, while ignoring many other crucial elements, in a model of the original which is (in Bloom's immortal Dublin phrase) 'the same, only different'. As Joyce was later to show in *Finnegans Wake*, the same can somehow manage to be the new. Not for him the gloomy elegance of Beckett who opened a novel with the line: 'The sun shone, having no alternative, upon the nothing new'.[11] For Joyce, everything changes even as it remains itself and the differences give the repetitions point and meaning. Many of the deviations from *The Odyssey* are tragicomic in implication, as Hugh Kenner has pointed out – tragic when Stephen refuses to pray for his dying mother, unlike Telemachus who was tactful and considerate; comic when it dawns on the reader that Mrs Bloom is something less than a faithful Penelope.[12] But most of the differences are finally crucial in allowing Joyce to redefine the nature of heroism for the modern world. There is a heroic honesty in Stephen's refusal to pray to a God in whom he does not believe, and a heroic wisdom in Bloom's refusal to take revenge on Boylan, unlike Odysseus who slaughtered those who tested the purity of his wife.

So it is in *Faith Healer*, where Friel's heroic myth is creatively misinterpreted so that he can redefine heroism for the modern Gaelic world. In the ancient legend, Deirdre's name meant 'troubler' or 'alarmer', and she was remembered for the prophecy at her birth that many would die because of her beauty. Grace, the modern Deirdre, is heroic not so much for the suffering she inflicts (though she has some of the cruelty of the ancient heroine) but rather for the pain she must endure. Similarly, Teddy is not allowed the easy 'heroic' option of instant death for the man and woman he worships, but is more realistically left behind at the end to pick up the pieces that remain, in a life of quiet desperation rather than heroic enterprise. The ultimate realism is to deny Deirdre the fake glamour of a romantic death such as she had in medieval versions, and instead to give her a lonely death in a bedsitter as a nervous wreck. In this respect, Friel returns to the oldest versions of the tale, which had Deirdre dash out her brains on a rock, the hopeless act of a woman crazed with grief, a year and a day after the execution of her lover. Perhaps most significant of all is Friel's decision to give Hardy the central role, just as Naoise was the pivotal figure in the oldest version from *The Book of Leinster*.

Underlying Joyce's depiction of Bloom as a modern Ulysses, Friel's of Hardy as a modern Naoise, is the conviction that primitive myths are not impositions of a culture but innate possessions of every single person, who professes to be a unique being but is in fact a copy, consciously or unconsciously emulating the lives of more original predecessors. Hence, the characteristic modern *malaise* of inauthenticity, which assails men sophisticated enough to sense the frustrations of a life lived in quotation marks. Hence, also, the supreme importance to Leopold Bloom and to us of those small differences with which history repeats itself, for they are our sole guarantee of individuality. And what applies to people is true also of authors. Friel retells an old story, borrowing characters, situations, even phrases from the tale – and to that extent, like Francis Hardy, he is a con man. But, like Hardy's pretence that his wife was barren and could not bear a child, he also remoulds his tale and his people to some private standard of excellence of his own – and, to that extent, he is indeed an artist. It adds to the poignancy of Hardy's life that he is quite unaware that he has re-enacted the story of Deirdre and the Sons of Usna, just as it adds to the poignancy of Leopold Bloom's plight that he is never for a moment aware that in his wanderings through Dublin he re-enacts the voyage of Odysseus. But that heroism, like saintliness, is quite unaware of itself as such.

14. Theatre as Opera: *The Gigli Concert*

I reland is a land of song; and Irish art, more than most, aspires to the condition of music. The playwright Synge had always hoped to be a concert violinist and abandoned the aim only because his extreme shyness left him unable to perform in public: but he compensated as best he could by treating his play scripts as musical scores and writing words such as 'andante' or 'allegro' against chosen passages. James Joyce's literary career, glorious though it became, was also embraced as a second-best option. He would have preferred the life of a singer and in his youth had such a fine tenor voice that it took the legendary John McCormack to defeat him (Joyce actually came third, as he could not sight-read music) at the competition for vocalists at the Feis Cheoil. (Reportedly, Joyce took a savage revenge by remarking to his rival 'John, you sing a good song well, and a bad song wonderfully'.)[1]

The conversation in Joyce's great short story 'The Dead' is dominated by reminiscences of opera singers whose greatness seems to grow in direct proportion to their distance in the past. Joyce's interest in the techniques, as well as the history, of opera was obsessive. He opened the 'Sirens' chapter of *Ulysses* with the verbal equivalent of an overture in music, filling it with brief, exemplary excerpts from the following narrative, in order to put the reader into the right mood. He was convinced that a verbal equivalent could be found for almost any musical device. For the staccato effect, he wrote 'Will? You? I. Want. You.' For the fermata by which a final note is indefinitely held, he wrote 'endlessnessnessness'. 'Sirens' is full of musical quotations, especially from *Don Giovanni*, and with these, in a parody of the Bloom–Boylan–Molly triangle, Joyce creates the irony of inappropriate song.[2]

Throughout *Ulysses* Leopold Bloom uses his experience of opera as a kind of touchstone for measuring the quality of a fully lived life. When an acquaintance in the newspaper office remarks that Red Murray has a face like 'our saviour's', the non-Christian Bloom rephrases the idea by saying 'Or like "Mario", the Italian tenor?'[3] Simon Dedalus opines that Italian is the only language to make love in and Bloom notes that 'tenors get women by the score'. All their fantasies about romantic Italy are brought to earth during the encounter in the cabmen's shelter of 'Eumaeus': there Bloom praises the lyric qualities of the Italian language, only to be curtly informed by Stephen that the Italians at the next table are haggling over money.

Despite such moments of wariness, Joyce never ceased in his attempt to compose the sort of operatic sentence in which the sound might match the sense. In the 'Nausicaa' section of *Ulysses*, Roman candles explode in mid-air as Gerty MacDowell leans back to watch, revealing more and more of her shapely leg and driving Bloom to orgasm:

> And then a rocket sprang and bang shot blind and O! then the Roman candle burst and it was like a sigh of O! and everyone cried O! O! in raptures and it gushed out of it a stream of rain gold hair threads and they shed and ah! they were all greeny dewy' stars falling with golden, O! so lively! O so soft, sweet, soft![4]

The deliberate patterning of O-sounds rises to a crescendo as Bloom reaches a climax, but the romance of the moment is cruelly deflated some lines later by the terse account of Blazes Boylan's ejaculation into the vagina of Molly Bloom: 'O, he did. Into her. She did. Done. Ah!'[5] Here the innocent, open sound of the ecstatic Os is replaced by the more knowing, somewhat accusatory 'ah', a shout of guilty disclosure rather than of rapt passion. Nor is that the end. Some paragraphs after the climax of Os, that sound is itself repeated, just a single anticlimactic time, as if its echo is a hollow mockery of Bloom's earlier ecstasies at the sight of Gerty's bared leg. For now he discovers: 'Tight boots? No. She's lame! O!'[6]

That half line stops and starts four times, in re-enactment of her limping departure. In a moment such as this, Bloom is revealed as an unconscious poet, whose inner acoustic is perfectly tuned to the world around him. If there is a silent music of the mind, then Joyce expertly captured it again and again, which was why that other music lover, Samuel Beckett, made the comment that his friend's writings were not about something but were that something itself, a perfect incarnation of content in pure form.[7] In *Finnegans Wake*, Joyce's last work, the very notion of content surrendered fully to the exigencies of form and style.

Such passages might be read now as relatively early samples of what is known as performance art, for they are based on a notion of art as a structure beyond ideas or opinion, a pure performance. It is that tradition which is taken up and perfected in the dramatic mode by Tom Murphy's *The Gigli Concert*. Here the 'self' is not presented as a fixed, unitary entity so much as a provisional complex at a point in time. The nature of that self may best be revealed, and most usefully defined, in performance: literally through its chastening encounter with available forms. Murphy's central character is a successful builder, unnamed as 'An Irish Man', for whom £2 million is not enough. He will not be able to live at peace with himself until he has sung like Beniamino Gigli.

According to Richard Poirier in his book of that name, '*The Performing Self* is the release of energy into measured explorations of human potentialities. . . so as to probe all those things which the self might be'.[8] He compares it to the way

[A] sculptor not only is impelled to shape his material but is in turn shaped by it, his impulse to mastery always chastened, sometimes made tender and possibly witty by the recalcitrance of what he is working on. Performance comes to fruition at precisely the point where the potentially destructive impulse to mastery brings forth from the material its most essential, irreducible, clarified and therefore beautiful nature.[9]

Just as the sculptor is educated by the chosen stone, so is a singer shaped and defined by a chosen song. The encounter of mind with available form leads to a release of energy, as at the climax of *The Gigli Concert*, but the fear of such energy may take the form of a 'repressive analysis', often disguised as psychotherapy, such as is practised in the earlier scenes of the play. Yet it is to the final release of energy that Murphy's masterpiece moves: that moment when, not the builder but his quack analyst finds in himself the strength to sing like Gigli, to validate a self by a sound.

Criticism is notoriously abashed, even disabled, by such a moment, as were the reviewers on the play's opening night in 1983: unable to reduce the work to a summarizable meaning.[10] That may have been in part because all performance art exists not so much in eternal time as for the duration of its own enactment. Being a process rather than a product, it lacks a definitive, final form. This problem is especially acute in dealing with the work of Tom Murphy, who from his beginnings as a playwright has shown a distrust of the analytic intellect. Born in Tuam, Co. Galway in 1935, he shot to fame in the experimental theatre of London during the 1960s and returned to his native country in the 1970s, offering dramas which implied a scathing rebuke to the 'rational' values that seemed to accompany society's modernization.[11] The procedures of psychoanalysis are enacted in *The Gigli Concert*, but only at the level of grotesque parody, as when the quack JPW King indulges the pretence that past sexual failures are the real key to the builder's problems. Murphy's plays are, however, critiques of pure reason – another is called *Too Late for Logic* – and they examine those zones of feeling which mere reason can never illuminate.

It is clear from the outset that part of what attracts the builder to King, rather than to a more orthodox therapist, is the fact that his analyst, far from being a measured professional, is a man as confused and helpless as himself. He is therefore someone who will not be able to probe too embarrassingly into those areas his client wishes to remain unseen. An Irish Man, as his premature resignation from the therapy shows at the end of the play, seeks only an investigation of a strictly limited kind, and certainly not one based on notions of rationality, since it is the rationality of the business world which has driven him all but mad.

Hence the importance of music, not just because it has charms to soothe the savage breast, but because it affords a more sensitive less invasive way of reading and defining a self. Joyce said that if a person wished to understand obscure passages in *Ulysses*, all that was needed was to read it aloud and the inner music would be revealed. Patrick Mason, director of the first production of *Gigli*, made a similar remark: 'Tom Murphy hears sounds as character or he expresses character as sound. All his characters make individual sounds – they have individual patterns.'[12]

In the play, An Irish Man says that he does not need to understand the words of an opera to know the feeling: 'I could always size a man up more from the sound than from what he's saying.'[13] This may not be as radical or innovative as it seems. The idea that a play might be constructed on the same principles of onomatopoeia that govern a lyric utterance is at least as old as Shakespeare. A major trend of modern criticism has been the swerve away from a Bradleyan study of a play's characters to the understanding that every Shakespeare play is a poem, with its own iterative images, contrapuntal melodies, vocal registers and so on.[14] Character has been redefined, no longer merely revealed by something that Hamlet says but also by the way in which he chooses to say it. Hamlet is a telling example, since he is obsessed by the relation between character and performance as he coaches the players, punctures the disguises of false courtiers, or tells his mother to assume virtues she may not have in the hope of finally living up to them.

The two playwrights who did most to clear the way for this conception of drama as musical performance were Murphy's Irish predecessors Bernard Shaw and Oscar Wilde. Shaw first came to prominence as a music critic. Ever afterward, he tried in plays to register clashes in character or even in national types by tonal contrasts. In *John Bull's Other Island*, for example, he contrasted the bass of the Englishman Broadbent with the higher-pitched voices of the nervous Irish; and in *Arms and the Man* he set the terse staccato logic of the bourgeois Bluntschli against the overblown posturing sentences of the aristocratic Petkoffs. He explained:

> In a generation which knew nothing of any sort of acting but drawing-room acting, and which considered a speech of more than twenty words impossibly long, I went back to the classical style and wrote long rhetorical speeches like operatic solos, regarding my plays as musical performances precisely as Shakespeare did.[15]

The danger for Shaw, as later for Murphy, was the fear of being accused of over-rhetorical, over-determined writing. 'I was therefore', recalled Shaw, 'continually struggling with the conscientious efforts of our players to underdo their parts lest they should be considered stagey.'[16]

Patrick Mason solved this problem by encouraging actors in *The Gigli Concert* to overplay rather than underplay their roles, to surrender absolutely to the emotional extremism of opera. So, in the final scene, when King sings an aria, it is from an opera in which a lover mourns the death of his beloved, before he goes out to commit suicide himself. Critics of the play who argue that Mona's revelation of her terminal cancer in the previous scene is a cheap theatrical shot may be forgetting that it is out of just such blatant emotionalism that opera is always made. Taking another instance, An Irish Man's tearful account of his childhood was *his* aria, his moment to dominate the forestage with his gestures and words. Perhaps the most operatic feature of all – as well as the most Shavian – is the constant resort to melodramatic reversals, which leave the unmasking JPW King himself unmasked.

It would not be an exaggeration to describe Murphy's play as a verbal opera. The term was first used by W. H. Auden in an essay on Wilde's *The Importance of Being Earnest*, which he dubbed the only pure verbal opera in English. By this he meant a play in which every other element was subordinated to the effect of the dialogue. Wilde, he contended, 'created a verbal universe in which the characters are determined by the kinds of things they say, and the plot is nothing but a succession of opportunities to say them'.[17] Here, character is subordinated not just to plot but to the demands of a pure, elegant language: and this in a play which, like *The Gigli Concert*, deals with the Double, a character split into a real and metaphorical self, who seeks, by the sheer intensity with which he lives out his fiction, to make the two into one.

That sort of fusion is sought in Murphy's play by a surrender of the ethical imagination to pure form. As so often in western literature, that relaxation of the moral for the sake of aesthetic beauty is described as a Faustian pact. King quotes Marlowe's *Doctor Faustus*: 'This night I'll conjure.' King is, of course, fixated on his own impossible Helen, the woman at the other end of the telephone line: and the voice of Gigli is the diabolical Siren song, the pure form taken by the devil to win over his soul. Some moments earlier in the play he had invoked God, but only momentarily, for like Beckett's tramps he feels a grudge against a God with whom he severed all connection some time ago. Instead, he makes his bargain now with the satanic powers below, like Hamlet, who asserted that, if he could not invoke heaven, then hell would serve as well.

Tom Murphy bears a grudge against God which is quintessentially Irish – what Kenneth Tynan once called 'a very Irish grudge against God which the merely godless would never feel'.[18] For Murphy, art is one way of answering the iniquity of the world which God has created. Whereas traditional religion (such as he had known while growing up in Tuam) offered man a sense of continuity and a way of taming the demonic, Murphy, like other artists, now seizes the initiative lost by religion: and, far from suppressing the daemonic, he explores and exalts it as a source of creativity. He is, in that strict sense, an aesthete who believes that life at its highest can be as intense and value-free as a work of art. Life for him finds its ultimate justification in a chosen form and all living is but a search for that ideal form. Within such a system, experience in all its aspects, sublime or base, becomes a supreme value, and the lived life is a chronicle of extreme sensations, deliberately sought and prolonged. The impact on the self rather than the moral consequences for society becomes the yardstick used to measure any action.

It is to this precise point that An Irish Man has come when the play begins. He is by then in revolt against the world of work, effort and reward, a world which he has mastered only to discover that such triumph is hardly enough. Though not a sociologist, Murphy proves himself to be a keen observer of social and cultural conditions. Throughout the nineteenth century, the Protestant ethic had taught men to save money and to be modest in their accumulation of goods. Once the transcendental tie with God was broken, however, hedonism was given free rein and soon all kinds of sensation could be purchased on the instalment plan. Work could no longer be cast under the aegis of divinity: and so it lost much of its traditional value and meaning. This is what the builder means when he complains 'There's too many facts in the world. Them houses were built out of facts: corruption, brutality, backhanding, fronthanding, lump labour and a bit of technology' (*GC* 16).

So now he comes to JPW King in search of his lost sensuality, his lost artistry, his anima – all those aspects which years of graft and money grubbing had led him to suppress and deny in himself. It all goes back in his mind to a day when his older brother Danny scorned his offer of flowers and belittled his childlike question as to which, the daisy or buttercup, was 'nicest': 'And Danny said "nicest" like a knife. "Nicest? Are you stupid? What use is nicest?" Of what use is beauty, Mr King?' (*GC* 56).

If An Irish Man has trouble in relating to his own wife, that is first and foremost because he has spent years suppressing the feminine dimension within himself. Only when his wife takes herself and their son away does that dimension erupt into his full consciousness, demanding his attention.

Nor is JPW King much further developed on this score. He has removed his ideal Helen to a remote zone of pseudo-spirituality, at the end of a phone line, from which distance she can be safely worshipped without any disillusioning firsthand contacts. Such *amour courtois* worship is merely a fancy way of repeating the builder's sin and avoiding a real relationship. If the builder abuses his wife with obscenities, King mistreats his fantasy women with heavy breathing phone calls. The appalling gap between King's utopia of domestic bliss in a clematis-fringed cottage run by an aproned angel and the sordid brutalities of the builder's actual home life is a proof that, for both men, the world of fact and the world of value have moved too far apart. All the facts are now brutal in the same proportion that all dreams are unreal. There is no remaining connection between the *is* and *ought*, between the realities of their lives and their aspirations. *Is* and *ought* occupy wholly separate zones. The desire to sing like Gigli is nothing other than the desire to reconnect them, to shape a moment when the literal and the metaphorical might coincide.

Though outwardly opposed – the builder being rich, worldly and repressed, the quack being poor, idealistic and impulse-ridden – the two men at a deeper level share many problems. Within a few minutes, each has separately voiced apprehensiveness about surviving the day; and when the builder mentions his Mandrax sleeping pills, King seems to have a remarkable familiarity with their clinical history, even down to the fact that they have been recently taken off the market. Throughout the play that ensues the initiative in the relationship between the two men will ebb and flow, until at times it seems as if it is the builder who is healing King rather than being healed by him.

At the most obvious level this is what happens, since at the close the quack, as a consequence of the transference, manages to sing like Gigli and, having done so, seems free at last to leave his claustrophobic room and go back into the world. However, this happens only *after* King has helped the builder to heal himself – as far as he wishes to be healed, which is as far as abandoning his career but not to the extent of singing like Gigli. An Irish Man fears an analysis which might excavate too much; and so, at an advanced stage in the treatment, he resigns from it, leaving King to make the final jump alone.

There are many ways of reading this. At a biographical level, Murphy himself is known to have aborted an analysis with the psychiatrist Ivor Browne on the grounds that a successful conclusion might indeed cure his pain but only at the risk of resolving those very complexes which provided him with his art. An Irish Man may represent, therefore, the canny, controlling aspect of Murphy's own personality: his shrewd sense of limits which must not be transgressed, his eye for the main chance, and above all his intuition that it will not serve an artist to become overly self-analytical. That kind of analysis might sterilize the impulses which it investigates. Murphy is one of those Yeatsian artists who is at his best when probing material only half-understood and when allowing that material to speak through him, resisting all attempts to control or master it.

The builder, of course, is not an artist and does not, therefore, have an artist's excuse for one kind of failure of nerve, which is displayed by withdrawal from therapy. He is simply a timid, bourgeois soul, and it is clear from his own testimony that he has been through a process of depression and recovery many times. On this occasion, King has brought him so close to resolution that he is unnerved, scurries into retreat, and then threatens the therapist with exposure to the police, before attempting to buy his silence with wads of cash:

> Look, Mr. King, be warned. I could have you locked up, like that, one telephone call. But why go throwing good money after bad? And it was my own fault. I just can't get over what possessed me to come into a place like this when I can cure myself like I did last time... (*GC* 62)

Having been to the river Styx, the builder turns back each time. He is accordingly terrified by King's account of how he engages in criminal acts such as stealing books from Eason's to assist his client. These satanic activities do not conform to the self-image of a solid citizen. And so, having flirted briefly with his own *anima*, he decides once again to repress it back into his subconscious and demonize it accordingly.

The repressed feminine principle is never so easily denied, and invades the room in the shape of Mona, the vulgar trollop and faithless wife, who is to King's world of facts as his idealized Helen is to his world of values. His endless skulking in his room is a symbolic portrayal of his refusal to face the world as it really is. Mona, however, comes repeatedly in from that world, bringing news of it, as well as practical help.

The original production of *The Gigli Concert* ran almost to midnight (from eight o'clock), prompting inevitable complaints that the play was too long. Much of the criticism focused on the character Mona, who was considered superfluous to the play's real drama between King and An Irish Man. Richard Kearney, on the other side, argued that Mona was a symbolic necessity to the Anglo-Irish sub-theme, since she came from the north and occupied an intermediate zone between Irish itinerant-hater and English quack who thinks he can solve intractable problems. In that reading of course, Mona's terminal illness would be part of the point.[19] Murphy had lived for a number of years in England between 1962 and 1970, and he married an Englishwoman. There is much curiosity in his plays as to the meaning and destiny of Anglo-Irish relations. The English quack seems more honest and likeable than the Irish builder, and ultimately just as unable to cope: and Kearney sees the northern Mona as 'a sort of neglected gobetween: the woman victimized by the male-dominated struggle for power'.[20] That interpretation would also explain the builder's parting advice to the English muddler: 'Go home, Jimmy. Forget that – Irish colleen. . . You are a remarkable man. I know there's kindness in the world, but they'll kill you over here. . . Go home' (*GC* 734). Nor is that advice nastily intended. Far from it, since the builder has just thanked King for all his help, and King has reciprocated by insisting that it is he who is grateful to his client. It would be only stretching matters a shade further to see in this Anglo-Irish process a disguised version of the relationship between Tom Murphy, Irish image maker, and his English-born director and dramatic analyst, Patrick Mason, who puts a structure on those wayward instincts latent in the play and reveals its inner harmonies.[21]

All these readings are valid up to a point, but they leave out more than they let in. The true justification of the character Mona has little enough to do with politics or Anglo-Irish relations. Rather, it concerns the fact that she represents the return of the repressed feminine principle, the hope of creative possibility in the midst of despair – or what she calls 'bouncing back'. As a broken housewife turned prostitute, as a mother who in her teens lost a son to adoption, and now as a victim of lymphatic cancer, she should by rights be as depressed as the men. Instead, she brings kind help, batteries for King's shaver, and so on – and this despite her pained awareness that King worships not her but the Helen of the phone line.

Near the end, 'Helen' phones to accuse King of being a dirty dialler at just the moment when Mona arrives with the batteries. For the first time, King realizes what real love is and that the builder was right to declare that the romantic kingdom is of this world. The next scene, preceded by the music of *Lucia di Lammermoor*, reveals the lovers in bed together, a classic conjunction of Love and Death, as she breaks the news of her illness and he asserts the importance of seizing every possibility in the here and now. Kearney has pointed in this context to the Greek word for 'possibility', *dunamis*, as the basis of King's philosophy of dynamitology.[22]

This would certainly account for King's obsession with the mistranslation of the message of the Old Testament God as 'I Am Who Am' instead of 'I Am Who May Be', that principle of pure possibility which, according to philosophers, is glimpsed only on the other side of despair. According to this principle, only when King has known the utter negation of rejection by 'Helen' and then the strange joy of love for a woman who will soon die, is he ready for his own journey to the abyss at which he may sing like Gigli, transmuting all that pain into the balm of art.

It is fascinating that all of this should, in a sense, stem from a retranslation of a key phrase of the Bible. The philosopher who did most in the twentieth century to give meaning to that retranslation was Ernst Bloch, a German predecessor of liberation theology, who used Karl Marx's description in a letter to Ruge in 1843 of a revolution which derives from the poetry of the future rather than the nightmare of the past to reinterpret the Bible as a truly utopian document. Bloch's philosophy of the 'not-yet' saw the world as an open process rather than a concluded system. He sought to identify and analyse the 'unconscious' dimension of the future which slumbers in the present, in the belief that the arts, more than any other facet of life, contain below the level of consciousness a dream of all that is to come. He shared with Walter Benjamin the conviction that every age not only dreams the next but, while dreaming, impels it to wakefulness. Popular art, in particular, Bloch saw as both reflective of social realities and as projective of human betterment. He was in fact the original dynamitologist: and his greatest book, *The Principle of Hope*, is a three-volume demonstration, written under the shadow of fascism, of how the principle of hope may be discerned in documents which might superficially prompt only the darkest despair. Bloch was, with Yeats, one of the very few thinkers of the twentieth century who formed a clear idea of the shape of the future, to which he looked with a degree of confidence. That confidence derived, however, not from analytic thought so much as from a sense of the redemptive strangeness of art and from a conviction that in the achievable human community every man and woman would be an artist.

In his essay 'Art and Society', Bloch actually resorts to the image of a dynamite explosion to explain the underlying idea:

I am talking about an anticipatory illumination that could never be realised in an ideology of the status quo but, rather, has been connected to it like an explosive, as though it could always engender the most stimulating surplus beyond the ideology.[23]

This is what, elsewhere in the essay, he terms the 'ideological surplus of genius', something that is not an ideology at all because it surpasses the particular epoch in a utopian way by a mode of transformation commonly called *genius*. According to Bloch: 'The ideology in great work reflects and justifies its times, but the utopia in it rips open the times, brings them to an end, brings them to that end where there would no longer be a mere past and its ideology, but rather where it would be shown *tua propria vera res agitur*'.[24] In other words, a future could be demonstrated to be opening up. At the centre of his essay, Bloch concedes that all of this is but a reformulation of an idea of Marx, who said:

> [T]he reformation of consciousness only consists in letting the world enter one's consciousness, in waking up the world form the dream about itself...Then it can be shown that it does not concern a large hyphen between past and future, but the completion of the idea of the past.[25]

In short, there is no contradiction between tradition and utopia, the Bible and the revolutionary community, the imagined past and the actual future. The phrase about letting the world enter one's consciousness while waking that world from a dream about itself is a perfect anticipation of the final scene in Murphy's play. There JPW King arises from the floor, prays to his dead mother not to leave him in the dark, and pinches himself awake by letting up his window blind, before re-entering the actual world which he had scorned for so long. 'It's pretty bad out there, isn't it?', he had said to the builder only moments before, to be told 'Oh now' (*GC* 72).

The use of light to welcome the new morning is clear. Light and dark images are employed at every major phase of the play, most obviously in the fact that An Irish Man appears repeatedly in the doorway as a shadow or silhouette, complete with Italian hat and overcoat in the gangster mode (Murphy in another play, *The Blue Macushla*, has equated Irish businessmen with Chicago criminals of the 1930s). The silhouette is of one with no name, known only as

An Irish Man: and it may be appropriate in that context to interpret it as a version of the *doppelgänger* in literature. That reading is validated by the many phrases and experiences which the two men, for all their superficial differences, share. The builder cannot be named, perhaps because he is simply a projection of King's imagination. Hence, when King claims to have stolen books from Eason's, he can blithely argue that he did this for the man, and so heap onto his double any feelings of guilt which may ensue.

This is the classic psychological manoeuvre which gives rise to the double. In the account of Erich Stern, the process 'causes man to transfer responsibility for certain deeds of the self to another self, the double; since his tremendous fear of death and damnation leads to a transference to the double'.[26] In folklore, men are seized by conflicting impulses when confronted by their shadows. On the one hand, if the shadow is seen as representing a hideous past self which clings, it can produce an urge to rid oneself of it, as at various moments King tries to dismiss An Irish Man. Such attempts to deny a darker aspect of one's self are often prevented, as here, by a recognition that the life of the shadow and that of the person are too intimately linked for this sort of facile dismissal. The shadow, of course, may also portend death: the folk belief that if a double sights a shadow, the person will die within a year, and so forth. There are playgoers who believe that King does indeed die at the end of *The Gigli Concert* and is resurrected on the far side of death – that, in effect, his song is a swansong.

However, beliefs about shadows are often contradictory, since in many cultures it is held that a man who casts no shadow will soon die. (That is why sick people are frequently carried into sunlight). This seems ultimately a more useful approach to the closing scene, in which King lets in the sunlight and so for the first time casts his own shadow, instead of seeing his shadow living at one remove in the person of An Irish Man. Now, at the latest possible moment, he has reintegrated himself and can therefore dismiss that shadow.

While acknowledging his indebtedness to it, he can now proceed on his own.

In some European folktales, men who see their shadows wish to rejoin them – perhaps in a death wish – but are not allowed, since the shadow must always come forward to meet them, as in *The Gigli Concert*.[27] Men are often described as being afraid of their own shadows, afraid of the dark, repressed, hidden aspects of self which erupt threateningly from time to time. One temptation, at the moment of such eruption, is for the haunted person to identify totally with the shadow side and to engage in persistent assertions of unworthiness: and another, as indicated, is to offload responsibility for everything onto the shadow, as King seems at times to do. All of these ambiguities are reflected in the constant accusations and recriminations through the play, as each man accuses his *doppelgänger* of being 'the one to falter' (GC 48–50, 64–5).

The shadow, like the double, can also epitomize the soul, and in *The Gigli Concert* there is much talk of the soul which, like that of Marlowe's Doctor Faustus, seems to escape into the firmament. Otto Rank, in his book on *The Double*, argued that it was man's need for immortality which led to the primitive concept of the soul as a duality, person-and-shadow, one aspect of which betokens immortality (King) and the other death (An Irish Man). The artist, in this scheme of things, is a version of the hero, since he wins immortality through art: and, unlike the neurotic, the artist manages to present the double in an acceptable form, 'justifying the survival of the irrational in our over-rationalised civilisation'.[28] This, again, might be taken as a perfect account of Murphy's achievement.

Within the structure of the play, there are some modifications to this scheme. An Irish Man could have been created as the outcome of JPW King's pathological self-absorption. In that sense, King's shadow is indeed his vanity and a force which, in Rank's terms, 'epitomises that morbid self-love which prevents the formation of a happily-balanced personality'.[29] This is indeed the crisis state in which King lives: self-enclosure which leads to an inability to reach out to others or recognize love when it is offered to him. As Rank elaborated on the syndrome:

> The pathological disposition towards psychological disturbances is conditioned to a large degree by the splitting of personality, with special emphasis upon the ego-complex, to which corresponds an abnormally strong interest in one's own person, his psychic states, his destinies. This point of view leads to the characteristic relationship to the world, to life and particularly to the love-object, with which no harmonious relationship is found. Either the direct inability to love or – leading to the same effect – an exorbitantly strained longing for love characterise the two poles of this over-exaggerated attitude towards one's own ego.[30]

King's exorbitant strain for love focuses on 'Helen', even as his inability to love is perceived by Mona who, at the start, counts it a triumph when he manages to use her name. By the end, however, she has cured him by her offer of a love without conditions. She penetrates his self-absorbed exterior and, at that moment, it is possible for the shadow, An Irish Man, to disappear for good. This was the shadow whose sense of hurt went all the way back to that moment in adolescence when he was not allowed to sing the part of a girl soprano and who has lived ever since in a world of macho achievers. The shadow can now disappear because of the restoration of the feminine principle.

This was an important moment in the evolution of Tom Murphy's career, for until its arrival he had been accused, with some justice, of writing largely masculine plays about the repressed hurts endured by males and of writing no strong parts for women. It can hardly be a coincidence that not long after writing *The Gigli Concert* he produced in *Bailegangaire* one of the major female roles in contemporary writing.

15. Frank McGuinness and *Observe the Sons*

The ferocity of the Irish Republican Army's bombing campaign in the 1970s and 1980s led many Irish nationalists to re-examine their commitment. Most were horrified at the thought that such deeds could be perpetrated in their name. Calls for the abandonment of the constitutional claim on the six counties of Northern Ireland (a claim seen by some as validating the IRA campaign) came thick and fast, but equally urgent were attempts to come to a deeper understanding of the unionist tradition. *Observe the Sons of Ulster Marching towards the Somme*, which was first staged in Dublin in 1985, seemed to capture that new mood, for in it a playwright from the staunchly republican county of Donegal set out to confront 'my own bigotry' and to introject his unionist Other.[1] The drama was an immense success not only in Dublin but also in Belfast. Although some initial reviewers in Dublin took it for a scathing exposé of unionist hysteria, it has come to be regarded as a genuinely sympathetic, if critical, exploration of the minds and hearts of young men who fought on 1 July 1916 at the Battle of the Somme.

That battle is, of course, a milestone in the history of Ulster loyalism. Over 6,000 members of the Ulster Division were killed in a single day of fighting. Entire streets of Belfast and small villages of Antrim were left without young men, because the authorities had made a point of bonding new recruits with neighbours from their own communities. That policy died the death after July 1916 but while it lasted it meant that recruits were deeply committed to one another as they went over the top. They had to be, because an edict just before the battle confined commissioned officers to headquarters.[2] This meant that many units going into battle had nobody above the rank of captain leading them. 'In the end, we were not led, we led ourselves', says the sole survivor, Kenneth Pyper, at the start of the play: 'We claimed we would die for each other in battle.'[3]

By a strange kind of irony, much of the IRA campaign in the streets of Belfast and Derry in the decade before the play seemed to feed off similar feelings. The journalist Mary Holland reported the insistence of a Derry IRA man that he was dying not so much for a united Ireland as to protect the neighbours in his street. It is also true that many loyalist gunmen saw themselves as community defenders. Moreover, the idea of an independent Ulster, as a real alternative to integration with either Britain or the Irish Republic, had been openly considered by many loyalist leaders. This was in keeping with the growing awareness of regional cultures which had developed not only as a response to the ever larger bureaucracy of the European Economic Community but also as a direct consequence of the introduction of local radio and publishing houses committed to the study of local history and culture. McGuinness's play was as much a product of the 1980s as it was a study of an Ulster mindset which achieved definition all of seven decades earlier. For perhaps the greatest irony of all about the soldiers at the Somme was their discovery of a version of their own Irishness. Back in Dublin, over the previous two years, Patrick Pearse and Desmond FitzGerald had feared that the very notion of an Irish identity would disappear in the trenches of the Great War:[4] but quite the reverse happened.

New and unprecedented ideas of Irishness emerged, as so often in the past, as a consequence of an intense experience overseas. In the muddy fields of the Somme, a generation achieved a form of self-definition.

Observe the Sons is open to many interpretations. Some have read it as a suggestion that a repressed homosexuality underlies unionism.[5] This possibility might have troubled some minds following the Kincora Boys' Home scandal of the early 1980s, when the attempt by loyalist politicians to hush up the exposure of coercive sexual activity with boys in care made headlines. It might even be possible to think of McGuinness as reversing the famous process by which the British authorities of 1916 imputed homosexual behaviour to the patriot Roger Casement, before executing the nationalist leader for high treason. Such readings, though clever, would slight the tenderness with which the playwright renders the homoerotic feelings between the male characters. These men are at their best in moments of personal integrity, which are set off against the horror of the war itself.

The action opens with the elderly Pyper preparing for his own death and recalling the deaths of those he left behind at the Somme. This first section is titled 'Remembrance'. The word echoes the familiar Armistice Day slogan 'lest we forget' and it also questions the amnesia of the southern state, which for many decades had allowed the memory of the 150,000 who fought in that war to be extirpated from the official record. Many of these had joined up in defence of the rights of small nations, actuated by the belief that Home Rule would be the reward for their loyalty when hostilities ended. By 1985 their role had been all but forgotten, and even the rebels of 1916 were no longer commemorated with the fervour which once they had aroused. There was a real danger that all the dead would be forgotten.

The boys and men of the Ulster Division had very different hopes from those of their southern counterparts in the British Army: they wished, by their loyalty and bravery, to stave off Home Rule. 'Who knows', asks a historian, 'how many had felt cheated of a fight with the menace of Irish nationalism by the suspension of Home Rule at the outbreak of the war?'[6] This may be why McGuinness has the soldiers imagine their unseen, unknowable German enemies as Fenians and Catholics. The battle, after all, was to fall on 1 July, at the height of the Orange marching season and a date which some believe to have marked the actual Battle of the Boyne. Such a symbolic coincidence could only have increased the ardour of those who wore sashes and shouted 'No Surrender' as they faced the German gunners.

'I do not understand your insistence on my remembrance' (OS 73), opens Pyper, but to whom? One critic has suggested that the dying man is defiantly addressing his God, with a rebuke for the mass slaughter orchestrated in his name.[7] Certainly, the opening monologue, which threatens to become endless, sounds remarkably like that issueless Protestant confrontation with conscience on which many of the texts of Samuel Beckett are based.[8] Pyper searches with similar compulsiveness for the liberating and exact phrase which would bring his suffering to an end, and also his monologue. But that monologue may also owe something to the overture to James Joyce's 'Sirens' chapter of *Ulysses*, for key phrases in it will be repeated and elaborated in later sections.

Pyper appears to be rebuking contemporary unionist leaders, who honour his comrades, or perhaps even castigating this playwright, who exploits him for his own artistic purposes. He wishes to deliver no celebration of slaughter: 'Invention gives that slaughter shape. That scale of horror has no shape' (OS 12). Nobody has the right to excuse such suffering in the act of making it a lesson for others. McGuinness is imagining the resistance of the dead to assimilation into any narrative written at the mercy of the present moment. He conceived of the play when he saw the names of dead soldiers on a memorial and began to imagine them back into life. In effect, his work seeks to restore the possibilities of their youth, before public events fully swamped their private lives. The title is a deliberate echo of an old Ulster saga, *Oidhe Chloinne Uisnigh*, or *The Fate of the Sons of Usna*, one of 'the three sorrows of storytelling'. In it the warrior Naoise and his brothers must leave their home province for love of the beautiful Deirdre. They, rather than she, are the focus of the oldest accounts, exponents of a blood brotherhood according to which all actions are performed under *geasa*, as injunctions based on honour rather than on clear psychological motivation. The tale will end when the king's promise to receive them back in Ulster as esteemed friends is cruelly broken and the old knightly code is exposed in all its bankruptcy, revealing the brave warriors as mere pawns in an aristocratic game.

McGuinness's revisionist version needs little straining to recast itself in terms of the First World War. By late June 1916, before the commencement of the battle on 1 July, over 170,000 shells had been fired at German positions and soldiers were assured that the capture of those few enemy operatives still at their posts would be a formality. However, the lies of army propagandists were already under scrutiny and 'not all of the men accepted the confident prediction that they were destined for little more than a lively summer stroll'. One young man wrote back home to the secretary of his Orange Lodge: 'When you receive this note I will be dead'. Rations and rum were issued in generous measure to men who feared they were being fattened for a sacrifice. 'I enlisted in the hope of death' (*OS* 19), says Pyper. Already he sounds not unlike his southern counterpart, Patrick Pearse, who admitted as much in a Gaelic poem:

Thugas mo ghnúis
ar an ród seo romham,
ar an ngníomh a chím,
is ar an mbás a gheobhad.

I have turned my face
to this road before me,
to the deed that I see,
and the death I shall die.[9]

As if to confirm that implied equation, the aged Pyper is soon laying claim to other elements of Pearse's mythology. Cuchulain is 'ours', because his people fought to defend Ulster; and so also is the Sinn Féin title because 'it is we, the Protestant people who have always stood alone' (*OS* 10). This was a point which had often been made by Bernard Shaw: that Protestant notions of self-election were far more in keeping with the Sinn Féin ideal of self-reliance than were the universalist pretensions of Roman Catholicism. By 1985, advocates of an independent province, such as the Ulster Defence Association, had not only adopted a mural of Cuchulain in their head office, but also much of the old nationalist rhetoric of exceptionalism, of exterior threat and of a code in imminent danger of eclipse. They were becoming in their way just as anti-English as some of the more extreme nationalists had once been. They were caught in a syndrome described and diagnosed by Douglas Hyde: Anglophobes who were also Anglophiles, eternally denouncing the culture they rushed to imitate. Their assertions of independence could never fully compensate for a humiliating sense of dependence on an England that scarcely cared twopence for them. The debacle at the Somme seemed perfectly scripted to capture at once their spurned loyalty and utter vulnerability.

Kenneth Pyper returned from that humiliation, denied the death he had so strenuously sought. No longer was he flippant about the gods of his loyalist forefathers, for now he wanted only to serve them: 'The world lay in ruins about my feet. I wanted to rebuild it in the image of my fellow companions' (*OS* 10). He gave up the life of a sculptor and jester, opting instead to manage his father's estates and the workings of the province. But to all intents he was one of the living dead, sleepwalking through life, for his heart was left with his dead comrades. In order to honour their sacrifice, he had to subscribe to the cult of loyalist courage and quell all doubts as to its value. The death wish of the 1890s poets was consummated in the trenches and the old Pyper is stark in the lesson he deduces: 'That is hate. Deepest hate. Hate for one's self. We wished ourselves to die and in doing so we let others die to satisfy our blood lust' (*OS* 12). All he can do now is summon the ghosts of fallen friends, including that of his younger self, so as to hear what they may have to say to him. It is a wan parody of the classic homoerotic encounter between a wise old man and an initiate in search of his level of understanding.

Other responses to the carnage might have been possible. Many young Britons died at the Somme and those who survived saw it as a reprise of the old story of cannon fodder sent to certain death by a cynical and manipulative elite:

> After World War One the British ruling class would never again be able to despatch slum dwellers and peasant labourers to perdition en masse. But the unionist psyche chose to ignore that exploitation and betrayal and turn the sacrifice of the Somme into something more positive. It became an affirmation of Ulster Protestant loyalism.[10]

A class-driven analysis could never have made headway among estate owners like Pyper, and it was they who set the agenda. Yet that radical analysis provoked real pain, even when it was made among socialists of the British left, for it implied that the sacrifices made by beloved brothers, fathers and nephews had been quite pointless. Those like Pyper who returned from war felt a terrible guilt for surviving at all, along with the dire necessity to confer some meaning on the carnage. Pyper's ambivalence perfectly captures the conflicting interpretations. It is the vestigial radical in him who insists that the slaughter not be given a consoling shape, yet he also feels obliged to draw some sort of conclusion: 'Ulster has grown lonely' (*OS* 11).

Nor was it in Ulster alone that survivors supplied such a shape. The Somme was unusual in the appalling number of casualties, but in general most soldiers who took part in the war survived it. Yet the cult created around the warrior dead proved invaluable to comrades as they faced a new world which had little inkling of what they had been through: and it also became a means of accounting for the mediocrity of the present.[11] The older Pyper's disillusion with the state of his society would have had its counterpart in the bitter disappointment of many veterans of the Easter Rising at life in the Irish Free State. One way of coping with such frustrations was to insist that the best, bravest and brightest had been the ones mown down by enemy guns. In those respects, too, the symbolic meaning of 1916 for loyalists and republicans was remarkably alike. The only major difference was that in the Great War the lingering theme was of 'doomed youth led blindly to slaughter by cruel age',[12] whereas in the Easter Rising the young, if anything, sent out a call to their elders. If July 1916 was sought by Pyper and comrades as an escape from the discontents of modernity, Easter 1916 was a confrontation with such modernity, as the young in Dublin sought to impose their ideas on the old. The Rising might never have happened were it not for the First World War, and the *dulce et decorum* rhetoric was common to both enterprises. But abiding differences remained. One of the major objectives of the Easter rebels was to take their compatriots right out of the carnage of the Great War by reminding them, in effect, that each had a nation and a people of his or her own to defend. The Rising was, among many things, a protest against a war that was claiming hundreds of Irish lives each week and which had little enough to do with Ireland.

The second section is titled 'Initiation'. In it the young Pyper appears as a type of the artist and jester. With cryptic wit he exposes the stolidity of his army comrades to searching criticisms, as they arrive for enlistment at a makeshift barracks. At times he sounds like a doomed Elizabethan clown who speaks that bitter truth which will unnerve all others:

CRAIG: You're not in your grave.

PYPER: You're making yours.

CRAIG: What? (*OS* 13)

The histrionics are blatant, for all wars fought by conscripts must have a theatrical element. In real life, these fellows are millers, black-smiths, clergymen, so it follows that military life, with the doffing of civilian garb for strange costumes, must be an act.[13] Moreover, the newly recruited soldier must suddenly assume virtues which he may not actually possess and these are the virtues of an out-and-out actor: nerve, coordination, self-reliance and timing.[14] Pyper, by his near hysterical challenges, might be seen as discomfiting his mates, but also as initiating them (in the manner of a slightly deranged sergeant) in the rituals of the military life.

It emerges that he may have homosexual longings and that he is also an artist. The artist in him sees through everything – the body of David Craig and the apple he carves before Craig's eyes. He cuts his hand and asks Craig to kiss it better, but the recruit refuses. The invitation is not just sexual; it is also a primal urging 'to eat of the tree of knowledge and re-examine the tenets of inherited faith' in the warrior world of *blutbruderschaft*.[15] The blood on the hand portends the sacrifice to come. It is the first of many leitmotifs of the mythical Red Hand of Ulster: but it also evokes the great symbolic test of friendship and male bonding enacted when Rimbaud plunged a knife into his hand to prove his love for Verlaine. Pyper has been to Paris and knows the value of such gestures among the community of artists. Later attempts by Pyper to repeat such a moment will prove more successful. For the present, he contents himself with looking intently at the body of Craig as he undresses. 'Did you not join up to die for me?' (*OS* 15), he asks, with an obvious pun on the Elizabethan meaning of die ('have sexual intercourse').

No superior officer appears onstage in the play, as if to suggest that they are not a felt force in the men's lives. Yet Pyper is soon impersonating a spit-and-polish version of the type. He does it so convincingly as to open the possibility that he is the sort of theatricalized man who can play everybody else's assigned part (soon he is playing Craig) but who will never be able to identify, much less play with conviction, his own. His effeminate quality disturbs the other recruits: 'I have remarkably fine skin, don't I? For a man remarkably fine' (*OS* 17). Never having engaged in physical toil, he may impersonate officers with ease because he shares their background in the upper class.

A good deal of stage business is organized around anxieties of masculinity in the ensuing scene. Told that he must make his own bed, the UVF man named Moore scoffs: 'Woman's work. You don't join the army to do woman's work' (*OS* 18). When Pyper tells his mate Millen that he is fit for dying and wants it over quickly, the Coleraine man objects to such silly chat as 'more fit coming from crying women' (*OS* 20). Millen, it transpires, is a chef: 'Give him a skirt and he'll run you up a four-course dinner' (*OS* 24). This nervous jocularity has a darker, misogynistic side. Craig's father finds that his way of life as a blacksmith is threatened by the motor car and his skill is dying, but his way of coping is to take refuge in crude quips against his wife: 'You should meet the father. My ma often says he should have married a greyhound. He tells us behind her back he married a bitch, so she got her wish' (*OS* 23). The next arrival is Christopher Roulston, once a preacher as Pyper was once a sculptor. Craig recalls his hot-gospelling in Enniskillen: 'You certainly shocked us into changing our ways' (*OS* 25). Now, Roulston appears to suffer from nerves. There is an element of neurosis in the air.

Millen asks each newcomer whether he sleeps on his right or left side: and the Belfastman Anderson smells a Taig (Catholic) in the barracks. Pyper chooses this moment to tell the story of his sojourn in Paris as an artist. Up to now his smart-alecry has been designed to unsettle his comrades' prevailing ideas of masculinity and femininity, but now he also begins to poke fun at their religious certainties. The play is all about the need to transgress fixed boundaries and to challenge psychosocial partitions; and so Pyper asks the men to believe that in France he met a nun turned whore possessed of three legs. They take the tale in literal earnest, though it sounds as if the whore may have been a transvestite male (the middle leg proving shorter than the other two). She 'died' on the wedding night, jokes Pyper, because he felt it his duty as a Protestant to saw her middle leg off and then he ate her.

Later, praising the beauty of French women, he is asked by Craig: 'Men or women?' His answer, 'What's the difference?' (*OS* 31), dismantles the neurotic, Manichean thinking off which loyalism, like nationalism, seems to feed. Pyper wishes to elude definition: for him a fixed identity is a barbarism. Yet some sort of individualism is necessary; it was in search of it that he fled the gods of loyalism for Paris. Those same gods can easily repossess his spirit. His byplay with the penknife may have been intended as a reprise of the Rimbaud/Verlaine exchange, but it threatens to lose that valency for a more fixed, Ulster meaning.

Pyper's energy verges on violence ('What are you like in a fight?' (*OS* 35)) and he actually strikes Anderson in the groin, before slitting his left hand with the penknife. On this occasion Craig needs no invitation, but bandages the wound:

CRAIG:	Red hand.
PYPER:	Red sky.
CRAIG:	Ulster.
PYPER:	Ulster. (*OS* 37)

The image of one youth bandaging another has its source in the poetry of Walt Whitman and Hart Crane, but the fact that this wound is self-inflicted suggests that loyalism may ultimately destroy itself by the very energies it draws on. The account by Moore and Millen of the beating of a Catholic in Coleraine is not a good portent.

Part III, 'Pairing', presents the eight men home on leave after five months of exposure to war. The pairs may emphasize their difficulty in achieving individual identity but also the possibility that any one coupling has within itself the potential from which a wholly new society might be remade. They recall the pseudo couples of Beckett (Didi and Gago), O'Casey (Joxer and Boyle) and Wilde (Algy and Jack). Although they have left the field of battle, it has not really left them. Pyper seems somewhat resentful of the fact that Craig in the intervening period has saved his life in battle: his tone is rather reminiscent of the character in Beckett's *Murphy* who says: 'You saved my life. Now palliate it.'[16] Craig makes no claim to heroism: he just did what his friend might equally have done for him. He brings Pyper to Boa Island on Lough Erne, a place famed for its hermaphroditic figures, in hopes that they may inspire him to create and sculpt again. The stage is divided into four scenes, each of which maps the 'pairing' between two of the men. Crawford, in another part of the stage space, urges a terrified Roulston to cease depending on traditional religion and leave the church a self-reliant man. Elsewhere, Millen encourages Moore to go across a rope bridge and conquer his fear of the drop by looking straight ahead. And McIlwaine and Anderson conduct their own private Orange march to the Field at Finaghy. There McIlwaine learns a further meaning of the Red Hand motif: that if he is to play the Lambeg drum his flesh must bleed. In the course of their visit, they lament something rotten in the growing relationship between Pyper and Craig. They, for their part, are inspecting the figures on Boa Island, which could be either male or female or both.

Each man experiences something akin to an epiphany in these expeditions. Pyper confesses that the personal care of Craig for him as a friend has brought him back to himself:

> I turn people into stone. Women and men. Into gods. I turned my ancestors into protestant gods, so I could rebel against them. I turned my face from their thick darkness. But the same gods have brought me back. Alive through you. (*OS* 47)

Already, however, the various men are asking guiltily why they have been spared. Roulston suggests it may be God's will, but Crawford assures him that he was stunted by his church:

> I'm a soldier that risks his neck for no cause other than the men he's fighting with. I've seen enough to see through empires and kings and countries. (*OS* 48)

Millen tells Moore to rely on the hand which is holding him up and to cross, but Moore sees only dead people, not living souls, on the other side. The rope bridge might be taken as leading back to the war, but it could also symbolize a frail and now threatened connection with England, which leads them to war. Even their deaths may not be enough to secure the connection.

There is no woman in the play, no character other than the soldier-comrades. The pairings have been cemented by the shared experience of a war which is incommunicable to anyone else. The lives of those at home and those in the trenches bore, in the words of one veteran, 'no relation to each other'.[17] What the soldiers home on leave felt for civilian society was an emotion closer to contempt. In the words of Philip Gibbs: 'They hated the smiling women in the streets. They loathed the old men.'[18] It probably suited the rulers of society that soldiers found their front-line experiences incommunicable: for Lloyd George was sure that if the war were ever described in accurate words, people would insist that it be stopped at once.[19] Yet the shells that burst on the battlefield continued to burst in the ears of the men on leave, and McGuinness is enabled to show how combatants 'work through' their battle experiences in a home setting.

McIlwaine suggests that 'we're all going mad' (OS 51). Crawford, who has by now confessed to having a Fenian mother (thereby confirming Anderson's wily suspicions), suddenly asks Roulston to hear his confession. That confession is devoid of Catholic overtones, yet it may serve to prove that no matter how suppressed the confessional impulse within Protestantism, it will erupt at moments of pressure. There is a sense in which the whole play is Pyper's confession to himself, yet another version of that never to be concluded Protestant confrontation with the single question: why did we do it? In these scenes the younger Pyper develops a more credible account of his sojourn in Paris: his wife killed herself 'because she was stupid enough to believe I was all she had to live for' (OS 56). That sounds like an accusation about what he and his comrades are about to do for their Protestant gods. The escape to Paris was no escape at all: the 'non serviam' was followed not by creation but by a repetition of 'Carson's dance' which he had gone there to avoid: 'When I saw my hands working they were not mine but the hands of my ancestors, interfering, and I could not be rid of that interference. I could not create. I could only preserve.' So he rejected the woman who would continue his breed. Instead, he hoped to kill and die in their name. This would be his nihilistic joke, his revenge for fate's jest 'in making me sufficiently different to believe I was unique, when my true uniqueness lay only in how alike them I really was' (OS 57). The tradition of loyalism speaks most eloquently through those most sure that they had transcended it. But then Pyper met Craig, the unseen obstacle to his deep desire for death.

Some of the early reviewers of the play assumed that it was suggesting a link between an Ulster Protestant identity and a cult of death.[20] Very probably it was, but only such a link as had already been made by, for example, Seamus Heaney between Mother Ireland and the self-sacrificing Sons of Irish Republicanism. McGuinness appeared to postulate, even more radically, a necessary link between all stabilized identity and death. The Protestant tradition was strongest in Pyper when he was least aware of it and it pointed straight towards his own death. The *blutbruderschaft* was founded on a warrior code whose ultimate validation was death, a fact registered by D. H. Lawrence with excited repulsion at the height of a war he was declared 'unfit' to fight: 'And even this terrible glamour of camaraderie, which is the glamour of Homer and of all militarism, is a decadence, a degradation, a losing of individual form and distinction, a merging of the sticky male mass.'[21] Pyper, on the other hand, is 'fit' for the grave. So were the Easter rebels. But Pyper seems fixated on the state of dying and being dead; the Easter rebels wished to look not just at but through death, to a future in which their revolt would carry a weight of meaning. The Ulster Division seems to be dying for nothing. Hence their jealous mockery of the 1916 rebels. The real blood sacrifice of 1916 was the loyalist one.

Such sacrifices also have a personal dimension and it is this which is brought out in 'Pairings'. Against the awful backdrop of war, the tender care of battle-scarred men seems not just miraculous but positively beautiful. The act of love between Pyper and Craig on Boa Island offers a positive countermelody to all the carnage. The deepening friendships between the other men are typical of the 'sublimated forms of temporary homosexuality' which Paul Fussell has found in many memoirs of the period.[22] The unprecedented levels of emotional self-exposure by one man to another seemed like a rehearsal for the moment when each would go 'over the top' and expose his body recklessly to German soldiers. 'There was extraordinary exaltation', wrote Wilfred Owen, 'in the act of slowly walking forward, showing ourselves openly'.[23] One rehearsal was that enacted by Pyper and Craig in the waters of Lough Erne, which allows Craig 'to wash the muck of the world off myself' (*OS* 58) as a prelude to healing. In the poetry and paintings of the First World War, the 'Soldiers Bathing' motif was endlessly recurrent, for reasons documented by Paul Fussell: 'There's hardly a better way of projecting the awful vulnerability of mere naked flesh. The quasi-erotic and pathetic conjoin in these scenes to emphasize the stark contrast between the beautiful frail flesh and the alien metal that waits to violate it.'[24] All the scenes enacted on the divided stage of 'Pairings' might be subsumed under the heading 'Pastoral'. Many of the soldiers who fought in the trenches carried a miniature copy of *Palgrave's Treasury* in their rucksacks: they were perhaps the first fully literate army in the world and their favourite poems emphasized green fields and blue lakes as a version of the home values for which they were staking their lives.

Home for most of the men in the play was an urban setting, Coleraine or Belfast, but their ideal images were of a field such as that at Finaghy, 'the holiest spot in Ulster' (a deliberate echo by McGuinness of Pearse's description of Bodenstown). The idealizing of rural life was part of a more general revolt in the years before 1914 against the catastrophic onset of modernity. Edwardian writing in particular had been filled with Arcadian images of the English countryside, in the novels of E. M. Forster or the childhood stories of Kenneth Grahame: and the most popular poets of the Great War were those who developed the theme. Rupert Brooke, for instance, presented himself as a sort of Pan. According to Granta in 1910, 'he plays simple tunes on a pan pipe, bathes every evening at sunset, and takes all his meals in a rose garden'.[25] Brooke suffered from severe confusion as to his sexual identity and a subsequent nervous breakdown. His life and struggles can be seen to inform the portrayal of Pyper (the name is a giveaway), who shares his view of the long peace as a weary 'sleeping' which could end only in the clarity of death. Even the narcissism of Pyper ('For a man, remarkably fine') has its part in the pattern so described. 'Prolonged threats to the integrity of the body heighten physical self-consciousness and self-love', says Fussell,[26] and the poetry of the period, from Pearse to Brooke, offers a recurrent complex of emotional immaturity and melodramatic self-sacrifice. It may be no coincidence that Craig, and not just Pyper, begins in certain scenes to sound suspiciously like Pearse: 'Sometimes I look at myself and I see a horse. There are hounds about me, and I'm following them to death. I'm a dying breed, boy' (*OS* 57). This Cuchulain complex might be characterized by asceticism, adolescent brooding and a repression of instinct. Its roots lay in an anxious masculinity which found itself in flight from the feminine values of the domestic world so thoroughly disparaged in the recruits' opening exchanges. The alternative to that domesticity (which threatened to overtake all men now that machines were doing the work once reserved for the strong) could be found only in a world of empire and war. As Anderson chants near the close of the act: 'They will die for it. Die, die, die' (*OS* 59).

The chant sounds like one from *Lord of the Flies*. That the attendant psychology may be no more sophisticated is suggested by Anderson himself when moments later he collapses and asserts: 'It's all lies. We're going to die for nothing' (*OS* 59). Each man will perish alone and the separation of space all through the act has served only to emphasize that loneliness: 'I'm on my own here, you're on your own there' (*OS* 59). Such a sense of isolation need not have been a negative factor, if the surrounding context had been more supportive. Hannah Arendt has captured the exhilaration felt by men in the early years of the twentieth century who sacrificed all for empire:

> Playing the Great Game, a man might feel as though he lives the only life worthwhile because he has been stripped of everything. ... Life itself seems to be left in a fantastically intensified purity, when man has cut himself off from all ordinary social ties.[27]

The Ulsters fought with superhuman bravery at the Somme, going over the top in broad daylight: but their gains against huge odds 'were of no military consequence as they could not be exploited, so widespread had the failures been elsewhere'.[28] Their own immediate objective was reached, 'though with such dear sacrifice of men that there was won nothing but glory'.[29] All along the lines, hundreds of thousands of men had sacrificed their lives 'to accomplish precisely nothing'.

Part IV of the play shows the men in a Somme trench, engaged in the final act of 'Bonding'. Pyper's background in the privileged classes has now been revealed, but his fighting abilities are nonetheless admired: 'Nobody's watching over me, except myself' (*OS* 63). He has blotted his copybook and is on his own with all those other persons put to their shifts. McIlwaine decides to relieve the tedium of waiting for the attack with a zany anecdote about events back in Dublin. It concerns 'this boy Pearse' who 'took over a post office because he was short of a few stamps' (*OS* 64). His account is tendentious. The rebels were crybabies, unable to spell the word 'republic' and quite unwilling to take the predictable punishment for traitors. Pearse cries that he has a widowed mother, but as he is led away the old woman grabs a rifle from a Tommy and shoots her son herself, shouting 'That'll learn him, the cheeky pup. Going about robbing post offices' (*OS* 65). Fenians, McIlwaine contends, cannot fight and are a disgrace to the male sex.

The tale is bizarre, distorted, full of unexamined prejudices and half-suppressed phobias. Anderson may be dimly aware of just how much the *mentalités* of the Somme and Post Office have in common and the jocular yarn may be a way of warding off that difficult analogy. But deeper still may lie a pained recognition that Pearse and his comrades had a definite sense of a future republic which would give their deed its meaning. They were in the moment of truth able to imagine each death as part of a much wider pattern. The soldiers at the Somme were undergoing a more terrifying experience, which would make it hard to believe in any values outlasting the life of the individual. Experience in the trenches was entirely ad hoc, at the mercy of the moment, and the lesson of the Somme was that the ruling class had no grand plan which might give the deaths a shape.

This was the ultimate nightmare of the First World War. Its destruction of a developmental notion of history outraged even the more intrepid intellectuals of the time, such as Henry James, who wrote with deep concern that it was all 'too tragic for words'.[30] The deepest wrong lay in the fact that the Protestant bishops had blessed the soldiers who went off to fight in a war which would destroy all respect for authority figures, including those same ecclesiastics, while the Catholic hierarchy in Ireland denounced the Easter rebels, who nonetheless found the courage to evolve an alternative theology which gave their act its moral sanction. (Many ordinary priests, of course, privately blessed individual rebels as they went out to fight.) The effect of both official church policies, despite their differences, was to weaken the teaching power of hierarchies. The young men of the Somme had at least the comfort of visiting the churches of their fathers without guilt before their final sacrifice. The official religion of Protestantism has always been more fully integrated into the loyalist ideology than was the code of Catholics into the republican philosophy, with the consequence that much unionist hatred of the enemy is theological, while most nationalist hatred is political.

No Catholic appears in the play, yet it is made abundantly clear that the whole identity of the Protestant recruits relies on the existence of such people, for (in the words of Barry Sloan) 'anti-Catholicism is not viewed merely as a negative posture' but as 'an essential mark of Protestant identity, a sign of God's chosen people'.[31] So Pyper must pretend that Germans speak Gaelic 'for badness' and that their army is infiltrated with Fenians. (There is some evidence that the rebels were seeking a military alliance with the Germans, but it amounted to little enough in the end.)

The myth of Ulster loyalism requires a definite enemy in order to guarantee its own continuing existence. When McIlwaine and Anderson arrive at the Field on their private re-enactment of the 'Twelfth', they find it quite empty – Ulster is always lonely, empty in Pyper's view, and they are risking death for nothing. The disaster of the Titanic in 1912 seems emblematic of the ways in which the certainties of a complacent pre-war world have been sunk, but it was a world erected on hatred with every rivet hammered into the ship as into the coffin of a Fenian.

The Arcadian moments of remembrance by McIlwaine and Anderson in Finaghy Field represent the myth of a golden age which may contain within it the blueprint for a utopian Ulster. However, it is a wish that is unrealizable because it is based on an emptiness, on a golden moment which never really existed and therefore cannot be revived. So it must convert its search for perfection into a crude assault on manufactured enemies who can then be blamed for preventing its implementation. The only golden moments in Arcadia are those available to such as Pyper and Craig, who are willing to make a separate, personal peace.

The emptiness of Ulster may not be peculiar to that place, however. It may simply reflect the hollowness of the imperial enterprise in its original form. All of the misogynistic lines in the play arise out of a terrible urge to seek male self-sufficiency in conditions which free men from dependence on women, yet such is the smothering effect of a mother's love that most of the men (apart, to some extent, from Pyper and Craig) cannot overcome the trauma of maternal loss and establish a fully adult homosexuality.[32] Hence the narcissism of such figures as T. E. Lawrence, Rupert Brooke or, in the play itself, Pyper: all seem to be in flight from emptiness at home, which may (as much as the search for raw materials or markets) be an explanation for much military adventurism. Boarding schools in which boys learned to drop rank, bear discomfort and do without their mothers were clearly a rehearsal for the army barracks.[33]

Yet the culture of imperialism asked men to offer their lives for the motherland, Britannia:

> Fashioned in the narcissist's dependency on his mother and struggle to be free of her, imperialism offered an outlet for an infantile unbounded desire. The son's sacrifice of his own life for his mother would not be wasted if history afforded him the omnipotence he longed for.[34]

Then, by the usual reflection, the woman can be 'blamed' for the warrior's death.

The closeness of such a process to the emotional world of Patrick Pearse would be astounding were it not so predictable. His attraction to boys remained *croyant* and 'wholly innocent of lasciviousness'.[35] His was an example of that chaste, sublimated trench homoeroticism described by Fussell. He remained always 'ill at ease in the company of women', yet utterly enraptured by the physical beauty of male youth:

> *Tá cumhracht id phóig*
> *Nochar frith fós liom*
> *I bpógaibh na mban*
> *Ná i mbalsam a gcorp.*

> There is a fragrance in your kiss
> That I have not found yet
> In the kisses of women
> Or in the honey of their bodies.[36]

Pearse also wrote a famous final poem to his mother in which his voice is obliterated by her own. It is as if, even at the defining moment of his life, Pearse could not speak for himself, but had to borrow what authenticity he could from the intensity of a mother's love, which drains her sons of identity even as it celebrates their tragic achievement. It may be assumed that a similar ambivalence attended many of the soldier heroes in the British Army of the time.[37] In that context, the play's jocular account of how Pearse's mother 'really' shot her own son (effectively doing the firing squad's work) carries a bitter autobiographical undertow, which cannot fully be dissolved in the humour of the telling. The projection of the soldier's own mother-hatred onto the 'boy' Pearse is all too embarrassingly obvious.

The frequency with which the question of Ireland and the question of homosexuality seemed to interlock has often been discussed. The same Edward Carson who founded the Ulster Volunteer Force in 1912 was the man who had baited his former Trinity College class-mate, Oscar Wilde, in a London courtroom during the playwright's trial; and Roger Casement would in the very year 1916 find his name blackened by diaries which were probably forged by the British authorities. *Observe the Sons* is based on the accurate perception that 'the formative years of unionism coincided with the judico-legal formulation of homosexuality',[38] in both of which enterprises Carson played a prominent part. If the idea of Ulster proves less stable and singular in this play than he might have wished, so also do the ideas of masculinity and femininity and also the still potent code of muscular Christianity. Christopher Roulston chooses to fill the time of waiting with a hymn which begins 'From the depths'. The words recall the prayer for forgiveness and reconciliation 'De Profundis', but that in turn evokes memories of Wilde's long letter of accusation and appeal to Lord Alfred Douglas, an upper-class youth who had beguiled him. The projection of homosexual activity onto Catholic or Irish persons by a nervous British establishment was an old imperial tactic.

So also was the pretence that the business of empire was all a Great Game. Physical-contact sports at schools had been seen as a suitable preparation for the conditions of war, so it is hardly surprising when Crawford urges his pals to find time for a football match. One of the more unusual aspects of the First World War was the number of regiments which went over the top with a football. The tactic was even employed at the Somme, when Captain W. P. Nevill gave a football to each of his four platoons, urged his amazed men to dribble the ball and offered a prize to the platoon which first got a football over the German lines. Although Nevill was dubbed by some 'the battalion buffoon',[39] such nonchalance helped to feed the hope that the attack would be a walkover. One survivor recalled:

> As the gun-fire died away I saw an infantryman climb onto the parapet into No Man's Land, beckoning others to follow. As he did so he kicked off a football. A good kick. The ball rose and travelled well towards the German line. That seemed to be the signal to advance.[40]

Nevill died almost immediately, but two of his footballs were preserved in the Imperial War Museum. The entire episode is rather reminiscent of Thomas MacDonagh's attempt to persuade a captured British soldier who shared his love of cricket to bowl googlies at him with a tennis ball during a lull in the Easter Rising.[41]

The major device adopted by McGuinness's combatants as they await the order to advance is the mock repetition of a joust between King Billy and King James at the Battle of the Boyne. Here two men act the part of horse and rider (the gay implication by now unavoidable) for each side, although the craziness of the situation is highlighted by the fact that the half-Catholic Crawford is to enact the Protestant leader astride his white horse (the blonde Pyper). 'And remember', insists Anderson with a warning note, 'King James, we know the result, you know the result, keep to the result' (OS 70). The same men who played fast and loose with the facts of the Easter Rising want no inaccuracies on this occasion. Yet this is precisely what happens: Pyper falls and unseats King Billy, leaving the other side victors. For those who found the coincidence of July dates promising in its symbolism, it is 'not the best of signs' (*OS* 71). History will not submit to the shape given it by folklorists, whose motto is 'to hell with the truth as long as it rhymes' (*OS* 71).

That feeling of unease is soon dispelled by a debate about the respective merits of the various Ulster rivers. The soldiers may not have known it, but as each asserted the claims of his own locality, he was re-enacting one of the most famous of all Gaelic poetic sequences, *Iomarbhá na bhFile*, on an identical theme. Just as the *Iomarbhá* indicated that regional piety overtook loyalty to any larger form of identity, so also here the feeling is that a commitment to any entity beyond one's immediate neighbourhood is hard to achieve. Yet that is the nature of the bonding required of these men. It is brought about when Pyper, against his previous form, suddenly delivers a speech which brings the men's differing loyalties into common focus.

By that stage the thoughtful Craig has realized that there is no future worth knowing, even for the survivors of that moment: 'Whoever comes back alive, if any of us do, will have died as well. He'll never be the same' (*OS* 74). Even as the men merge into a shared identity, they also recognize that each is on his own: and even Roulston learns that his religious life makes no great difference to one who is no better or worse than the others. Only Craig sees the shape of the future with any accuracy. Pyper had always longed for his body and had claimed to see right through it to the plain sky, that red sky at morning which portends catastrophe but which was also the 'only visible theatre of variety' available to trench-bound soldiers, with the 'power to persuade a man that he was not entirely lost in a common grave'.[42] Now it is Craig who, sensing a shift in his friend from integral individual to purveyor of a communal fantasy, claims to see right through him into a future for him as leader of Ulster's march into nothingness. 'Damn you', he says to his comrade, 'after listening to that little bit of rabble-rousing,

I saw through you. You're wasted with us, man. You're not of us, man. You're a leader. You got what you wanted. You always have, you always will' (*OS* 76). But the leaders of Ulster, he darkly suggests, will be those who have learned how to lie most fluently about this betrayal of the men, even before it has fully happened. For the Somme proved an ambiguous symbol: it fed the unionists' sense of belonging to and betrayal by the British and taught the sharper-minded among them that the one experience might easily be confused with the other. Pyper, by the close, is hopelessly mixed up. His youthful experience has taught him that only personal bonds last, yet he continues through old age mumbling the public platitudes in which he had so early lost faith.

McGuinness's play has been read as 'both homosexual and homophobic, both pro-unionist and anti-unionist'.[43] Desmond O'Rawe has argued that the homoerotic in it often has a negative association, and so does the violent intolerance in forms of Ulster unionism. Yet it is not enough to leave the analysis at that. For one thing, those negatives are all qualities which unionism may hold in common with the nationalist tradition. For another, the play offers a sincere elegy for doomed youth and an attempt to discover some positive values which might be salvaged from Ulster's ruin. By suggesting that all borders are fuzzier than people think, and by emphasizing points of contact for southern audiences, the play might seem to endorse some sort of 'United Ireland' philosophy. Yet it hardly goes so far. Rather, it makes a more qualified set of suggestions. It proposes that all fixed identities are dangerous and deathly, but that to live without some form of identity is impossible. That is the dilemma of Pyper, whose 'bonding' with his companions leads him to defend precisely the sort of society which had once rejected him.[44] Yet some progress is made, for the older man who refuses to meet the expectations of his hearers declines to repeat the rabble-rousing speech made at the Somme. He refuses, in short, to give it all a shape.

McGuinness suggests that unionism has been able to declare Irish rebels, German soldiers, French women and even English homosexuals its Other because it never dared to articulate or interrogate its own code. Equally, those liberal Protestants who disavowed loyalism by seeking attachment to one of these other codes did little or nothing to advance the analysis, because they simply dismissed a unionist belief as a thing of no account. Neither response allowed for the sort of honest debate initiated in this play, which tries to make some sense of the 'deserted temple of the Lord' which is Northern Ireland. In suggesting that unionist identity is constructed around a lack, it did no more than repeat the widespread critique of identity in 1980s critical theory, but in doing that much it implicitly asked nationalists to consider the same possibility as well. It also insisted that a loyalty to Ulster might be replacing that given to the British connection, and that, in this very process, another nationalism might be being born.

In all that it also revealed the common ground on which Irish people of seemingly antagonistic traditions might meet. Only ten years after the play's success, a leading representative of Sinn Féin took part in the annual Goldenbridge commemoration of the 150,000 Irishmen who died in the First World War; and three years after that the leaders of both nationalist and unionist communities signed their names to an agreement which recognized that people on the island might feel themselves to be 'Irish or British or both'.[45]

16. Derek Mahon's Lost Worlds

The dandy confronts the deteriorations of modernity with a face which registers no tremors, but that impassivity is just a pose: inside, the heart is breaking. Derek Mahon wears his rue with a difference. He addresses modern decline with a sense of real outrage, but the indignation is itself a pose. For one thing, it leads him to a fascinated detailing of the minutiae of modern life, beyond whose listings he seldom likes to move; and, when he does make such a move, he takes such a long historical view that he is hard put to sustain a sense of crisis. Things, he sighs, have ever been thus. If they are not getting very much better, analogies with the ancient world also suggest that they are not getting very much worse:

> Now we are safe from monsters, and the giants
> Who tore up rocks twelve miles by six
> And hurled them out to sea to become islands
> Can wrong us no more. The sticks
> And stones that once broke bones will not now harm
> A generation of such sense and charm.[1]

Up to a point perhaps. These lines were written in all innocence before Northern Ireland erupted into renewed violence.

The ruined dandy, like the destroyed Gaelic bards, knows that his life is over; and yet, inexplicably, it goes on. What is the appropriate grammatical tense to capture such a state? Like Samuel Beckett's Molloy, the poet feels himself already dead, yet somehow he can hear the song of the birds. One ear is tuned to the melody of the present moment, the other to the distant sounds that come in on the strange frequencies of a long-forgotten civilization. Such a long view compels the poet also to imagine the future, for if the past was once somebody's hoped-for civilization, so the anticipated future will turn out to have been some even more evolved people's past. In 'An Image from Beckett' the poet contemplates the fate of Matthew Arnold's optimistic version of culture and places it in balance with Beckett's mordant view of a life created astride the grave, gleaming for an instant before it is gone:

> But in that instant
>
> I was struck by the
> Sweetness and light,
> The sweetness and light,
>
> Imagining what grave
> Cities, what lasting monuments,
> Given the time.
>
> They will have buried
> Our great-grandchildren, and theirs,
> Beside us by now. (*NCP* 41)

The bleak, glittering images are austere in their bare intensity, as stripped and reduced as the shards of phrasing in Beckett's own writing; and the anticipatory nostalgia of the speaker indicates a longing to release the present moment, in its capacity to condense all past and future meanings. The landscape, however, is imagined as soon enough bereft of our human presence, which throws the value of this poetic utterance into question:

> Still, I am haunted
> By that landscape,
> The soft rush of its winds,
>
> The uprightness of its
> Utilities and schoolchildren –
> To whom in my will,
>
> Thus, I have left my will.
> I hope they have time,
> And light enough, to read it. (*NCP* 42)

Andrew Marvell, in 'To his Coy Mistress', had asked for 'world enough and time',[2] but Mahon fears also that there may not be enough 'light'. Every poem is supposed to emit the light it can be read by, but he is not so sure. Even Matthew Arnold, who believed in 'sweetness and light', was not convinced that the ancient values of the Aegean world would survive in a bleak northern latitude.[3]

Yet, if being ignored by posterity is one risk, being condescended to is quite another matter. The speaker of 'Lives' (a poem dedicated to Seamus Heaney) began as a torc of gold, buried in the earth for 2,000 years:

> Till a labourer
> Turned me up with a pick
> In eighteen fifty-four

– but he becomes by the close an exponent of what E. P. Thompson has called 'the enormous condescension of posterity',[4] which is to say an anthropologist, equipped with the latest gadgetry, tracing facile connections between the experiences of one era and another:

And if in the distant

Future someone
Thinks he has once been me
As I am today,

Let him revise
His insolent ontology
Or teach himself to pray. (*NCP* 46)

The danger of anthropology is its conversion of past people into mere artefact, its reduction of human life to a discourse of connoisseurship. Respect for life might be less common than a poet hopes, but so also is respect for the dead. When bodies are repackaged as educational entertainment, the culture of the exhibit in a museum takes over from the reality of a felt life. This would be a theme explored by Heaney in 'Bog Queen', but here this writer imagines that the current generation of anthropologists, fancying themselves as enlightened – but so did the peer's wife who exhibited the Bog Queen – will themselves be anthropologized by some equally cold-hearted, irreligious scientist of the future.

An Irish proverb says 'you will be a long time dead when you're dead'; but if consciousness can survive that death, then the chastening effect of the grave may be bracing. Yeats held that the dead may not even know that they are dead:[5] and Beckett developed the insight in having a character say that dead voices can sound like leaves, like wind; 'to have lived is not enough for

them. They have to talk about it.'[6] In 'Consolations of Philosophy'
Mahon writes:

> There will be time enough to live through in the mind
> The lives we might have lived, and get them right;
> To lie in silence, listening to the wind
> Mourn for the living through the livelong night. (*NCP* 50)

Yet the words of such dead people are modified, as W. H. Auden
said, in the guts of the living. So Mahon can rewrite the lament of
the Gaelic poet Anthony Raftery:

> *Féach anois mé is mo chúl le ballaibh*
> *Ag seinnm ceol do phócaí folaimh.*[7]

as

> Is it empty
> Pockets I play to? Not on your life. (*NCP* 51)

– yet the current reality of a two-seminar week as writer-in-
residence seems a betrayal of the tradition. Provincialism in space
can be accompanied by provincialism in time, the illusion that all
of history has been a lead-up to the present moment and that no
perspectives other than those of enlightened secular modernity are
possible. In 'Afterlives' Mahon writes:

> What middle-class shits we are
> To imagine for one second
> That our privileged ideals
> Are divine wisdom, and the dim
> Forms that kneel at noon
> In the city not ourselves. (*NCP* 57)

The effect of these multiple perspectives is to make any reality seem provisional, to heighten the nomad's sense of transience in a degrading world. The scrap metal in the poet's own garden is not so different from that of the gypsies, his intercontinental intellectual travels an upmarket version of the tinkers on the roadside. The rubbish accumulated in a consumerist lifestyle may be despicable but could itself be endowed, like the *objets trouvés* of surreal artists, with an entirely alternative consciousness. So Mahon writes in 'The Mute Phenomena':

> Already in a lost hubcap is conceived
> The ideal society which will replace our own. (*NCP* 76)

The very refuse of a lost civilization may contain somewhere within its hidden pattern the master-narrative of a new dispensation. There may even be an intervening period of no civilization at all, as nature reasserts its claim in the absence of any human presence. The deserted Rathlin Island prompts the same question as that raised by the gay holiday lights of the seaside resort of Portrush:

> What did they think of us
> During their brief sojourn?
> A string of lights on the prom
> Dancing mad in the storm –
> Who lives in such a place
> And will they ever return? (*NCP* 91)

Even poetry – and the very words in which it is written – will not survive; and perhaps language itself will die. The imagination of apocalypse informs many poems by Mahon. It is as if the fear of nuclear catastrophe, so pressing on his student generation through the Campaign for Nuclear Disarmament of the 1960s, has chastened every act of creation on his part, but never wholly annulled it. The excavation in those years of lost cities in Africa and South America may have awakened in him, as did the work of Eliot and Auden, a sense that the great cities of modernity may one day be a tale.

The impulse in Mahon's poems, as in the writings of J. M. Synge, is a 'terrified search for some sign of the persistence of the person'.[8] The present exists only to be swallowed up into the black hole of the future. The waste of earthly resources – another theme of the 1960s pointed up by Rachel Carson in *Silent Spring* – leads to a plea to Gaia for more light ('Remember life on earth!' (*NCP* 312)) and to a conviction that all things must be rebuilt. The noisy fridges in these poems may preserve some organic life for the immediate future, as they do for the old Hag of Beare, 'The Widow of Kinsale'. But most acts of preservation seem inadvertent, strangely random, as when in 'A Disused Shed in Co. Wexford' a thousand mushrooms, waiting since the time of the civil war, incline towards the rays of light that come in through a keyhole. The expropriated owner never returned and, apart from the still strong fungi nearest the door, the others have grown wan in the dark – reminders, like all mute phenomena, of the need for somebody to speak on their behalf, as for all the lost ones of history, those burned alive at Pompeii or Treblinka. They appeal to the insouciant poet:

> · 'Let not the god abandon us
> Who have come so far in darkness and in pain.
> We too had our lives to live.
> You with your light meter and relaxed itinerary,
> Let not our naïve labours have been in vain!' (*NCP* 82)

Hugh Haughton has argued that this poem evokes not only junked objects but dispossessed people, and that it is a sort of descent into the underworld, such as happens in epic, but with the strong implication that all is not yet fully lost. The opening line, 'Even now there are places where a thought might grow' (*NCP* 81), can be read as suggesting no final conclusion, an ending still withheld.[9]

That might be true for someone taking the long view across generations, but for those on the sharp end of history's cruel decisions there is always less time. In the sixty years between the foundation of the Free State in 1922 and the publication of 'A Garage in Co. Cork' in 1982, one in every two people born in Ireland had to emigrate. Mahon's most powerful poem of all is a protest against this emptying. It takes its tone from a joke postcard of a derelict petrol station, the joke being the family name 'McGrotty's'. Rather than punning on the name, the poet treats the picture as the kind of photograph taken of a people-free site currently the scene of a criminal investigation. The man with the light meter has returned to a spectacle of human loss, but on this occasion the metre is not light. The opening word 'Surely' carries echoes of W. B. Yeats, but whereas Yeats intoned it to celebrate ancestral mansions ('Surely among a rich man's flowering lawns') or to mark immense historical change ('Surely some revelation is at hand'), Mahon administers the word as a mild rebuke – to the photographer, perhaps a casual by-passer, for a world insufficiently imagined:

> Surely you paused at this roadside oasis
> In your nomadic youth, and saw the mound
> Of never-used cement, the curious faces,
> The soft-drink ads and the uneven ground
> Rainbowed with oily puddles, where a snail
> Had scrawled its pearly, phosphorescent tail. (*NCP* 121)

History will move too slowly for the 'curious faces', whose owners are already gone, their interrupted lives signified by the unused cement, the snail's long-drawn scrawl a marker of the way in which human technology gives way once again to nature.

But what makes this Mahon's greatest poem, apart from the

stateliness of its metre, is its unconditional sympathy with suffering humanity once rooted in this spot, now gone forever. The snail might even be an image of his own earlier allusion to his luminous if streaky destiny. The sense that many of the amenities created in the Ireland of the 1950s and 1960s were part of some tourist's film-set – and not a real world built to last or to accommodate a thriving population – is terrifyingly conveyed:

> Like a frontier store-front in an old western
> It might have nothing behind it but thin air. (*NCP* 121)

This is what Fanon meant when he described the postcolonial state learning how to consume but not how to create wealth, producing not a simulacrum of a modern goods-driven society but its caricature. It is, literally, all front and no back, a testament to the failure of the industrial revolution to take root for long in many parts of rural Ireland. The family, which invested its hopes in this modern project, is gone, as are many of those motorists who might have filled up their car-tanks there. The site is a ruin of industrial modernity, as remote in its way as a dolmen or cromlech, for nothing seems as distant from us as the recently abandoned past. Over a century after the Great Hunger, one can still hear (in the words of Mahon's friend, Brendan Kennelly) 'an awful absence moping through the land'.[10]

For this spot was somebody's actual home: Nirvana. No longer a sight for tourists or for the sore eyes of moralists decrying neglect, nor indeed a 'site for improvement', the space is filled with sound: the cries of children, a family eating and sleeping, resurfacing the area. But no sooner are they evoked in all their fragile, everyday decency than they are gone. To South Boston? To Cricklewood? The nostalgia they will feel for a lost home will tilt the place towards a mythic realm ('such as Noah knew' (*NCP* 121)), but one rooted in the miracle of the ordinary – hens, thyme, an overgrown cart track and a single blackbird. That solitary bird forever sounds the note of elegy over heroes in Fiannaíocht lore but also over dead or dying people memorialized by Mahon.

The postcard was a typical 1980s artwork. In those years, as Ireland lurched into a crisis made worse by the hike in oil prices of the previous decade, emigration soared. Photographers developed a technique of juxtaposing the old land of Marian shrines and Celtic crosses with rusting motorcars or abandoned washing machines. Articles appeared in learned journals like *The Third Degree* on the beauty of such discards as kitsch. There was a feeling abroad that photography was somehow catching up with James Joyce, learning how to set the mythical and matter-of-fact into some kind of creative tension. But the truth was rather more complex. Joyce had not only aligned the mythical and the everyday: he proceeded to show how deeply one was penetrated by the other, to such a point indeed that they might appear indistinguishable. Most of the fashionable photographs were a lazy juxtaposition, staging (and many were 'staged') as pointless a clash between tradition and modernity as any of the pre-orchestrated disputes that then filled the airwaves.

Mahon is rather sardonic about these montage techniques, which may belittle the efforts of country people to bring some order to precarious lives:

> Left to itself, the functional will cast
> A deathbed glow of picturesque abandon (*NCP* 122)

But he moves the poem through a number of gear changes, in order to make those lost garage owners live forever in their chosen spot:

> A god who spent the night here once rewarded
> Natural courtesy with eternal life – (*NCP* 122)

– so that now an old man and his wife have been transformed

eternally into the two surviving petrol pumps out front, while a virgin who eluded that god's clutch now surveys the townland from the safety of her Marian shrine. This postmodern tale of human life converted to some other form is as old as the Children of Lir; and that tradition of shape-changing arises from the way in which ever-altering cloud formations constantly cause a single spot of land to undergo many metamorphoses in appearance. The clouds which have that effect were mentioned as the poet recalled the filling of a cream Lagonda with petrol while 'A cloud swam on a cloud-reflecting tile' (*NCP* 121). The effect of making one landscape go through endless mutations, so that a single home may become an everywhere, is beautifully captured: 'We might be anywhere but are in one place only' (*NCP* 121).

The story of a god turning old folks into petrol pumps might appear condescending – a glib postmodern flip on old legend – but it is just a way of capturing their sense of being (in Yeats's words) 'rooted in one dear perpetual place'.[11] The state of grace allowed them is a reward for their display of the greatest Yeatsian virtue, 'natural courtesy'. It is as if this is the legacy on which they might indeed have settled for themselves. The sense of specific place inheres not just in the *dindshenchas* of Gaelic tradition, whereby every poet was expected to recite all the lore surrounding a place name, but also in the lives of ordinary people. That sense grows ever more acute after emigration.

Some commentators see this 'reward' by the gods as a savage irony on Mahon's part – as if the stasis which would have been their lot at home, with a celibate daughter, has been averted.[12] However, the lyric in its concluding couplet settles, as surely as would the family, for the limitations of a thinly peopled world, which had the grace and luck to know itself for exactly what it was:

Not in the hope of a resplendent future
But with a sure sense of its intrinsic nature. (*NCP* 122)

Irish Language

The Gaelicization of Ireland, a major aim of the founders of the Free State, was advanced, on some fronts more than others, by the 1970s and after. Gaelic football continued to soar in popularity in most counties, but the ancient game of hurling, though still practised to high levels of skill in certain regions, was nothing like as extensive in reach. The revival of traditional folk music continued apace, with tens of thousands present every year at the annual festival, the Fleadh Cheoil. Competitions in the disciplines of Irish dancing were intense; and after the success of Riverdance as an intermission entertainment in the Eurovision Song Contest in 1993, traditional dancing went global.

The fortunes of the Irish language, however, were more mixed. Students who took their state examinations in the language could in theory get ten per cent extra in marks; and special government grants were given to Gaeltacht dwellers who set up shops where business was conducted in Irish. But such affirmative action measures often proved counterproductive. Grant money given to boost economic activity in, for instance, the Connemara Gaeltacht was increasingly being spent in English-speaking shops in Galway city. And levels of unemployment, during the early 1970s, were even higher in Connemara than in the gerrymandered city of Derry.

While leaders in Dublin paid lip service to Irish (employing only a ritual opening or closing phrase in speeches given mainly in English), the Gaeltacht seemed to be dying. A group of activists, inspired by the civil rights movements in Northern Ireland and the United States, founded in 1969 a group named Cearta Sibhialta na Gaeltachta. And it reformulated Irish not as a national piety, but as an element of the countercultural movements that flowered after the student rebellions of the late 1960s.

Meanwhile, in the cities, parts of the bourgeoisie, which had once found in Irish the basis for the claim to a separatist nationhood, began to lose interest. Many parents felt that their children would be better served learning a continental European language. But in areas of social deprivation, attitudes were often very different. Groups of concerned parents established all-Irish language schools, recognizing that these would be free of church control and yet might become centres of excellence, assuring upward social mobility for their offspring. In the north as well as the south, these schools became the nuclei for a new kind of urban Gaeltacht (in the north the prisons in which republicans learned Irish were soon renamed the Jailtacht). Through the 1970s a revival in the writing and publishing of Irish flowered, augmented by the establishment of a Gaeltacht radio station. It was followed by the emergence of local publishing houses made possible by the new technologies of the 1980s. The Innti group of writers at University College Cork – led by Michael Davitt, Nuala Ní Dhomhnaill, Gabriel Rosenstock and Liam Ó Muirthile – sometimes held poetry readings which attracted many hundreds to a single session.

Yet the plight of Irish was ambiguous. As these advances occurred in literary culture, it was obvious that the language was under pressure. The spread of bilingualism in the Gaeltacht meant that few spoke Irish with the range of vocabulary or precision of idiom of their forerunners. And the decision of the coalition government in the mid-1970s to make a passing grade non-compulsory for those who wished to gain a certificate in state examinations appeared to some as the final betrayal. Irish was still a compulsory subject of study for all but a handful of students at primary and secondary level: but there were increasingly strong arguments that while making it an optional subject might result in fewer students, the voluntary element might arrest the sharp decline in the standard of written and spoken Irish in schools. People still felt that Irish was crucial to the national identity, but few had the will to learn it properly. Those who mastered Irish often asserted that there was a demonstrable link between cultural self-belief and business success: an entire course, Fionntar, at the pioneering Dublin City University was based on that understanding. And the 1990s saw the establishment of a television station in Connemara, which became one of the few non-metropolitan sources of news in Western Europe (the death of the English Princess Diana featured as the fifth item among headlined events on the day in question). The station, staffed mainly by energetic and creative young people, became a sort of default arts channel for the Irish broadcasting service, providing excellent documentaries on writers and on history, as well as offering expert commentary in Irish on continental soccer leagues. It was hard for anyone to say for sure what Douglas Hyde would have made of such a development – but it was certainly interesting.

17. Nuala Ní Dhomhnaill: *Pharaoh's Daughter*

Some poets of the Irish language, notably Biddy Jenkinson, refuse point-blank to allow their work to be translated into English. They insist on being read in the original – or not at all. They know that whenever Irish has been put into English in earlier times, translators have shown too much respect for the target language and not enough for the source. The brilliance of J. M. Synge was that he allowed Irish to remould English, by using it with the myopia of a second-language learner, whose discovery of its potentials had the excitement of surprise. If nineteenth-century translators turned Irish into English fustian, Synge recast English until it became a kind of Irish, with a truly Gaelic syntax and rhythm. He allowed his English to be massively disrupted and rerouted by the base-text. Synge really did make English over into Irish, whereas other Victorian and Edwardian translators made Irish sound like it was halfway to being English anyway.[1]

When Ní Dhomhnaill was a small child, her parents sent her for fostering with an aunt in the Kerry Gaeltacht, where she learned Irish. In later years of childhood, she attempted poetry in English but found that her improvisations in Irish were far better.

Her initial impulse was to resist the compulsion to master Irish, but she soon found that it was mastering her. Much more difficult was the attempt to justify that choice, given the hypocrisy of a state elite which paid lip service to the *cúpla focal* (couple of words), but had no intention of making the full, arduous return to the native language. Like Beckett in his adoption of French, Ní Dhomhnaill may have been half-consciously submitting herself to the process of language shift, undergoing by choice what so many had undergone perforce in the nineteenth century. Others who fled English offered negative reason – its overload of rhetoric; the tiresome wit and wordplay expected of Irish writers; its occasional vagueness. Perhaps some of them also felt intimidated by the achievements of a Yeats or a Joyce or a Synge. There is, however, no sense of such a strain behind Ní Dhomhnaill's decision.

Yet it was a strange call: 'mad', according to her mother.[2] During the Revival period, writers of the national theatre were constantly asked why they did not write in the national language. But now that question was reversed. Ní Dhomhnaill was often asked why, given her excellent English, she bothered to write in a tongue used by just tens of thousands. And who among that small sub-group would ever take up a book of poetry? In 1969 the great prose writer Máirtín Ó Cadhain, lecturing in the town of Nenagh where Ní Dhomhnaill lived, remarked rather mordantly on the ambiguous experience of writing masterpieces in a language likely to die before he did.[3]

It was a fair point. Ó Cadhain also used the occasion to complain that too much poetry was written in Irish by people with little gift for the language. A public spat ensued with the poet Seán Ó Ríordáin, after which Ó Cadhain got so inebriated that he lost his false teeth in the heat of the argument. (On the following morning, when he sheepishly enquired of a barman whether his teeth had turned up, he was offered a choice of three sets, deftly laid out for inspection on the marble bar top.) Sitting in the audience through these debates was the schoolgirl Nuala Ní Dhomhnaill. She was not fazed. For one thing, she already knew that when a book of poems was published in Irish, it could sell 1,000 or 1,500 copies: as many, anyway, as most books by an Irish poet in English. The audience might be small but the impassioned debate just heard by her proved it could be an intense interpretative community. She might also have consoled herself with the famous letter written by W. B. Yeats to *The Leader* in 1900: 'the mass of Irish people lost touch with poetry when they lost touch with the Irish language, which is the language of their imaginations'.[4]

That was a way of registering one dire after-effect of the Great Famine. In reducing so many to silence, it robbed them also of the gift and comfort of poetry. Subsequent clearance of cottiers also marked the end of a centuries-old tradition of recitation and performance. The world of written texts was one which anxiously policed its own activities in a manner often over-deliberated. Great poetry might still oftenest be found where there remained speakers and listeners, for literature must have the urgencies of speech. Only in those parts of rural Ireland where the spoken and written arts confronted one another – perhaps for a last, blessed time in cultural history – might a meaningful fusion be possible. After that the antiquity of all the spoken poetry would be lost.

Ní Dhomhnaill sensed from an early age that she had been lucky enough to write Irish on that cusp. Whereas artists like Joyce and Beckett had to struggle to access the inner stream of consciousness, she found that the tale-tellers of the Kerry Gaeltacht could do this without any act of will, just by speaking: 'And the spoken word, by its very nature and spontaneity, has a plumb-line into the sub-conscious, which, except for the very best fiction and poetry, literary activity very rarely has.'[5] The diminished capacity of literature to render experience has been blamed on the unspeakable horrors of warfare and mental illness: but what if that diminishment is due to an excessive faith in the capacity of print culture to contain all that pain? Ní Dhomhnaill quotes Wendell Berry on this:

> It is not the written word that impairs memory, but dependence on the written word to the exclusion of the spoken. Some experience cannot be put wholly into writing. And so as dependence on writing grows, the communicated experience suffers a corresponding attenuation.[6]

If a language enjoys the kind of global 'triumph' achieved by modern English, it risks losing expressive capacity through overuse. The idiom of computers, airline bookings and business transactions could slowly be exhausting the language of Shakespeare and Austen.[7] At the same time, dozens of lesser-spoken languages (some with no texts whatever) are dying in every decade. As a critical traditionalist of a 1960s hue, Ní Dhomhnaill invested her hope of expressive freedom in a minority language. The Innti poets of University College Cork (of whom she was one) attracted thousands to their readings in the early 1970s. Irish was becoming cool, not as a nationalist piety but as an element of the counterculture against globalization. 'Small is beautiful', said hippies. 'Nothing is great but the minor',[8] wrote Deleuze and Guattari in extolling the genius of Kafka. In Ireland, the Innti poets could all remember Patrick Kavanagh's version of that idea: 'there is nothing as dead or as damned as an important thing'.[9] English was being steadily provincialized by its apparent triumph. While its texts were rapidly translated into Estonian or Greek, dozens of brilliant texts appeared each year in languages of which sole readers of English were quite unaware. The Innti revival was such an instance, because to most readers of poetry in Ireland it remained a closed book.

Ever since the government investigation of 1975 had found that over ninety per cent of people considered Irish a key to their identity, but that less than twenty-five per cent thought it would survive as a community language, the ambivalence of public attitudes had become even more marked.[10] (There had been no official report in the half-century after independence because of fear – lovers of Irish feared that levels of opposition to compulsory Irish in schools would be too high, while despisers of the policy feared there might be strong sentiment in favour of the language. Both groups, in a sense, were proven to have a point.) Some groups had long wished that the language as a test case for Irishness (it was compulsory until the 1970s to pass it in state examinations) would lose traction. As early as *Literature in Ireland*, the critical masterpiece by Thomas MacDonagh published shortly after his execution in 1916, it had been argued that English was now the viable literary discourse in Ireland and that, once all major Gaelic texts had been published in it, it could go forward free of such translations.[11] Even a poet as sympathetic to Gaelic tradition as Thomas Kinsella remained convinced that Irish as a fully expressive community language had died in the mid-nineteenth century: those who now composed in it were like medieval church leaders sending documents to one another in Latin.[12]

Ní Dhomhnaill, while cheerfully admitting that ghosts have a tendency to speak in dead languages, and that Irish was too often taught as if it were Latin, denies that she is a ghost. She knows that responsibility for reviving Irish was passed onto schoolchildren by a wider citizenry reluctant to speak it; and that some who taught it suffered from personality disorders and found its complex declensions, conjugations and irregularities 'character-forming'. She admires Biddy Jenkinson's tenacity in the face of demoralization, her insistence on not being translatable:

[W]e have been pushed into an ironic awareness that by our passage we would convenience those who will be uneasy in their Irishness as long as there is a living Gaelic tradition to which they do not belong.[13]

That is, when you think about it, a richly ambiguous sentence, for it refers with equal sarcasm to essentialist revivalists and out-and-out anti-revivalists. The problem with revivalists is that something must be dead if they are to be seen to revive it. They are really morticians, imbuing a corpse with the appearance of life.

Unlike Jenkinson, however, Ní Dhomhnaill has remained open to translation, in the hope that readers will be sent back with renewed curiosity to the original poem. The ideal translator should be like a good lover – faithful without seeming so. But the fear is that the translator will be traducer and that poetry will get lost in the translation. Yet this seldom, if ever, happens in the versions of Ní Dhomhnaill. Here is the final poem from the parallel-text collection *Pharaoh's Daughter*, 'Ceist na Teangan':

> *Cuirim mo dhóchas ar snámh*
> *i mbáidín teangan*
> *faoi mar a leagfá naíonán*
> *i gcliabhán*
> *a bheadh fite fuaite*
> *de dhuilleoga feileastraim*
> *is bitiúman agus pic*
> *bheith cuimilte lena thóin*
>
> *ansan é a leagadh síos*
> *i measc na ngiolcach*
> *is coigil na mban sí*
> *le taobh na habhann,*
> *féachaint n'fheadaraís*
> *cá dtabharfaidh an sruth é,*
> *féachaint, dála Mhaoise,*
> *an bhfóirfidh iníon Fharoinn?*[14]

And here is Paul Muldoon's version:

'The Language Issue'

I place my hope on the water
in this little boat
of the language, the way a body might put
an infant

in a basket of intertwined
iris leaves,
its underside proofed
with bitumen and pitch,

then set the whole thing down amidst
the sedge
and bulrushes by the edge
of a river

only to have it borne hither and thither,
not knowing where it might end up;
in the lap, perhaps,
of some Pharaoh's daughter. (*PD* 155)

It is a free enough version. Moses, named in the penultimate line, is not cited by Muldoon; and the word 'Ceist' in the title means 'Question', but that translator prefers 'Issue'. For Ní Dhomhnaill the poem expresses the trust she places in Irish to survive the dangers of the world; for him the idea of the fate of the poem itself, the 'issue', may be to the fore. Yet, crediting poetry and trusting Irish may amount to much the same thing, if Yeats's equation between the two in 1900 still holds firm.

Through Ní Dhomhnaill's poems, mothers abandon or surrender their children, by choice or by force. The poem may attempt to understand the thinking of a mother who fostered her out to Kerry.

The mother of Moses could have handed him over to the imperial Egyptian army, who might have cut him in two, separating head from body. For that is what colonizers do, even when they perform no physical violence on the person, contenting themselves with mental coercion. Ní Dhomhnaill endorses Ngugi's diagnosis that a colonial child, in being asked to identify with a distant regime, is also expected to distance itself from the immediate environment:

It is like separating the mind from the body so that they are occupying two unrelated linguistic spheres in the same person. On a larger social scale, it is like producing a society of bodiless heads and headless bodies.[15]

That is sometimes the problem with trying to live in two cultures for the price of one: and it has set up in many people a dispute between intellect and emotion, leaving many dead from the neck down, denatured, unable to harmonize their bodily rhythms with those of nature. But the problem may have roots that go back much further than colonialism.

Ní Dhomhnaill has often asked why the Negative Mother archetype (rather than a more nurturing form of goddess) should predominate in Celtic mythology. The head was the icon of the Celts, forever cut off in warlike acts by a culture which devalued the feminine, so that 'it may be that our head-hunting Celtic forebears played a role in perverting the moderately life-enhancing qualities of the message of Christ into the virulent life-denying force that has come to be Irish Catholicism'.[16] Faced with the possibility that her child might (literally) lose his head, the mother in the poem understandably chooses the lesser evil and entrusts him to the great river of life, sensing that he might some day, having been himself saved, become the saviour of the Jewish people. Gaelic poetry, as far back as Feardorcha Ó Mealláin in the time of Cromwell, had seen an equation between the bondage of Ireland and the captivity of Israel:

Clann Iosraeil a bhain le Dia;
Faoin Éigipt cé bhí i mbroid
Furtacht go grod a fuair said.

The children of Israel who stood by God:
Although they were in bondage to the Egyptians,
Suddenly they found freedom.[17]

The vessel of conveyance may be rough and improvised (sealed only with bitumen and pitch), but it performs the task – as does any good poem – of transporting its fragile cargo. The risky buoyancy of the long voyage is emphasized by the question mark that concludes Ní Dhomhnaill's poem: but Muldoon prefers a hither-and-thither zig-zag journey, a statement of the possibility that some kind foster mother, daughter of a potentate, will have not just the power to rescue the creature but the knowledge to interpret the meaning of the image. A child of the colonizing force may even be the rescuer.

The poem is an example of its own process: an account of how an image, once created, must be let go, because it cannot indefinitely remain the possession of its creator, just as a child cannot always be the captive of its parent. Expression, pressing-out, involves a sense of loss and severance; if a poem makes a claim on the world, it may be of a kind not predicted or anticipated by its maker. There must be a fundamental trust in nature, in prophecy, in the future, and in the rights of those into whose laps a poem, person or language falls to use as best they can. It was hard for Ní Dhomhnaill to feel that trust when some earlier hopes of the Irish language revival had failed, but, even as it floats precariously on the surface waters of the English language, the lyric may be achieving its destiny.

For value can be added, as well as lost, in any translation. 'Ceist na Teangan' may suggest that, the more translated a work is, the more likely that work is to perfect its destined form. The positive ideal of the translator is to reach back, after the divisions into multiple languages caused when the Tower of Babel crashed, to some divine harmony. During the Irish Revival, many concurred with George Moore's quip that if you translated Irish word for word into English, the result inevitably was poetry. He compared the English so produced to 'a jaded townsman refreshed by a dip in the primal sea'.[18] Moore suggested to W. B. Yeats and Augusta Gregory in 1901 that the proper way to modernize the story of Diarmuid and Gráinne was for Moore himself to write it in French, for Gregory then to put it into Hiberno-English, for Tadhg Ó Donnchadha to convert the result into Irish; and, for Gregory, only then, to translate it 'back' into English. The act of translation, far from seeking some essence of a national language, expresses the hope that Bohemia is transnational and that a transnational Bohemia is the artist's only native country.

Translators appear humble, avowedly secondary; but there is always an element of arrogance about their humility, a sense that they may hope to exceed the potentials of their models, which can become literally pre-texts for greater inspiration in their own languages.[19] A risk is run by any author who leaves a text for extraordinary rendition by another. *The Odyssey* is a powerful foundational text, but who is not to say that it is trumped for our time by *Ulysses*? The entire Irish Revival was an act of continuous translation, of energies which seemed to ebb in the native language being carried over (as MacDonagh observed) into English, a retelling of old tales in new forms and styles. A thinly veiled aggression sometimes lay behind the formal external homage offered by the translator: a covert desire to displace and exceed the original text. That desire is not always covert in Muldoon's versions.

All of which raises a question. Exactly what role do translations of Ní Dhomhnaill play in the creative agendas of Paul Muldoon, Seamus Heaney, Michael Hartnett and eleven others (all but two male – the exceptions being Medbh McGuckian and Eiléan Ní Chuilleanáin). There is a high old irony in this, given that *Pharaoh's*

Daughter appeared in November 1990, just months before *The Field Day Anthology of Irish Writing* was published early in the following year and denounced for containing mostly male contemporary poets (the women poets included McGuckian, Ní Chuilleanáin and Boland).

Is Ní Dhomhnailll seeking an even wider fame through validation by these authoritative figures? Are they offering some sort of condescending, protective (mainly male) embrace to a vulnerable Gaelic poet? Or are they, like so many poet-translators, 'blocked' in some sort of writing impasse and using the turbo-charged lyrics of Ní Dhomhnaill to rekindle the creativity within themselves? Renato Poggioli once argued that the translator, in finding the author without, liberates the author within.[20] Over many years, Heaney and Muldoon had vied in producing translations from the Irish. These could be read as conscience-stricken gestures by poets who would have preferred to be composing in the native language, but can more convincingly be interpreted as ways of reigniting the spark or extending their poetic range. Poets in general are not lacking in ambition or self-belief; and there may well have been something honourably self-interested in their willingness to do this work.

One thing is sure. Ní Dhomhnaill denied absolutely that she was offering herself as 'the male poet's Muse: they were my translators'.[21] The notion put about by Cork-based poets from Ó Ríordáin to John Montague that woman is poetry and men its communicators had no appeal for her. Ní Dhomhnaill has in fact been quite scathing about those texts in which a female voice, or 'anima', is given poetic utterance by a man, as in *The Hag of Beare*. She has insisted on an absolute distinction between a woman producing a text (herself) and 'a woman described as a poet in a text produced by a man'.[22] So much for the famous androgyny of the Irish male artist from Yeats and Joyce down to Beckett, giving tongue to Crazy Jane, Molly Bloom or Winnie. Yet dicing with the anima must be one reason why a Muldoon or a Heaney was attracted to this work.

For instance, it allowed Heaney, who was sometimes accused of being macho, to cross gender lines in 'Mo Mhíle Stór':

Fós i mo chuimhní
tán tú bachallach,
tá dhá chocán déag i do chúl buí
cas. (*PD* 48)

But in my memory the curls grew on,
twelve coils in the ripening
crop on your head. (*PD* 49).

– and it permits Muldoon to do the same thing, even by the introduction of a fruit (the quince), which is neither male nor female in his version of 'An Crann'.

All that said, however, it makes more sense to think of the primary poet as a Celtic queen, lording it over her supplicants, those (mostly male) poets brave enough to partake in her inner world. If in 'Ceist na Teangan' she recognizes that she must give up any final, controlling claim upon a poem, so must they. They do indeed generate poems of their own but, as in molecular theory, one glances off another, releasing a wholly new energy, which may have been latent but never fully expressed in either. In the white space on each opening of the book between both versions, there may lurk an implied Hiberno-English poem, even more beautiful and expressive than either of the official languages between which it almost, but never quite, stands.

Since few people at the start of the twentieth century had a formal training in Irish, the revivalists saw translation as a necessary manoeuvre. Douglas Hyde's *Love Songs of Connacht* was a best-selling volume after publication in 1894, not just for the beauty of the lyrics but because underneath each poetic version in English was offered in extended footnote a free translation into

Hiberno-English prose (intended as a crib for language learners but actually far more beautiful than anything above it).[23] The hope was that eventually the carry-over would be complete and, either that the English literature of Ireland could exfoliate without further cross-fertilization from Irish, or else that most people, having learned Irish, would no longer need secondary English versions.

These theories, however, did not fully address the real complexity of the situation. By translating old texts, many Irish writers saw them as if for the first time – as did their readers. To translate them was, in effect, to revive them; and to revive them was to translate them. Throughout much of the eighteenth and nineteenth century, translators were often foreign scholars, compiling anthologies which contained the 'greatest hits' of a culture (often as a psychological aid for those who ruled over its producers). But, as time went on, and especially after Hyde's success in 1894, the Irish embarked on a campaign to translate one another, to translate themselves. No longer content to exist in intellectual ghettos created by outsiders, they wished to design structures better suited to themselves, to write and then rewrite their own history.

If it would be a sin to leave a good poem untranslated, another sin would be to repeat it exactly. The apparent collapse of Irish in so many places created a felt need for translation: but an element of tokenism disabled many nineteenth-century anthologies, which were often made from languages which sophisticated readers would never be expected to learn. Moments of such repressive tolerance might have shadowed the project behind *Pharaoh's Daughter*. Most of the translators are world-famous. If Irish provides the framing source, English offers the framing device, for the overall volume is packaged by cover-blurb and publication details in English only. If Irish represents imaginative impulse in this enterprise, English is the language of the critical reader. Yet, when all is said and done, these troubles dissolve and are forgotten upon an actual experience of the texts. Most translations throughout history are of works important enough to deserve such treatment, and today, when so many texts never make it into English, the significance of those which do make it shines brighter than ever. It is a rare, probably unprecedented, compliment to the art of Nuala Ní Dhomhnaill that so many other artists wish to engage with it. For the translator invariably comes to know a text more intimately than any other kind of reader.

As far as Ní Dhomhnaill is concerned, every person in the world is already translated anyway, already an effect of translation. Because she believes in an otherworld, anything in this world – especially her own poetic creations – are simply renditions of some prior and parallel reality. Or, then again, they may not be. The *slua sí* or fairy folk are at once there and not there, throwing into question the notion of an original. Does the reproduction create for the first time the notion of an original? Or are poems on facing pages like twins who resemble one another, in which case it is possible to ask which gives which its similitude? (As in the case of twins, we can know which was born first.) But if every poem is itself a translation of some other entity, then why would Biddy Jenkinson bother to outlaw a translation of a translation? If every public performance of a poem by an actor or a reader is itself a version, a sort of translation, then the logical extension of the Jenkinson position would be to ban all performances, except by the poet herself.

Ní Dhomhnaill has written most of her prose essays in English. She might have chosen to write poetry simultaneously in both languages, as did Brendan Behan and Michael Hartnett. Yet, for each of them, sooner or later, the option to work in Irish or English reduced itself, for a period at any rate, to a choice between expressing or exploiting material. Whenever Behan wrote in Irish, for instance, his tendency was to keep his eyes trained on the subject matter, even at the risk of losing his audience; whereas when he wrote in English, he kept one eye on the audience, with the consequent risk of losing possession of the material.[24]

For Ní Dhomhnaill there is a sense of remembrance, of re-member-ing, in the work of writing Irish, and hence a link to ideas of redemption. She feels in particular a need to translate the voices of silence from Famine times. 'One might for example speak of an unforgettable life or moment', said Walter Benjamin, 'even if all men had forgotten it. . . for its translatability is what is important.'[25] Ní Dhomhnaill believes that the pain caused by the Famine is transgenerational, not yet fully worked through. The sign that the Irish are still colonized may be found in 'the prevention of that trauma from being expressed as it needs to be – in anger and forgiveness', with the consequence that 'it remains impacted into the psyche'.[26]

The sense of disconnection from the past is a major effect of the Famine. Yet every child who learns a language is learning, however slowly, to reconnect with that past. The child learns words used by dead predecessors, sharing known words in the attempt to acquire unknown ones. That is why acts of translation within one's own language are so critical – why self-translation is no different from the translation of others. A poem translates the voices of silence, as surely as a writing renders the spoken word, or a landscape maps an inner terrain of the mind; yet each enters into a strange vibration with that which gave rise to it. This is what happens in *Pharaoh's Daughter*. The versions in English transform our understanding of the originals, even as each one exists as the mercy of its own creator, its own moment of utterance.

Ní Dhomhnaill is too sophisticated to believe in any simple-minded 'return to the source'. She knows that the much-vaunted native speaker (*cainteoir dúchais*), mistaking himself for an authentic bearer of tradition, is just an effect of a prior colonial translation. The literatures of Ireland suggest that the idea of a singular origin is delusional: Beckett's French may in the end be as Irish as anything by Máirtín Ó Cadhain or Elizabeth Bowen. No matter the language in which one writes, there will always be another one staking its claim. Those who can live on a cusp between two languages embody Scott Fitzgerald's definition of first-rate intelligence: the capacity to hold opposed ideas in the head without losing the ability to function.[27] There is a sense in which the poems of *Pharaoh's Daughter* are themselves already pre-translated, crafted by one who grew up using English for most of the day, even if she would have preferred not to. Máirtín Ó Direáin once said that a modern poet in Irish was compelled to a process '*go ndí-bhéarlaíonn sé an tábhar*' (until he deanglicizes the subject):[28] but re-anglicization must be a constant process in a world dominated by English-language media. In an ideal moment of poetry, Gaelic and Anglo elements may fuse to produce an enhanced persona, but there is also the danger that they may sometimes cancel one another out:

> and the sheer effort of maintaining a standoff of the warring parties is deeply exhausting, All my energies get sucked down into the sub-conscious, with a depression characterized by overwhelming lethargy as its most obvious physical manifestation.[29]

The condition of the Irish speaker in the current generation has much in common with the plight of Beckett's characters: a fish out of water, caught hilariously 'out of role'. For Beckett, the humiliation begins with our loss of immortality at birth. For Ní Dhomhnaill that first loss was re-enacted with her forced removal to the Gaeltacht, and then being forced to leave it once she had learned to love it. Every setting exists to be lost and every relationship is beset by separation anxiety:

> *Ansan d'imís ar bord loinge,*
> *chuireas mo mhíle slán i do choinne.*
> *Chuireas suas le bruíon is le bearradh*
> *Ó gach taobh...* (PD 48)

When you sailed away
My goodbyes were the gulls in your wake.
I put up with rows and with blame
From every side... (*PD* 49)

That is the voice of the women in *Love Songs of Connacht* lamenting a lost young man. Perhaps it is also an elegy on the Irish language, forever won and lost, again and again, whose service costs friends and comfort, a beloved whose hair turns grey even as the passion grows.

'Separation anxiety' – whose elements were defined in a classic psychological study by John Bowlby[30] – is as good a description of post-Famine Ireland as any other. Like the mermaids who found themselves gasping on land, no longer swimming confidently in the waters of the unconscious, the Irish have learned to adjust and survive by denying their origins: '*ag tabhairt cúl le dúchas*'. Learning to live in a strange new landscape called for many transitions, a repression of past memories and ultimately of the memory of language-change itself. The first generation 'on land' was so busy adjusting to new realities that it had little incentive to remember old ones: but the genius for adjustment came at a huge cultural cost across the generations – bad health, denial of the body, fear of the beguilements of music and dance. In the final analysis, there came a fear of dreaming or of art, a censoring of imagination, out of terror at the buried truths which they might expose.

Throughout the 1970s and 1980s, many novels made eloquent connections between contemporary political troubles and those of the war of independence: J. G. Farrell, John Banville and David Thompson were among the writers.[31] But Ní Dhomhnaill followed Beckett in tracing the trauma further back to the experience of the Great Famine, the change of language and climate, the disruptions of migration. Ní Dhomhnaill's subjects, like Beckett's, often suffer from borderline personality disorder and have difficulty in recognizing boundaries between self and other: a problem exacerbated by catastrophic adjustment over a few years from a medieval to a postmodern mindset.[32] The Negative Mother who bestowed on her child a dress, a horse, a harp and then took them all back might be an image of Irish tradition. That tradition relies, in the words of Laura O'Connor, on 'the enabling myth of the disabling mother', whose hostile nurturing becomes nonetheless a source of art.[33]

Whether that false mother is the Irish state (with its hypocrisy towards Irish) or the historic nation (a hag destined again to become a queen) scarcely matters. Ní Dhomhnaill's way of honouring the tradition is to attack it, as in 'An tSeanbhean Bhocht' ('The Poor Old Woman'), translated by Ciaran Carson:

> is gur ag dul i mínithe is i mbréagaí atá gach dream
> dá dtagann, gach seanrá a thagann isteach i mo chloigeann,
> aon rud ach an tseanbhean bhaoth seo a choinneáil socair. (PD 130)

> Folly, I'm saying, gets worse with every generation:
> Anything, every old cliché in the book, anything at all
> To get this old bitch to shut the fuck up. (PD 131)

The passing of the baton in any race is never smooth. Yeats's and Gregory's old woman had the walk of a queen, O'Casey's a surly gob on her; and since their time the *aisling* mode has been thoroughly inverted. This old woman does not re-blossom as glorious maiden: she just gets older and battier. The figure of the crone, from 'The Hag of Beare', through Joyce's milkwoman, Friel's Cass McGuire, Tom Murphy's Mommo, McDonagh's old lady of Leenane, Beckett's final texts, is a surprisingly persistent one.

As a student of Carl Jung, Ní Dhomhnaill knows that age-old repression of the feminine will leave that force in a raw, mutinous state: 'the Hag energy must erupt'.[34] The negative connotation of the word 'animus' in Jung's essays is proof enough of that. But the author here, as in no other case just cited, is a woman, who claims to combat a sexist nationalism by 'using the poems themselves to turn that tradition on its head'. Yet her vocalized tirade sounds remarkably like the ones now familiar on the stage of Friel, Murphy, McDonagh. Perhaps on this occasion the statement is as much autobiographical as accusatory. The lines are coiling in upon themselves, as if they too are unstoppable, ungoverned, what happens when any repressed being is given back a voice. The handover of tradition, like the passing of the baton, is never trouble-free. 'An tSeanbhean Bhocht' may be an account of a second childhood and of its characteristic language. Adam Phillips has argued that Ní Dhomhnaill's poetry explores what happens afterward to 'the languages we learn as children'. He understands that she has no trust in a myth of origins: 'it is something far more disturbing than innocence or order that she wants to recover'.[35]

Every excavation of a past confronts a people with the foreignness of its origins, just as any good translation can make the base text glow with a new strangeness. An artist will reach back to a lost universal harmony, but only in the sure knowledge that it can never be regained. To translate is to invent something all over again. The figure of *bean an leasa*, the changeling of the fairy fort, recurs through folklore as through the poems of Ní Dhomhnaill:

'An Crann'

Do tháinig bean an leasa
le Black and Decker,
do ghearr sí anuas mo chrann.
D'fhanas im óinseach ag féachaint uirthi
faid a bhearraigh sí na brainsí
ceann ar cheann.

Tháinig m'fhear céile abhaile tráthnóna.
Chonaic sé an crann.
Bhí an gomh dearg air,
ní nach ionadh. Dúirt sé
'Canathaobh nár stopaís í?
Nó cad is dóigh léi?
Cad a cheapfadh sí
dá bhfaighinnse Black and Decker
is dul chun a tí
agus crann ansúd a bhaineas léi,
a ghearradh anuas sa ghairdín?

Tháinig bean an leasa thar n-ais ar maidin.
Bhíos fós ag ithe mo bhricfeasta.
D'iarr sí orm cad dúirt m'fhear céile.
Dúrtsa léi cad dúirt sé,
go ndúirt sé cad is dóigh léi,
is cad a cheapfadh sí
dá bhfaigheadh sé siúd Black and Decker
is dul chun a tí
is crann ansúd a bhaineas léi
a ghearradh anuas sa ghairdín

'Ó', ar sise, **'that's very interesting'**.
Bhí béim ar an very.
Bhí cling leis an -ing.
Do labhair sí ana-chiúin.

Bhuel, b'shin mo lá-sa,
pé ar bith sa tsaol é,
iontaithe bunoscionn.
Thit an tóin as mo bholg
is faoi mar a geobhainn lascadh cic

nó leacadar sna baotháin
líon taom anbhainne isteach orm
a dhein chomh lag san mé
gurb ar éigin a bhí ardú na méire ionam
as san go ceann trí lá.

Murab ionann is an crann
a dh'fhan ann slán. (PD 36, 38)

or in the version by Paul Muldoon:

'As for the Quince'

There came this bright young thing
with a Black & Decker
and cut down my quince-tree.
I stood with my mouth hanging open
while one by one
she trimmed off the branches.

When my husband got home that evening
and saw what had happened
he lost the rag,
as you might imagine.
'Why didn't you stop her?
What would she think
if I took the Black & Decker
round to her place
and cut down a quince-tree
belonging to her?
What would she make of that?'

Her ladyship came back next morning

while I was at breakfast.
She enquired about his reaction.
I told her straight
that he was wondering how she'd feel
if he took a Black & Decker
round to her house
and cut down a quince-tree of hers,
et cetera et cetera.

'O', says she, 'that's very interesting.'
There was a stress on the 'very'.
She lingered over the 'ing'.
She was remarkably calm and collected.

These are the times that are in it, so,
All a bit topsy-turvy.
The bottom falling out of my belly
as if I had got a kick up the arse
or a punch in the kidneys.
A fainting-fit coming over me
that took the legs from under me
and left me so zonked
I could barely lift a finger
till Wednesday.

As for the quince, it was safe and sound
and still somehow holding its ground. (*PD* 37, 39)

This poem concerns depression; and yet, although most theories
of art suggest that such melancholy can be contained and purged
by means of poetry, this does not happen here. The fairy woman
could be a hallucination on the part of the speaker, a myth of self-
harm and self-disablement. Or she could be, as changelings often

are, a substitute, a rival for the husband. The speaker could herself be imagining things. It is odd that the other woman speaks in English in a poem otherwise written in the native language; and interesting, also, that Muldoon, unlike the author, does not care to italicize her speech. He makes fast and loose with his source by adding the Latin tag 'et cetera et cetera' (this time in italics). Whether this is to express his lofty condescension to the source text (whose ten line stanza he has impatiently reduced to eight), to the paraphrased husband's discourse, or to the offending fairy woman is left deliberately unclear. The speaker may be mad, repressed, depressed: in the words of one critic, 'where repression is, *she* is'.[36] Ní Dhomhnaill suggests as much about the people of the otherworld: 'I'm interested in why we invent them, the need we have for them, and what they say about levels of our psyche that are not available to us through the modern rational view of the world.'[37] The uncanny thing about that last sentence is that it reads like an almost literal, word for word translation from the Irish.

The fairy woman in the poem not only speaks English, but she also does a rather colonial thing – she cuts down a tree with a new-fangled machine saw. The curse seems mysteriously to have been transferred to the innocent party; or else the blame for an otherwise unaccountable melancholy has been projected onto the fairy. One thing is clear: nature has survived (despite the machine saw) in somewhat better shape than the humans who over-invest in it.

Women's Movement

The 1968 papal encyclical forbidding contraception was the last straw for many women, especially those who were burdened by large families as well as coming under the usual strains imposed by a more expensive consumerist lifestyle. Yet a considerable number of women would continue religious practice for many more years. The country was, nonetheless, ready for radical change: for instance, the right of women to remain at work in the public service after marriage was restored.

Through the 1970s, women's movements asserted the right to contraception, and some even opened family planning clinics which were in clear defiance of the law: they therefore charged for the advice rather than the contraceptive. Such legal loopholes were constantly exploited. One male leader of the Family Planning Association was arrested at the Louth border for importing 5,000 condoms from the North: his wily lawyer helped him avoid jail on the technicality that they were all 'solely for his personal use'. The right of married couples to use contraceptives in family planning had been vindicated by the Supreme Court in 1973, but it would be some years before contraceptives became more widely available (restricting availability to those who could produce a certificate of marriage was famously described by Charles Haughey as 'an Irish solution to an Irish problem').

Both Haughey and Garret FitzGerald held the position of Taoiseach at various points in the 1980s; and both were naïve enough to believe that a constitution was an appropriate document in which to solve the complex question of abortion. In 1983, a ban on abortion was written into the Irish Constitution (Bunreacht na hÉireann) after a bitter, divisive debate, in which the voices of secular fundamentalists and narrow-gauge Catholics seemed to dominate over any more subtle contributions. Three years later, FitzGerald tried to rescind the ban on divorce and until a late point in the debate it seemed that he might succeed. However, a campaign based on the slogan 'Hello Divorce, Goodbye Daddy' convinced some women, frightened about the implications for property inheritance, while many male farmers were terrified that the legislation might cost them part or all of their land under a settlement with an ex-wife, and the proposition was lost. Yet, within a decade, a Fianna Fáil-led government would decriminalize homosexuality and make divorce legally available without any rancorous public debate. The dire predictions that divorce would 'open the floodgates' never materialized. Many couples whose marriages broke up chose not to incur the expense of formal separation or divorce proceedings, because of the prohibitive legal costs. The average number of children in a family had dropped between 1971 and 1991 from four to two.

The present century has seen further reforms: reforms in which the contributions of the women's movement have played a crucial role. In a 2015 referendum, sixty-two per cent of voters opted to ratify gay marriage. It was a spectacular example of Ireland as exponent of both the archaic and the avant-garde. The familism that had remained strong even after legislation for divorce was now invoked as an Irish tradition which should not be denied to gay people.

In the 1990s and after, women began to emerge even more strongly as prominent participants in the workforce; and the dependency ratios, so appallingly high in the 1980s, fell spectacularly as something like full employment was achieved.

18. Eavan Boland: *Outside History*

As late as the 1930s, newspapers in Dublin referred to 'the Irish poet, W. B. Yeats'.[1] It was as if some were trying to reconnect ideas of nation and poetry which he had started to detach from one another over two decades earlier. 'I did not see until Synge began to create', he observed, 'that we should renounce the attempt to build a Holy City of the imagination and express the individual.'[2] The fate of Synge had raised the issue for Yeats: 'whenever a country produces a man of genius, he is never like its official idea of itself'.[3] Having minted a romantic Ireland in youth, Yeats spent his middle and old age fighting hard against narrow-gauge versions which denied the freedom of the artist, but he never abandoned Ireland as theme.

That trajectory was repeated four generations later by Eavan Boland. In her twenties she co-wrote (with Mícheál MacLiammóir) a book titled *W. B. Yeats and His World*.[4] Such was her sense of vulnerability as a woman, when confronted by the masculine poetic tradition which he so awesomely embodied, that she did not notice how deeply his struggle to protect poetry from the claims of a simple-minded nationalism anticipated her own.

After the success of *New Territory* (1967), she went from being 'the poet Eavan Boland' to becoming 'the woman poet'; and in a series of essays sought to explain why the coupling of these words was still necessary, if only to demonstrate new forms and themes closer to the experience of Irishwomen than those practised by male poets. Appalled by the violence in the northern part of the island, and worried that forms of nationalism had led to enactments of violence in more domestic spheres, she challenged the image of Ireland as female, whether crone or beauty, forever calling on young men to die or kill for her – but also to trust her as object but seldom as subject, as image but seldom as author. Nations seemed invincibly gendered: if Germany had a fatherland, France was Marianne, *la patrie*.

Few of the feminized nations went to the extremes of the Irish. Under the humiliations of colonial rule, many men had asserted a reactive masculinity, linked to a notion of a woman whose honour needed vindication in battle. So potent did the myth remain that Eoin MacNeill, Gaelic historian and leader of the Irish Volunteers, felt obliged to remind his men during manoeuvres that there was no such person as Cathleen Ni Houlihan: just a country and its inhabitants for which they might have to fight.[5] But the linkage of Ireland and woman went right back to *aisling* poems, in which a wan woman might be revived by a male saviour. It went back further still to bardic notions that a chieftain was somehow married to his land, which might be bountiful or barren depending on the quality of the relationship. Boland could not possibly have overstated the masculinist discourse in Irish poetry. For an artist whose access to national identity had been arduous and uncertain (she lived through some childhood years in England), it was troubling on recognition as an 'Irish poet' to discover the ways in which that tradition ignored her immediate experience. Yet she never abandoned the idea of Ireland. Where other women like Augusta Gregory had inverted old male myths, she probed the secret lives which they conceal, not least her own.

In doing so, she remained alert to the ways in which weakness rather than strength lies behind male assertion, including the fact

that the very idea of the nation may be an epitaph for the death of
the Irish language:

> This is what language is:
> a habitable grief. A turn of speech
> for the everyday and ordinary abrasion
> of losses such as this.
>
> which hurts
> just enough to be a scar.
>
> and heals just enough to be a nation.[6]

The scarring is felt in the ways the spoken rhythms push against
and abrade the line units; and the woman's experience of secondary
scar tissue after a painful birth becomes a way of recognizing the
communal experience. 'Mise Éire' repeats Patrick Pearses's *odi
et amo* ambivalence about a nation betraying itself. Yet, where he
began in pride ('I bore Cuchulain the valiant') and ended with the
image of a mother betrayed ('My own children sold their mother'),
she moves from negation ('I won't go back to it') to a complete
identification with the pain of a migrant mother huddling a
half-dead body:

> mingling the immigrant
> guttural with the vowels
> of homesickness who neither
> knows nor cares that
> a new language
> is a kind of scar
> and heals after a while
> into a passable imitation
> of what went before. (*NCP* 129)

Here the title, 'Mise Éire', remains in Irish, untranslated, as if to suggest that any imitation, even though passable, must be regretted; and that the experience, though it can be guessed at, cannot find expression in any poem commensurate with it.

The poet of women's lost lives feels forever belated, happening as if by accident on the emptied scene of some almost forgotten crime:

> How slowly they die
> As we kneel beside them, whisper in their ear.
> And we are too late. We are always too late. (*NCP* 188)

Even the dead might not be safe from conscious-stricken descendants.[7] James Joyce had anticipated the thesis – that the idea of nation is a myth structured around a lack – when he dubbed the Irish 'the most belated race in Europe'.[8] But all artists feel themselves belated in their grappling with intimidating antecedents: the conviction that history has long since happened, elsewhere. In seeming to give voice to those who were so traumatized as not to be fully present even when history happened to them, the poet is just admitting candidly to marginality. Marginality but not helplessness, because 'the very injustices which made it inevitable that an Irish writer would write in English can be addressed in the writing'.[9] Nevertheless, we have already noted Jacques Derrida's observation that one should never pass over in silence the language in which the question of the language is raised.

Gaelic poetry was shared intensely across the community until the decades before the Great Hunger: but the misfortune for a woman poet of the mid-twentieth century was that, by the time she had been recognized as a member of the band, poetry itself has ceased to be communal. Worse still, because they were saying new things in new forms, women had to create the very critical understandings by which their poems could most adequately be judged, in effect doing the work of two.

Some of Boland's new themes were very old, seeming radical to a generation raised on a poetry built around Victorian ideas of nation, empire, public life. She practised a lyric of small things – children's combs, tea-caddies, domestic objects. That had in fact been the aesthetic of nature poets as described by Kuno Meyer in *Selections from Early Irish Poetry*.[10] In rebellion against the moralism of religious texts which they scribed, the ancient writers often entered doodles in the margins of their texts – about cats, food, or their own distractability from the big themes:

Mo náire mo smaointe
A mhéad éalaíd uaim;
Is eagal liom sceimhle
Lá an bhrátha bhuain.

My shame my own thoughts
And how they escape me;
I fear terror
On Judgement Day.[11]

Like Boland, these dissident scribes, though aware that they might be adjudged trivial, took a perverse kind of pride in their rootedness in the everyday. As she would try to do, they rendered the concrete image with an exactitude at once laconic and rich.

Boland knew the Celtic poets, but she would have been aware of how the patriotic English-language lyrics of *The Spirit of the Nation* in the works of Thomas Davis and Charles Gavan Duffy represented a less focused type of lyric. These ballads and poems were published in 1848, yet she claims that no word in them 'refers to the crisis of the Famine',[12] so detached had poetry become from the people in whose name it was written. The poor in coffin ships were outside patriotic balladry as well as outside written history.

Her hope was that their experiences, recoverable through oral tradition, might animate a redefined Irish poetry.

The writers of the nineteenth century enlisted her sympathy. For a young woman who, as the child of a diplomat, had a nation long before she felt a country, it was too easy to credit 'the rage and anxiety of a long nineteenth-century hunt for a place'.[13] The noble desperation of men whose nation was a high abstraction, as they lived their lives 'within sight of the gibbet',[14] recalled the precarious lyric intensity of a Wyatt or a Raleigh. But to her, Young Ireland had worked in an out-of-date mode. She was closer by far to T. S. Eliot with his descriptions of the sights, sounds and smells of a city settling down to its ordinary evening, as in 'Ode to Suburbia':

> Six o'clock: the kitchen bulbs which blister
> Your dark, your housewives, starting to nose
> Out each other's day, the claustrophobia
> Of your back gardens varicose
> With shrubs make an ugly sister
> Of your suburbia. (*NCP* 66)

The celebration of Boland as the laureate of women – titles such as 'Night Feed', 'Mastectomy' from the 1980s are indicative – has obscured an equally radical innovation: her introduction of suburbia, in which more and more Irish people lived, as a setting worthy of literature. That would, of course, enable a rising generation of novelists like Roddy Doyle and Dermot Bolger, intent on capturing the life of housing estates which managed (like Ireland itself) to seem at once unfinished and used up. Like them she came to know the eerie life of incomplete rows of houses built on the side of some mythic hill, where legendary heroes once had provided the material for some fantastic tale. Her poem 'The War Horse' of 1975 is perhaps the first of many texts to register the surreal surprise of a wild mountain horse creating minor havoc in suburbia. Eventually, the image would be hackneyed to the point of self-parody in the work of others, with the appearance of a white horse in a high-rise elevator on a northside Dublin housing estate: but it was Boland who made this world possible for poetry, as surely as Kavanagh did the same for the stony grey soil of Monaghan. There is a quotation from Adrienne Rich to which Boland recurs, which captures the poet's search to secure new territory for art: 'a difficult and dangerous walking on ice, as we try to find language and images for a consciousness we are just coming into and with little in the past to support us'.[15]

Boland worked through the 1980s in 'the equivalent of a labor-atory in the garage',[16] an image which links her to younger artists of that decade from Bolger to Bono, who also wrote about suburbia from such locations. If her example gave many women courage to write their lives into poetry, her themes seem to have even more often been reworked by young men into prose. There was, of course, a major precedent for this chronicling of everyday life in Joyce's *Ulysses*, a book in which the making of a cup of tea in a kitchen takes on a heroic dimension. Nobody and nothing comes from nowhere. Even 'Night Feed' has some distant precedents in Yeats's 'A Prayer for My Daughter', though it is hard to imagine the Nobel laureate administering the bottle himself at two in the morning. Anne Yeats once remarked drily of a famous photograph of her as a very small girl with the poet: 'you can tell that father cannot wait to get his hands back on a book'.[17]

All of this shows a Boland more influential, and more precedented than some of her more extreme followers (and detractors) would like to think. Her aim was to renew the Irish tradition, not destroy it; and she understood that the best way to revivify an inheritance was to critique it. Her object was the same as that of Jane Austen: to find a mode of existence for her critical attitudes within the prevailing order rather than outside it. She is forever returning to the matter of Ireland, despite 'the power of nationhood to edit the reality of womanhood'.[18] One danger lay in submitting to the stereotypes of the suffering, passive *spéirbhean* or skywoman; the other (arguably more scary) lay in movements of excessive reaction to such images. By the 1980s the anti-nationalism of most intellectuals was axiomatic, given the murderousness of the IRA campaign and the British security response: but it took a certain courage to hold to the national idea.

Boland could no more transcend her gender than her nation. To her the notion of a transcendent human identity was 'an extremely suspect concept',[19] a sentimentalization by new radicals. Yet her poetry exists always in a fruitful tension with the national ideal. The very neutrality of the state, which her father defended through the Second World War, becomes for her an example (however questionable) of a balance that must be kept by a poetry confronted by the latest atrocity:

The night he comes to tell you this is war
you wait for him to put on his dinner jacket.
The party is tonight.
The streets are quiet. Dublin is at peace.

The talk is of death but you take
the hand of the first man who asks you.
You dance the fox-trot, the two-step,
the quick step. (*NCP* 175)

This is an honest way of reducing the distance between poetry and actual experience: but it does so by probing a zone of silence, of necessary unknowability between the one and the other. The suffering women of history cry out for some commemoration, yet the hardest of all lives to realize may be your own, to bring text and life into alignment. The risk of the actual, as Kavanagh showed, might be the most exciting risk of all. It called for a complete reimagining of the poetic persona, away from the self-regard of someone bearing a national idea: a childhood watching diplomats had probably alerted Boland to the possibility that whoever claims most loudly to represent a nation is most often the one least qualified to speak for it. Against all that, she was convinced that style was a world elsewhere in which a real change of heart can be found.

There are various ways of dealing with an old story. One can just retell it as known: but nobody does that, because writers will use a story to give utterance to some secret within. Or you can show how it repeats itself in our everyday lives as Joyce did, whenever food is prepared or a child loved. Men and women think they are telling the myths, whereas all the while the myths are telling them. Or you can, in showing the secrets it tells about ourselves and our ancestors, probe also what it occludes. Virginia Woolf, confronted with the tale of Shakespeare, began to imagine a life for a possible sister of his.[20] Boland often tries to give a shape to lost moments in the lives of her ancestors, poor women living on the edge. Her prose work *Object Lessons*, surely the most beautiful Irish autobiography since *Reveries Over Childhood and Youth*, repeatedly offers such virtual histories, while also proofing itself against the condescension of posterity. It recognizes the sad fact that most Irish people have been bystanders of their own history, blown here and there by forces never fully understood. The peasantry were themselves as disempowered as women, objects of an art which never for a moment suspected that they might one day be its subjects. But they were also – men and women – the ones who shaped those legends whose occlusions and blind spots are now so troubling.

In 'Listen. This is the Noise of a Myth', Boland offers a pictorially seductive version of the elopement of Diarmuid and Gráinne. Such persons may have existed, she speculates, but over time the actuality got encased in the emblematic art of a story. Yet the tale was told over and over by real enough people, whom it may have helped to sugar over the pain of migrations, forced marriages, lost loves. This was one of those poems produced by Boland in her suburban garage laboratory: and it is accordingly sceptical about the fixed version assumed by the tale. No sooner has she begun her retelling of a man and woman under a willow tree than she interrupts it, as if to suggest that the line of history can be bent and even broken by a free artist's will:

> They are fugitives. Intimates of myth.
>
> Fictions of my purpose. I suppose
> I shouldn't say that yet or at least
> before I break their hearts or save their lives
> I ought to tell their story and I will. (*NCP* 152)

But her retelling of the couple's hard travelling under winter conditions brings her back to the point of origin under the willow. The tale seems inexorable, the myth more powerful than the poet's scruples; and yet suddenly the costume drama of repetition is abandoned for a piercing set of questions:

> Legend, self-deception, sin, the sum
> of human purpose and its end; remember
> how our poetry depends on distance,
> aspect: gravity will bend starlight. (*NCP* 153)

The light from those stars is sourced far back in time, yet even it can be distorted in transmission:

> Forgive me if I set the truth to rights.
> Bear with me if I put an end to this:
> She never turned to him; she never leaned
> under the sally-willow over to him. (*NCP* 153)

But this is just a storyteller's trick, to gain the interest of her listeners; and to free Gráinne of 'the bereavements of the definite' in a story of lovers that was 'never mine': 'She may or she may not. She was or wasn't' (*NCP* 154).

All that can be said for sure is that these tales are 'poultices' placed over old sores – 'evicted possibilities', 'displaced facts' (*NCP* 154): they conjure up those stories of travel and pain from the past which leads contemporary tellers, in some desperation, to evoke them. Boland in the end accepts the story as a story with some reparative functions, rather as she accepts the creation of a nation as the scar tissue over the wound of a lost language: 'And when the story ends the song is over' (*NCP* 154). The problem with art is that it prettifies even the worst suffering, because distance gives permission for the process to begin; and the attempt to get back closer to the moment is often unavailing.

Nevertheless, Boland persists in the attempt, worrying that her suburban poems led merely to creation of a new myth, which deflected into that world of change and family growth the sadness of another way of being outside history – a process which would underlie and ultimately explain the collapse of Tiger Ireland.[21] The frantic new consumerism was at once an unprecedented form of 'monetary nationalism' and a denial of the national past.[22] In an interview in 2010, Boland confessed that: 'I'm not sure we're going to know for years where our so-called private lives begin and where the life of the nation ended.' The question for her now is whether 'we're less Irish or, worse again, were never Irish in the way we thought we were'.[23]

Not that she was ever sure of what being Irish might entail. Robert Emmet, romantic hero and scientist, had said in his oration from the dock that his country had yet to be made and to take its place among the nations of the earth: 'then and not till then let my epitaph be written'. But Boland asks an even harder question: what if the nation is itself the epitaph on the very impulses that gave rise to it?

Her condition is paradoxical: 'By imagining a nation, I was beginning the very process, awakening the very faculty that would bring me into conflict with it.'[24] For her, as for Emmet, the nation has yet to be made. It lies up ahead, in the uncreated conscience of Joyce's Stephen, in the noble house of Pearse's thought, in the life of Gráinne as one of the undocumented. No wonder that Boland is haunted by Emmet's later, more cryptic, words on the scaffold. Three times the executioner asked: 'Are you ready, sir'? Eventually, Emmet said 'not yet', at which point the trapdoor was sprung. And in that moment, says Boland, Emmet disappears: 'he becomes a legend and excuse'.[25]

19. John McGahern's *Amongst Women*

Whenever a world is about to disappear, a poet emerges to utter it, and through that poet it achieves a comprehensive articulation. If that world has been self-enclosed or cut off by the facts of nature from a wider society, then it often reaches such a point of artistic refinement through its own inner resources. Tomás Ó Criomhthain on the Blasket, J. M. Synge on Aran, W. B. Yeats on Anglo-Ireland, Kate O'Brien on the Victorian Catholic upper class – all these became elegists for a dying culture. In every case it was a culture that remained so separate and so sequestered as to evoke that intense form of writing that is poetic, even though it is formally offered as prose.

John McGahern was born in Dublin in 1934 but grew up in Ballinamore, Co. Leitrim, where his mother was a teacher. The father, a police sergeant, lived thirty miles away in the barracks at Cootehall, Co. Roscommon, and it was to these that the boy was moved following the death of his mother in 1945. Encouraged by a local Protestant family, the Moroneys, to enjoy the run of their library, he developed a love of reading. Yet the early experience of death and removal was crucial.

McGahern is the major contemporary inheritor of a durable mode of Irish writing: an artist of the self-enclosed world. Another name for this kind of work is 'epic'. In his books he attempts, like Yeats in *On Baile's Strand*, to study the fate of those heroes who survive to live in the wan afterglow of a heroic engagement. In *Amongst Women* (1990), that engagement is the Irish War of Independence itself. The central character is Moran, a man who experienced the frustration of an incomplete revolution but who must now live through the long diminuendo of the death of his revolution. The guerrilla fighters, of whom he was a great and successful leader, have lost their old glamour and been replaced by a cunning breed of priest, politician and doctor. Doubtless, all this was inevitable, the sad destiny of revolutions everywhere, but Moran, who had always expected to die in action, must now endure the indignities of an ignoble peace. 'What was it all for?', he asks; 'the whole thing was a cod.'[1] Only seven of the twenty-two men in his flying column lived to witness the truce, and they were in most ways the unlucky ones, doomed to live like aliens in the new land that they had brought into being.

The portrait of Moran owes something to the one truly great autobiography to emerge from the war, Ernie O'Malley's *On Another Man's Wound* (1936). O'Malley also never expected to survive the battles and found the post-heroic world quite underwhelming. In a subtle comment on O'Malley's other major book, *The Singing Flame* (1978), which treats of the civil war, McGahern has observed: 'There is a pervasive and sad longing throughout for the clarity of action, as if action in itself could bring clarity to the confusion and futility of friends and former comrades fighting one another.'[2]

Moran bears the name of one of the defeated, immobilized protagonists of Samuel Beckett's trilogy, and his search, like theirs, is for a tense appropriate to a man whose life seems over, even while it still goes on. He seems to live entirely on prospects and even more on retrospects, but he can never submit to the sacrament of the present moment, being cursed always to take long views. The past is a storehouse of memories to rebuke the mediocrity of the present. The future is only what that mediocrity will become. All of McGahern's central characters have a sort of second sight by which the shape of a future life becomes discernible, but that shape is seldom consoling, and they would do far better to live without that knowledge. The trick, seldom mastered, is to realize the present, to submit to the immediate moment. This is all but impossible in a culture so denuded of sustaining traditions: the world of Moran has divested itself of the old folk and musical lore, but the vacuum has not been filled by a more modern version of civility or culture. Rituals of death abound in a landscape that otherwise knows only the death of ritual. All the old institutional supports to human decency have been stripped away.[3]

This state of things poses the major technical problem for McGahern. If the short story is the form appropriate to the hunted outsider figure, the novel is the one calibrated to a fixed and settled society. Yet post-independence Ireland had scarcely evolved the sort of layered social fabric from which a novelist might draw some threads: this may account for the sense of loneliness and isolation in McGahern's world. The novel implies a sense of social amenity, shared discourse, even collective leisure, such as Ireland was beginning to settle into at the mid-century, but the very choice of that form implies a defeat for Moran's world of outlawry and heroic dissidence. *Amongst Women* may have begun as a short story about such a figure, only to turn into a novel whose real focus is on his daughters: it is with them that the narrative begins and ends.

The simple opening sentence indicates a new social order: 'As he weakened, Moran became afraid of his daughters' (*AW* 1). They epitomize the complexity of a modern life to which he has never fully submitted, yet they also carry its stigmata of anomie and alienation that leave them longing for 'home'. Even after years of married life in great cities, they will think of Great Meadow as their still centre. In those cities they are but 'specks of froth' against the passing scene, whereas in Great Meadow they feel themselves aristocrats of 'a completed world' (*AW* 2). The discrepancy is akin to that predicted by an aunt for the nine-year-old William Yeats, as he set out from Sligo for London: 'Here you are somebody. There you will be nobody at all.'[4] Great Meadow confers the shape and structure of a life on the Moran daughters, and they cannot allow their father to die until his life also assumes the contours of a real meaning. However obscurely, he resents their refusal to let him slip away, sensing in it a version of his own fear of death, now far deeper and more demeaning than in the days of the flying columns.

The narrative of those days requires the epic boasting of the short, self-contained anecdote. As Moran and his former lieutenant regale each other with accounts of ambushes of English forces who seemed almost to court defeat, they lament the lost splendour of that epic world. Moran notes, 'For people like McQuaid and myself the war was the best part of our lives. Things were never so simple and clear again' (*AW* 6). Moran was not sociable, and he was unable to make the sort of friendships that advance a peacetime career: the closest he got to any man was when he saw him through the lens of a rifle. He has not prospered in the new business order to anything like the same extent as McQuaid, a cattle dealer who drives a Mercedes. Yet even McQuaid has done his utmost to recreate his jobbing world in the image of the flying column. As exploitative as Moran of his women, he abandons his wife and home without explanation for days on end, only to burst suddenly into the house with demands for feeding and watering: 'there's six men here with lorries' (*AW* 13).

Their accounts of the fighting are almost Homeric in the detail accorded to passing engagements and also in the telescoping of major events: 'Next we had the Treaty. Then we fought one another' (*AW* 18). Moran has the gift of few words and of telling understatement, but it is a mode that seems to be ratified by the surrounding narrative, for the dialogue is never a record of how the characters speak, so much as a shorthand summary of their way of speaking. The supreme economy of McGahern's writing, which never draws attention to itself and always gives exactly the image that it receives, is achieved in the taut, telegraphed conversations. Neither the characters nor the writer would regard word play or manipulations of language as anything other than self-indulgence. It is as if the characters themselves have come to understand the artistic principle that the most effective utterance is that which leaves out more than it lets in.

The anecdotes told by Moran and McQuaid to the girls at the outset are really a collection of war stories. So, in a deeper sense, is the book as a whole. Its epic quality owes much to McGahern's deep immersion in Tomás Ó Criomhthain's *An tOileánach* (*The Islandman* 1929), the classic account from within of Blasket Island life in the late nineteenth and early twentieth centuries, for the world surrounding Great Meadow is never described, since intimacy with it has already been assumed.

If every artist is to some degree a translator, in the sense of one who knows how a tradition may live in the very lament for its passing, then this is especially true of McGahern, who has always recognized that no lament is ever final. In Ireland the account of the eclipse of one dispensation may itself provide the narrative form that enables its own successor. If the novel is in ways a domesticated version of epic, then *Amongst Women* may also be read as an attempt to assess what happens when certain epic values are 'translated' into the discourse of a more modern world.

The mythic element is present in the refusal of the narrative voice to set *Amongst Women* in a very particular time or place (although references to Boyle and to Elvis Presley suggest the north midlands of the late 1950s or early 1960s). McGahern has praised this element in *An tOileánach*, that 'could as easily have taken place on the shores of Brittany or Greece as on the Dingle Peninsula'.[5] For him the truly great writers are characterized by the same virtues and the same abiding themes: only journalists and local colourists are seekers of difference, people who mistake variety for truth.[6] By this method, the writer manages to be utterly faithful to his immediate world of Roscommon/Leitrim, yet by keeping the references to that region vague and sparing, he can treat it as an everywhere.

The great evil to be avoided – as it was avoided by Ó Criomhthain – is to treat the events narrated as part of some portentously national narrative. All literature for McGahern, like all politics, is local: he once joked that Ireland is an island composed of thirty-two separate, self-governing republics called counties.[7] It follows that the style of the narrative will be less an expression of the author's personality than a strict expression of the reality of the social world that it is asked to record. The subject, in short, determines the style, and it would be an act of near criminal egotism for an author to develop a personal signature that might then come between the reader and the reality to be presented. Which is not to imply that the author lacks personal feeling or opinion about all that he records. Yet these are expressed only seldom, and therefore to some telling effect. In that, at least, McGahern is at variance with Ó Criomhthain, who rarely offers a personal view and never one that rejects the conventional wisdom of the island.

Much of the authority of McGahern's writing derives from its combination of felt intimacy and achieved distance: he writes again and again of the power of local custom, but often having captured that power, he analyses it with the steely language of a somewhat bemused anthropologist, convinced that there must always be some practical explanation for patently strange behaviour. At times it is the sense of intimacy that is uppermost, even in the course of a cool analysis: 'Moran was neither rich nor poor but his hatred and fear of poverty was as fierce as his fear of illness which meant that he would never be poor but that he and all around him would live as if they were paupers' (*AW* 10). On other occasions the distance is positively interstellar, as if a Martian newly landed were reporting to people back home on the behaviour patterns of civil servants in Dublin, when confronted suddenly with a runaway brother: 'Such is the primacy of the idea of the family that everyone was able to leave work at once without incurring displeasure. In fact their superiors thought the sisters' involvement was admirable' (*AW* 106). Yet, even in such moments (which are rare enough to be worthy of comment), there is little sense of authorial self-assertion: rather, the method recalls that of Joyce's *Dubliners*, in which 'people, events, and places invariably find their true expression'[8] because material and form are inseparable as water and a bucket.

In *An tOileánach*, Ó Criomhthain expresses a deep, primordial fear of the day when he must draw that most modern of blandishments, a state pension: 'I have only two months to go till that date – a date I have no fancy for. In my eyes it is a warning that death is coming, though there are many people who would rather be old with the pension than young without it.'[9] The same fear may, at least in part, account for Moran's unwillingness to draw the Irish Republican Army (IRA) pension to which his exploits entitle him: McQuaid berates him for a false pride that denies his daughters good money that might further their education. But no Cuchulain ever took a state pension. Beneath the surface camaraderie of the two former soldiers lurks the old warrior desire to be top dog. Moran may be unconsciously envious of McQuaid's material success, and so the last reunion between them erupts into bitter recrimination. McQuaid notices his comrade's need to bask in the glow of perpetual attention (which he takes as a kind of cosmic ratification), and he quits the house, in terminal irritation at Moran's compulsion 'to have everything on his own terms or not at all' (*AW* 21). Before leaving, however, he says very simply, 'some people just cannot bear to come in second' (*AW* 22). It is, perhaps intentionally, as good an explanation of the causes of the civil war as has yet been given.

Thereafter, Moran senses that his doom is sealed. His long periods of withdrawal from family life, periods in which he often takes to the bed, seem to indicate a sullen revolt against the waning of his powers. He is in his way rather like those plates that his daughters broke on the kitchen floor out of sheer nervousness: 'Anything broken had to be hidden until it could be replaced or forgotten' (*AW* 10). And so he resigns himself to the loss of his last remaining comrade, turning to the family structure for a compensating sense of himself: 'in a way he had always despised friendship; families were what mattered, more particularly that larger version of himself – his family' (*AW* 22). This seemingly innocuous sentence may also be the best reason yet formulated for the fetishizing of family in the constitutional debates of the 1930s: it was less an assertion of the social bedrock than a flight from the very idea of society as such.[10]

The fear of the pension is really a *timor mortis*, and to stave that off, Moran resolves to marry again. His courtship of Rose Brady is conducted in the local post office, to which he goes on a daily pilgrimage in fruitless hope of a letter from his son Luke, now in England. Only later will it transpire that Luke left following a beating by the father which took him within an inch of his life. The normally unsociable Moran must visit the family of Rose Brady: 'though her mother disliked him, the custom of hospitality was too strict to allow any self-expression or unpleasantness' (*AW* 28–9). Rose is attracted by his sense of separateness, his superiority and self-containment. Her worried mother asks his children (whom she likes) about the rumours of beatings, but loyally they deny that these are worse than usual.

At a barn dance, where once he had been king of the night, Moran refuses to take a lesser place: 'He would not take part at all' (*AW* 37). Soon he no longer bothers to shave before his visits to the post office, showing that 'he had gone as far towards Rose as he was prepared to go' (*AW* 31). At the wedding he wears no new clothes, only his brushed brown suit, and he shames his daughters by walking the last furlong to the church in breach of a local custom that calls for a car, much as he appals the Bradys by insisting that the wedding feast be held in their home. In years to come even the simplest gatherings of that family were held in hotels, as if to exorcize the terrible memory of that violation of social decorum, and this even though the officiating priest had praised the 'outstanding simplicity' as a return to old ways (*AW* 43). This is the sole reference to the priest in the novel, as if in this walk-on role he were no longer a real spiritual force in the lives of the people, whatever his social éclat. Moran, who despises priests and doctors as the illegitimate beneficiaries of his revolutionary activities, is strangely serene on his wedding day, 'as if he needed this quality of attention to be fixed upon him in order to be completely silent' (*AW* 45). Yet he will recur more than once to the failure of the priesthood to provide a secure prospect of eternal life. That, even more than social parasitism, is the inexcusable offense: 'Strange, to this day I never met a priest who wasn't afraid to die. I could never make head or tails of that. It flew in the face of everything' (*AW* 74). That fear of death was really part of their denial of life, a denial characteristic of those who had lost the tragic sense and who could never look beyond death to what comes after. In this, they contrasted utterly with Ernie O'Malley, who was supremely confident that his enemies could never triumph, because dead men would help to beat them in the end.

After the marriage, Rose soon establishes the house as a place of warmth and nurturing, which it had never been under Moran. Soon the children are co-conspirators, as she paints all the walls and brings plums and eggs from her old home. They can sense that the patriarchy epitomized by the father, far from being a sign of his strength, is an outward covering of his male weakness. For he is a man who feels not at all at home in the world. Under Rose's benign and loving care, even his daughters come to seem like aliens, members of another species entirely. In theory the women are mastered by this paterfamilias, but in practice 'they were controlling what they were mastered by' (*AW* 46). Moran lives in fear of the life-instinct that they epitomize, and he comes to resent his younger son Michael's nurture of pretty flowers: 'I suppose one of these days you'll be getting yourself a skirt' (*AW* 65). This sentence turns out to be prophetic, in ways that Moran never intended. The flowers offend his heroic sensibility, for they have no use or value, seeming redundant in their beauty; better by far, says Moran, to plant vegetables, maybe carrots. Yet already Michael has learned to view his father's brutal labours on the farmland through an alternative frame of reference, seeing them as 'voluntary slavery' (*AW* 65) – just what the revolution he fought for was designed to avoid. Moran's attempt to recruit his son to his own scheme of things amounts to no more than enlisting his help in the felling of trees (a war on nature initiated by the English Puritans of the seventeenth century): 'this man and me are after slaughtering a few trees out there', Moran says (*AW* 47). The hatred of beauty among the men of Moran's generation was attributed by McGahern to the fact that they could never fully convince themselves that they owned it.

Chastened by the rebuffs, Rose increases the number of her visits to her former home, bringing apples from Great Meadow and returning laden with eggs and plums. Moran seems to notice only what she takes: his racial fear of the poorhouse is so ingrained that he panics at the thought of lost produce. Deeper than that, however, is the sense that any departure was a threat to the proud self-enclosure of his aristocratic world, an acknowledgment of social interdependence. It is probably this that leads him to deliver the third and most bitter rebuke to Rose: 'we managed well enough before you ever came round the place' (*AW* 69). Her grave and dignified reply – that she would not live where she was no use – is delivered with the quietness and desperate authority of someone who has discovered that 'they could give up no more ground and live' (*AW* 71). At this very moment, in the confusion that is as close as he will ever come to an apology, Moran realizes one of the great mysteries of his marriage: he knows less about his wife now than he did when first he met her as a stranger in the post office.

In one sense this is simply a wise recognition on Moran's part that while he may be able to categorize acquaintances, it is impossible to do so with those who share our daily lives. But in a more profound way, it is also McGahern's reminder that his characters all have depths that are hidden not just from one another but most of all from him. His duty is to honour the mystery of their being, and this is done by the eloquence of a powerful reticence that constantly reminds readers of how limited our knowledge of any person can be. *Amongst Women* is filled with vivid, rapid portraits of the main characters, such as might be made by an IRA outlaw, whose very life might depend on such powers of summation, but the book's ultimate focus is less on this or that person than a study of the bonds that form individuals into a 'whole', represented by 'the house'.[11]

If *An tOileánach* is characterized by the rhythms of 'a continual setting out and a returning',[12] then so is *Amongst Women*. Patrick Kavanagh claimed no less for his own aesthetic, suggesting that the truth of 'going away' was matched by that of 'returning' and that the latter was the ultimate in sophistication.[13] The first such return happens when Maggie comes home for Christmas, to share the story of her adventures in London and to compare them with those of Rose some years earlier in Glasgow. Moran, no longer the centre of things, soon becomes listless and bored. His only interest is in news of his 'lost' son Luke, who seems more vivid a presence in his troubled imagination than those loyal children by his very side. Even the reduction of London to a sort of dormitory suburb of rural Ireland holds no fascination for him. The younger girls, Sheila and Mona, are spellbound by contrast, 'so poised on the edge of their own lives that they listened as if hearing about the living stream they were about to enter' (*AW* 80).

The phrase that echoes Yeats's 'Easter 1916' is very deliberately used, for Moran represents (as do the republican rebels of Yeats's poem) a heart with one purpose that seems 'Enchanted to a stone / To trouble the living stream'.[14] Yet the image is more complex than is often allowed or than Yeats may even have intended: the hearts may only 'seem' enchanted to a stone, for without that stone in its fixity, no ripples could form and move around it at all.[15] By their refusal to change, the rebels have changed everything, 'changed utterly', and Yeats is honest enough to admit that. McGahern's use of the image is similarly open: while it would be tempting to think of Moran as 'the stone's in the midst of all',[16] a hero holding fast against a sea of troubles and seeking to arrest the living stream, the same is true of his children. They also try to hold back time, to prevent their dying father from slipping away, to prolong the vivid feelings of childhood. Yet the very structure of the book, in which there are no separate chapters but a succession of events linked seamlessly to one another, suggests just how futile is this attempt.[17] Everything in the book is somehow magically and rigorously linked to everything else: the visit to Strandhill by the elder couple is repeated by a younger couple, and the repetition of leitmotifs produces the oceanic flow and resonance of the finest music.

There are certain redeeming moments when it seems possible that the attempt to hold back time might just about succeed, and these are the occasions on which the family members seize a day out of the flow of their lives in order to save the hay. In such passages the writing expresses, even if it can never quite explain, the mystery of life as a process beyond all human comprehension and the power of nature to heal maimed lives. These moments are Hardyesque in their intense beauty, and they may owe something to that author's observation, near the close of *Far from the Madding Crowd*, that work (even more than pleasure) may bind men and women or even entire communities together. The nightly rosary, decreed by Moran, is less a religious ritual than a means of asserting family unity ('the family that prays together stays together' was an old motto), but it is out in the fields that the children discover the old Benedictine truth that to labour is to pray anyway: 'They loved the sound of swishing the sheaves made as they were stooked, the clash of the tresses of hard grain against grain, the sight of the rich ears of corn leaning delicately out on the shoulders of the stooks' (*AW* 68). It is of moments like these that Moran is thinking when he says: 'Alone we might be nothing. Together we can do anything' (*AW* 84).

Inexorably, time's flow works to undo such hopes. Sheila and Mona achieve fine results in their examinations and leave for secure jobs in the city. At home the girls had served as a protective screen between Michael and his father; now that they are gone, the pleasure of Michael's cosseted existence is replaced by raw exposure to the old man's being. His interest in the flower garden turns out to be so flimsy that it cannot survive without their praise, and he soon embarks on a reckless love affair with an older local woman newly returned from America. He plays truant from school and drives with her in her car across the countryside, like a motorized version of Diarmaid with his Gráinne, and eventually he leaves home rather than face the naked whipping that led Luke to flee the house. Helpless, Moran can only thank the girls for what they did for Michael in Dublin before he went on to England. 'They're all gone now' (*AW* 125), he broods sadly, in the manner of Synge's old Maurya, who has lost her children to the seas of life in *Riders to the Sea*.

The echo of Synge is as deliberate and as resonant as that of Yeats. The lesson of *Riders to the Sea* is that not even the family can provide anything more than a fragile bulwark against the forces of nature. The wind and sea themselves could invade a country kitchen, proving that there is no safety in the domestic role. Not even the home was a fully secure haven, for it could not but reflect the processes at work in the outside world. The rosary as led by Moran is no more potent an answer to the superior force of the elements than was the holy water sprinkled by Maurya:

A wind was swirling round the house, sometimes gusting in the chimney, and there was an increasing sense of fear as the trees stirred in the storm outside when the prayers ended. For the first time the house seemed a frail defence against all that beat around it.

The prayers had done nothing to dispel the sense of night and stirring trees outside, the splattering of rain on the glass. (*AW* 90)

In that context, the children's feeling that within this shadow and these walls they would never die might seem to show a lack of real intelligence: as long as they sojourn in its embrace, they share in the delusion of its owner that time itself can be set at naught. That is why they try with utter futility to recreate the spirit of Monaghan Day, when the dead McQuaid last visited, but their attempt merely serves to remind their father of his losses rather than his glories.

Claude Lévi-Strauss once remarked that people often imagine in their conceit that they are the narrators of their fondest myths, whereas all the time the myths are narrating them.[18] In other words, the resources of an individual are as nothing when compared with the power of the general culture: that is why self-expression can sometimes seem a crime against one's ancestors. The force of custom may become so great as to be self-sustaining, as in those Gaelic tales wherein characters act under *geasa*, some compulsion which is not explicable in terms of modern psychology but which has its own inscrutable inner logic. Ó Criomhthain never bothered to ask why people behaved as they did: 'what happens is all'.[19] McGahern's own texts seldom argue, judge or assign motives, leaving such things to be inferred. This is true even of the interior monologues of his central characters: coming as they do from a culture that is rich in emotion yet poor in social and intellectual life, they might be expected to have active inner lives. Yet, with his usual discretion, McGahern often refines a Joycean interior monologue down to the merest sentence or two, as if there might be something indecent about any deeper exposure.

There is no real sense of an achieved society here, any more than there is in the world of Joyce, which may explain why the writing can often seem so close to poetry; but there is an assured implication that beneath the surface drama of the family unit (which is really the widest unit available for inspection by the writer), each character has a reasonably complex inner life that can never be fully articulated but may often be deduced or guessed at. If Ó Criomhthain had read Joyce, this is surely how he would have written. Moran's pain is that he wants to be in an epic but is entrapped in a novelistic world. He would wish to conduct his battles alone against the forces of nature but is inexorably drawn into a social network. McGahern has often quoted the classical anthropologist E. R. Dodds on the linked clash between the essentially *religious* consciousness of a Moran and the *moral* awareness of his children. 'Religion', wrote Dodds in *The Greeks and the Irrational*, 'grows out of man's relationship to his total environment, morals out of his relations to his fellow man'.[20] The problem is that the religious and the moral sense are, despite the popular misconception, utterly opposed to each other and (as we have noted Yeats observe) likely to destroy each other in the end.

Within the 'moral' scheme of things it is perfectly right for Luke and Michael to leave home and make their way in the world, but to the 'religious' mindset, their going must seem like a breach of *geasa*, an abandonment of the household gods, a denial of their own father's right to the immortality that permits a man to live all over again in his sons. This most ancient of myths speaks through Moran as surely as the land itself seeks articulation through his tiring body: 'Instead of using the fields, he sometimes felt as if the fields had used him. Soon they would be using someone else in his place. It was unlikely to be either of his sons' (*AW* 130). The conflict is Oedipal but also 'Cuchulanoid', and its tragic irreconcilability is summed up by Luke, who says 'Either I'm crazy or he is' (*AW* 146) and refuses point-blank to return home. To Moran, the quality of self-reliance and individuality that Luke felt necessary to a successful career in England appears as no more than a brutal apostasy, yet, as in Yeats's dramatic treatment of the myth, there is a strong implication that it is the women who really impel the narrative from start to finish and that it is the men's inability to live for long at peace with the feminine principle of life that leaves them at war among themselves.[21] Luke is too like his father for any rapprochement to be possible. Yet Michael is reconciled, even to the point of returning regularly to be affirmed in his frail existence by the Great Meadow.

The later stages of the book are enacted at a fast pace, with some loss of intensity in the writing, but on the understanding that the living stream is now unstoppable. Maggie returns with a hard-drinking, leather-jacketed young man, who is attracted by her 'separateness' yet appalled when finally confronted with its source. Though Mark is of Irish background himself, he views the rituals of Great Meadow through the uncomprehending eyes of a rank outsider, breaking all its protocols when he asks for the loan of Moran's car and then again when he invites Moran and Rose to the pub. 'That's going to be their life', observes a prescient Moran, 'gather money, then a spree' (*AW* 139). It is this penchant for taking the long view that prevents him from endorsing Mark's commitment to extracting the maximum from the present moment: he sees too deeply into the potential of that moment for its meaning to be tolerable. Many of Synge's characters show a similar affliction and try as best they can to make the present participle real, but Moran cannot do that. For Mark, Great Meadow seems more like a war area than a home. It is an astute perception of what it is like to live in the backwash of a heroic world, where people with new information are intent on keeping it from others. The world around Great Meadow is one where people can be fully themselves only in the company of others, yet everyone is a potential enemy of everyone else, and no final privacy is possible. At home, Maggie seems divested of the confidence and singularity that had so impressed Mark in London.

As he cuts the grass in the great field, Moran inadvertently supplies an image of the family's condition, cutting the legs off a hen pheasant. 'I know', he apologizes breezily to Rose, 'You can't see them in the grass. Anyhow the hares escaped' (*AW* 159). If (as William Blake once wrote) the cut worm forgives the plow, then perhaps also the hen pheasant absolves the harvester. This is one version of the workings of tradition: that the wound of an animal will start at once to heal even as the body is dying of the shock. Another is offered by Rose to Michael just before he runs away for the last time: 'He'll not change now. All you have to do is appear to give in to him and he'd do anything for you after that' (*AW* 122). She alone of all the characters in the book has learned the wisdom which holds that all traditions must seem to die in order to be reborn in some newer form. As the arranger of what sweetness is to be found in the Morans' botched lives, she becomes a surrogate for the artist – and so for the workings of the creative principle.

The task of the writer, as McGahern sees it, is 'to pull the image that moves us out of darkness',[22] that darkness in which it was missing, presumed dead. To write the image is to remember it in the literal sense of that word, to recall it to consciousness, and to liberate its once despised but now real expressive potential. The process is like Walter Benjamin's redemptive time or Marcel Proust's involuntary memory: while it is vain to try too consciously to redeem the past (as the sisters do on their ill-fated Monaghan Day), it is perfectly proper to unleash old energies once trapped within a buried image.[23]

Moran's own version of Irish tradition is quite different from these. He sees it as a state of eternal dissidence, and it is this view that leads him to identify with the Protestant Rodden, who as a member of a beleaguered class fed Moran's own instinct for rebelliousness: 'No matter how favourably the tides turned for him he would always contrive to be in permanent opposition' (*AW* 163).

Even as a paterfamilias, Moran never acted as if he were really in anything more than a temporary occupation of a safe house. Rodden, more assured, feels at home in a world that may see him as tangential, cheerfully and efficiently adjusting the harvesting machine to the actual contours of the local earth.

The scene in which the entire family (minus Luke) gather to save the hay is another Hardyesque set piece of ecstatic communal labour: timeless, seasonal, mindlessly beautiful. On this type of occasion alone does Moran learn how live one day at a time and to redeem life's harvest. In this he might be seen as a version of Tomás Ó Criomhthain, who saw the experience of a person as 'a succession of single days'[24] not to be squandered, in McGahern's own reading of the book, and who knew that 'there is nothing more difficult to seize than the day' (*AW* 106). Yet even in the midst of that blessedness, the family experiences what seems like a violation. Sheila's new husband, Sean Flynn, grows exhausted by the manual labour and returns to the house with his wife, and there they make love, to the consternation of all the others. Even the rakish Michael feels that the true virginity of the house has been lost in their selfish absorption. It is a mark of how deathly the house has become that the simple lovemaking of newlyweds should seem like a betrayal of what it stands for.

'I suppose it'll be long before the house is ever as full again', opines Rose after the last of the children has gone (*AW* 168). Moran looks as if it were unlucky to say such things, yet he himself has shown no compunction about making gloomy prognostications for the other. In *An tOileánach*, Ó Criomhthain suggests that it is best to take each day at a time, because 'to plan ahead is as useless as to look back in regret'.[25] Perhaps Moran, while he faces into the end, is searching for a similar wisdom. 'There seems to be a superstitious fear of predicting events', says McGahern of *An tOileánach*, 'as if the very human attempt itself may be enough to incur the wrath of nature'.[26] It is in these circumstances that Moran achieves his miraculous epiphany. As his bodily powers wane, he grows ever more respectful of nature, even while despairing of humans.

One day he struggles out to lean on a post and survey the Great Meadow. McGahern writes, 'He had never in all his life bowed in anything to a mere other. Now he wanted to escape, to escape the house, the room, their insistence that he get better, his illness' (*AW* 178). Out in the fields, faced with the fresh growth and the blue tinges in the green grass, he suddenly feels himself at one with the world, even as he is about to leave it. He begins to live as he conceives of life not as an epic but as a tragedy: 'To die was never to look on all this again. It would live in others' eyes but not in his. He had never realized when he was in the midst of confident life what an amazing glory he was part of. He heard his name being called frantically' (*AW* 179). This scene resonates beautifully, and contrapuntally, with two preceding ones. In the first scene, Moran had shot an annoying jackdaw and the children had called out in terror to ensure that he had not killed himself; and in the second, Michael, suddenly indifferent to his garden flowers, chooses to ignore that same 'glory' that now entrances his father.

That epiphany is hard won. Even on the day of his wedding to Rose, Moran had felt numb – as if his life were passing before his eyes rather than being fully lived. He had been described as walking the fields 'like a man trying to see' (*AW* 130). Now that he has been vouchsafed one glorious vision at the end, he can die reconciled to nature. His children, like the daughters of old Maurya in *Riders to the Sea*, have no inkling of the transformation that has overtaken their feeble parent and simply lead him away in the belief that his mind is disintegrating. In Synge's play the old woman, so long guilty of self-absorption and self-pity, managed to transcend all merely personal feeling in offering a prayer for all souls left living in the world. Here in this climactic passage, the man who slaughtered trees now learns to put himself at one with the glory all around him. Throughout his life, Moran owned but could never really see his land. Now he sees it for the first time, even as he is about to lose it. The tragic trajectory had, as we have observed, been followed long before Moran: when the Anglo-Irish governed the land in the nineteenth century, then too the owners could not see it, and the seers could never own it. Moran, for most of his days, never deeply felt the field to be his, but in that last scene of blessedness, owner and seer are briefly and wondrously one.

Which is not to say that he dies fully reconciled. The 'shut up!' with which he aborts the rosary he once so studiously recited suggests that his anger with the priests is unappeased. At his funeral there is no firing party, but the tricolour is folded and removed when a little man 'old and stiff enough to have fought with Finn and Oscar came out of the crowd' (*AW* 183). This is the only overt reference in the novel to the world of Celtic epic, which lingered still in the countryside of McGahern's youth, 'but as a whisper'.[27] Yet the epic strain in the Irish novel has never been more definitively affirmed. No sooner is that affirmation concluded than the victory of the novelistic mode is asserted, as the daughters, remarking on the return of their menfolk from the funeral, compare them to a crowd of skittish women coming home from a dance.

What is embodied in *Amongst Women* is nothing less than a total world, whole unto itself, a world that exists on its own terms and in its own style. People are presented in their full outline, but with that same tact and discretion that would have been necessary for them to live with one another: far more is suggested that can ever, or should ever, be said. A kind of reticent but steely poetry allows for the same comprehensive representation of a dying culture that was achieved by Ó Criomhthain: if the energy of life is its desire for expression, here a world that remained inarticulate from the time of William Carleton becomes suddenly eloquent. Its intimate knowledge of its landscape and people confirms Synge's view that a work of art is possible only to one person at one time and at one place, yet its anthropological attitude assumes a universal readership.

In that sense, it is yet another example of a radical traditionalism, because its documentation of the power of custom sits somewhat oddly with its interrogation of customs grown oppressive.

To some eyes this might seem downright eccentric, were it not for the fact that the eccentric is usually possessed of a deeper than average perception of the true nature of reality. For McGahern every civilization is constructed against the fact of death. Each person moves simultaneously in two quite contrary directions: toward emergence as a distinct individual (a process that can be painful and exhausting) and toward the dissolution of death (a moment even harder to contemplate with equanimity). Institutions such as the family (or literature itself) offer to referee and even reconcile these conflicts, affirming a margin of hope for the persistence of some personal distinction in return for a surrender to the customary demands of tradition. Yet people die anyway, despite the modern tendency to deny most evidence of human mortality.

The civilization that was rural Ireland in the mid-twentieth century had many flaws and many apologists – chief among the latter being Éamon de Valera with his vision of frugal comfort amid pastoral beauty. McGahern's account is more poised and balanced than that of most other prose writers. It captures the warm humanity of country people such as Rose Brady and the Moran children, but also the intellectual torpor of a society that regarded women doctors as exotic and even unhealthy phenomena. It recognizes the direct link between the warmth and the narrowness, because it finds a tremendous intensification of the fundamental realities of life in an enclosed and separate world. This is a world in which not just men and women seem to belong to different species but parents and children as well. All seem self-enclosed. Its children – McGahern included – would wish to feel the intensity of emotion but without the shadowside of terror and fear.

Patrick Kavanagh had made a similar attempt at distinguishing the one from the other and had gone to Dublin to write his way out of that conflict, only to conclude that a city of which he expected more than any city can give would never afford him the solid ground on which to stand while he conducted his analysis. In the end he was drawn back to a sort of late, delayed homage to the stony grey soil of Monaghan. McGahern learned the lesson well, and so he never abandoned that world, even when the provocation of censorship might have made such abandonment understandable. That censorship left him with the reputation of a dissident, yet his underlying aim was to affirm (and in affirming, examine) the values of the very society that so cruelly repressed his work. Even at an early stage, before the banning of *The Dark*, he enjoyed the status of an 'official writer', garlanded with prestigious prizes. He remained ever afterward a wonderfully ambiguous figure, a real Tory anarchist, at once a hero to the dissident intelligentsia and yet the deepest and most sympathetic recorder of a world that most members of the intelligentsia have affected to despise. He wrote that world from within, with that absolute attention to detail that is in its own way a kind of prayer and might even be one of the private languages of love.

All of which is to say that McGahern's was in part a genius for translation, for translating some elements of an ancient, heroic Gaelic culture into the form of an English novel, a form often considered by some narrow-gauge nationalists to be inherently inimical to that old culture. Yet, even in the act of transfer, more may have been gained than lost. For in Ireland everything must first seem to die before it can be reborn as something slightly different.

20. Between First and Third World: Friel's *Lughnasa*

S et in Donegal during the late summer of 1936, Brian Friel's *Dancing at Lughnasa* asks a question: who is to inherit Ireland? That question is implicit rather than explicit, however, in a work which is thoroughly addressed to the integrity of the local moment. The long decline of rural Ireland over the previous century has almost come to an end, and the five Mundy sisters are just about clinging onto a way of life that cannot last. The oldest, Kate, is a local primary schoolteacher and her income holds the home together. She played a part in the War of Independence, but neither that nor its outcome is ever discussed. Two of the sisters, Agnes and Rose, earn pin-money by knitting gloves at home. Another, Maggie, keeps house. They are in their thirties. The youngest, Chris, is twenty-six and mother of a seven-year-old boy named Michael. He is the offspring of an affair with a travelling salesman, Gerry, who returns twice during the action. Michael appears both as a boy and as the young man who narrates the events over a quarter of a century later.

Apart from a passing line urging people to vote for de Valera, there is no reference to the politics of the new Ireland. In fact, there is more interest in the wars in Abyssinia and Spain. Yet the very lack of a visible political structure in a Donegal well remote from the affairs of Dublin opens the way for a deeper set of questions as to whether, in that condition of vulnerability, the received culture of these sisters might sustain them. There is something strangely exhilarating, as well as terrifying, about their raw exposure to the resources of culture as they face into the future. Like Edward Said's Palestinians, they live at those frontiers 'where the existence and disappearance of peoples fade into each other, where resistance is a necessity, but where there is sometimes a growing realisation of the need for an unusual, and to some degree, an unprecedented knowledge'.[1]

These people's access to the traditional interior of the ancestral culture – the fire festival of Lughnasa celebrated in the back hills of Donegal – has been blocked by the codes of a prim Catholicism, epitomized by the censorious but not bad-hearted Kate. So they attempt to find a margin of hope and of culture, by which to locate themselves. There is little reference to the past by the sisters, other than a brief recollection of a local dance and of the moment when their mother waved an unsmiling farewell to their older brother, Jack, as he left for the African missions. It is as if all their energies must be invested in holding onto the present moment, prolonging it just a little, before it disappears. For the war clouds gathering over Spain are paralleled by the hairline cracks appearing in the little world of Ballybeg. 'Uncle' Jack has now returned, an apparently sick and dying man, in such disrepute with his church as to threaten Kate's continuing viability as a teacher employed by the parish priest in charge of the local school.

'I had a sense of unease', says the narrator, 'some awareness of a widening breach between what seemed to be and what was, of things changing too quickly before my eyes, of becoming what they ought not to be.'[2] Even a child, confronted by a fatherless landscape, could sense something amiss. The transfer of power at the start of the previous decade had been no more than a transfer of the crisis facing rural communities. The flight from the land was a global phenomenon in the 1930s, but in most other countries, whether the United States or Uganda, it meant simply a shift of poor people from the countryside to the nearest big city. Even in East Africa by 1936, one in every six people was living outside the rural areas in which they had been born.[3] In Ireland, that shift meant, more often than not, a flight out of the country itself; and this migration masked to some extent the huge transformation that was taking place, as rural ways yielded to urban living. What seemed like a crisis of overpopulation in the 'congested districts' of the west was really a failure to produce goods and distribute food more efficiently. The managers of the crisis invariably referred to it as a painful but challenging period of transition. What it led to, in fact, was a growing sense of conflict between country and city. Power – cultural as well as economic – was wielded in the cities and it was there that the leaders of the emerging societies ran the business.

Friel's narrator has a clear memory of the ways in which these factors worked: 'Irish dance music beamed to us all the way from Dublin', by means of the new wireless set (*DL* 2). Thus did the new rulers create a sort of retro-nationalism by means of electronic technology. As in Africa, the new state might appear to be the product of a vibrant national movement, whereas in fact the reverse was often the case. Political nationalism was a product, not always well fitting, of the pre-existing state.[4] In any tussle between them, the forces of the state could be guaranteed to win. Poor people, such as the young Kate Mundy, were exploited to advance the nationalist cause, and then cast to one side. The entire county of Donegal was a blatant example of the wider pathology; hence Kate's silence on the independence struggle. The thought was just too painful to contemplate.

Michael recalls how his mother and his aunts took to the radio. Sets had been sold widely in Ireland just four years earlier, so that loyal Catholics could tune into the Eucharistic Congress celebrations broadcast from Dublin. It was in the course of one of these programmes that Count John McCormack's rendition of 'Panis Angelicus' became the most famous challenge to male tenor voices across the land. Whether the leaders of the Catholic Church were making wily use of the new technology or the manufacturers of radio sets were cashing in on a people's devotion to religion has never been fully clear, but the technologists got the better deal. The sets remained in houses long after the praying had ceased, with the consequence that a boy like Michael can watch 'Marconi's voodoo change those kind, sensible women and transform them into shrieking strangers' (*DL* 2). The modern, far from putting an end to mythology, turns out to be the most potent myth of all and may help to explain the sisters' forgetfulness of their parents and of past events. 'The electronic whirlpool', it would soon be observed, 'far surpasses any possible influence father and mother can now bring to bear.'[5] Radio technology encouraged the involvement of the listener: by it youth could learn once again how to live mythically as part of the global village.

The radio is brand-named Minerva, but the sisters christen it 'Marconi'. The other classical deity who presides over their lives is the god Lugh, in whose honour the August festival is held. In mythology, Lugh was believed to have been the father of Cuchulain but that paternity was never fully clear-cut, for other names were canvassed too as likely fathers for the Celtic hero; and, indeed, other offspring were attributed to Lugh. Michael has his own reasons for recalling the summer of 1936, because it brought the revelation of his father ('and for the first time in my life I had the chance to observe him' (*DL* 2)), who would also turn out to have other children in another family. Gerry is himself at once a down-at-heel Romeo, unable to hold even the most tenuous of jobs, and a presence filled with mythic possibilities. Apart from the pagan Lugh analogy, he may also evoke the Christian St Patrick, the poor boy from Wales transported to rural Ireland and there put to his shifts. Kate seems vaguely troubled by that distant echo. Accused by the emotional Chris of not calling him by his familiar name, she retorts: 'Don't I know his name is Gerry? What am I calling him? St Patrick?' (DL 34).

The search for expressive freedom on the part of the sisters has been frustrated even before it begins. The drab overalls and aprons of the period lie like straitjackets on their bodies, degrading clothes to the level of seedy costume: and father Jack's resplendent uniform of a British army chaplain simply confirms, by way of contrast, that here are people who will never wear their own clothes. His uniform and hat are pure comic opera, in recognition of the fact that, wherever the British upper class went they gave the impression of a people at play, impersonating those higher home types they could never hope to be. In Jack's case the impersonation continues even after his return home.

The youngest sister, Chris, opens the play with a telling query: 'When are we going to get a decent mirror to see ourselves in?' (DL 2). This evokes many previous moments in Irish writing, from Maria Edgeworth's fear that the people would only smash any glass which offered an honest reflection of their condition to Synge's Christy Mahon, who rails against the devilish mirror in his father's home, which 'would twist a squint across an angel's brow'.[6] In Ulysses, Stephen Dedalus had suggested that the cracked looking glass of a servant was a fitting symbol of Irish art. Synge's use was perhaps the most radical of all, for he had seen in the image the limits of a literary realism which could render only social surfaces but give no deeper account of the psychic condition of country people. In his eyes all mirrors were problematic, since they afforded only a distorted image of the self, the distorting factor being an image of the power of public opinion. For him, a true freedom would be possible only when the mirror was thrown away and people began to construct themselves out of their own desires. The Mundy sisters are still far from that insouciance, being greatly exercised by what the neighbours think of them and of Jack. 'The only way to avoid seven years' bad luck is to keep on using it', says Maggie (*DL* 3). Yet what the cracked looking glass will reveal is the multiple, fractured state of the family that peers into it.[7]

The impression is soon conveyed that postcolonial Ireland has not been transformed by political independence: it is rather a place filled with emigration and arguments about votes. De Valera seems almost as remote as Gandhi: but the sisters know that they are expected to vote for him: 'Will you vote for de Valera, will you vote? If you don't, we'll be like Gandhi with his goat. . .' (*DL* 4). The parliamentary system is nothing more than a race for the spoils of office: what is actually done with the power is never discussed. Ownership of the system rather than its transformation turns out to have been the issue all along. Or, as Kwame Anthony Appiah would put it: 'When the postcolonial rulers inherited the apparatus of the colonial state, they inherited the reins of power; few noticed, at first, that they were not attached to a bit.'[8] The world of the Mundy sisters is filled with absences brought on by emigration – Danny Bradley's wife and children have gone, leaving him as the only sexual opportunity for the 'simple' Rose. All the men with get-up-and-go have got up and gone. As in Synge's *Playboy*, there is a sense of bristling sexuality just below the surface of the women's demeanour, along with a curious tendency to impersonate the absent men. 'I'm your man' is one of Maggie's turns of phrase when Chris suggests that they go to a dance (*DL* 3), but the same Chris has just tried on Father Jack's surplice. Her own childhood friend, Bernie O'Donnell, has been in London for eighteen years, and has just come home on a visit 'the figure of a girl of eighteen', making her look like the sister of her own daughter (*DL* 18).

This is another feature of the play: its dissolution of the borders which ordinarily separate adult from child. As a narrator, the actor who plays the adult Michael also uses the same voice to represent the seven-year-old child he once was; but the effect is to suggest a premature ageing process, brought on in the boy by excessive early exposure to the cares of the grown-up world. Conversely, some of the adults behave in a fashion more common among children: Maggie with her riddles and Father Jack playing with the kites. The man-child and child-woman meet in Ballybeg, as if to suggest the impossibility of real childhood under such conditions, but whether the blame lies with modernity or tradition remains radically unclear. When Maggie hears of Bernie O'Donnell's ravishing good looks and beautiful daughters, she silently confronts those thoughts already voiced to the boy: 'Just one quick glimpse – that's all you ever get. And if you miss that. . .' (*DL* 14). But she looks out the window so that the others cannot see her face: only at the very end of the play will she and they face the audience with that knowledge fully decipherable in their bodies.

Meanwhile, optimism and pessimism are held in a fragile balance. Maggie wagers that Michael's kites will never leave the ground, but Kate still hopes to fix up the old bicycle for future use. (It may have fallen into disrepair because of priestly injunctions in the Congress year against provocative young women who rode bicycles.) Agnes decides also to accentuate the positive, resolving to attend the local harvest dance: 'I'm only thirty-five. I want to dance' (*DL* 13). But Kate will have none of it: the spectacle of mature women dancing might leave the whole countryside mocking them. Still, there is a seasonal madness in the air. Up in the back hills, the old fire rituals of Lughnasa are still observed by wild people who light fires by spring wells and drive cattle through flames as a way of casting out devils. Some of the young people, crazed with drink, dance around those flames in a reprise of the old rituals of St John's Eve, recorded by Synge in his travels through the west.

Perhaps it is some distant intimation of this holy frenzy which grips Maggie at this moment. As a céili band beats out 'The Mason's Apron' on the radio, she rises with her face daubed in white flour and animated 'by a look of defiance, of aggression' (*DL* 21); 'a crude mask of happiness', she launches into the dance of 'a white-faced dervish'. Taking up her mood of carnivalesque masking, Chris dons the priest's white surplice and joins in. 'But the movements seem caricatured', insist the stage directions, 'and the sound is too loud; and the beat is too fast.' White may be the colour of innocence: but there is something not quite right about the scene. Eventually, even Kate joins the other sisters, but like a more modern dancer improvising in her own space, she dances alone. The impression is of women 'consciously and crudely caricaturing themselves' (*DL* 22). There may be a feeling of release and defiance in their gestures of energy and physical self-expression, but it comes with a bitter anger at their condition. For the dancing is furtive, enclosed in the kitchen rather than performed as ritual in a public space; and, worse still, it is over all too soon, as the radio peters out and fails to prolong the promised orgasm. Even the modern myth fails them: 'It's away again, that aul thing' (*DL* 22). Far from being a male fantasy of sexually voracious dervishes, the scene depicts a world in which the radio, overheated, wilts like a man who cannot satisfy the sisters. Their search must be for a further surrogate, which will be no more satisfactory: 'Wonderful Wild Woodbine. Next best thing to a wonderful wild man' (*DL* 23).[9]

This great climactic scene in Friel's oeuvre comes in the middle of the first act. All that follows is a slow, dying fall – a long slide into nothingness. This is a huge technical risk on the part of the playwright, but the sense of anticlimax created is wholly effective. The suggestion is that all the educational and cultural training of these women has been a preparation for something that will never quite happen. The emotional graph already traced by Joyce in *Ulysses* or by Yeats in his *Autobiographies* – a rising curve of expectation followed by frustration and disappointment – is shown here to apply to women as much as to men. For the rest of the action, the sisters will be seen holding onto a way of life which, although it should not be despised, just has to go. The fact that so much is distorted even in their dance suggests that already they feel a degree of removal from their own experience: and since most of them are no longer young, they feel that sense of distance all the more deeply. Their dance is a defiance of the ageing process and of a society which offers them so little emotional scope – a swansong before its final break-up.

What should be a harvesting of the fruits of independence by a 'risen people' is revealed as anything but. At that very moment in distant Dublin, the Taoiseach Éamon de Valera is preparing a new constitution for ratification in the following year: this will give the rural Irish family its destined recognition as the foundation of Irish society, but at that very moment when thousands of such families are being broken by emigration.[10] Previously, the young had gone rather than defer to a hated British law; now they were leaving because of sheer boredom. Yet *Dancing at Lughnasa* manages also to suggest that something good is being lost, and even more tantalizingly, that the society depicted had within its reach the sources of its own renewal.[11]

Apart from teaching or manual labour, rural Ireland has no work to offer the Mundy sisters commensurate with their talents: yet by focusing on five unmarried but sensuous sisters, Friel brilliantly avoids the usual stereotypes – mother, martyr, virgin. The dance expresses a longing for a world that passed them by. It might even be seen as a validation of Chris's brief rebellion against the mores of Ballybeg, which left her with Gerry Evans's love-child. Yet the céili music to which they move is scarcely more venerable than the Cole Porter hits which also issue from the radio set: for Irish dance music is another 'invented tradition', dating back no further than the 1890s. Against the fire ritualists of Lughnasa, it may seem to offer a paltry, private experience. Even if Chris manages to subvert the clerical order by donning the robes of a priest, her gesture has no meaning for the wider community. In earlier decades country kitchens were places where a community gathered to sing and dance, but this is a purely private rebellion – a compensation for the fact that the sisters will not be taking part in any public festivity.[12]

Chris is normally a mild person, not likely to be fooled by the empty promises of her lover: but under the influence of the dance she assumes a different identity. Which is her true self? The submerged buried one might seem so, but, like her sisters, she appears to be sheepish and embarrassed when the music stops. The fade-out of the music before its proper conclusion seems indicative of much else in the Mundys' world – the kites that will not fly, the bike that never goes, those sentences of Uncle Jack which peter out, even the memories of Michael the narrator, which never quite come to a clarifying point. It is as if everyone has difficulty in telling or living a story from start to finish, as if all impulses are arrested before they can fructify, as if the very festival of Lughnasa becomes a mockery of their unharvested desires. The old integrity of experience has been replaced by a search for mere sensation: and this is why the very idea of a past seems all but untransmittable. Jack wishes to tell the sort of story which might feed the collective illusion, but he fails repeatedly to shape one. Michael struggles to disentangle the real from the illusory and succeeds, but only to a limited extent, coming in and fading out like a distant radio signal.

The outside world appears to hold all the aces. Already, it has erased Jack's Irish and Gerry's Welsh accents. The new technology has left the members of the family all focused on distant sources of authority which their own local culture seems unable to provide. They are more than willing to participate in its schemes: songs like 'The Isle of Capri' and 'Anything Goes' resonate as freely through the kitchen as jingles for Wonderful Wild Woodbine Cigarettes. There is no central myth or coherent theory to hold the traditional Ballybeg society together anymore, and no way of telling what belongs to it and what does not. 'Anything Goes' may be a myth of the modern, but could equally well have been said of the Festival of Lughnasa.

The sisters, because theirs is a world of shreds and patches, have mastered the art of speaking through the available materials ('the most exciting turf we have ever burned'), but in such angular ways as to leave them sometimes a mystery even to themselves.[13] The songs which provoke their curiosity also serve to leave them feeling restless: and the technology of radio and gramophone, coming at the primitive phase of a wholly new civilization, appears to be at once pagan and modernist, but in either guise quite at odds with approved local codes. The new gadgets are helping to abolish the very idea of 'home', since their traces can be left anywhere in the world. Joyce had made this mythical potential of radio one of the major elements in *Finnegans Wake*, recognizing that it was a new sort of tribal drum. Field Day, under Friel's guidance, had been derided for its old-fashioned naturalism as a pre-electric movement,[14] but the playwright here shows that if anything, the reversion to mythical experience is now a frankly postelectric phenomenon. The spread of jazz rhythms across the western world in the 1930s, often by performers who were themselves happily illiterate, was a further illustration of that truth. Many decades later, in the 1980s, what was still left of local communities would learn how to use radio for such people's own expressive purposes.[15]

In the 1930s this was not yet possible. What was broadcast from national transmitters in the great capital cities was what a people's lords and masters wished it to hear. The signals emitted from Dublin exemplified the cultural confusion of an elite uncertain as to whether to promote a distinctively Irish music or to submit to the forces of the international market. So céili faded into Cole Porter. The Mundy sisters are just old enough to have been educated into a world of print technology in classrooms as rigid and stratified as a factory conveyor belt (for which they were the logical preparation). Print itself was, after all, the first of millions of 'assembly lines' and a mastery of its processes was an essential precondition for work in the new knitting factory near Ballybeg. The hand-knitting crafts of

Agnes and Rose are by 1936 as obsolete as the old weaving of a text by oral tellers in the form of a rhapsody: and their flight from the fate of factory life is a final protest against the new dispensation. But before they go, they connect via radio with an even more advanced technology which carries within itself a promise of a return to the mythical. This they love, as much as they hate the other mode.

The vibrant response of the sisters to the music of 'The Mason's Apron' indicates the ways in which electronic media serve as extensions not only of the body but of the central nervous system, involving the person as a whole rather than this or that organ.[16] Something of that ecstatic power is unleashed in the dance... and the theatre audience, which was first struck through the eye by the spectacle of a golden field of August corn, now submits to the aural experience of the music, as the democratic ear takes over from the hierarchical, surveying eye. Yet so persistent are the old print modes that once the moment of excitement has passed they reassert themselves: and so Maggie can suggest that they put roses on Jack's windowsill 'with a wee card – ROSES – so that the poor man's head won't be demented looking for the word' (*DL* 27).

And *that* is the nature of cultural transmission: one new form does not necessarily kill off another. Gerry, now selling Minerva gramophones, attests to the fact: 'People thought gramophones would be a thing of the past when radios came in. But they were wrong' (*DL* 29). Even cows with single horns have survived the onset of modernity; and a form as ancient as spoken drama can contain both the radio and the gramophone, as well as the short story. But the handover is always difficult and the strain is likely to show in a world where the climax comes always too soon. 'Suddenly', says Kate, 'you realise that hair cracks are appearing everywhere, that control is slipping' (*DL* 35). To her this loss of control is manifest in exactly those zones where her ancestors might have thought themselves to exercise it: in the ritual sacrifice at the Lughnasa fire, the sacrifice of a goat. The Sweeney boy was 'doing some devilish thing' with the animal when he fell into the flames. Now, some hope of peace is to be derived from the knowledge that he has been 'anointed' by the parish priest (*DL* 35).

That same priest, however, makes no appearance on stage, as if to suggest that he is not a force in the spiritual lives of a people. This may be a homage to Synge, who tended to keep his priests offstage in order to show that the instincts of rural people were of more ancient lineage than the Christian scheme of things. The only priest allowed to appear is more in the tradition of Shaw's Peter Keegan, a holy fool defrocked by superiors too obtuse to appreciate his deeper vision. Father Jack Mundy has just returned after more than two decades on the East African missions. If Gerry Evans is a sort of latter-day St Patrick on a mission to convert the Irish to Minerva gramophones, Jack embodies the more traditional notion of the Irish missionary seeking to found a spiritual empire for his people beyond the seas. Such young men and women went out, perhaps, with a somewhat patronizing idea of converting the heathen (including the 'buying' of 'black babies'), but they were in the main animated by a desire to help poorer peoples. The Irish missionary campaign had no ulterior political imperial motive, such as disfigured other European efforts; and this meant that its exponents were more willing to identify with the struggles of native peoples for self-development. Both sides were involved, after all, in the attempt at decolonization.

Even those who went as missionaries with the British forces were more likely than imperial administrators to find themselves exposed to local cultural rays. A soldier or governor needed only to know how to issue orders, but a missionary needed to understand the natives' souls (if they were to be transformed). E. M. Forster had noted how in India, as a consequence, administrators travelled first class in rail carriages, while missionaries went third, among the ordinary people. His novel *A Passage to India* investigated the confrontation between a European and non-European mindset:

would the result be a happy confluence or sickening conflict? Would each group take the best from the other, or would the discrepant codes cancel one another out, removing all self-restraint and opening a cultural chasm into which the credulous might fall? Forster, like Joseph Conrad, tended to be pessimistic.

Father Jack's return should, in theory, have been a moment of triumph for the Mundy family, for local newspapers had long celebrated his work and local parishes had saved pennies to support it. At first the sisters were worried that his mind might have been unhinged by prolonged exposure to African ways, but soon they decided that his problem was linguistic: after twenty-five years of speaking Swahili, he had forgotten most of his English. Their task was simply to teach it to him again. Kate, however, broods on the question after the doctor assures her that Jack's mind is far from confused and 'his superiors probably had no choice but send him home' (*DL* 35). The implication is that he has gone native. He frets about his mother's impassive face on his departure in 1911. Kate says that simply indicated her knowledge that she would never see her son again:

> JACK: I know that. But in the other life. Do you think perhaps Mother didn't believe in the ancestral spirits?
> KATE: Ancestral – What are you blathering about, Jack? Mother was a saintly woman who knew she was going straight to heaven... (*DL* 38–9)

Jack tells the story of a fellow priest addicted to quinine who had been given up for dead, but was cured by a medicine man and lived to eighty-eight. He fully approved of ritual sacrifices of animals to appease ancestral spirits. The English District Commissioner in Uganda befriended Jack and rebuked him for going native. In accordance with imperial policy, this DC offered Jack money for schools and hospitals in return for cooperation, but Jack refused.

Although beguiled by the British uniform, Jack kept faith with the ideals of those Irish missionaries who refused to implicate their programme of spiritual renewal in the colonial agenda. The DC must have been fond of Jack, however, for on departure he made him a present of the last governor's ceremonial hat.

In Ryanga, where he worked, Jack tells Chris that women are eager to have love children: and seems mock-surprised at her confession to having just one. The harvest rituals of Donegal and Ryanga appear to have become hopelessly entangled in his head, leaving him a cross between Joseph Campbell and Edward Casaubon, armed with the key to all mythologies. He seems to be using his knowledge of Africa to parody the ancestral Irish culture which sent him out there. The overlaps between the sacrifice of animals and the birth of love children are too exact to be mere accident. By the early decades of the twentieth century, German scholars had established that ancient Irish society (with only rare exceptions) regarded all children as legitimate and that its women were keen to bear children to admired men in the knowledge that such offspring would be seen as a blessing.[17]

If Jack is being mischievous, it is possible that his mischief is of long duration. Friel's use of a comparative ethnography goes clean against the trend of cultural nationalism, which had always seen Ireland as a unique and privileged place, like no other on earth. The myth of Irish exceptionalism, much reinforced by its island status, was augmented in later years by the reluctance of scholars to engage in comparative literature or comparative politics, such matters being the preserve of creative rather than scholarly minds. By implying an extended set of comparisons between Ireland and Africa, Friel is enabled to put a larger question: whether the exodus of young missionaries in the first half of the century was brought about not only by idealism but also by boredom? Perhaps that was why Jack's mother looked so stern and unforgiving as her son flew the nest? In like manner, it could be argued, against the orthodox

Marxian explanations, that much colonial activity by Europeans was motivated less by economic imperatives – the search for new materials and markets – than by an intolerance of *ennui* and emptiness at home.

The search for a meaning to life might be conducted with greater intensity in some faraway place. At all events, this would tally with the illuminating remark of Chinua Achebe concerning the disinclination of West African tribes to proselytize: 'I can't imagine the Igpos travelling four thousand miles to tell anybody their worship was wrong.'[18] A cultural motivation would always leave missionaries open to the counter-claim by those natives too serene for self-assertion.

Michael's next narrative is a sudden flash-forward which works to almost brutal effect: it warns that Rose and Agnes will leave and Kate will lose her job in the school. The audience by now shares with the characters the desire to hold onto each moment a little longer, to slow down the march of time so that the present might be made real. As if to confirm such unreasoning optimism and to prove that not all predictions are necessarily correct, Gerry falsifies Kate's prophecy by returning within days. He and Chris dance silently together on the boreen, while their son watches from behind a bush; what he sees is, in effect, their wedding ceremony. The vows there exchanged are felt with sufficient depth for Chris to experience no depression, no urge to sob, on this occasion after Gerry goes.

The second act opens with further revelations about Ryangan life. Its people have blended old and new in a living tradition. They have blended the sacrifice of the Mass with offerings to Obi, the earth goddess, so that their crops may flourish and so that departed ancestors may be contactable for their counsel. The Ryangans have not been relegated to the back hills, like the devotees of Lughnasa (no better than savages, according to Kate), but have been true to their beliefs, singing local songs and making no false distinction between the religious and the secular. Maggie is less than convinced by all this propaganda for an effortless hybridity in what is, after all, a sick bay: 'A clatter of lepers trying to do the Military Two-Step' (*DL* 49). But the alternative is outright surrender to a life on the conveyor belt and endless commuting by bus to a factory in Donegal town.

Already the daily life of the Mundys is on fast-forward: their neighbour Vera McLaughlin is too old to work in the factory at forty-one. On his return visit, Gerry climbs the sycamore tree and seems to see ahead into a distant future, but Agnes, already sensing her doom, calls up: 'The tree isn't safe, Gerry. Please come down' (*DL* 53). She sees that it can be dangerous to know too much of the future, for such knowledge can unfit people for life in the present. The fear of that future is, of course, wholly linked to the sisters' nervousness about the past, for to plant coordinates in either zone is to remind themselves of just how sickeningly fast their history is now moving them.

As if to embody that felt pressure, the older Michael's narrative breaks in ever more insistently, as one urgency overrides another with a grim, inexorable violence. 'The Industrial Revolution had finally caught up with Ballybeg' (*DL* 59). It is at this moment, more than any other, that the formal arrangements of the play become most effective. Throughout the action, even during the kitchen dance, there had been a problem of synchronization. The beat was stronger than the melody, or the music itself went too fast for the dancers. Four sisters sang and shouted, while Kate remained utterly silent. Gerry and Chris danced when there was no music at all. Gerry smiled when feeling terrible. But, above all, everything seemed somewhat distorted (like the expressions on the boy's masks), as if some elements of life were more developed than others. Such effects may have owed something to the expressionist depiction of war scenes in Sean O'Casey's *The Silver Tassie*: but in this case they are also the signs of that uneven development which afflicted many postcolonial societies. In the years before Friel completed his play, many books had been written exploring the problem: one even bore the title *Uneven Development*.[19] Put simply, the thesis was that Ireland contained elements of both a First World and Third World economy, the former manifest in middle-class urban enclaves and larger farms, the latter among unemployment black spots of the urban and rural proletariat.[20] Their problem of internal synchronization reflected a wider global issue: the fact that the modernizing countries of the Third World were being asked to undergo in a single century a catastrophic set of adjustments to modernity which in most 'developed' countries of the northern hemisphere had taken three or four centuries to achieve.[21]

The structuring devices of *Dancing at Lughnasa* have a beautiful, even an astonishing, formal appropriateness in this context. The clinging of the sisters to the present moment is their response to being hurtled into the future at breakneck speed and the uneven pace of the narrator and dramatization perfectly renders the reality of lives lived at different speeds. It is as if the older Michael is impatient to give history a forward shove, while the actual *dramatis personae* do their utmost to retard it. While Friel worked on the play, a famous advertisement for Industrial Development Authority at Dublin Airport proclaimed: 'Missing out on the Industrial Revolution was the best thing that ever happened to Ireland' (this by way of celebrating its accession to the age of clean industry). But the lesson of *Dancing at Lughnasa* is that if you miss out on some historical phase, you have to catch up on it at a horrific speed which leaves little room for intelligent choices. The problem of synchrony is the tragedy of uneven development.

The Sweeney boy is reported by Rose as having made a full recovery from burns: but whether it is due to the Catholic anointing or the ancestral Lugh will never be known. Rose looks radiant and young, following her ramble through the back hills in the company of the dreaded Danny Bradley. It is as if, freed of the family designation of being 'simple', she can become her true, destined self: but when next we hear of her, in Michael's narrative, she is dead, a quarter century later, in a Southwark hospital for the destitute. Michael only pieced small details of her life together with the greatest difficulty: the sisters worked as toilet cleaners, until Rose's health broke and they ended up sleeping rough on the Thames Embankment. As they quit the farm, Agnes wrote: 'We are gone for good. This is best for all. Do not try to find us' (*DL* 60). Those lines are a bleak epitaph on whole generations of emigrants who by leaving solved two sets of problems. In the first instance, they gave themselves a chance of material improvement in a new world; and, in the second, by removing themselves from the scene, they ensured that those who stayed had greater comfort. Put at its most brutal, the three eggs laid by the Mundys' pullet would have been divided more neatly among the three sisters who remained. Had those who emigrated stayed on, they would have been a drain on Kate's domestic purse – and Ballybeg would have looked even more like Uganda.

After such knowledge, what forgiveness? Against all odds, Jack's health rallies, but he never says Mass again. Gerry Evans falls off his motorbike during the Spanish Civil War but survives with a leg injury. Years later, he dies in Wales, assisted by the wife and children whom Chris never knew he had. It is a strange revelation, adding to his mythical dimension, a little like the disclosure that there may have been two St Patricks. It also confirms Father Jack's contention that polygamy may be for some a more natural way of life than such furtive, deceptive liaisons. As if to bear him out, Gerry is already making eyes at Agnes before he leaves for Spain.

The flash-forward technique puts immense pressure on the actors in these final scenes. The audience now knows all that can ever be known of their fates, such as the fact that Chris worked in the Donegal factory to her death, hating every day of it – but the characters do not know such things. The effect is identical to that achieved by Yeats in 'Long-Legged Fly': the future which still lies before these people is already a long retrospect to the audience. It sees the characters in a moment of vulnerability, of jeopardized solitude, of sheer insouciance. Somehow, the acting must restore to these late moments the openness they truly had, before hindsight: yet it cannot escape the available foreknowledge. Roland Barthes observed that once you have been shown a photograph of a man who died at thirty years of age, that fate seems to proclaim itself to the viewer in every line of his face, even as the picture is snapped.[22]

This adds immeasurably to the bittersweet poignancy of those closing scenes, much as a similar technique conferred a retrospective aura on the actions of Stephen Dedalus in *Ulysses*. He is depicted in its pages as fully aware that all future reconstructions of his past life will be made at the mercy of their immediate moments: and in the National Library he muses: 'So in the future, the sister of the past, I may see myself as I sit here now but by reflection from that which then I shall be.'[23] Like the Mundy sisters, he feels himself at a remove from his own gestures, already storing them up for these future savourings. The whole thrust of *Ulysses* is to restore to a moment many years earlier a sense of its multiple potentialities before life gave to subsequent developments the look of inevitability:

Had Pyrrhus not fallen by a beldam's hand in Argos or Julius Caesar not been knifed to death? They are not to be thought away. Time has branded them and fettered they are lodged in the room of the infinite possibilities they have ousted. But can those have been possible seeing that they never were? Or was that only possible which came to pass? Weave, weaver of the wind.[24]

Although Friel's characters do not know their fate as they walk like somnambulists through the closing scenes, perhaps there is a sense that this is the moment when each embraced a destiny, even though it would not be revealed as the time of choice until much later.

The ability to step back from experience even as one submits to it is recommended by Jack as a way of being at ease with the world. He involves Gerry in a ritual exchange of hats, swapping his imperial headgear for his friend's tricorne: and he suggests that they both place them on the ground and take three steps back, as 'a symbolic distancing of yourself from what you once possessed' (*DL* 69). The moment is both sublime and absurd, having analogies in Beckett and the Marx Brothers, and also in customs of marginal tribesmen exchanging precious objects (or nowadays jeans). Jack's equanimity may be more apparent than real, however, for it transpires that he is most likely the one who slaughtered Rose's pet rooster in a private ritual of sacrifice. Maggie remains as unimpressed by the two weak men in their borrowed costumes as any O'Casey woman was with her strutting male peacocks (*DL* 69).[25]

That so much of Jack's gesturing and his sisters' language is parodic suggests that they have already achieved a measure of distance from their past. The final movement is a gentle farewell to the lost world, with all characters assembled onstage swaying ever so slightly side to side, as in a wistful wave. The nostalgic beauty of this hazy tableau is undercut somewhat by the young boy's kites turned at last to the audience, which sees the working of his imagination all through the play: and on each is a cruelly grinning face, primitively drawn.[26] Any illusions of a gentle childhood among doting adults are violently dispelled: and in so far as the kites fly, they do so only to add a tinge of tart mockery to the closing tableau. The note of bitterness amidst such sweetness helps the older Michael to express the essential criticism of the nostalgia to which even he finally submits.

Feminist readings have seen in Michael a Frielian device of control – that of the male narrator who frames a female experience. But if there had been no male presence, the action would have been not only incredible but also monotonous. Moreover, there is a strong implication that the anarchic, subversive energies of these five women will be more than a match for the framer: by making his narrator male, Friel may be simply recognizing his own authorship.[27] The very fact that Michael is split into two characters – child and man – is hardly an assertion of unproblematic male power: and the tendency of directors and actors to play up the positive implications of the kitchen dance (ignoring darker aspects) is a sign of just how easy it is for such figures to elude all attempts at an honest valuation.

Michael as narrator admits at the end that his recollections are likely to be false. Through the preceding action, he was the weakest of all the figures framed, a seven-year-old child, observed by others who did not understand him, even as now he, the grown man, observes and does not wholly comprehend that experience. The others exist in his remembering more at the level of atmosphere than of incident, as in a photograph where everything is at once actualized and illusory:

> [E]verybody seems to be floating on those sweet sounds, moving rhythmically, languorously, in complete isolation; responding more to the mood of the music than to its beat. When I remember it, I think of it as dancing. Dancing with eyes half closed because to open them would break the spell. . . (DL 71)

He admits that the characters may be projections of his imagination, yet he also honours his characters, according to each an autonomy, a free space. Through the play, his memories had seemed at times to race against the pressure of actual experience, but he was also content at certain moments to see them exceed his own designs for them.

The pattern is like that enacted in earlier masterpieces by Irishmen who adopted a female voice in projecting an *anima*: and it asserted itself at a rather similar moment in Friel's career. He was in his fifties as he worked on the play, which is in many ways a response to those critics who accused him of privileging male voices in his work. By then he had enjoyed success with *Translations* and *Faith Healer*. It was almost as if the censors which had kept his *anima* firmly under control were finally relaxed and the voices and repressed energies of women came pouring out. Yeats had an analogous experience with his Crazy Jane persona: another female voice unleashed by an artist in his fifties. And Beckett's Winnie in *Happy Days* could be seen as coming in that tradition, much like Mommo in Tom Murphy's *Bailegangaire*. Having been kept under wraps for so long, it is hardly surprising that their voices should be powerful, menacing, even sometimes (in Yeats's word) 'unendurable'.[28] And, since the feeling of manliness is less assured in men than the sense of womanliness in women, it would not amaze should a male author seek to retain some illusion of control in the face of the onslaught. Clearly, some male anxieties are revealed in those nervous references to surplices worn by women and to the garish sweaters donned by Father Jack. But this is no more than to recognize that the holy man, like the artist, is an androgynous shaman. After all, to become a writer in a macho culture was to expose oneself to certain ridicule for being effeminate: and the use of male narrators is an attempt to assert a virility which the very act of writing may have thrown into question.

If Michael is honest enough to raise doubts about the veracity of his narration, similar questions need to be raised about Father Jack's. Perhaps in his version of Ryangan culture there is more dreamy atmosphere than hard incident. After all, his devotees were lepers and presumably their people were also being modernized by radios and factories. Like the Irish they would have wished to know the benefits of modernity as much as the liquidation of its costs, and to have held on to what was valuable in the past even as they moved confidently into a better future. But they also had been colonized. This meant that they should cease to uphold their native traditions, without ever becoming fully English: in the words of Basil Davidson, 'the British were the most systematic in imposing this sentence to nowhere'[29] on Africans for whom there was not even the empty promise of assimilation.

This condition of nowhereness is, however, also endured by the sisters in the early decades of an independent Irish state; the late assimilation of two of them to London will merely be the *coup de grâce*, of a battle lost way up the line. They, rather than Jack, are the ones living in something like a cultural vacuum after discrepant codes have cancelled one another out: and so they cannot enjoy the elementary liberty of taking the surviving shreds of their culture for granted, but must instead practise the dance in secret, as if they were functioning like an underground movement in their own country. The play is in some sense a prehistory of the new marginals who will crowd from colonial peripheries into the great cities of the First World, there to live 'at once within, between and after culture'.[30] It is perhaps symptomatic that neither the Ryangan nor the Lughnasa festivals can be directly presented: instead they are merely reported, like the denouement of a classic tragedy, as something which happens always elsewhere.

Even though there are no overtly political themes in the play, it is a reminder of the ways in which public events such as the Spanish Civil War or great economic forces like multinational capital leak into personal lives, becoming also distinctly personal experiences. One implicit irony of the action may be found in the fact that the 1930s were the years when even relatively strong European nation states were brought under the control of the emerging neocolonial order. De Valera was leading an economic war against the rulers of Westminster at the very time that people like the Mundy sisters were being ever more closely assimilated to the world of the Thames Embankment. The nation state had been turned to by Cosgrave and de Valera as one possible means of controlling, or at least softening, the catastrophic onset of modernity. Its failure to do that left the Mundys even more pathetically exposed to economic forces and with fewer cultural resources to contest them. Yet the one comparison which Friel steadfastly refused in his own artistic anthropology is that between Ireland and England: in earlier work, the comparisons are with the United States, in later with Africa, but never with England, perhaps because he considered its stresses to be those of a colonizing force rather than of a colonized people.

In portraying the sisters as caught in a no-man's-land between cultures, Friel seems once again to be doing what he did so effectively in *Translations* and *Making History*: writing out the last gestures of a Gaelic Ireland. The displacement of the sisters from their ancestral culture may be less intolerable in London than in Donegal, where the estrangement is all the more glaring. Yet most audiences will feel at the close that Rose and Agnes would have been better off staying in Ballybeg. There is clearly nothing for them in London but an even more extreme loss of all ideas of ritual and ceremony. Such rituals may be deeply distrusted by those who call themselves modern, yet they are indispensable to humanity: even the feasting on crumbs in hungry Donegal could generate the improvised menu 'eggs Ballybeg' and a planned meal is the start of a return to real ritual. Without such ritual, life declines to mere routine and people are compelled to construct themselves only by props, possessions and settings. What Friel seems to be hinting at is a superior survival of such ritual in an Africa that was less than fully penetrated by the colonials and the hope that similar zones may persist in Ireland, such as the 'back hills'. This was the implication also of postcolonial critics such as Basil Davidson, who wrote in the 1990s:

Now, with disaster having followed on colonial dispossession, it must be useful to look at what was seldom or never discussed before: at the possibly permanent and surviving value of the experience that came before dispossession. Not as colourful folklore, nor as banal assertion of Africa's possessing a history of its own, but as a value that may be relevant to the concerns and crises of today.[31]

The spiritual values which underwrote the Irish Revival at the start of the last century contained within their codes ideas of sovereignty which had little enough to do with political structures as such. A study of the Celtic past, in particular, animated most of the great leaders of that movement, whether they were politicians or intellectuals, from Eoin MacNeill to W. B. Yeats, from de Valera to Hanna Sheehy Skeffington. They staked their claims in the spiritual and sociocultural sphere, regarding political nationalism merely as a means to achieving them (and not as an end in itself). Long before the 1916 Rising, they had defined the cultural values of the risen people, much as the Sinn Féin courts were to set up a virtual republic within the British scheme of things, which they broke like the exterior casing of a shell. What happened after that is too well known: the maintenance of one of the means for implementing that cultural freedom became an end in itself, and those Celtic practices which were to provide a set of principles remoulding the new polity were soon expelled to the margins, as subjects of arcane study by learned professors. It is a mark of the depth of that defeat that most audiences of Friel's play had never even heard of Máire MacNeill's classic book *The Festival of Lughnasa* when first it was staged.

In the play, Kate recognizes that what is at issue is Jack's search for a world whose rituals and symbols answer real human needs. In that he is no different from his sisters, whose desire is less for a self than for a viable culture. Friel conspires in that search, by presenting as the focus of his drama not any particular individual but an entire social group. What is depicted is the fate of a community – and of one boy communally mothered. In some ways this might be seen as a return to the techniques of Sean O'Casey, whose mockery of male heroism was reinforced by his refusal to supply in his Dublin plays the sort of central character with whom audiences could easily identify. In a testy response to Yeats's criticisms, O'Casey said: 'God forgive me, but it does sound as if you peeked and pined for a hero in the play. Now, is a dominating character more important than a play, or a play more important than a dominating character?'[32]

Friel's reasons for adopting the same approach go well beyond the political and into the domain of culture. The qualities of the individual sisters are subordinated, as in Synge's *Riders to the Sea*, and for similar reasons: to permit a deeper anthropological search for some sign of the persistence of a viable common culture. Traditional forms – whether African or Celtic – are no longer fully available to the sisters, and the new state scarcely connects with any of their needs, the need (above all) for ceremony. Nor can the Catholic Church fill that vacuum, since its priests seem implicated more in systems of power than in a search for true authority. Stripped of ritual, denied ceremony, the sisters have to improvise these things in snatched moments – in the posing of riddles, the telling of stories, the sudden dancing in the kitchen. These are the utopian instants when ritual might be reborn and the culture might heal itself.

The African analogy is important solely because of the encouragement it affords in such moments. This is not just a matter of ticking off useful comparisons between the loose familial structures in Ryangan Africa or Celtic Ireland. More fundamentally, it concerns the openness of peoples to the numinous; what impressed all missionaries in Africa was the readiness of even its radical political thinkers to embrace a spiritual dimension. As Kwame Anthony Appiah reported their saying in Ghana: 'There are no atheists or agnostics in Africa.'[33] The rediscovery of pagan or Celtic spirituality in the 1990s and the attempts to link it with more recent Christian forms suggest that Friel's own 'search' resonated with many. Beneath the flux and desolation of modern living, a more real life was continuing to go on, a life which might even in its moments of blessedness see the ancestral spirits subtly intervene in the daily surfaces of things.

Friel wrote this play towards the end of the 1980s, a decade which had witnessed intense debate as to whether Ireland itself might be a Third World country. Economic stagnation and rampant unemployment reopened the question of whether the 'experiment' of political independence had been a success,[34] or even a good idea. During every year up to 1988, over 40,000 people – most of them young – left Ireland for work overseas, as factories closed. If the cottage industries of Donegal had been dying a full seven years before de Valera's speech on cosy homesteads, the postmodern equivalent was the shut-downs of the local factories which had replaced them.

The horrific carnage in Northern Ireland also raised the common postcolonial issue of how wisely the old departing elites had redrawn the political borders. In the republic the new managerial class, intent on further Europeanization, proved resistant to these suggestions, but artists were more responsive. A young novelist like Roddy Doyle constructed *The Commitments* (a successful movie as well as novel) around the thesis that the Irish were the blacks of Europe: and the leading part taken by Irish musicians such as Bob Geldof in African relief led many young people to commit themselves to 'development' work on that continent. At the same time, many missionaries who had spent lives of hardship and dedication out there returned in a more purposeful frame of mind than Father Jack's, imbued with the principles of liberation theology and intent on reforming the ecclesiocracy and on introducing more democratic procedures to parish structures. Meanwhile, postcolonial theory was on the rise in the world's universities, and some of its leading exponents, such as Edward Said and Fredric Jameson, wrote pamphlets exploring the cultural analogies between Ireland and the Third World. Among the young there was – especially after the collapse of the Soviet empire in 1989 – a turning way from political to cultural nationalism, epitomized above all in a renewal of interest in Irish dancing, and a rediscovery of radio as a medium for higher culture.

All these elements formed a complex weave in the tapestry of *Dancing at Lughnasa*, a play which uses the 1930s to explore the 1980s.

Some productions have been unashamedly pastoral and have neglected the bleaker emphases in the text. By 1971, more Irish people lived in cities and towns than in the countryside, giving a new lease of life to nostalgic depictions of country living: but the undeniably affectionate celebration of that life by Friel was finely balanced against an honest depiction of poverty and cultural loss.[35] The play's astonishing success with audiences across the world suggests that it not only captured the meaning of its cultural moment in 1990, but answered many felt needs. It provided many emigrant communities overseas with a myth of self-explanation at just the time when the presidency of Mary Robinson began to reconnect them to the greater Irish nation, for 1990 was also the year of her election. That president found a healing way in which to combine the Europeanization of the managerial elite with the postcolonial analysis favoured by some of the intelligentsia. Mrs Robinson's presidency began with a campaign video containing grainy footage of men and women dancing at a country crossroads: it evoked a nostalgia for a lost Ireland, while launching a youthful female president purposefully into the new one.

Friel's play worked in similar ways. It confronted very honestly the pain and the defeats of the past, the hairline fractures and the sad removals, but its experimental form was buoyant, vibrant and beautiful. The sheer bleakness of the content was somehow contained and defeated by the astounding energy with which a contemporary artist framed it, and a reinvented Ireland at last found a way to cope with both its colonial past and European present. The method of that coping was very familiar. The play which most fully embodied the themes and projects of Field Day was presented at the Abbey Theatre in Dublin. Field Day did not die, but its agendas were broadened until they filled a national canvas: and this also was prophetic of the ways in which the problem of Northern Ireland would once again be seriously reimagined by all the peoples in Ireland, north and south, at home and overseas.

21. Roddy Doyle: *Paddy Clarke Ha Ha Ha*

A lthough it describes the world of a ten-year-old boy in 1968, *Paddy Clarke Ha Ha Ha* would hardly be described as a book for children. Yet over almost 300 pages, it maintains the voice, vocabulary and restricted understanding of such a child. Its first-person narration is a remarkable technical achievement, less the speaking voice of Paddy than the inner voice through which he thinks things out. There are few sustained inner monologues in children's literature or in the literature of childhood, but this novel conveys the mind of Paddy Clarke awakening to its own processes in a world that is increasingly strange to him. Children do, of course, conduct interior monologues – babies babble, five-year-olds prattle as they walk along a footpath – but these sounds are usually directed to an imaginary playmate or to their own selves, not the wider world.

Children's literature as written by adults allows kids some access to adults' knowledge and desires: in a sense it coaches children in roles, suggesting what their mature carers believe or want them to be. Roddy Doyle's novel, however, works in the opposite way: it is a work written about a child for adults, offering its readers a deeper understanding of a way of seeing that is childlike. Its main character has read thirty-four of the 'William' books by Richmal Crompton. Doyle's novel, when it won the Booker Prize in 1993, appealed as a fictional autobiography aimed at those last adults to grow up in a mainly print culture, one in which television was still a background element and in which a favourite parlour game was to cross a room with a book balanced on your head: 'If it fell off I would die... I knew all the books in the house. I knew their shapes and smells. I knew what pages would open if I held them with the spine on the ground and let the sides drop. I knew all the books but I couldn't remember the name of the one on my head.'[1]

The generation whose childhood is described in *Paddy Clarke* is also the generation which bought most copies of the volume. In its chapter-free randomness and sequence of seemingly unrelated vignettes, it is one of the finest attempts to recreate the aimless immediacies of a ten-year-old boy. For that very reason, however, it might bore an actual child, who would want separate chapters, episodic climaxes, a clear unfolding plot. It is far more likely to appeal to an adult looking back on the hours and days of a childhood rendered without mediation. Yet, precisely because of this lack of significant mediation, it does permit the reader the sense of being a ten-year-old once again. Paddy's parents are not seen as they would see themselves, but only through the baffled, partial understanding of the child; and other children are rendered in shadowy ways, existing only in certain restricted roles on the fringes of the boy's consciousness. Girls – for this is 1968 – hardly feature at all.

The action is set in Doyle's fictional suburb of Barrytown, on the edge of a developing Dublin and on the fringe of the countryside. A character in Conor McPherson's *The Seafarer* will remember 'when it was all fields around here... all around all up to Donaghmede, all up to Sutton, all up to Howth'.[2] It is still semi-rural in 1968 but less and less so. The recently constructed estate feels at once incomplete and used-up, but the boys are more interested in exploring the open land. They think of themselves as being on some kind of frontier, of the sort depicted in clashes between the cowboys and Indians on television screens. They call one another names like Geronimo and they whoop like wild horsemen as they ride their bikes through the neighbouring suburb of Bayside. The horse, indeed, being a nobly rural animal, is one of the keys to their mythology; and so they devise a version of the famous Grand National steeplechase, which requires them to race through gardens, vaulting over walls and hedges, from one end of the street to the other. But they can sense, for all their wildness, the growing suburbanization of Dublin:

> Our territory was getting smaller. The fields were patches among different houses and bits left over where the roads didn't meet properly. They'd become dumps for all the waste stuff... There were no farms left. Our patch was gone, first sliced in half for pipes, then made into eight houses. The field behind the shops was still ours and we went there more often... (*PCH* 146–7)

The boys belong to a gang, staking out territory but smart enough to yield ground to a stronger rival group. As part of their territorial claim, they inscribe their nicknames all over Barrytown on the drying cement of walls and pathways. They start malicious fires, as if in some half-conscious desire to prevent further building or development. Paddy puts some of the fuel from his cigarette lighter into his brother Sinbad's mouth. This seems cruel because it is, as is his refusal to call his brother by his proper name of Francis; but it may be an offloading onto his brother of the stress felt in their parents' marriage back in the family home. The outside world of gangs and japes, recorded in the early part of the book as if of intrinsic interest in itself, is eventually revealed to function as a distraction from the pangs of family life. Yet the figure of the suffering Sinbad, his eyes wet from crying after the lighter-fuel incident, is a constant reminder of that jeopardized world: 'I hated him' (*PCH* 6).

The moments of tenderness with the estranged father grow rarer and rarer, and thus infinitely precious, explained word for word: 'No one's fingerprints are the same as anyone else's. Did you know that?' (*PCH* 11). The narration moves randomly, from one scene to another, just as a child might (and then... and then... and then...); but the adult reader, apart from feeling some nostalgia for a lost world, attaches more and more importance to the happy moments of bonding, sensing they will be short-lived. A child reader might be indifferent to such events, wondering whether they were enough to sustain interest at the level of plot. All through the book, the father is prey to sudden, inexplicable surges of emotion. Such infantile bouts of rage and tenderness in an adult can terrify children, inducing a sort of premature adultification in them: and the book is filled with such fragmentary moments, not generating a clear interpretative line – as if all the characters, old and young, are at the mercy of experience rather than in control of it.

The absence of separate chapters and this lack of clear emplotment accounts for a felt precariousness in the experience of childhood. Few moral coordinates are supplied either by past national history or by present religious faith (though both are extensively described in their more absurd guises). The teacher at school reads the Proclamation of the Irish Republic in 1916 and Paddy claims that the rebel leader Thomas Clarke, on the commemorative tea towel, is his grandfather. Miss Watkins makes him read the writing; 'executed by the British on 3 May 1916' (*PCH* 22). Standing corrected, he then tells people that his grandfather Clarke is alive and living in Clontarf, but his father corrects this misunderstanding too: 'Granda Clarke's dead... Do you not remember?' (*PCH* 24).

If Paddy's sense of the family past is too weak to sustain him, so also is his sense of religion. Although he thrills to the account of Father Damien in the missionary leper colony, its appeal is as an adventure story rather than for its spiritual content. His father castigates his mother for encouraging such rubbishy religion, at which point she tries to untie her apron knot in a staged threat to leave. Religion has declined from a grand narrative of faith to a paltry kind of rule-keeping for the sake of social decorum.[3] The dead baby sister has been saved for heaven from an eternity in limbo by virtue of the baptismal water spilt over her head before she died (a tale of consolation for the distraught mother). The theft of a copy of *Football Monthly* from the local newsagent might cause a boy to burn in purgatory for 4 million years; but if he died after making a clean breast of things in a good confession, he would go straight to heaven. Paddy gets so caught up in this complex system of punishments that he finds in it an outlet for his growing frustration with his father. He times the interval between the man's eating of a fried breakfast and his taking of communion at half-eleven Mass, discovering it to be less than the hour required under the relaxed but still clear-cut rules after Vatican Two. 'I kept it to myself. If he went up for communion, I'd see what happened. I knew and God knew' (*PCH* 155).

Without any clear sense of the past, Paddy Clarke cannot develop any hope about his personal or family future; and a rule-bound religion offers not comfort but judgement. Like many boys of that time, he yearns for the worldly authority of the priesthood, but this amounts to little more than cutting strips of Vienna roll to serve as communion wafer at pretend Masses. The ultimate importance of Sunday is that it is hedged in by even more rules and prohibitions than other days. When Paddy asks whether you are allowed to wear casual jeans on the Sabbath, his father (in a moment of black comedy) says no; but the mother says more sensitively 'he's just asking. . . he doesn't have any jeans' (*PCH* 61). With so little support from the traditional sources of meaning and comfort in Irish life, Paddy is aware of fragility and transience. The children around him live in a climate of rumour about early death: a boy dies of polio contracted from seawater at the local swimming pool. Paddy (who cannot remember big things, like his grandfather's passing) is obsessed by the short memory of little things: 'the memory of a goldfish is eight seconds' (*PCH* 71); and haunted by the brief life cycle of tiny animals: 'the life expectancy of a mouse is eighteen months' (*PCH* 44). These – like the record score in a professional soccer match: Arbroath 36, Bon Accord 0 – are just the sort of nerdy details which impress a ten-year-old.

Parents often feel free to criticize in their children just the sort of weaknesses which they fail to notice in themselves. The mood swings of Clarke senior towards his children are rather like those of Paddy towards Sinbad: and, although the children can sometimes recreate their father's flaws in their dealings with one another, they know that they must always tread warily lest the mood of the head of the family changes. One minute he refuses to allow them to watch television (too much viewing was considered demoralizing in 1968), but 'the next minute he'd be sitting on the floor beside us or watching it with us, never for long though' (*PCH* 37). This sort of behaviour calls into question the very notion of a binary contrast between child and adult as categories. The adult's illusion of control provides a space of inadvertence in which children can explore and criticize the adult codes to which nevertheless they are made to conform.

Because the work of the father is done miles away from the home, he becomes less and less visible to his son. Since he cannot pass on the basic skills of his trade as in former times, all he can offer is his love; and when the current of that feeling fails, all is lost. He appears more and more as a fake: the 'autograph' of George Best is just a version of the footballer's name which he had printed himself. The family's favoured songs, like so many people's, covertly point to a half-admitted crisis in their life: 'I married another, she's worse than the other' (*PCH* 84). Perhaps the father is using the songs to alert Paddy to the looming break-up. When he urges him to sing 'I'm Gonna Wash That Man Right Out Of My Hair', the mother puts a stop to this. Later he turns down the television newsreader and plays a Hank Williams song as if the man on the box is mouthing it: 'Now you're looking at a man that's getting kind o' mad, I've had a lot o' luck but it's all been bad' (*PCH* 90). Everyone roars at the childish prank, but one can imagine (even if Paddy cannot) the mother's silent scream.

Or maybe Paddy *can* imagine such a thing. He has after all recorded the ambiguous moment: and he seems to notice a lot – the pointless solidarity of the family in a photograph, holding their smiles for so long that they ceased to be smiles (with poor Sinbad actually looking down at the ground). When they all sat to table, the father's feet were steady, but the mother's could not be still, as if her world was growing far less stable. There is violence not far below the surface of her anger; and it emerges in strange, passing moments, as when she uses an old-style mangle to crush the water out of a sheet. The father, like many fathers when corporal punishment was still used in schools, feels entitled to use violence as a way of disciplining his children; and Paddy explains that the best way to minimize the blow was to back into it, giving the assailant less room in which to swing. There is a good deal of casual cruelty in a world where grown-ups are invariably served in shops before children and in which most of the children's games replicate the violence endured in the school classroom.

A boy named Kevin bullies members of his group into using bad language, 'a curse on your family', yet he beats them up if they use a mere 'bloody' (*PCH* 223). The system of capricious autocracy has built a replica of itself in every child's head. Subtle differences of age count for as much as the hidden injuries of social class, with the consequence that the children feel free to mock a boy whose mother must work in the local chocolate factory or another whose mother has run away from her family with an airline pilot. And boys at school, even as they are becoming aware of a secret life in their sexual parts, take a vicious pleasure in trying to damage one another's testicles. As an irate teacher points out, this seems like a half-conscious attack on the very idea of their future.

Yet, for all that, there are moments of unalloyed joy in their lives. They relish football games in the schoolyard so deeply that they continue to play while eating their lunches. In their altered rules, even goalkeepers are allowed to score. They knick-knock on hall doors and run for their lives. They can buy broken biscuits in the local shop and have an outdoor feast. Like all play, these actions are enjoyed as activities without any object beyond the pleasure afforded by the moment; and this is an aspect of the book's wider aesthetic. There is no need for an episode to be brought to a climax: in fact, it is far, far better when there is no melodrama. So the entire family celebrates the purchase of a car by taking a short trip of a mile or so to Dollymount Strand, where they all simply stare out to sea. The locale of the legendary scene in *A Portrait of the Artist as a Young Man* in which the young Stephen Dedalus saw a brazen girl in the water and discovered his artistic vocation[4] has no equivalent here. It is as if Doyle's denuded world cannot provide such a moment of intense clarification – and as if it is sweeter so.

There is, however, one clear link to Joyce's book: the depiction of a child's increasing control over language. Paddy has a fondness for repeating multisyllabic words like mantras of a personal religion:

Ignoramus. Ignoramus. Ignoramus. (*PCH* 128)

These words often voice a dire judgment on human fallibility:

Substandard. Substandard. Substandard. (*PCH* 128)

They can even be used to express a good-natured contempt for the warren of houses in the adjoining suburb of Bayside:

Labyrinth. Labyrinth. Labyrinth. (*PCH* 128)

Paddy recognizes that the blind rages tearing at his father are somehow linked to the man's sense of powerlessness and to his attempt to triumph over it with a mastery of words. He often disappears behind his newspaper, as if rehearsing his withdrawal from the family's shared life, yet the struggle to read can so exhaust him that he falls asleep, even as his cigarette burns nearer and nearer to his fingers. When awake, he would move his mouth laboriously in time to his sounding out of the words. Or he would tell his wife something he had just read and she would say 'very good', even though she never sounded like she meant it. The boy, supersensitive to language above all, can tell towards the end that she is just going through the motions of a good wife. She reads her own magazine, *Woman*, 'not really reading, turning the pages' (*PCH* 208); and Paddy yearns for his father to notice her frustration, but the father just continues to emit the low noise with which he read: 'I hated him for doing it. Newspapers were bastards' (*PCH* 208).

The hidden promises of language, nonetheless, hold for Paddy until the very end the possibility of redemption. As all else disintegrates, the father remains keen that Paddy should extend his impressive vocabulary. The parents ask their son how to spell certain words, how many syllables they have; and the boy in turn tests his father, all the while looking for traces of tell-tale lipstick on his collar. The implication is that Paddy may yet succeed in zones where the father did not. The language game even allows Paddy to create a sort of surviving collaboration between his parents. He is asked jocularly how many syllables there are in the word 'bed':

I stood up quick.
– Okay.
I wanted to go while it was nice. I'd made it like that. (*PCH* 211)

It becomes clear in the later stages of the book that Paddy has intuited the repressed elements in the relationship of the parents. A child, as Melanie Klein observed, will often tune into what is happening (or, more desolately, *not* happening) between parents. Paddy is not sure whether his mother is good-looking, but he is certain that she is far more sensitive than her partner: 'She listened to him much more than he listened to her. . . I knew she was better at talking than him' (*PCH* 202). He senses her desire to protect her eldest son from the visible signs of her husband's violence, as when she does not come down the stairs one morning or when she does not wash the dishes. The songs sung in the house acquire dire, secondary levels of meaning, which Paddy begins to decode:

> I'll tell me ma, when I go home,
> The boys won't leave the girls alone.
> They tossed me hair, they stole me comb,
> But that's all right, till I get home. (*PCH* 191)

He sees a clear link in his mother's bruised face, yet it is still hard for a ten-year-old to understand what is happening: 'I loved him. He was my da. It didn't make sense. She was my ma' (*PCH* 191). He puzzles to find a reason for his father's aversion to his wife: 'I wanted to be on both sides/ He was my da' (*PCH* 252) – but it is unfathomable. All he can sense is that the bafflement is somehow shared by his mother, who embraces her children: 'But she wasn't cuddling us; she was hanging on to us' (*PCH* 222). This may be one of the very few moments in the novel when a somewhat more grown-up language is overlaid on that of a ten-year-old, a moment when direct experience may be yielding to memory.

The stress of it all suddenly makes Paddy aware of how he looks to Sinbad, for his red eyes and white face had been noticed by everyone else, from his mother to his teacher. Now that the parental split is out in the open, his feelings about his brother change from irritable aggression to protective love. He even begins to call him by his real name, Francis, as if he no longer needs to glory in his power over him. Instead, he advises him to button up before he zips his trousers. Paddy gets caught up in more and more fights and eventually learns how to beat up the boy who was bullying him, much to his mother's pleasure.

Deeper down, however, he no longer cares what his peer group make of him. They may say 'Paddy Clarke. Ha. Ha. Ha.', but 'they were only kids' (*PCH* 281). He has long been rehearsing a parental role, now recognized by his mother. Even though the action has taken just a few months, and he is still the ten-year-old he was when it began, he has grown up, not by choice but out of sheer necessity. He has gone from being a carefree child to a supportive companion for his mother. While a child reader might enjoy that moment when she calls him 'the man of the house now' (*PCH* 281), it is doubtful that most child readers would have stayed with the book until this point. It is a volume which, rather, reminds grown-up readers of a state they might once have known and, indeed, of how and why they ever learned how to read. When you love your friends, and cannot abide them at the same time, you are ready to disappear into a book.

Peace Comes Dropping Slow

As the Troubles of Northern Ireland continued into the 1980s, ten Republican prisoners starved themselves to death in a campaign for political status, which would give them the right to wear their own clothes. The response in the South was muted but in the North thousands of new recruits joined the IRA/Sinn Féin movement. Since only a minority could be used in military activity, it was inevitable that Sinn Féin (the political wing) was destined to become a main player in the politics of the North, and soon its candidates had won forty-two per cent of the nationalist vote. Politicians in London and Dublin took note. After some jaggedness in Anglo-Irish relations (mostly caused by Margaret Thatcher's suspicion of Irish intentions), an agreement was signed at Hillsborough in 1985, recognizing that Dublin would have a consultative role, especially in monitoring infractions of the civil rights of Catholics or nationalists.

As Sinn Féin support grew, its leaders launched a peace process, based on the IRA's recognition (shared by British army intelligence) that neither side could hope for outright military victory. The visionary SDLP leader John Hume began a complex but fruitful dialogue with Sinn Féin's Gerry Adams. The British government began to repeat a familiar mantra: it had no long-term strategic interest in Northern Ireland and would stay only as long as a majority vote indicated that wish. More and more nationalists, though disenchanted with the northern state, seemed increasingly indifferent to the prospect of unity with the South and seemed ready to settle for some sort of power-sharing arrangement. All this talk of peace did not prevent continuing outrages – a 'shoot to kill' policy among British agents in pursuit of Republican militants and the massacre by the IRA of eleven Protestants at a Remembrance Day commemoration in Enniskillen in 1987. The release of the Guildford Four and Birmingham Six, wrongly imprisoned for bombings in the 1970s, increased public distrust of police and army.

By 1993, politics seemed to be in the ascendant: a jocular newspaper columnist suggested that the Derry brigade of the IRA might be nominated for the Nobel Peace Prize. In the event, a few years later, that prize was shared by John Hume and David Trimble (leader of the Unionist Party). Despite setbacks – including bombings in Britain – a peace agreement was achieved. In 1998, ninety-four per cent of citizens in the Republic voted to ratify the Belfast Agreement, which recognized that the six northern counties were British or Irish or both. This recognition of the multiple nature of identity was a triumph, in its way, for those writers of the Field Day Theatre Company who had posited a 'fifth province' beyond current conflicts. It was primarily, of course, the outcome of skilful diplomacy from Washington, London and Dublin. The vote in the southern referendum was especially notable: a rare example in the modern world of a people opting to reduce rather than increase a traditional territorial claim. As such, it seemed more like a gesture out of the twenty-first century than the twentieth.

Eventually, the SDLP and more moderate Unionist Party would pay a price for their willingness to negotiate, as Sinn Féin and the hard-line Democratic Unionist Party under Ian Paisley topped the polls. But by some minor miracle (not unconnected with the desire for restored local power and for generous cash subventions from London), the two more extreme parties went into a power-sharing executive, headed by the so-called 'Chuckle Brothers', the Rev. Ian Paisley and former Derry IRA leader Martin McGuinness. It was a striking example of the middle being displaced by both ends. One mordant commentator (the fiercely intelligent SDLP politician Seamus Mallon) called it 'Sunningdale for slow learners'. By now, over 3,000 people had died in the conflict, which appeared to have been resolved on terms roughly similar to those which governed the 1973–4 power-sharing arrangement. But there were differences too. The old industrial power of loyalist workers had disappeared in a new era of soft industry after the closure of ship-yards; and the nationalist community was making huge strides forward in all aspects of public and industrial life, now making up a majority of students at Queen's University. The southern govern-ment had a definite input into policies, also carefully monitored in London and Washington.

The loyalist fear that its adherents might one day be out-bred by Catholics receded, as contraception in the minority community took effect. But the power-sharing executive had its share of problems, collapsing in acrimony over a series of scandals in the winter of 2016–17, mainly caused by a return of the old kind of unionist arrogance.

Meanwhile, in a 2016 referendum, the British had voted to leave the European Union (Brexit), a move opposed by many northern unionist farmers as well as by Sinn Féin, which increasingly played the role of a moderate party, devoted to achieving consensus. At elections in spring 2017, Sinn Féin came within a single seat of the DUP; and for the first time ever there appeared to be a majority among northern voters against the union parties. No major party in Dublin seemed anxious to restore the territorial claim or to call (as John Hume once had done) for a same-day all-Ireland plebiscite on the national question. Compared with the fears unleashed by Brexit, and the possibility of a break-up of the United Kingdom (since Scotland, like Northern Ireland, had voted to stay in the European Union), they had other, more pressing, difficulties to confront.

22. Seamus Deane: *Reading in the Dark*

The crisis in Northern Ireland was kept well below the radar in the 1940s and 1950s, the years treated by Seamus Deane in *Reading in the Dark* (1996). Every Twelfth of July, Orangemen and police drove the inhabitants of the Bogside in Derry back into the foyer of the local cinema and beat them all – adults and children – up. Such brutalization of the Catholic nationalist minority went all but undocumented in the mainstream British press. In 1936 the National Council for Civil Liberties drew an analogy between politics in the Northern Ireland state and the Nazis in Germany. In 1962 Prime Minister Verwoerd of South Africa said he would gladly exchange all his own state's apartheid legislation for one clause of the Northern Ireland Special Powers Act.[1] Like *North*, *Reading in the Dark* is not so much about relations between nationalist and unionist communities as it is about life among the minority community. The pain inflicted by the other side, though bad enough, is as nothing compared with the suffering visited by members of the oppressed minority upon one another. The system has built a replica of its own harshness within that community.

As a city, Derry was a less vicious place than Belfast.[2] In Derry even enemies were somewhat intimate. The despised police in Deane's novel are not just the Other but also mind-readers, decoders of all things. Like the boy narrator, they are themselves readers in the dark. Sergeant Burke, though a member of the Royal Ulster Constabulary, is a Catholic and at key moments he tries to assist his enemies to achieve a measure of civility. This may also reflect the mellowed politics of Derry in the years of the book's gestation. Two years before its publication, Eamonn McCann noted the disappearance of republican militants and British army patrols from the city's streets.

Reading in the Dark is a Gothic novel, centring on ghosts, apparitions and the power of dead men walking. In the Ireland of the later nineteenth century, such writing was done mainly by Protestants as they confronted social decline under the Land Acts. The books were about possession and dispossession among a pressured minority, which felt itself (like Bram Stoker's Dracula) to be quickly running out of earth for its coffins.[3] But in the twentieth century, Gothic became a preserve of writers from a differently stressed minority: the Catholics of Northern Ireland, who also faced dark fears of perpetual dispossession in an oppressive state.

The boy narrator tells his story from start to end, but to strange effect, because he remains shadowy, a mystery to the reader as much as to himself. Despite this intelligence, he never analyses himself, remaining content to report observations and conversations in chapters as brief as school essays or diary entries. Each section comes headed by a precise date, month and year. This may afford the illusion of control over elusive material, but that attempt to 'fix' things comes with problems. Even as the dates hurry forward to a wished-for solution, each individual section pulls the narrator further and further back in time; and yet it suggests, withal, that a future is forming in which things might be put right. The dates, with their finicky precision, suggest a positive unfolding of past events through the present, but also that every analysis is conducted under the constraints of that present. Moreover, the dates are misleading. Though marking a day on which the boy is told something, they rarely mark a simple happening. It is as if they are anchors to a present which keeps slipping back into the past, a past which will not allow this boy to live his own life.

In Northern Ireland, the unionist majority believed, as Protestants do, in the power of text. Their claim to power in the here and now was underwritten by the Ulster Covenant of 1912, signed by hundreds of thousands. Nationalist claims had a more oral basis, rooted in tradition rather than textual history. Nationalists looked far back to a time when the lost land was theirs or forward to a utopian world in which it would come back to them again. One of the narrating boy's main aims, therefore, is to write down in a clarifying sequence all of the rumours and stories he has pieced together, in hopes of achieving the authority of a written narrative informed by oral memory, the authority of history chastened by tradition. In effect, he is trying to write himself right out of the entire conflict.

There is, of course, a problem. To write a *Bildungsroman* is not possible. The family conflict of father and son is not one that produces social progress, since neither father nor son has hands on the levers of social power: that conflict risks simply lapsing back into the intensified squabbles of family life. The boy is given no name, because he cannot even begin to grow until the very end of the novel, when he leaves Derry. Even as he is leaving, he has not fully pieced the story together and still lacks an identity. But if he has no identity, how can he possibly tell the story?

Before that conclusion he portrays himself as a mere reader in the family dark, a decoder of the ancestral/parental situation. In order to make a true reading, he must suspend all personal investments, keeping his own emotions at a remove, like those exponents of the tradition of 'practical criticism' in which Seamus Deane was trained at college. This is (in the words of Liam Harte) a portrait of the artist as a young critic.[4] In the protocols of close reading pioneered by practical criticism, the political backdrop to a text was often repressed or excluded as evidence. This meant that there was seldom an enabling social context supplied to the young critic, which might provide clues about his investigation. So it is here. It would be difficult to tell from the novel's pages what the politics of its author might be. One senses in the boy a desire to read, and a resolution not to be read. He may be an informer but he refuses to be decodable.

During the years in which he worked on this novel, Deane also edited Joyce's *A Portrait of the Artist as a Young Man*.[5] Joyce's book offers a model for shaping 'the uncreated conscience of my race', but such ambition is not achievable in 1940s Derry. The narrator must rest content with being a historian rather than a creator, an observer rather than an activist. Derry seems claustrophobic, its narrowness and intensity reinforcing one another. Its interest for the outside world is limited. When a British army chaplain invites the boys at school to imagine the vast strategic importance of the Foyle basin in the global fight against communism, this is too much for his listeners, caught up at ground level among streets and landmarks over-familiar for years. They can live only their own lives.

Although Derry is indeed a cathedral city, it is still heavily ruralized in culture, not least in the obsession of its citizens with ghosts, spirits, supernatural hauntings. This is doubtless connected with the forms taken by Catholicism in the area but also with the extreme degree of repression in people's lives. It is a world of appearances and disappearances, of hidden forces at work not far beneath the surface. A clown at a circus appears and then disappears, much like the narrator's uncle Eddie, who seems to have vanished in America: the narrator's father will not speak of this. Early in the tale, a diocesan exorcist cleanses the spirit of an unquiet sailor once betrayed by his wife.

The sequence of short, sharply rendered chapters is like a series of still photographs, imposed on one another with the effect of a palimpsest. The ghost mentioned in chapter one is exorcized in chapter three; and the killing of a boy by a lorry anticipates by many pages the death of a soldier in the same space near the end of the book. These early episodes, for all their observational naivety, show exactly how stories in such a community are constructed. A policeman vomits at the sight of the crushed boy's body, but it seemed wrong to feel sorry for this man, since everybody hated the police. At first, the narrator feels nothing for the boy's mother or the lorry driver, until the story is recast as a police atrocity, narratable in a more familiar fashion.

The language in which such stories are told seems to have an autonomy all of its own. The names of childhood illnesses – scarlatina, rubella, polio – sound like those of Italian soccer players; and some can evoke deep fear: 'meningitis' had 'a fight and a hiss to it'.[6] Death is one cause of separation anxiety, as when the boy's recently deceased sister Úna appears before him as a ghost: his brother strongly advises against telling their mother. The father's daily work at a British naval base causes the boy to fear that he might vanish overseas, like uncle Eddie, but 'every day when he came back, I was relieved that he had changed his mind' (*RD* 15). It becomes difficult for the young detective to decode people's faces: at his sister's funeral, all faces are set in such a stern expression that even the handsome and the ugly look alike. Easier, perhaps, to read in darkness, under cover of bed sheets, a book concerning the 1798 rebellion, about a heroine named Anne to whom the young reader pledged undying love. Against these high melodramas, the essay by a country boy describing an evening meal and read aloud to the class had a powerful, honest exactitude: 'That's just telling the truth' (*RD* 21). The narrator feels guilty for including words like 'cerulean', 'azure', 'phantasm' in his own effort, though they would appear often enough in later writing by the country boy-genius who was Seamus Heaney.

A priest named Regan tells the boys in a sermon of a man who once killed a policeman, in reprisal for the killing of a friend. The man held that going to confession was no use, because he felt no guilt about what he had done. He wanted, however, to tell someone, not as a confession (for he was deeply anticlerical) but as in confidence. Yet he went to his death unshriven. This was wrong, says the priest: but he assures the boys of the existence of a higher power, 'a law greater than the laws of human justice', beyond this corrupt world 'where the unjust hold power and the ignorant rule' (*RD* 26). This story reflects that of the boy's maternal grandfather, now sick in old age. Did he do such a thing? The family is tainted by this suspicion, leading the police to raid their home in search of a gun: father, brother and narrator are beaten up. The father divulges to the police the whereabouts of the gun, but they do not believe him. Perhaps, in the convoluted codes of intimate enmity, they are going through a charade (one designed to leave the father with some protection).

Did Uncle Eddie evaporate in the big fire of Chicago? The boy asks too many questions. Was Eddie like the boy's father? The mother accuses the boy of being possessed: he should let the past be the past: 'but it wasn't the past and she knew it' (*RD* 42). In this family, people feel violated by a past which should in theory uphold them. There is little enough sense of a national narrative of songs, stories, books (*The Shan Van Vocht* must be read in the dark). Donegal is the largest meaningful world elsewhere, both utopia and dystopia, a place just up the road in which the surplus energies of Derry life may be carried off, either harmlessly or (more often) harmfully. Although an urban people, the characters in the novel are vulnerable to the visiting chaplain's phrase (taken from Karl Marx) on 'the idiocy of rural life'. The boys attempt to laugh at all the old superstitions and beliefs, yet they seem the most haunted of all.

The father's own world had been swept away in a week during his thirteenth year, with the death of his parents and disappearance of his brother. He could thereafter never believe that freedom could be found in such a place. What you wanted to do and what you should do could seem close enough but in such toxic conditions *is* and *ought* remained as far apart as ever. When the boy's father rescued his own sisters from work as slaveys in Donegal, his dead mother appeared as a smiling ghost at the foot of his bed, pleased with him: but the boy could not help feeling that there was 'a deeper sorrow in the family than I could yet know' (*RD* 51). The sentence resonates with the epigraph to the novel from the famous folk-song 'She Moved Through the Fair':

> The people were saying no two were e'er wed
> But one had a sorrow that never was said. . .

The unionists of Derry annually commemorate the siege of 1689, in the course of which the town's apprentice boys held out against the army of King James II. Like all settler communities, its members do indeed feel besieged by the armies of their surrounding enemies and also by the disapproval of the outside world. But the feeling can be catching in a small place. Nationalists also feel themselves under siege in this book by illness, by the police, by the power of the past to erupt into the present, by the very myths that otherwise sustain them. The boy narrator learns of the Field of the Disappeared, where birds vaporize if they try to fly across it, their cries sounding eerily human. 'I think it's all made up' (*RD* 54), scoffs the boy, who is a sceptical reader, anxious not to credit nonsense; yet this selfsame anxiety will cause *him* to disappear at the end, rather than stay in the community to be further decoded by the police.

Each of the short chapters in *Reading in the Dark* conveys a sense that, properly expanded, it could have the makings of an entire novel, and a novel even denser in potential than this one. The impression conveyed is that there are even more tales untold than told. Each story may, in a way, be a version of another. The bodies of the dead Fianna sleeping beneath the stone fort of Grianán evoke also the Disappeared. The man who went mad when locked in the fort anticipates Crazy Joe's state of perpetual childhood (the secret of the insane). In this order of things, children take on many of the woes of adult life, while some adults are reduced to the high dependency of children, forever arrested by some trauma in an infantile state. The story told by Aunt Kate, of a boy and girl whose hair and voices changed under the malign influence of their dead parents, and who themselves disappeared when they stood before a mirror, comes straight from Henry James's *The Turn of the Screw*: it is an entire novel reduced to an oral anecdote. Most of the *major* texts employed in this book concern the attempts by amazed, unnerved children to decode a fallen adult world – *To Kill a Mockingbird* (whose Boo Radley lies behind Crazy Joe), *What Maisie Knew* (the other source in the work of Henry James), and, of course, *A Portrait of the Artist as a Young Man*. Joyce's book seems, unlike the others, to haunt every page – in its depiction of the intensity of mother–son relationship which the son needs to escape, but also in its great set pieces (chilling sermon; nerve-tingling classes; clashes with authority figures; furtive discovery of sex).

Alongside these literary references are placed dozens of stories from oral tradition – so many that the text is at once a novel and a collection of short stories. The stories appear in the guise of a novel, much as Derry itself seems a collection of tight villages somehow strewn together to make a city. No wonder that the cultural codings of the surrounding countryside exert such an influence. If the short story based on outsider figures is the appropriate form for an unmade, still rural society, the novel with its varied social classes is the genre for a made, increasingly urban network (however fragile or toxic). Every anecdote here carries reverberations of other ones. There is a constant implication that seemingly supernatural events, which sometimes reduce people to silent numbness, may be caused by unrecorded political repression.

The narrator vomits (like the shocked young policeman at the road accident) when he sees two tinkers copulating in a field. Later, he will wonder whether you need to know Latin to engage in sexual acts (semen, vagina, ejaculation, etc.). In general, he does not think much about sex ('I'm normal' (*RD* 152)). Or, if he does, it is all mediated through his intense experience of language, an extreme vulnerability to individual words which he shares with some of the more deranged characters. Crazy Joe asks a good question about the way in which meaning shifts in sentences with the changing location of prepositions: 'Why is it sad when I ask what will become of you and not sad when I ask what will you become? Is the word 'of' sad?' (*RD* 85). No wonder the boy tries to acquire through his growing control of language a sense of freedom, when so little in his world is controllable. Joe's mind is filled with stories of men whose imaginations were so undisciplined that they could never find the language to report their confusions with any clarity. He tells of Larry McLaughlin who, on the night before his planned marriage, was seduced by a fairy woman (or *leannán sidhe*); she vaporized, leaving only a fox in her stead, staring at him from a nearby hedge. Thereafter, McLaughlin could never marry or have a child, but spent his days looking up the street where the meeting occurred:

> And like a love-sick *leannán sidhe*
> She has my heart in thrall,
> No life I own nor liberty
> For love is lord of all. (*RD* 45)

This is another aborted *aisling*, the dream of a fairy woman which is not carried through to liberation: in psychological terms, a case of analysis interrupted, or terminated before resolution. McLaughlin is just one of many repressed persons in this community who project an unlived experience onto the figures of spirits. The boy's own mother does this most of all.

The major set piece of the book is 'Maths Class'. It has the elegant lucidity of a theorem; and yet it turns out that the boys, straining at all times for exactitude, have been collectively working on the wrong problem. Some critics have questioned whether such virtuosic anecdotes have a developed connection with the wider tale. But that itself is the wrong question. The episode in the class is a microcosm of the book as a whole. Every boy who contributes to the attempted solution is at the mercy of his own position in the sequence, curtailed by what has gone before even as he constrains the possibilities for those who follow. Each boy functions at the mercy of mistakes made by previous boys. And all the while they may be torturing themselves by seeking to answer a question never asked, a question that (as in classical tragedy) should never have been put. For in the Greek drama, some question is raised the answer to which might at once illuminate and shatter a being.

Every narrator is a necessary 'informer', but this narrator is accused of a more literal version of that crime, which aligns him to his Uncle Eddie, who was once accused of that wrong. (As in the case of Eddie, his presence is so upsetting to the family that he, also, will have to go away). Right now, he is accused by the bully Willy Barr of collaborating with the police, who arrest him. Sergeant Burke says that people will say that the reason the police left the gun in the family home was because it was a house of informers. . . but the sergeant knows something more:

> Barr's got it wrong. I'll say your daddy has it wrong too. Maybe you should ask your mother, now her daddy's got sick – none too soon either. Still, there you are. Once an informer, always an informer. That's what they'll say. (*RD* 99)

That last phrase recalls 'The people were saying' from 'She Moves Through the Fair' – about that unadmitted sorrow which dogs every uneven relationship but also about the distorted forms which can be taken by unexamined social consensus. Only a part of the truth can ever be grasped by each person, but never the whole story: and yet in order to function, the community needs to agree to believe in certain lies. The real reason Larry McLaughlin went mad was because he was the one who executed Uncle Eddie, who did not die in America at all but was dispatched as a condemned informer in the field of Grianán. And Crazy Joe is crazy because he has had to carry the knowledge of that awful injustice. The boy's mother believes that her family is cursed: when he protests that he did not talk to the police but threw a stone at them, she sighs 'same thing' (*RD* 101), as if in conditions of intimate enmity every communication is a collaboration. So the boy tells his father that the police were on top of them before he was born ('Blame Eddie, not me' (*RD* 103)), at which point the father strikes him. By way of response the child uproots all the father's garden roses, as if he is trying to tell him something more; but the father simply cements over the garden plot, a gesture which suggests that he wishes to have done with the past. The past cannot be so buried. In their innocence, the authorities believe that they have burned out the rats in the trenches and shelters left after the war, avoiding the recognition that the vermin (like the repressed nationalists) can never be finally put down. They will remain 'breathing their vengeance in a dull miasmic unison deep underground' (*RD* 80).

The local Catholic bishop invites the boy to discuss a possible vocation to the priestly life; but the interviewee adroitly uses the meeting to suggest that the prelate has pulled rank to send a message cautioning Sergeant Burke to tell no further lies about him. The grandfather, as opposed to church as to unionists, tells his grandson that Eddie was executed as an informer on his direct orders: 'I left him and went straight home, where I would never talk to my father or my mother properly again' (*RD* 126). At the start of the book, his mother had seen a ghost on the landing which her son would not see, but now he is beginning to discern its outline. The refusal of the father to make this story his own compels the boy to confront it. Setting out like W. B. Yeats to write an autobiography, he finds himself deflected instead into writing the untold story of his father's people. Now he begins to understand why his brother did not want him to tell their mother when he sighted the ghost of the dead Úna. A restless boy, the narrator believes that what seem like mysteries can be rationally explained; that early disappearance of the circus clown was a trick he wished to analyse, although everyone else seemed content to accept it as a teasing mystery.

The boy's persistent analysis may be admirable but, in a world based so comprehensively on denial, it is also disruptive. He is sent to his grandfather as a sort of punishment for asking about Eddie's role as informer, but the punishment deepens when he learns from the old man that Eddie was not the informer at all. That information is numbing. A past as untransacted as this one simply immobilizes the next generation. Worse still, he has learned that the real informer was McElhinney, his mother's one-time lover and husband to his Aunt Kate. Though he and his mother may never talk, they are nonetheless 'pierced by the same shaft' (*RD* 127). There is little of sun-lit pleasures and childhood joys in this book, such as may be found in the poems of Deane's classmate at St Columb's College, Seamus Heaney: rather there is the slow unfolding of trauma. In Joyce's *Portrait* other characters are shadowy and unclear, existing only on the fringe of the narrator's consciousness; here the narrator is the shadowy one, nervously vigilant, anxious always to distance himself from all the pain lest it overwhelm his good judgement. Yet this very capacity to intellectualize everything causes him further pain, bringing also the burden of adult knowledge and responsibility. When his brother asks the father how Eddie died, the narrator protectively wants to stop the conversation: 'For once, I knew more than he did. Than either of them did. It was like being a father to both of them, knowing more' (*RD* 133). Eddie, before his death, had been interrogated in the very farmhouse where his sisters worked as skivvies. The father tells his sons that Eddie died an informer's death.

The stigmata of all this grief has reduced the mother to madness, leaving her abstractly touching the walls of her home or staring vacantly through its window, for she had loved a man other than the one she married. No surprise that her husband should ask her in her moments of derangement where exactly she has gone. He probably knows more than he suggests; certainly, he speaks wisdom in telling his children that there are few real Christians or real republicans.

Crazy Joe, confided in by the mother, becomes a sort of second father to the boy, educating with the riddles of a Shakespearean fool. He was the one who identified McElhinney as the informer, and the result is that he will always be the same age. He understands how much pressure the lad must register, caught between what he knows and what he feels. Because of the silence of the adults, the boy is obliged to fill the gaps himself by intelligent deductions. As Derek Hand has shown, he gains knowledge but, perhaps because of the constant stress, cannot be said to achieve wisdom.[7] He wishes his mother would fill out some details – but she cannot. She knows that her son knows the truth and she dislikes him for knowing it, but she refuses to tell her husband: 'Was it her way of loving him, not telling him? It was my way of loving them both, not telling either' (*RD* 187).

Yet tell the tale he does, albeit in his own strange way. He writes it in English, translates it into Irish and then destroys the English version. He reads it to an uncomprehending father, who says it sounds wonderful, as the mother watches angrily. This is a parody of the way in which the 1937 Constitution of Ireland was composed (drafted in English, then put into Irish, as the 'superior' version in law) – the document which, even as it made a territorial claim on the six counties of Northern Ireland, recognized that state's existence for the first time.[8] It was a postmodern fantasy worthy of Flann O'Brien, who pointed out that in the event of a legal dispute between versions, the one in Irish would prevail over the source in English even in the event of a mistranslation, for the same document proclaimed Irish the first official language.

The wisest characters in the novel turn out to be Sergeant Burke, Crazy Joe and the boy's father. Burke reveals himself to have deep reserves of compassion: he knows how much the family has suffered, and so he let them off on the night of the gun raid, simply hitting the men of the house for show. He may even be a better detective, a smarter sifter of clues, than the wily narrator. And he understands that the lives of people in Derry are being deformed by the past. The grandfather, in freeing his own mind by confiding events to his grandson, has redoubled the burdens of the child; yet that child also knows that the 'disgrace' of belonging to an informer's family has no basis at all. The father, who had seemed to wink at the antics on the night of the gun raid, perhaps knew more than his child understood.

Crazy Joe, who discovered that McElhinney was the actual informer, was too smart to approach the IRA with this information, choosing instead to share it with the boy's mother. Now, after his release from the lunatic asylum, man and boy seem inseparable. But the father, who cannot understand that strange bonding, may have known far more than he let on: by holding and containing his pain within him, he may have protected his wife and their marriage. 'Staying loyal to my mother made me disloyal to my father' (*RD* 225), says the narrator, who knows that he will have to leave, if his mother is to feel once again free to love her husband. Imploring him to go away, she has observed that people in small places make big mistakes, or mistakes which are made to seem bigger by the sheer intensity of living in small places. The sense of entrapment is absolute, between the nightmare terrors of Donegal and the imperiousness of the local Protestant overlords. So overwhelming are these constraints that one might wonder whether the narrator has had a childhood at all. At the end the narrator leaves for college in another city, but notices how the father continues to believe that it is sometimes best not to tell all the truth. When the parents of an

English soldier killed in their street visit to view the spot at which their son lost his life, he tells them that the trooper died instantly.

The conflict between nationalism and unionism is ultimately less significant than that between the parents. The boy wishes that his mother's sobs would turn into articulate words, but they do not. He finds it hard to speak himself, except by indirections. After his father dies, the mother loses the power of speech – the very secret she silenced may now be silencing her. So the history of the family 'came to me in bits' (*RD* 225). Sergeant Burke thinks it better that children should not know such a story, but it is futile to try to prevent its telling. Better by far to come to terms with it as fully as one can, knowing that no version can tell all.

The boy who confused names in *The Aeneid* earns no name himself, and even at the close cannot fully understand the role played by his father. The cry 'oh, father' betrays, as Derek Hand has said, a depth of emotion that has been repressed (or absent) for much of this account.[9] The lesson is harsh. Those who can think may not be able to feel; and those who feel may not be able fully to think. We come to know little of the narrator, because he has scarcely had the serenity in which to achieve a knowledge of himself.

He may also be less clever than he thinks. The precise datings come to seem frankly incredible: could anyone, short of a manic diarist, retain so many years later all such numbers in the head? They relate less to actual events than to changes in the boy's awareness of things. He never seems to wonder whether his older brother might know much of what he is privately researching: in this he may epitomize the narcissism of the critic. He questions ghosts but may be the biggest ghost of all himself, forever watchful, spectral, inactive. His attitude to his nearest and dearest is like that of a colonial anthropologist, who wants to read others but disclose nothing of himself. Like a child in an adventure story by Enid Blyton, he tries to solve the mystery by knowing more than bumbling adults. He notes repeatedly the childlike qualities of adults, but may underestimate the actual level of their knowledge. The cementing over of the rose garden raises a question: is it better to uproot the past or to pave it over? The narrator's excavations cause more trouble than enlightenment: and his knowledge is not socially useful to the community (which probably has it all anyway). But it means that he has to disappear.

Yet he has fulfilled the aim of combining in narrative a written and an oral version: no grand narrative but a series of linked stories. The problem with oral lore, from the outset, is that it can impose a shape where there may be no conclusive pattern. The real 'truth' lies somewhere between written Irish and English accounts, in a language of silence.

23. Reading Éilís Ní Dhuibhne

'There's no there there any more',[1] Gertrude Stein sadly said of Oakland, California, after she had returned to it; but the same observation might have been made of the Donegal Gaeltacht in 1972. Supposedly a repository of traditional Gaelic culture and values, to which four Dublin girls are sent for a summer sojourn to improve their Irish, it turns out to be a surprisingly modern place. Its teenagers are more sexually precocious than the visitors from the capital; they sport 'fast' platform shoes; and they use the same mass-produced furniture in their bedrooms.[2]

Éilís Ní Dhuibhne in *The Dancers Dancing* has produced one of the most compelling and understated exercises in the female *Bildungsroman*. Her Dublin girls cannot learn the Donegal dialect from their hosts – a skill which, if mastered, would anyway make them ridiculous in a capital city whose elites speak a 'civil service' Irish, stiff with correct grammar and syntax. But they can learn other lessons – about the hidden injuries of social class; about the cultural gap that separates northerners and southerners at the height of the Troubles; and about the hybrid nature of a national identity which has already been sufficiently expanded to include English mothers as well as Irish fathers, Protestant fathers as well as Catholic mothers.

Ní Dhuibhne's book was first published in 1999, a year after the Good Friday Agreement announced that a county such as Derry might be British or Irish or both at the same time;[3] but its narrative shows that such a redefined Irishness had to be learned in youth before it could be proclaimed in middle age. Her chapter headings can make play with this double layering of time: 'The truce is over (but not to worry it's 1972)'.

If the form of Irish taught in Dublin has little use value in the Gaeltacht, this is true of many other aspects of education and upbringing too. Orla, the central character of the four, comes from a family intent on bourgeois proprieties: her bricklayer father must now be styled a building contractor. She herself seems at times less interested in reviving Irish than in stamping out such Hiberno-English expressions as 'youse' (second person plural of 'you').[4] Yet the crowded house of her *bean-an-tí* in Donegal reminds her all too pointedly of the fact that, when her father was on strike, her own mother had to take in lodgers so that she might receive a good education at secondary school.

That education, though strong on theory, fell short on practice, and Orla's mother, for all her carefulness, did not think to alert her daughter to the likely onset of her menstruation. More generally, the Dublin girls know next to nothing about the war being enacted in Derry, not far from their Donegal setting, during the prosecution of Operation Motorman by the British army. In that summer of 1972, the journalist Mary Holland interviewed an IRA volunteer who insisted that he was dying not for Mother Ireland but simply to protect the neighbours in his street.[5]

The girls from Derry whom Orla meets are thin, fast and derisive of southern attitudes: and their background in nationalist enclaves of dire unemployment suggests a possible equation with Gaeltacht dwellers, who suffered from the same condition.[6] The northern girls are undernourished but modern. They are already aware of their bodies, but not so good at Irish. They talk with utter freedom only when together, yet they know how to manipulate adults. When one of them goes on hunger strike, it is not hard to feel the force of the implied equation between Gaeltacht and ghetto.[7] In the end, the differences between the southerners and northerners come down less to matters of nationalism than to questions of social class. And the southern girls, like honest young people everywhere, try hard to understand.

Orla, being the complex child of an Irish–English marriage, longs to build a bridge between worlds, between the labouring poor and respectable middle class, between Galltacht and Gaeltacht. But the Gaelic values into which she is inducted often seem hopelessly abstract: Irish dancing, in those pre-Riverdance days, is less a sensuous challenge than a sort of Euclid theorem performed with nervous legs. Worse still, the headmaster of the Gaeltacht college believes so little in his own mission that he reverts to English whenever he has a crucial message for his charges, 'so youse will all understand' (*DD* 207). The novel is haunted by that very Hiberno-English which the respectable are intent on abandoning: yet whole sentences and paragraphs written in it suggest that, at its best, such a dialect is filled with expressive potentials, and, moreover, that those who still use it are often much more quick-witted than the politer sorts. If respectable people still think in English while using halting Irish words, then others who still think in Irish are capable of using beautiful English phrases. No wonder that poets from W. B. Yeats to Tom Paulin have argued that Hiberno-English posed the 'real' language question for modern Irish people, too ashamed to recognize the beauties of a hybrid language which had evolved out of the desperate bargain struck between English and Irish in the nineteenth century. Yeats believed that all prestigious activities, from the writing of editorials to delivery of church sermons, should be done in Hiberno-English,[8] but that the Irish were too colonized in their minds to do this.

Orla herself is often ashamed of her eccentric Aunt Annie, about whom she feels (as many do about Irish) that 'something' should be done (presumably by other people). She avoids Annie, much as southerners avoid issues raised by the northern conflict – but, inevitably, a confrontation of sorts with both deferred national questions must occur.

Deeper still, however, is Orla's confrontation with her own emergent womanhood, against the natural backdrop and secret potentials of that hidden place called 'the burn'. It is here, in the presence of the female divinity of the river, that much is resolved, so that the Euclid theorems may be cast aside to make way for real dancers really dancing. Near the end, by a subtle shift of voice, Ní Dhuibhne adds further depth to this narrative of growth and demonstrates how a woman can take power by the simple but audacious expedient of writing herself. This second look at experience can transform a person from one imprisoned by it to one freed of it.[9]

The subtlety of this marvellous *Bildungsroman* lies in its refusal of any sense of a grand narrative. There is no major catastrophe, because everything happens elsewhere, further up the coast, in Derry, or back in the past. This is, after all, an account of a relatively happy childhood, and a happy Irish childhood at that, delivered with tenderness of touch and an utter exactitude of language. Perhaps, in an age of angst-ridden exposes of parental tyranny and youthful trauma, there can be no more subversive or more honest a story than that.

24. Making History: Joseph O'Connor

O f all topics with which a modern Irish author might deal, none is more daunting than the Great Famine. It reduced most of those who survived it to silence. It was a cataclysm so immense, indeed, that it destroyed those very instruments which might have measured it.[1] As is true in many instances of trauma, its effects went largely unreported, even long afterwards. But one effect was plaintively recorded by Malachy Horan, an old man of county Dublin: 'It wasn't that it left the people poor – because they were right used to that – but it left them so sad in themselves.'[2]

An artist writing on such a theme runs a risk. The danger is that he or she will be accused of appropriating extreme suffering and filtering out some of the trauma in order to give a viable shape to the tale. And that risk is compounded if the writer chooses to do this in the form of a novel. Some might say that this genre had its heyday in the 1840s but it seemed quite unable to cope with the privations of Ireland's poor (the vast majority of the people). As a form the novel was considered more appropriate for the depiction of upper and middle classes. Societies which had not yet produced a fully functioning bourgeoisie were deemed unsuitable for such treatment: in the words of one famous exponent of the genre, 'how can you write a novel of manners about a society that has none?'[3]

Nevertheless, Joseph O'Connor has done what many would have considered impossible. In 2002 he produced a novel that does full justice to that terrible event, and to all the sorts of persons who found themselves caught up in it, whether they were landlords, tenants, witnesses, sailors, victims or hangers-on.

His unit of investigation is a very old one, as old as the Christian Bible and probably older than that. He takes a ship full of people en route to the New World after the holocaust. Because he is a dialectical thinker, as well as a natural storyteller, he shows just how interwoven are the destinies of all on the ship. By the end he has established a comprehensive and convincing picture of both Britain and Ireland in the 1840s. *Star of the Sea* is as ample in scope and resonance as anything produced by Charles Dickens or Anthony Trollope. In fact, Dickens has a cameo walk-on role at the close of one chapter, where he is suddenly given the idea and name of his great rascal Fagin for *Oliver Twist*; and there are lots of clever references to another great book of the 1840s by someone called Ellis Bell, who is presumed to be a clergyman from the north of England.

In no way, however, does *Star of the Sea* return us to the narrative methods of the 1840s: rather, it combines an amazing variety of types of writing in a postmodern fashion. O'Connor, as always, does social comedy with great verve, being especially adept on the strange psychology of the Irish male.[4] He combines documentary journalism with political thriller and vernacular letter writing. Previous books of his had been accomplished essays in one or other of these modes; but here the full range has been deployed for the first time in a work of astonishing amplitude.

O'Connor can fuse the kind of writing found in *Cowboys and Indians*, *Desperadoes* or *The Secret World of the Irish Male* because of one strong conviction: that the world of the 1840s is not so very different from his own. In both decades, market forces were proclaimed the way to happiness in a society which reconciled itself blithely to the idea that only the fittest could deserve to survive. Again and again in the novel, the reader on its publication in 2002 would have been reminded of recent events which had featured in the national news, from commissioned acts of murder to the accidental death of refugee stowaways in container ships plying from ports in mainland Europe to Irish harbours. The book opens with a victim of the Great Famine who became monstrous – in fact, a contract killer – but he is used as an analogy for the free market: 'A man called X would have to die. And a man called Y would have to kill him. You could call it the dictum of the Free Market of murder; the exigencies of supply and demand.'[5]

In a similar parallel between Victorian and postmodern worlds, there is a deeply affecting chapter about the decayed bodies of a young man and woman found smothered in the recesses of a ship, having stowed away there as they moved in hope towards America. That image connects powerfully with television pictures of refugees from Eastern Europe found asphyxiated in container trucks rolling off ships in Rosslare harbour.

The dilemma of a journalist who must sometimes choose between telling a story or saving a life was nothing new in 1847 – and is nothing new in the twenty-first century. O'Connor's method is dialectical in the deepest sense, for not only does it explore the strange interdependencies of rich and poor in an era when Karl Marx was propounding his analysis of the relation between base and superstructure, but it also suggests many terrifying analogies between then and now.

In certain ways *Star of the Sea* recalls the other indisputably major novel written about the Great Hunger, Liam O'Flaherty's *Famine*. That book was published in 1937, as the first production of Victor Gollancz's Left Book Club, at a time when many conservatives were calling for an end to hunger marches and industrial strikes and a return to the Victorian world. O'Flaherty, being a socialist, did not agree. He told a story which proved that private charity, no matter how good, could never be a substitute for organized justice. In doing that, O'Flaherty provided Aneurin Bevan with one of the slogans which would prove serviceable a decade later during the creation of a welfare state. It is based on a perception similar to that voiced by Grantley Dixon at the end of *Star of the Sea*, when he characterizes the relationship which might have existed between Pius Mulvey and David Merridith: 'One was born Catholic, the other Protestant. One was born Irish, the other British. But neither of these was the greatest difference between them, One was born rich, the other poor' (*SS* 397).

For all its deep dialectic, this book is never solemn, recognizing that the discrepancies in human destiny often produce moments of sheer hilarity. A figure in Newgate Prison decides to beguile the time by reading the poetry of John Milton. He attempts to cast an imagined production of 'Paradise Lost' using only the warders and inmates around him (much as many young people, when bored during long religious services, tried to cast an entire production of Shakespeare's *Hamlet* from those sitting in plain sight in nearby pews).

O'Connor is suavely acerbic about those ascendancy types who seek to cross over and 'pass' as Connemara peasants. There are definite traces of the founder of the Gaelic League, Douglas Hyde, in David Merridith, a moving portrait of a complex man. And O'Connor is mordantly witty about the Victorian male's obsession with data, number and quantification. At a moment of maximum vulnerability, a starving peasant in Connemara remarks with sophisticated derision that the king of England invented time one afternoon in Greenwich: 'but we'd all have been a lot happier if he hadn't' (*SS* 75). Nothing, as Beckett joked, can produce more fun than unhappiness.

Music was often the food of those who could find nothing more substantial in their mouths. O'Connor knows the Irish song tradition far better than most and marvels at the cynicism of balladeers who, in order to sell an existing song to a prospective bidder, would simply change the words to match the buyer's prejudices. Thus the very old could be recycled as the utterly new. So the song 'Arthur McBride', with its eloquent refusal by Irish republicans to take the king's shilling, is subtly rejigged and resold as a cockney ballad in London:

Oh, the nancies we chases are sweet as the air,
The doxies of Dean Street and sweet Leicester Square;
But you'd lug us to Ireland with nary a care,
Where we could get plugged in the morning.

So we'll stay 'ere and play 'ere, flash-lads in the know,
Where sweet Thames flows slowly from Richmond to Bow;
And with sad benediction we bowed very low
And bade him be buggered this morning. (*SS* 189)

That cynical strategy recalls the barefaced cheek shown by the Irish-language poet Gofraidh Fionn Ó Dálaigh in a rather eloquent poem written in the heyday of the bardic system:

In a poem for the Gael
We promise that the foreigner will be expelled from Ireland.
And in a poem for the foreigner
We promise the expulsion of the Gael.

If society is shown not to have changed all that much since the 1840s, the writers of that decade are shown to be caught in exactly the same vortex of cynicism as the ancient *filí*. In *Star of the Sea* a London publisher advises a would-be novelist how to write about Ireland: 'Make a collection of impressions of the Emerald Isle. Mist on the lakes. Jolly swineherds with queer wisdom. Pepper it up with a few pretty colleens. Do it in your sleep. Don't know why you won't' (*SS* 47). A book so willing to ironize its own procedures may be the only way to deal nowadays with this difficult subject. There is a noble discretion in its closing pages, the energy of a powerful reticence, as O'Connor leaves us with some of the few actual accounts of the Famine which survived. All of them suggest what Amartya Sen has demonstrated: then, as now, the problem of hunger is never one of supply but of distribution – and the real villains are those middle-men who prevent supplies getting through quickly to those who need them most.[6]

O'Connor's novels of the past are written out of a conviction that there can be no history, only histories. In his subsequent American tale, *Redemption Falls* (2007), set in the Wild West of 1865–6, he has produced a choric novel narrated through the actions of Irish rebel James O'Keeffe, but also through the poems and ruminations of his loving but unhappy wife, Lucia Cruz-McLelland, the gossip of local townspeople, the newspaper diatribes of his enemies and the oral narrative of his black serving woman. The letters and reports of a whole retinue of officials are set into constant tension with ballads and come-all-yes, which offer many alternative versions, especially on the Confederate side. As in *Star of the Sea*, O'Connor remains unsentimentally alert to the fact that popular balladry is as likely to lie in extenuation of barbarism as is any government document.

When wars and famines end, the real trouble begins. The slave-holding American South had lost the civil war by 1865, but the psychic scars created by racism were carried, by white people as well as black, for more than a century after the abolition of slavery. A colonial power may be expelled by a movement of national liberation, yet habits of self-doubt and even self-hatred may persist long after the occupier has gone.

O'Keeffe is a freedom fighter who has escaped the hangman's noose and the life of a convict in Tasmania, finding fame and fortune in the land of the free, only to discover that his earlier sufferings are not so easily transcended. In the end, he may be sabotaged by his very virtues. The title of the novel indicates not only the name of the town in which much of the action is set but also these bitter, underlying truths. O'Keeffe, hero and anti-hero, is known as 'the Blade' (in the same way that Thomas Francis Meagher, on whose life his seems based, was known as 'the Sword'). He is at once a brave Irish rebel and tawdry showman, a fearless abolitionist and intermittent racist, a harsh dispenser of Reconstruction law and a sensitive soul having a hard time. All this against a background of anarchy and improvisation in the American West.

Such a tale has been retold in a vivid, Boys' Own style by Thomas Keneally in his devoted, scholarly study *The Great Shame* (2000) and in telescoped, dramatic form by Donal O'Kelly in *Catalpa* (1996). O'Connor opts for a more layered approach, which stresses the inner uncertainties of men and women who are anything but what they seem to others. In this world, heroes may be clowns, prostitutes can also be saints, cowards might prove brave and scientists turn out sentimental. Although *Redemption Falls* is written with the panoramic sweep of a classic Victorian novel – witness its repeated references to George Eliot and Charles Dickens – it is filled also with interior monologues and implied soliloquies, which could be written only by someone well familiar with the works of late modernism.

'History', it is often said, is what gets written in official narratives by the winners, whereas 'tradition' is what ordinary people, often life's losers, remember as having actually happened.[7] But what are we to make of lives when (as is so often the case) nobody really wins a war or can even say what winning or losing might mean? Then there are only histories, endlessly proliferating; and O'Keeffe bears the stigmata of every one.

By any measure, James O'Keeffe is a major literary creation. With each new version of him put into circulation, he becomes more fascinating and unfathomable, a man who in the end seems strange even to himself. 'People like not being able to understand things straight away', he muses at one point: 'What was life itself but an appearance not apprehended?'[8] There is mystery at every turn in this plot, but no lack of clarity, for O'Connor is incapable of writing an obscure sentence. However, he insists that in a world in which even our interior monologues may be as deceptive as a newspaper editorial, it is not enough to have one or two accounts. As Toni Morrison has said, a writer needs 'a whole community of memories'.[9] To have produced such a kaleidoscope is a superb artistic achievement, worthy of comparison with Morrison's own book *Beloved*.

Like *Beloved*, *Redemption Falls* deals with the voyage of a troubled woman. Eliza Duane Mooney travels in search of her younger brother Jed, one of the hundred thousand children drawn into the war. Like Morrison's *Beloved*, this child appears in the story as both victim and judge, as tormentor and liberator. Seemingly mute after many traumatic episodes, he is adopted by O'Keeffe as a surrogate for the son whom the Irishman guiltily abandoned in Tasmania. Like 'the Blade', however, the child becomes the site of endless ambiguity, a focus of gossip and speculation (the debt to George Eliot's *Silas Marner* is deftly and beautifully evoked in the text).

O'Connor shows well how the anxieties of adults about their own 'lost' values are forever projected onto the image of childhood; but that the image of childhood often returns sentimental adults to those very nightmares which led them, in some desperation, to evoke it. *Star of the Sea* used the reports of dead bodies arriving on 'coffin ships' in 1840s America to cast an angular light upon a contemporary Ireland in which refugees arrived asphyxiated in trucks opened at a port in Co. Wexford. With its tales of teenage soldiers pressed prematurely into battle, *Redemption Falls* presages a postmodern world in which mere boys often make up armies in Eritrea or Bosnia.

O'Connor has clearly based the book on massive research in New York archives; and the reader is struck by analogies between the vigilante mobs who threaten O'Keeffe and the Klansmen of later decades. That Irish persons, who might have known better from their own colonial experience, were drawn to take the side of slave holders as well as abolitionists is central to the theme.

Star of the Sea ended with the arrival of its shipful of disparate and desperate characters in America. This is a story set eighteen years later (Eliza Mooney being the link) concerning the instability of an Irish-America that never really knew which side it was on in the great debate of that age.

In recent decades, Irish-Americans have written fine novels and scholarly monographs, treating Ireland as a stable entity that can be assessed, controlled and ultimately contained by their 'objective', authoritative analyses. Here O'Connor brilliantly reverses that manoeuvre, demonstrating just how shaky and uncertain is the ground on which every Irish-American stands. He clearly loves and learns from many leading American novelists of the present – from the brooding but exact lyricism of Cormac McCarthy, through the trauma narratives of Morrison, to the garrulous oldest-widow-tells-all style of Allan Gurganus. But to this rich blend he has added a gift for storytelling, an explosive humour and an amplitude of language all his own.

The result is a big book filled with memorable, flawed but utterly real people. It affords all the pleasures of old-time nineteenth-century plot lines, but in a fashion that honestly reflects all of our twenty-first-century uncertainties about the power of storytelling to heal anybody or illuminate anything. O'Keeffe, the stage rebel, yearns to tell adoring audiences 'I am an imposter' (*RF* 84); but he knows that, although people distrust fictions, they cannot live without them. 'Only the wind stays the same in the end', we are told, 'and the bodyless who live in the songs' (*RF* 123).

Yet there is a surprising sting in the tail. After all the preceding horrors, it comes as a moment of mellowness and happiness. It demonstrates how even the most damaged persons can survive trauma and report it with clarity. This book shows O'Connor taking on the United States without in any way abandoning his Irish roots.

25. Fallen Nobility: McGahern's *Rising Sun*

There is a temptation to interpret the writings of John McGahern as one last, loving exercise in the old Gaelic mode of *caoineadh ar chéim síos na nuasal*, a lament for fallen nobility: but the writer is also shrewdly aware that the announcement of the death of a code is often the signal for a major attempt to revive it.

Although many of the characters in *That They May Face the Rising Sun* are poor in a material sense, and some are either gruff or completely silent, they bear themselves like ruined aristocrats, for whom the exchange of money is a vulgar embarrassment and custom far more significant than any law. 'No misters in this part of the world', says one of them early on in a beloved local mantra, 'nothing but broken-down gentlemen'.[1] In one sense, that line evokes the great elegists of a toppled Gaelic aristocracy, from Dáibhí Ó Bruadair to Aogán Ó Rathaille, and seems to suggest that it may not be possible to write a conventional bourgeois novel about such people. Yet, at a deeper level still, the remark recalls the rural villages of Jane Austen in the England of 1800, that mellow, fading world in which a few families shared scraps of news and gossip in the slowest of slow motion.

McGahern himself has observed that the decline of rural Ireland began as far back as the Act of Union in 1800; and that, in 300 years' time, historians may have come to see the Anglo-Irish Treaty of 1921 less as a qualified triumph for nationalism over unionism than as the moment when a native elite took over from foreign rulers the responsibility for 'managing' the crisis of rural Ireland. The image of fretful children peering up from the floors before being removed to England is what Joe Ruttledge recalls of visits by himself and his partner Kate to view 'For Sale' houses near Shruhaun, put up by families whose dreams were now 'in tatters' (*RS* 16). The x-mark scored through every day of the month on a calendar left hanging in the house the couple finally bought stopped on October 23, the day its owner died. This seems to be a community whose members are bound only for death or the emigrant ship. The return of the Ruttledges is almost perverse, an act which goes against the prevailing trend of people leaving the place. Their childless state suggests that only couples untrammelled by parental responsibilities – which is to say, only those without a personal stake in a communal future – can afford to stay. The few who achieved some wealth, such as Ruttledge's uncle (called the Shah), have done so by smartly avoiding the heavy demands of family life with many children. That celibacy practised by priests, far from being repressive, is viewed as the ideal social state and emulated by the Shah, who says ruefully of a girlfriend who tired of waiting for him and married another man: 'if she'd waited another few years, she'd have been safe' (*RS* 39). The logical outcome of these attitudes is narrated by Patrick Ryan, another singleton, who says that whereas once the countryside was walking with people, 'after us there'll be nothing but the water-hen and the swan' (*RS* 45).

Dirges like this have been sung in every generation and yet something of the old world always stubbornly remains. Telephone poles, television aerials and meat factories may change the look of the landscape, but its traditions manage to live on, even in the very lament for their passing. What is celebrated here is nothing like wild, untamed nature, but an altogether more Augustan notion of a countryside filled with civilizing human presences, such as the practice of bee-keeping.[2] Against such a neoclassical backdrop, the naked expressions of rudimentary passion by characters like John Quinn or Johnny seem like gross self-indulgence, bound to bring suffering and trouble, as when Quinn rapes his new wife or when Johnny quits a good life in that secure world to pursue an unrequiting lover to England. The sexual reticence of the Ruttledges, in a community which prizes the quiet life, begins to seem enviable rather than wan. The cultural alternatives to it are stark – the brutal violation of almost total strangers enacted by John Quinn, or the licensed version of his activity which passes for entertainment on the TV show 'Blind Date'. Soon, says a trusted neighbour named Mary, 'they'll be watching it on television rather than doing it themselves' (*RS* 189). It is as if the same fate awaits sex that has already overtaken darts.

The overall focus of *That They May Face the Rising Sun* is not on this or that individual, so much as on the community as a whole, and this is one of those very rare Irish books which, even as it insists on the community as the key to identity, avoids all hint of socialist moralizing. The lake around which most of the characters live is the force which organizes and governs their days, and as such it is more powerful than any person. It survives the coming and going of peoples as the ultimate hero of this narrative. So unimportant are individuals that McGahern leaves it deliberately unclear at certain points (for instance the scene on page 34) as to who exactly may be telling an extended story. In the end, it does not really matter who is the teller this time in a society where so many utterances, jokes and stories are shared. A man in such a dispensation has so little individuality that he 'can be taken out of the air like a bird if you had the mind' (*RS* 262). The impression is that the overall story is telling the characters far more than they are telling it. That may well be an unavoidable conclusion reached by any who live close to the land: like Moran in McGahern's *Amongst Women*, they may try to work the fields, while all the time suspecting that the fields are working them.[3]

The equation of man and bird in their shared vulnerability is not offered to belittle men: after all, it is the birds who may survive to lay a final claim to the lake (their song, which often charms humanity, is really an articulation of a territorial claim). All through this book, animals are approximated to humans and humans to animals, to the strange if surprising dignity of both. Johnny, heartbroken, shot his two magnificent dogs before leaving for England, but would have been better off if he had shot himself instead of the animals. The animals on the Ruttledge farm have a status halfway between lodgers and pets: the cat might some day order a breakfast and the shorthorn might soon be imagined putting on a pair of spectacles to read the *Leitrim Observer*. A republican rebel sheltered once by Jamesie's father never thanked the family which risked all to protect him, but the same man would not leave a dog to die alone. And the passing of a lamb is felt by the Ruttledges as a kind of family bereavement.

Because humans are equated with animals, there is no great sense of injury in the final victory of nature over some of the forms of culture in Shruhaun, for the dichotomy is shown to be almost meaningless. An ash tree grows in the room where Jamesie's wife, Mary, played cards as a girl (*RS* 88), but her father, on those dark nights when he rode tipsily asleep in the pony and trap which bore him home through the village, might have been rehearsing not just his own death, but the mindless, repetitive rituals of a nature to which all must return. The lake is indeed a whole world, determining everything, even those sentences which people share and gratefully repeat: 'How are yous around the lake? You were very good to come.' The herons which fly out of the reeds are in fact guiding those persons who think they are making their own way around the rim of the shore. If a lingering dissolution awaits such elderly invalids among the ageing population as Bill Evans, even that fate may also be taking its pattern from nature: 'his kind was now almost as extinct as the corncrake' (*RS* 15).

Nature is a beautiful foreground which creates – long before it reflects – the human mood. In *Amongst Women* it could sometimes seem like the enemy, rattling domestic windows – or driving desperate men to a victory in 'slaughtering trees'.[4] Like so many Irish after the Great Hunger, Moran could never bring himself to a full trust in a nature which had failed his own people. Yet the lesson of *Amongst Women* was that Moran's children might move to the great cities, environments which, though wholly constructed by humankind, left them feeling less at home than ever. The sentiment for nature in *That They May Face the Rising Sun* is more mellow and less conflicted, mainly because the experience of nature is in no sense 'knowing'. The lake and birds are simply there, not as projected metaphors for human moods, but in all their concrete immediacy, as in those early Celtic nature poems doodled by monks on the margins of their holy books. More than one passage of this text reads like an extract from the famous translations done by Kuno Meyer: 'the berries on the rowans along the shore glowed with such redness it was clear why the rowan berry was used in ancient song to praise the lips of girls and women' (*RS* 147).

The book as a whole, which has no divisions into chapters, none-theless provides a full account of the changes in nature through the calendar year, as if what is written is less a plot-driven novel than a book of hours and days. A feeling of harmony with nature leaves people like perfectly tuned instruments, clear as bells but too serene for self-assertion. Those who leave for the city, like Jamesie's clever son, may know some career success yet somehow find themselves dispossessed of all their vital energies. Only in the next generation, writes McGahern, will the effects of strong breeding show through in children less exhausted by the transition (a marvellous, if inadvertent, explanation of much of the energy which may lie behind the Ireland of the Celtic Tiger). The first-generation denizens of the city are so distracted by, and engrossed in, the demands of urban life that they lack true interiority (while, of course, endlessly agonizing about the pathology of the self).

Some readers have said that this book can hardly be called a novel, since nothing very much happens in it. In that complaint, they are hilariously like Jamesie, their surrogate, who loves to steal furtively into his neighbours' houses but is 'nearly always disappointed by the innocence he came upon' (*RS* 1). If Flaubert's ideal novel was a plotless affair, held together only by its style, then McGahern seems to extend that theory to the community of Shruhaun as a whole – a community which, for all its flaws, becomes itself a kind of perfected artwork, one which knows not how to mean but only how to be. If the early Celtic nature lyrics anticipated the modernist poetic in offering concrete images of nature without attendant moralizing (no ideas but in things), McGahern suggests here that there is no real need to go outside this community for reference or meaning. If you do, you may (like Johnny or Jamesie's son) be lost. Within the secure embrace of the community, everyone is a possible artist, as is Kate Ruttledge with her drawings, but this is never an art to be fetishized or reified. Her creations will never achieve the luminous interpretability of Lily Briscoe's in *To the Lighthouse*, because in McGahern's world (unlike Woolf's) nature is invariably privileged over art.

McGahern has often joked that the problem posed for an artist by Irish life is not how to liven it up for entertainment value but rather how to tone it down for purposes of believability. This may explain the rather rough treatment accorded in the narrative to J. M. Synge's *The Playboy of the Western World*, described by Mary as 'terrible eejity stuff' (*RS* 97). The implication is that a plotless book of days may be a more real, non-baroque version of the life Synge sought to record: yet there is also a sense in which McGahern takes from that great play one of his own central themes. This is voiced by Joe Ruttledge himself at the very outset when he avers that 'the way we perceive ourselves and how we are perceived are often very different' (*RS* 3). There are numerous examples of this insight, made possible by the author's focus on many different couples and individuals. For instance, at one point Patrick Ryan is castigated by Jamesie for cruelty in treatment of a borrowed mule, yet some pages later he shows how deeply grateful he was for the loan (*RS* 65). Or again, the Shah thinks that his niece Monica wants only drink and male company in the seaside hotel to which he brings her for a holiday, whereas it later transpires that what she wished for was the very absence of these things (*RS* 102). Such discrepancies can also be enacted by the entire community rather than individuals: Ruttledge is scorned by local farmers for treating lambs with human respect, yet on Monaghan Day it is the best-treated cattle that win the highest praise.

Although Synge's famous play is dismissed by the characters it claimed to describe, it is also rewritten by them, as when Ruttledge recalls the reappearance of Christy's seemingly dead father: 'we may all be the father at the window yet' (*RS* 123), a richly ambiguous sentence. For the past that seems dead has a way of returning, much like the despised play itself. Of course, the deeper affinity between McGahern and Synge is to be found in his respectful use of *The Aran Islands*, the quietest of Synge's masterpieces, written with that sort of spare, austere authority which provides a template for this book. In Shruhaun, as in Synge's Aran, each man can do two or three jobs (Jimmy Joe is undertaker and auctioneer, as well as republican insurgent; Patrick Ryan a mortician as well as a builder) in ways that betoken versatility of mind and body: and, as in Synge, the work of people changes with the seasons, in a manner which keeps them free from dullness.[5]

However much Synge may have admired the west of Ireland, he wrote of it as a dying civilization. The complex of old people's apartments built near Shruhaun in McGahern's account is called Tráth Nóna – evening time – as if to evoke the mellow, autumnal moments that must be followed by death. It is Tráth Nóna for the Ruttledges too, and for 'a whole new class neither in the world or the graveyard' (*RS* 148), people who might once have looked down their noses at the simple Bill Evans but now share his fate. This Beckettian condition, in which life is over but somehow still going on, might offer a pessimist's view of the rural culture recorded here, were it not for the rather upbeat quality of the Ruttledges' involvement with their receiving community.

The Ruttledges begin in the style of a Greek chorus, but a chorus which rapidly gets drawn into the action on which it had intended only to comment as objective analyst. Up to the half-way point, their involvement is somewhat conditional, partly because their neighbours are themselves unsure whether the couple can hack it. Contradictory interpretations abound, as to whether the quiet was something which attracted them to Shruhaun or something which would finally drive them mad (*RS* 295). When Kate Ruttledge is offered the chance to return to a good post in London, she thinks hard before closing the door, but even that closure 'was not a pleasant sound' (*RS* 177). Yet one of the main reasons for her staying is that the Ruttledges, though somewhat precarious in their tenure, have become the fulcrum around which so many other uncertain lives in this surviving community revolve – the Shah, Frank Dolan, Bill Evans, Patrick Ryan, Jamesie and Mary. It is as if their strange, reckless act of faith against all the evidence emboldens the others. 'You were like an angel, today', Kate tells Jamesie at the end, who scoffs 'I thought you didn't believe', only to be told 'there are lay angels' (*RS* 252).

That They May Face the Rising Sun is McGahern's defiant response to those who would question the viability of rural life, not least his own precursor Patrick Kavanagh, whose trajectory McGahern himself threw into reverse by returning to live as a writer in the north midlands.[6] The community around Shruhaun is in many respects a happy people, apparently as far removed from the 'death of rural Ireland' thesis as a people could ever be. But there is also a feeling of closeness to dissolution: when Jamesie and Mary lost their clever son to the university and thence to the city, the life left their place. And the condition of Bill Evans, who represses the memory of a traumatic childhood and is reduced to a simpleton, prevents any glib idealization of the earlier generations. Even the Shah's celibacy has its nervy aspect. Perhaps the Ruttledges are shown to stay because, in a subtle way, they have become the necessary props to these wounded but likeable neighbours, the Greek chorus which not only keeps the community visible to itself as such but also keeps it viable too. If Bill Evans in his derangement lives in an eternal now, allowing neither prospect nor retrospect, that is not so very different from the world of Kate Ruttledge, who says: 'The past and present are all the same in the mind: They are just pictures' (RS 73).

The great virtues, epitomized by the Ruttledges, are tact and trust: and the couple is esteemed by a community which itself places a premium on these two values. They are conflated in the repeated refusal of cash payment by people in Shruhaun. Patrick Ryan may unconscionably delay for years the erection and completion of a shed for the Ruttledges, but he would never dream of taking cash for work done as a favour to a neighbour; and the musicians at the wedding of John Quinn refuse all money too. Ryan is so nervous of cash that he pulls wads of it from his pocket in embarrassment whenever the parish priest comes into view, out of the guilty sense that he owes the man unpaid dues; and the priest himself takes only a minimum £20 fee for officiating at a funeral (and not the £100 he could easily command). These people are such natural aristocrats that they handle money only with extreme unease. When Ruttledge takes care of the Shah's savings and then returns them, he asks jocularly whether his uncle would not like to check the accuracy of the amount: 'I could have helped myself to thousands' (*RS* 103). In this plotless world, news is in fact a currency far more negotiable than any money and far more eagerly sought, as it can be given or withheld by mischievous rationers. And silence in that context may be the ultimate gold, worth more to the Shah than his thousands.

The Shah would never dream of counting the money returned by his nephew. Like Jamesie and Mary, he is one of those elect pictured in Giotto's *Flight into Egypt*, who bear themselves 'as if they had complete trust in the blessed light as they travelled to a place where nothing casts a shadow' (*RS* 108). The old Gaelic notion of *comhar na gcomharsan* has been denounced by some sociologists as a form of licensed mutual terror, but it was also a form of rural *noblesse oblige*.[7] It was well described by Synge in *The Aran Islands*, where he cast the employer more in the role of 'host' and the work more as a kind of 'festival'.[8]

Jane Austen herself created many memorable scenes around the notion of neoclassical tact: the need for people to exercise self-restraint, even and especially when in the presence of disagreeable persons. This was part of her wider attempt to find a mode of existence for her critical attitudes within rather than beyond society. For McGahern too, freedom assumes a similar form: there can be no freedom from, only freedom in, society. That society itself is, however, a precarious and even intermittent organism, existing only at privileged moments. And this is why the majority of people in Shruhaun, though disbelievers in its central mystery, still attend Mass in such numbers. When Jamesie's pride is hurt by the disapproval of his 'fast' urban daughter-in-law, everyone feels his smart as if personally endured: 'they were all too fond of him to say another word until he recovered and a path was found out of the silence' (*RS* 35).

Not that silence is always embarrassment: it all depends on the kind of silence one keeps. The Shah and his assistant, Frank Dolan, maintain a successful and productive collaboration over many years based on shared silence. Ruttledge feels happiest when working quietly with Ryan on the long-postponed shed. Work in McGahern's world unites persons far more completely than pleasure ever can. The exquisite tact of the Shah is absolute precisely because it is rooted in his need as a businessman to know exactly whom he may trust:

> Often he sat in silence. His silences were never oppressive and he never spoke unless to respond to something that had been said or to say something that he wanted to say. Throughout, he was intensely aware of every other presence, exercising his imagination on their behalf as well as on his own, seeing himself as he might be seen and as he saw others. Since he was a boy he had been in business of some kind but had never learned to read or write. He had to rely on pure instinct to know the sort of people he could trust. (*RS* 36)

This keen awareness not only of his own presence, but of how others appear to themselves, is what marks the Shah off from someone like Jamesie's daughter-in-law, Lucy. Though resident in Dublin, she is the ultimate provincial in Patrick Kavanagh's definition of the term: someone who has no sense of her effect on others, and no sense of other people's interiority precisely because she has so little of her own.[9] Those who lack this empathy are soon lost in the world of Shruhaun. Hence Lucy's visit with her children drives Jamesie onto an uncharacteristic alcoholic spree. In a life filled with repetitions, which can raise routine to the power of ritual, even the most fully rendered characters are capable of behaving unpredictably, and of taking themselves as well as others by surprise.

Novels, it is often said by those who remember their Tolstoy, can only be written about unhappy persons: the happy family seems proofed against any kind of narrative. Yet in this book McGahern sets himself the task of writing an interesting account of people who are almost all utterly at one with their world, even if they feel that their presence in the natural world is uncertain and provisional. The theme, however, is Proustian: happiness may be possible but can be known as such only in retrospect:

> The days were quiet. They did not feel particularly quiet or happy but through them ran the sense, like an underground river, that there would come a time when these days would be looked back on as happiness, all that life could give of contentment and peace. (*RS* 206)

The suggestion is that the only ideal tense is the future perfect: the tense in which one can say that this will have been a happy day.[10] The only paradise is, by very definition, the paradise that has been already lost;[11] and that loss may come about through an excessive 'knowingness'. The happiest people are those fully absorbed by their experience, but once the eye starts to look beyond that experience to the use that can be made of it, then integrity is lost:

> [W]ith a rush of feeling he felt that this must be happiness. As soon as the thought came to him, he fought it back, blaming the whisky. The very idea was as dangerous as presumptive speech; happiness could not be sought or worried into being, or even fully grasped; it should be allowed its own slow pace so that it passes unnoticed, if it ever comes at all. (*RS* 183)

This is the real reason why the book refuses the narrative structure of chapters. Better by far, it implies, to submit to the rhythm of the immediate day, without useless fretting about past or future. The past is after all a fiction, and the future unknowable (as unpredictable as the fact that every one of John Quinn's children proves to be charming, kindly and successful in life). The characters all seem to live in a version of Bill Evans's eternal now. Jamesie and Mary pass their days in a house where each of the clocks tells a different time, but Mary is reconciled to this: 'People we know come or go in our minds. . . whether they are here or in England or alive or dead. . . We're no more than a puff of wind out on the lake' (*RS* 115). In saying as much and as little, she becomes the author's own surrogate in the text (as her husband is the reader's), sharing in the yearning of the novelist to recapture lost time: 'it was as if she asked to touch and gather in and make whole those scattered years of change'. Immediately after this statement, however, the writer himself intrudes with unexpected bluntness, as if he had dared too much: 'But how can time be gathered in and kissed? There is only flesh' (*RS* 125).

It is the Shah who comes up with the nearest thing to a solution to this question. The day, he feels, is the unit by which to seize a life, 'turning each day into the same day, making every Sunday into all the other Sundays' (*RS* 41). When Patrick Ryan goes drinking with Ruttledge in town, he angrily refuses his companion's offer to buy his turn in the rounds: 'What the fuck matter whose round it is? All we are on is a day out of our lives. We'll never be round again' (*RS* 228). This echo of a leitmotif of Tomás Ó Criomhthain's *An tOileánach* – 'níl ann ach lá dár saol'[12] – is taken up and repeated by Ruttledge in a later scene when he tells Johnny that the Shah 'has much more now than he needs. There is only so much you can do with the day', to which the response is: 'It may be the whole show' (*RS* 267). This stoic philosophy of Ruttledge, who has no way of knowing whether there is an afterlife or not (*RS* 294), is appropriate in a book which itself offers no comfortable certainties about religion. It does, however, insist that human life is sacred, since it is all anyone can know for sure, and in that context the violence of political fanatics seems like an affront. For this is a work which expresses beautifully, even if it can never solve, the human mystery.

This helps to account for the deeply religious sense of yearning which permeates a text utterly devoid of devotional or creedal conviction. Even the ruined life of Johnny is brought to high dignity at its close, when the preparation of his corpse for burial affords him just the sort of aura he had never enjoyed in life. In the absence of Patrick Ryan, Ruttledge offers to do the work, only to find his handiwork savagely denounced by the returned Ryan on the funeral day: 'It was some face to give a poor man leaving the world... Some face to give him for his appearance in the next' (*RS* 277). Ryan, forever aware of life only as a performance, has no idea of who he is from one moment to the next, becoming his true self only on stage. He delays the completion of the Ruttledges' shed on the understanding that there is very little work that cannot just as easily be left until another day.

Students of pre-Celtic Tiger Ireland might smile sarcastically at this account of the sort of tradesman who perennially left a job incomplete. But there may have been deep wisdom in Ryan's tardiness. For one thing, it was licensed by the fact (already mentioned) that he would take no payment. For another, the rafters he raised made the sky seem 'human' by reducing the sense of its immense space: if the day is one way of controlling and seizing the meaning of life, then this building may be another. Ryan seems reluctant to appear at the scene of a death, in whose arts he is genuinely skilled; and by the close the Ruttledges come to fear the completion of their shed, as if the builder may know or sense something that makes him hesitate. Besides, there is the genuine pleasure which both he and Ruttledge take in silently shared labour: as if, were it to come to an end, so might their solidarity. So, at the very close, Ruttledge holds back from Kate the information that Ryan is coming next week to finish the job.

There is no mockery of last things here, but a cautious, if slightly baffled, reverence. The ancestral custom of burying people with their heads in the westward position, so that if they wake on Judgement Day they will face the rising sun, suggests not only the resurrection of the body but also its willingness to face nothing more than the start of a new day. It is an astringent ending to a very tender book, which captures a community in that moment of perfection which may be possible only to civilizations that are about to die.

26. Conor McPherson: *The Seafarer*

As the twenty-first century dawned and the country boomed, the Irish pub began to die. High prices paid for premises by incautious speculators were passed on to drinkers. At the same time people began to obey the laws against drink-driving. Off-licenses sprang up, offering beer and wine at bargain prices. Many people shifted the main scene of their drinking from pub to the home kitchen. Conor McPherson's *The Weir* – a huge global success in the 1990s – had been rejected initially by the Abbey Theatre on the grounds that its setting in a country bar was hackneyed 'pastoral'; yet almost a decade later, reflecting the new drinking locales of Tiger Ireland, he set *The Seafarer* in the kitchen basement of a house on Dublin's northside:

> The place lacks a woman's touch. It has morphed into a kind of bar in its appearance. Those who live or pass through here are so immersed in pub culture that many artefacts in the room are originally from bars; a big mirror advertising whiskey, ashtrays, beer mats, a bar stool or two somewhere. There is a cold store.[1]

This is not just a sociology of Baldoyle. It is McPherson's answer to his critics at the Abbey – showing that the other time-honoured Abbey setting (an all-purpose kitchen) can replace the shebeen. Public space is being eroded by Tiger Ireland. Even an activity as sociable as drinking has been relentlessly privatized.

Yet the characters are all veterans of the pub crawl. Every second bar on the northside of Dublin seems name-checked in the play, as if McPherson were mocking the fashion for brand placement of designer perfumes in contemporary sex-and-shopping novels. The variously named premises are intoned like ports of call from a sailor's past, with pub crawling presented as a version of the seafaring engaged in by the main character, Jim 'Sharky' Harkin, who once worked on boats. The play deals with what psychologist Carl Jung called the night sea journey of the middle-aged, people confronted by a crisis of meaning in their lives. Sharky is no longer allowed to work on the boats (because of the unreliability and short temper caused by his drinking), so he is one of those sea creatures attempting now to learn the art of living on land. The poem that gives this play its name concerns the lonely voyage on which every traveller must go, to the safe harbour of God:

> He knows not
> Who lives most easily on land, how I
> Have spent my winter on the ice-cold seas
> Wretched and anxious, in the paths of exile,
> Lacking dear friends, hung round by icicles,
> While hail flew past in showers. (*The Seafarer* c.755AD)

In ancient tales the sea represents the unconscious, an environment in which modern people can no longer live for long at a time, but which must be accessed if humanity is to survive. The four drinkers in the play, like all addicts, have a history of keeping on the move, from pub to pub (when affordable), from off-licence to shop (when money is scarcer). Why this restlessness? So as not to be seen in all their guilty pleasuring? So as to meet their own kind? So as to enjoy another drink, as if it were only the first of the day? Any port in a storm may assuage the addict's guilt.

There is also a sense that the drinker is in touch with the 'beyond' – a truth hinted at by Mr Lockhart, the diabolical debt collector, in a central aria:

> that's where I really am... Out on that sea. (*Short pause.*) Oh, you'd have loved heaven, Sharky. It's unbelievable! Everyone feels peaceful! (*Laughs.*) Everyone feels at such peace! Simply to exist there is to know an exquisite, trance-like bliss, because your mind is at one with the infinite! (*S* 128)

Sharky knows that experience of 'beyond', as does Lockhart, in the shame of abjection and repentance, but also in the early euphoric phase of a drinking spree. His fragile, intermittent but recurring connection to that greater power is symbolized by the Sacred Heart lamp which flickers on as inexplicably as it flickers off throughout the play. The boom–bust psychological cycle traced by the alcoholic seems in graphic ways to follow the alternation of loss and redemption, of doom and recovery, which has been the experience of many Irish Catholics. Lockhart epitomizes the demon in every person, driving Sharky after days of abstinence back on to the drink; and that in turn feeds the drinker's self-loathing and shame, curable only by grace and a sudden saving. 'The idea of forgiveness and redemption', says McPherson in an interview: 'I guess it is kind of the culture of the hangover, you know'.[2]

Abjection is very real for all four men in the play. If the basement lacks a woman's touch, that is because they are all shy of women, yet they claim to be bullied by them too! Sharky's wife is now with Nicky Giblin but 'with' is perhaps an exaggeration, since these are men who come together to share a sense of ill-use at the hands of female partners. The women are absent because they are distant points of authority, more potent than the broken fellows onstage. The men admire the women as guarantors of a better way of life which they might still know, but their self-pity imprisons them. The basement room becomes a sort of security zone which indicates their fear of encountering the world.

The blind Richard pees on the floor; and so he must project the guilt for that on to a group of winos who do much the same in the laneway outside the house. Whether these winos really exist except as a projection of his imagination may be doubtful. Even his blindness may be simulated, to license his need for spoiling by his brother Sharky. When the spirit moves him, he seems as able to run and fight as any other man. Yet, though he comes across as mostly ungrateful for his brother's loving care, he is also capable of acts of kindness and psychological insight. It is as if each man who cannot bear to love himself finds a measure of grace in showing some sort of concern for another. And when one like Sharky goes on the dry, every addict around him feels on edge, for him as much as for themselves. McPherson's interest in addiction can be traced right back to an early play about Coleridge and opium, *This Lime-tree Bower My Prison*. When, years later, he directed a film version of Beckett's *Endgame*, he treated it as a study in the co-dependency of addicts, who can neither bear one another's company nor split up either, and who are doomed to repetitive cycles of drinking or of obsessive-compulsive disorder:

> Beckett's characters are like sitting on the edge of a cliff at a table, and everything's laid out, and the cliff is crumbling and they are going to fall into the sea, but they're naturally concerned with using the right fork. It's these silly details that we're all concerned with, when in fact we don't know if there is a God and what will happen when we die.[3]

Richard is like Beckett's blindman Hamm, a melodramatizer of his own pain ('I have so little left to live for!' (*S* 73)), a tyrant and control-freak, and a man terrified by the evidence of human failure all around him. (The vomit deposited in the lane is probably his own.) If Hamm fantasizes about being served by a dog, so does Richard ('if they can get me one of those dogs that bring you your meals' (*S* 94)). He has the physical self-indulgence of the sadist Hamm, just as his Sharky recreates a Clov forever on the verge of walking away from the abusive relationship: 'And you can walk into the walls and spill Paddy Powers all down your horrible filthy whiskers and sit in your own stink 'cause you don't even know what day it is or what time it is. . .' (*S* 79).

Richard's gestures of kindness often have an element of self-interest about them, as when he extends his control over his brother by giving him a mobile phone for a Christmas present, 'that I could get you, you know' (*S* 151). He is sensitive enough to be appalled that his friend Ivan can sleep on the floor ('like an animal' (*S* 75)), yet he is profound enough to see in animals evidence of the miracle of creation. A bluebottle, whose two eyes constitute almost the whole of its head, came to him in a dream, each one staring at the other, communing:

> And there was such. . . comfort, in his blank unseeing regard for me, Mr. Lockhart. You just know that God is in a fly, don't you? The very existence and amazing design in something so small and intricate as a bluebottle – it's God's revelation really, isn't it? (*S* 123)

But the satanic Lockhart balances this optimism by reminding Richard that flies love shit.

Beckett's characters existed mainly in their need for one another. If *esse est percipi*, 'to be is to be perceived', they craved that satisfaction which comes when others confirm an existence by perceiving it. Hence the obsession in this play also with eyes, and with the relationship between blindness and insight. Ivan loses his spectacles for most of the action, as if he cannot bear to see the world around him as it is. Yet there may also be a kind of insight consequent upon blindness. Richard achieves a piercing vision into limited aspects of reality simply by blinding himself to the rest of it. He likes to have visitors to assuage his loneliness but also in whom he can confide it. Like Beckett's Pozzo and Hamm, he seems to have gone blind rather suddenly... or to have blinded himself to his world. But, like Ivan and like Sharky, he needs to feel needed too. He hopes to make some sort of difference, however small, in their lives; and to provide them with moments of gracious adjustment such as the bluebottle afforded him.

The play was premiered in 2006, at the height of the Tiger boom. It centres on a card game involving all four men, fuelled by alcohol and the desire to make some quick money. It would not be far-fetched to read into their carry-on a downmarket version of the casino culture which turned the entire national project into a game of chance. Even though the bust of 2008 is still two years away, prophetic intimations of the end of the Tiger abound. Lockhart is a debt collector, feeding off the plunge into penury of a people too heedless to sustain sudden wealth. Ivan won a boat in an earlier card game, a vessel worth €40,000; but because he is timid (and a night sea voyager), he did not use it. Instead he sold it for €12,000, to bankroll an epic drinking spree. The gambler who lost the boat was trying to ascertain information about the burning of a Wicklow hotel many years earlier... but Ivan never had to explain the point because he won the game: 'won it off a total nutcase that killed himself not long after. He drowned after driving his lorry off the end of the pier in Howth' (*S* 112). The suicides of many businessmen after the collapse of the Tiger are prefigured in that story, as is the random, chancy nature of capital accumulation in those glory years. And the tacky, 'bling' clothing that characterized this sudden wealth is worn by Nicky Giblin in his soiled, €3,000, dogskin Versace jacket (and accompanying shades). Such affluence as there has been is already gone.

The male hysteria of life in Tiger Ireland may have had other explanations too – a fear that the wealth could not be lasting and that those who enjoyed it could never make it endure. The past threatens to return and smother current initiatives. Sharky is trying to stay off drink but Lockhart returns as a figure from a distant Christmas Eve, when he helped the other man escape the rigours of the law. Lockhart had lost a card game and that was the price of Sharky's victory. Like many alcoholics, Sharky exists always on the verge of violent outburst, a tendency inherited from his parents (his mother once broke a chair on him). Their failure to bequeath him the house may have sentenced him to a life of wandering. Like Richard lashing out in bitterness at the winos, he is explosive – he himself once assaulted and killed one of his own kind, a vagrant named Lawrence Joyce. If Sharky managed to escape the rap on that, so also did Ivan on the burned-out hotel. There is a sense through the play that these social marginals, from an unemployment black spot on Dublin's northside, spent most of the pre-Tiger years on transitory odd jobs, desperately seeking to make some money in the prevailing 'compo culture', which has led Sharky to prosecute over long years a futile case arising from a back injury from a fall on a Dublin bus. The law in the play is depicted as an ass. That valuation is reinforced by the possibility that Lockhart (now in pursuit of debtors whom he expects to find in their homes on Christmas Eve) must have once been a lawyer with the power to get Sharky off.

He has now come back to claim this ultimate of debts. He is the devil in a high-stakes game for Sharky's soul, and for his money ('you're coming through the old hole in the wall with me tonight' (*S* 101)). There is something stagey, even preposterous, about Lockhart's name and his language; as if he just might be a hallucination conjured up by a desperate man with delirium tremens in the third day of detoxification. But then, ever since the

Old Testament and the primal scenes of *Paradise Lost*, devils have seemed over the top in their gestures, the ultimate actors and shape-changers. Richard knows just how easily addicts can hallucinate. A loud scream is all it takes for them to feel themselves in the presence of the banshee.

The card game occurs in a time-free zone of pure contemplation, in which every moment is like every other one. It is a process, in its way, similar to the trance-like state of the inebriate, for whom time and days cease to matter: for gambling also is an addiction. The heavenly sense of connection with the 'infinite' has a darker side too, a nightmarish capacity to make every instant a black hole into which a suffering person can easily fall, a state of absolute terror in the eye of non-being. This is hell in a basement, when hell is less the experience of other people than the state of being locked forever within a self. Lockhart knows this condition intimately, and feels the deep envy of the seafarer for all land-dwellers in their cosy homes: 'and you can't even deal with the thought that someone might love you, because of all the pain you always cause' (*S* 127). The feeling of self-disgust and worthlessness in the addict eventually precludes the possibility of being loved by God. Unable to value self, he finds it impossible to be valued by anyone else.

Yet at a crucial moment in mid-game, when Sharky relapses into drinking, his brother finds the courage to say 'I believe that he can change... back to the little fella that always had a tune on his lips' (*S* 131). Lockhart cannot bear the sound of music but Sharky has received a CD from his new girlfriend; and, for as long as he can think of playing it, he has hope. The game comes to a weird climax in which Lockhart and Sharky seem obsessed with one another, as a man might be with his shadow side. They play intensely and Sharky appears to lose all, even money he may not have – until the naive Ivan relocates his glasses and realizes that he, not Lockhart, has the winning hand. The fool, by that sort of self-protective power which inheres in the truly innocent, has trumped the knave; and in that process he has saved a friend. The action had been heavy with foreboding until that point, heavy with the sense that men like he and Sharky, who have been saved once, may not be spared a second time – as in the story of Maurice Macken who did not die when electrocuted but then went home from hospital only to perish in a blaze. Ivan is now the inadvertant, unintending saviour of Sharky; and the sulphurous, combustible Lockhart is shown to lack final power.

The play's director Paul Gottinger has said that the characters 'are not at all conscious of the fact that highly significant things are happening to them... it is only their love for each other that can save them from the devil, yet they would laugh at such a sentimental idea'.[4] This unconsciousness is at once their doom and their redemption. Their strange solidarity caries them through all the phases of a night's drinking, from initial vigilance, through a façade of friendship, then aggression, followed by numbness, self-loathing and (eventually) a confusion which can somehow be survived and reported with clarity. Lockhart, seeing humans as mere insects, is ultimately no match for the secret power of such insects. He condescends to that which Richard idealizes. Like Ivan, Sharky gets a second chance and the devil is deflected by those blind ones who still have an ear for beauty. He is reduced to the condition of an exposed dramatic gull, who must leave the stage, even as the more negative elements of Sharky can be repressed back into the unconscious, for the time being anyway. His brother points the moral as Christmas Day dawns ('You're alive, aren't you?') and suggests that they visit the local monks. This must be the only work of contemporary Irish literature which concludes with the protagonists setting out for an early Mass. The monks, celibates though they are, may be able to broker a peace deal between Ivan and his wife. The prevailing tone is of forgiveness for past acts of violence, which were themselves rooted in dispossession; and, although this attempted truce might unravel, there is at least a margin of hope.

Christmas is the season when ghosts revisit: but, because the play is cast in pantomime mode, such apparitions may end well. Yet the ghosts are conjured because not all past experiences have been fully lived through or enacted. For all the comedy, there is hint of menace – of spectral presences, of sentences left uncannily incomplete. A lot of lines in the play are uttered by someone offstage. McPherson's interest in the Gothic has antecedents and echoes in contemporary Irish writing: in work by Banville, Deane and Keegan. The reason that so many ghosts walk may be the same explanation for their prevalence in so many plays of Shakespeare's England. Once a secularizing, modern code proclaims the impossibility of ghosts under the new order, they tend to appear everywhere, a case of the return of the repressed. In the work of these other writers, however, they appear usually as hallucinatory, as manifestations of the uncanny: as a sort of dicing with the darker side of the human personality which no longer holds sway. But in the work of McPherson, these extra-human forces take on a redemptive potential which exists in direct proportion to their real menace (developing themes adumbrated in *The Gigli Concert* of Tom Murphy). McPherson is avowedly also a follower of Murphy in his use of a sudden aria, voiced by an otherwise tough guy (Richard on the bluebottle; Lockhart on heaven and hell). But he adds to Murphy's formula a postmodern inflection. Redemptive possibilities arise not from a full-blown creed but out of the objects of Catholic kitsch, such as the Sacred Heart lamp which can be unexpectedly reanimated.

The Seafarer is a sober, if hilarious, analysis of the rather poignant condition of the lad culture of the 1980s and 1990s, and of how well or badly it survives under the conditions of middle age in the later decades of its sponsors' lives. The responsibilities of home life, but also its amenities, begin to emit a siren call to men whose freedom is shown to be generally hollow. But that call is less to morality than to religion, less to an ethical regulation of relationship than to a moment of connection with the 'beyond'. The ghosts project the four men's diminished capacity for a transforming experience. Far more than the monks in the nearby monastery, these cellular men-without-women stand in dire need of a spiritual community. The ghosts they conjure arise out of a sense of loneliness and loss, even as a weird sort of company for those who crave connection. Whether God exists as anything more than an expression of this human need, people must care for one another.

The basement in Baldoyle anticipates in some ways those 'ghost estates' which deformed Ireland in the years after the crash of 2008; and in other ways it captures the loneliness of a privatized world in which even an abutting lane seems to be a no-go area. Although the references to northside pubs might cast *The Seafarer* as a localized narrative in the tradition of Roddy Doyle's *The Commitments*, there is hardly any sense of community such as can be found in his works – merely a longing for such a thing in the aftermath of its disappearance. There is certainly no sense of national narrative. Irishness is merely the experience once described by Conor Cruise O'Brien (in honour of whom McPherson was named) of being a reflection of 'an Irish predicament: a predicament which has produced common characteristics in a number of those who have been involved in it'.[5]

The decline of religious practice after the 1970s had left theatre as one of the few remaining sacred spaces of Ireland in which people could still confront a relationship with fate and destiny. Even those artists who had never thought of studying for the priesthood might see their texts as sublimated forms of religious ritual, just as the secular culture offered alternative forms of confession on radio phone-ins and of festive commemorations (such as Bloomsday). Though the return of Lockhart portends the plunge into debt by a people unable to sustain their wealth, there is a sense that all will be well, as the four drinkers, having smashed up the set, head for an early Mass. To appreciate the subversion of McPherson's concluding gesture, one must register the number of occasions in the past on which Irish playwrights had sought to break out of, rather than into, sacred spaces.

An Ireland addicted to drink and money had hit bottom and was starting to bounce back. The physical energy which wrecked the set may yet be transformed into human kindness, as the night journey of the seafarer is survived and reported with honesty. It was perhaps inevitable that plays such as this would reactivate images and rituals of a religion which had become taboo among most intellectuals. The desire of artists was to free the religious mind from entrapment in discredited creeds and outworn social systems. They returned to the oldest theme: the cosmic joke of a humanity thrown into the world without a clear, supplied script.

Like other works of McPherson, *The Seafarer* has had huge success with audiences in London and New York, as well as in Dublin. This has little enough to do with its Irish setting, but arises from a universal belief in the cathartic power of a re-enactment and containment of a past pain. Lockhart's reappearance compels Sharky to confront his earlier moment of dire weakness in December 1981, with a question implied: is he a stronger man now? This second consideration of past trauma may show him to be a man confined and defined by that failure; or else one freed by his power to frame and transcend it. That healing experience is brought (as in Tom Murphy's play) by art, once seen by some in Ireland as the handiwork of the devil but in more recent times as the national alternative to the confession box. The art of narrative is linked in the final scenes to the healing power of faith which – like the twelve steps taken by a member of Alcoholics Anonymous – may even be an illusion, but an illusion necessary for people to function. It is, like the Mass itself, an attempt to construct something upon which to rejoice. Even Beckett's Hamm said as much near the close of *Endgame*: '[U]se your head, you're on earth, there's no cure for that! Get out of here and love one another! Lick your neighbour as yourself!'[6]

27. Claire Keegan: *Foster*

The aristocratic families of ancient Ireland had a custom: to send a child to be raised for a time in the home of another chieftain. That child was a sort of hostage, whose presence in that other family would act as a guarantee against a war breaking out between chiefs. The more positive motive was the hope that the second family might educate the child more fully than might the first, in the ways of the world.[1] Even after the old Gaelic order disintegrated, the custom persisted among the poor. When yet another child was born to a hungry family or to an exhausted mother, one of the older children might be sent to live as foster child, either temporarily or permanently, with an aunt and uncle.[2]

The narrator of Claire Keegan's *Foster* is one such. Like most children, she is powerless and therefore notices everything. Uncertain, even abject, as she is driven in her father's car to stay with the Kinsellas, her aunt and uncle, who are childless, she sees herself not as she is now but 'wild as a tinker's child'.[3] She is deposited without food or clothes. Her father 'looks just like my father' (*F* 5), the implication being that the teller has changed, even if he has not. He is a feckless man, poor, improvident, coarse maybe to the point of being abusive. On their journey, he drives past the village of Shillelagh, where he once lost a red heifer in a card game. The image recurs through the story, as if to suggest an anxiety in the red-headed girl narrator's mind that she might also be gambled away (the man who won the heifer 'sold her shortly afterwards' (*F* 3)). That image was once used in the poem, 'The Lost Heifer', by Austin Clarke, known to generations of Irish schoolchildren, symbolizing the lost ancestral culture of the Gael.

The father, Da, seems to want her gone: and he speaks to his daughter with near despair, even bitterness: 'try not to fall into the fire, you' (*F* 15). Edna Kinsella offers a gift of rhubarb for him to take home. A stick of it falls to the floor but he does not pick it up. It is the uncle who rescues it, as he may perhaps rescue the girl (for the short story is a form radiant with anticipations). 'There now' (*F* 14), he says to her father, as if cajoling a baby. Already, John Kinsella seems like the sort of loving father the girl never had.

On the journey, she had used the family she knew in the attempt to imagine the one for which she is bound and the father she knew as a flawed basis for imagining the one she will meet: 'a square body like the men my sisters sometimes draw' (*F* 6). Her father lies that his hay is saved, yet this improvident man can also complain of his daughter's huge appetite, before eating his fill himself. She'll eat them out of house and home, he says, but they can work her hard. 'There'll be no need for any of that' (*F* 12), says Kinsella, who is domesticated enough to prepare the meal. The child, already mastering the visiting courtier's art of self-fashioning, begins to sense how her dress and dirty sandals must appear to her hosts; but with a flicker of hope she senses a world where there is plenty of room, 'time to think... money to spare' (*F* 13). Already, Keegan is subtly shifting the terms of the traditional fairy tale:[4] the aunt and uncle who take in a foster child seem the very souls of kindness rather than cruelty. And Keegan is also challenging a rigid tradition of Irish writing, for here it is the foster father (rather than his wife) who is the epitome of sensitivity and tact.

Yet adult readers, schooled in the old stereotypes, cannot but wonder whether they are being set up for a later revelation. The very vigilance of the child suggests something not quite right, a fear that past traumas may be repeated in the present with the Kinsellas: 'I'm glad, for some reason, that they sleep together' (*F* 17). The child cannot know everything, but somehow the feeling of past and possible hurt hangs in the air. Perhaps she has been abused by the man about to leave: 'part of me wants my father to leave me while another part of me wants him to take me back, to what I know. I am in a spot where I can neither be what I always am nor turn into what I could be' (*F* 11). The narration of all past events in a continuous present tense evokes the vivid immediacy of a child's summer idyll; but it could also suggest the recollection of a trauma so intense that it is forever being re-enacted in her mind. For the present moment is what this figure cannot live in – the past erupts and usurps it, while the future impinges (more rarely) as a possibility. The narrator's need to separate the two worlds, even as she has been mapping one onto the other, suggests a real sense of strain. The plight of being 'caught' between families and codes recurs; but she wants her Da gone, for 'this is a new place, and new words are needed' (*F* 18).

Keegan, like Deane, is working in a Gothic mode; and her use of the newly arrived narrator allows her to study the manners of a rural Wexford parish as if she were a Martian put down on a weird, undiscovered planet. The estrangement effect is everywhere. The interest in grotesques, in the flotsam and jetsam of an introverted, over-coded society derives in part from her study of Gothic female authors of the American South: Flannery O'Connor, Carson McCullers, Eudora Welty. Keegan had been taken on as an au pair – in a sense, fostered – by an American family in New Orleans; and during her time in the United States had come to read and admire these authors.[5]

But her work owes a great deal also to the art and ideas of Frank O'Connor, an Irish writer of short stories who saw the form as attuned to 'the lonely voice', the utterance of those who feel submerged and marginal in a social formation. Both O'Connors, Flannery and Frank, were fascinated by eccentrics, but mainly because they understood that the eccentric is simply a person with a deeper than average understanding of reality. They used the short story as the form which emerged on the cusp between oral narrative and printed text, often to chronicle the pleasures and pains of an individual becoming self-aware and modern. In *Foster*, the narrator will be taught by Kinsella how to read books: *Heidi*, *What Katy did Next*, *The Snow Queen*. The thrill is like that of riding a bike: it allows her to go to places she had not entered before, or to make up endings different from those in the books.

Learning to read is like learning this new family: you use the known world and word in order to infer those yet unknown. Some of what the child hears is forgotten; some passes her understanding but is remembered; and some more still is consciously processed. It is not clear when – or even if – her father will ever return for her. Likewise for the reader: the child never will clarify whether or not her home life was abusive. An encounter with water suggests purgation, as if her father had indeed wronged her: 'This water is cool and clear as anything I have ever tasted: it tastes of my father leaving, of him never having been there, of having nothing after he was gone' (*F* 23). Her vigilance in the new life suggests a child forever on guard. Aunt Edna says there must be no secrets in that house, because 'where there's a secret, there's shame, and shame is something we can do without' (*F* 21). The outburst comes hard on the aunt's invitation to walk to a well: but the child's impulse to cry suggests that she has her own past sufferings to contain also. A consciousness of adult pain seeps into and out of every childhood hurt, even as the darker intuitions of an adult world condition the child's own narrative method. The tale may be told about a child but the framer could be any age at all.

A world bound together by such unspoken pain must reduce adults at moments to the sort of dependency felt mostly by children, even as it converts its children at certain times into premature adults. As they look into the well, Aunt Edna holds the belt of the girl's trousers, so that she will not fall in and drown: but, walking back and holding her aunt's hand, the child feels that she is the parental one, keeping the woman balanced. In this strange world, opposites become complementary. People do not talk when they are happy, but nor do they talk when they are sad. The mud balls pelted by the girl's sisters against an outhouse wall back home eventually get softened by rain and return to clay. Already, this carries an implication that the girl will return to her own life, changed but not utterly: 'Everything changes into something else, turns into some version of what it was before' (F 26).

Still, it is a stressful transition. Attempting to sleep on her first night, the child is awakened by a sudden, unnecessary interruption by 'the woman' whose weight is felt upon the bed. The comment then made could mean anything: 'If you were mine, I'd never leave you in a house with strangers' (F 27). This could indicate menace, or a protective desire to comfort. Or it could emanate from a zone of deep desolation in the speaker. Next morning, when the mattress is found to have been urinated on by the fretful child, the aunt seems more kind than accusing: 'those old mattresses. . . they weep' (F 28). Too kind to make an issue of the incident, the aunt devises a remedy of her own: she feeds the girl shredded wheat (Weetabix) every night and there is no more bed-wetting. Already, her complexion is taking on the radiance of a healthy new life, a life of running through fields and eating good food. Yet questions asked in all kindness by the uncle (will you marry?) or complimentary comments by the aunt (you have nice toes) still carry an air of slight menace – or do they? Readers might begin to wonder whether the shame might be found in their over-interpretation rather than in any badness of the characters. But, if that is so, why is the narrator recalling such vivid details?

If every force in nature embraces its own opposite, then a child can become parental, or a girl become an honorary boy. Kinsella does not like the way in which his wife has dressed the girl in boy's clothes, so they travel to the town of Gorey, where a shop assistant tells the narrator she is 'the spit and image of her mammy' (*F* 45). Which mammy becomes clear only when Edna pays for a whole new wardrobe and is proclaimed a wonderful mother.

En route home, they attend a wake, which allows Keegan to raise a question often raised in her tales: are people upheld or smothered by their cultural practices? Such a question is posed by the very retelling of this story we now confront. For even as that telling may help to free the child of the experience (in the sense of 'containing' it), it may also function more in the mode of a flashback, simply repeating a prior distress. A wake permits a people to assert the bonds of community in the face of death: but death is hardly talked about (the conversation tending more to milk quotas and the like). A century before Keegan, J. M. Synge had been fascinated by wakes – the taking of whiskey and snuff, the attempt to redeem a life lost through good stories: yet he had also been struck by how redundant these gestures seemed to some, how meaningful to others.[6]

After leaving the wake, the child meets a gossip named Mildred, who asks probing, invasive questions – how rich are the Kinsellas; do they eat margarine or butter? Mildred mocks the new clothes as those of an adultified child ('Anybody would think you were going on for a hundred' (*F* 55)). Worse still, she divulges to the girl that the home in which she is a guest has a secret: the Kinsellas had a son who drowned in their slurry tank and the couple turned white overnight (a Gothic flourish, certainly, but perhaps no more than neighbourhood gossip). The revelation makes poignant sense, as if the narrator is made to wear boy's clothes to impersonate for the aunt the dead child: but it increases the sense of jeopardy too, for in folk tradition the wearing of the clothes of a dead person may prompt that spirit to return and claim the living one.[7] Hence Kinsella's distrust of it.

As the tale unfolds, Kinsella emerges as the strong, wise one. He may dandle Petal (the girl is named just once) on his knee or play games with her, but it is hard to believe that he could have any other agenda than love. He values her for herself, not primarily as a substitute for the lost boy; and when he takes her by the hand, she realizes that her father never once did that. As if that tenderness reminds her of all that her actual father lacks, she writes: 'Some part of me wants Kinsella to let me go so I won't have to feel this' (*F* 61). There is, despite the kindness, a sense that the Kinsellas' house, even as it provides an improvement on her home, is also a mirror of its darker elements. In the comparison and contrast, each place seems even more strange.

Kinsella takes the girl to a beach on the Wexford coast and explains that his wife has been over-trustful of the malicious neighbour. The subject need not be mentioned. His advice sounds rather like the manuals for the art of omission which characterize the finest short stories: 'Many's the man lost much just because he missed a perfect opportunity to say nothing' (*F* 65). This is the sentence which reverberates, forward and backward, through the tale. It stands in direct opposition to his wife's assertion that there can be no room for secrets, since a secret implies a shame. The ferocity of Mildred's commentary on the Kinsella couple suggests that their quietness about their loss has drawn on them the anger of a wider community when confronted by the mystery of an inexplicable death: but this, too, may be an example of a truth whose opposite is also true.

Mildred may, in all her coarseness, have made a telling point. To hide an experience is to imply that it carries a load of humiliation, a bad judgement from above. Secrecy in that sense may be bad: but the unspoken may betoken sensitivity and reverence. Yet, is there any ultimate difference? Alex Leslie says that there is and that *Foster* pivots on the distinction: 'a secret is something one hides: the unspoken is something that one doesn't need to be told'.[8] The death of the boy, like the narrator's home life, has no need of articulation: each of these is unknown to members of the other family. The storyteller must learn what to leave out in deciding what to let in. Having uttered his wisdom, Kinsella shows Petal three lights blinking across the sea, where previously there had been only two: 'And that is when he puts his arms around me and gathers me into them as though I were his' (F 67).

The letter announcing the birth of a baby brother, at nine pounds two ounces, is the signal for the guest to come home. She may have noticed how much more rigorously Kinsella completes farm tasks than her errant father, but she is her father's daughter nonetheless in her desire to complete a move, once it is planned: 'Now that I know I must go home, I almost want to go, to get it over with' (F 72). Yet she feels wounded when once Kinsella walks past her as if she had already gone. She goes to the well for water and the sentence which reports this has multiple meanings: 'it could be the last thing I do' (F 75). As she sends the bucket down, a hand like her own seems to come out of the water to pull her in, yet again she is caught by that same in-between stage, in which she had felt so trapped at the very start, of which she had said: 'I can neither be what I always am nor turn into what I could be' (F 11). In folk belief, the hand that pulls humans into water arises from the unconscious. It can portend death (as if the dead boy had come to claim his cousin for the otherworld), or it can merely be a practical warning that there is danger in the vicinity. But that hand's appearance is the epiphany of the tale.

The girl's previous walk to the well had been in the protective company of her aunt. Now, in venturing there alone, she may have taken on too much – it could be the last thing she does. Her distance from her birth family has given her the gift of individuation, but the process may have carried her well beyond all reasonable limits. Perhaps, she is half-consciously preparing for her return home – she can dice with death as a way of asserting independence. She must go home now, and know it as if for the first time. Its slatternly stability provides a measure of her own development, but that stability is also necessary to earth her in the world. Her growing capacity to imagine different endings for her favourite books suggests that she will from now on use words to control (as well as to narrate) her own life story.

Although she catches cold, she appears to be ever more confident. Her concoction of those different endings suggests that this tale too may have an open conclusion. The question of when and how to end has baffled all writers of short stories. The end-point cannot be arbitrarily chosen, but somehow it must deepen rather than resolve the central mysteries of the work, bringing closure but in ways which are not closed. Petal's mother tells the returned girl 'You've grown' (*F* 80), while her sisters, tongue-tied, look at her as if she were an English cousin. Her hoarseness prompts curiosity but she insists 'nothing happened' (*F* 83). In saying this, she is choosing not to tell of the incident at the well (which may have been a hallucination brought on by fever) or of the embrace on the beach.

Kinsella seems suddenly unable to cope with his emotions and wants to leave at once. His wife just weeps: for losing this girl is like losing her son all over again. The narrator knows that she need never mention whatever it was that happened: 'it is my perfect opportunity to say nothing' (*F* 86). This is the energy of a powerful reticence and it gives her an immediate authority. As her father walks towards her, she stares at him past Kinsella's shoulder as the uncle holds her in his arms, calling 'Daddy' (*F* 88). It is repeated as warning: 'Daddy'. She sees the father whom Kinsella cannot see, but whom he has all unknowingly remoulded to a new standard of parenthood, no longer Da but Daddy. This man will have to learn to 'read' himself now, to decode all that is not said but somehow known. And yet the call remains ambiguous and unclear: it could be made to Kinsella, as a warning that another person who pretends to be her father is coming into view.

If there has been abuse, the daughter who has now grown in independence has put him on notice: his new name carries different, fuller responsibilities. But there may have been no abuse: the subject which needs no mentioning could just be her growing intimacy with her uncle and aunt. The story was published in 2010, at a moment when allegations of child abuse in Ireland had reached a crescendo; and it appeared in *The New Yorker*, a magazine whose sophisticated readers might have been expected to be alert to such inferences. But it is set in 1981, during a hunger strike by the Irish Republican Army; and those inferences may be all in the mind of an over-suspicious reader, who might even feel manipulated at the end into a sense of unworthiness for harbouring such baseless suspicions.

The hunger strikes of 1981 may serve merely to locate the story in time: but in a tale so rich in reverberations they may signify something more than a date. The idea of hunger has stalked the narrative from the outset and is counterpointed by the sense of plentiful food in the Kinsella home. Yet the story returns to an endorsement of a kind of austerity, an aesthetic in which less is more and a little can go a very long way. If storytellers as well as children can gain power by doing without and knowing those things to omit, then the protestors in Northern Ireland may have some exemplary value. Many men in modern Ireland seem to lack agency – even Kinsella engages in a pretence of agency by tapping the roof of the father's car just before it goes. Likewise, the hunger strikers lacked a sense of agency other than the right to deny themselves food.[9] They invoked that right in search of another – they wished, like Petal at a certain point in this action, to wear their own clothes.

Walter Benjamin once lamented the decline of the storytelling capacity in modern culture; and he blamed this on the agonies endured by soldiers in the trenches of the First World War, agonies that were unreportable in any language.[10] The Irish, however, retained a belief in story as a form which could offer counsel and wisdom after describing the adventures of a protagonist in a strange place. Keegan suggests that a traumatic experience can best be reported, if it is inferred more than fully described. Her art is closer to that of the poet than that of the novelist. She cannot tell all of the truth, and so she offers just a bit at a time. Her story partakes of the non-moral world of the folk tale in its impassive listing of statements and incidents, but it treats that account with a postmodern wit and it ultimately leaves things to individual judgement by a silent reader.

If this story were simply paraphrased, it could read like a superstitious folk anecdote about the power of the otherworld, a power that is better transcended, as the girl flees the hand of the dead past. But a layer of sophisticated, tart consciousness has been added, that of a contemporary Ireland which qualifies magic by analytic realism. For this is a world which has moved straight from folklore to postmodernism without the long interlude of heavy industry or Victorian naturalism. The girl in the story, while learning how to read, is also illuminating all acts of readership. She has selected and omitted material, pitching her narrative in the first person, to convey the urgency and honesty of the speaking voice. In the tale she is the central character, far more central than either of the adult couples. Yet, being young, she must remain blind to the possible significance of some details, whose meaning in a wider scheme will be determined by the adult reader.

As in a lyric poem, some symbols are created within the unfolding tale – the lost heifer, the inappropriate clothes, the role of food. The characters are etched in vivid outline against the natural world and they say little enough. The perpetual present tense is heightened by rare, momentary returns in mid-paragraph to the past tense: but the pervasive narrative present, especially at the close, casts a shadow not just on time past but on time future too. The strangeness of our everyday world is Keegan's innermost theme: the need in embracing the stranger outside ourselves also to befriend the stranger within.

The portrayal by gossips like Mildred of people as Other arises from crass ignorance: but *Foster* nonetheless shows that people can learn about difference only after the experience of sameness. The rigid notions of family with which the narrator begins become the basis for a more expanded understanding. She had begun with some awareness of how she and her siblings appeared to the outside world. By the end, she returns to her family of origin with a heightened sense of how strange the outside world must seem to them.

By 2010, as this story was appearing in *The New Yorker*, the country had lapsed into a dire recession after the affluent decade of the Celtic Tiger. It may be that, in chronicling a character's short sojourn in a wealthy household and ultimate return (suitably matured) to a more austere life, Claire Keegan was writing the secret history of her country. Frank O'Connor had always suggested that the submerged populations and eccentric individuals who animate the short story may provide the basis on which a more communal society can be made.[11] Old Ireland may have been imprisoned by routine but it was also upheld by ritual. New Ireland sees how its women, in particular, can be liberated by storytelling, retelling in words and silences a life first experienced as the mere insult of the actual. Far from being an apprentice's form for artists practising to depict a fully achieved society in the novel, the story may in fact be the subtler and surer basis of a remade community, since it can only become a whole community again when it has room for its marginals and isolates, when it can let its own weirdness in. The classic novels of Ireland, from *Gulliver's Travels* through *Ulysses* to *Cré na Cille*, are, in fact, collections of stories about eccentrics strung together in the guise of an experimental novel about an emergent sense of the social.

As with all good stories, we have known from the start how *Foster* would end, but we read it as though we do not. Our positional superiority to the narrator makes us fretful for her betimes, until we sense the hidden hand of the author at work; and then we learn (as if for the first time) that we also are at the mercy of each immediate moment. Yet the tale is told about people who are shy of exposing themselves to the passing moment, and shyer still to narrate themselves. Their stories are mysterious enough to resist a further telling or an absolute silence.

28. Kate Thompson and
The New Policeman

Tiger Ireland emerged in the mid-1990s and lasted for about a decade. In its earlier, heroic period, before 2002, useful industries were created and reliable goods made – artisan foods, quality furniture, and so on. The incomers from Britain, mainland Europe and Africa took a pride in the culture they brought with them and showed a real desire to learn about the traditions of the land in which they had settled. One of these was Kate Thompson, a daughter of the English Marxist historians Edward and Dorothy Thompson.

Kate Thompson had for a time trained horses in England and later meditated in India, but her final resting point was the west of Ireland, where she studied traditional music and wrote children's books (though, like many children's classics, they were never confined to children in their appeal). Of these, *The New Policeman* (2005) is the finest: a steady, beady but loving meditation on the ways in which Ireland's present was now almost wholly separated from its past. For, after 2002, a new kind of incomer arrived into a very different 'bling' economy, devoted to quick profit and endless business. A virtual world of consultants and computers had replaced honest manufacture with spin; and the incomers, though condescendingly dubbed 'new Irish', cared little for the native culture and even less for that which they brought with them. If there were to be a rescue-job on jeopardized traditions, it would as likely as not come from one of the more serious-minded first band of incomers – much as T. S. Eliot, after his arrival in London almost a century earlier, had invoked the great old lyrics of Spenser, Donne and Marvell in the act of saving contemporary poetry.

E. P. Thompson and Dorothy Thompson had long had an English radical's interest in Ireland as a crucible of republican modernity: but they were first and foremost keen to repair the polity of their own country, restoring the traditions of levellers, diggers and leftist radicals. Edward had for many years edited a journal with an agenda implicit in its very title: *Past and Present.* Their daughter's novel centres on a fiddle-playing policeman, Larry O'Dwyer, who may be a fairy from another world and who feels a troubling sundering between tradition and modernity – except when he plays his music, which has the effect of happily 'linking his past to his present'.[1] *The New Policeman* concerns itself with the half-conscious attempt by a fifteen-year-old boy, J. J. Liddy, to provide a similar linkage for the entire community. His mother, complaining that there is never 'enough time' in the new Ireland, asks her son for the ultimate birthday present which will provide her with more.

Tiger Ireland's diminished sense of the past is clear in J. J. Though his parents are thoughtful antinuclear bohemian types, not formally married and happy to give their son the surname of the mother's family, J. J. knows next to nothing about his grandparents. Like other Tiger cubs, he lives in a depthless present: 'How was it that in his fifteen years of his life his mother had never spoken to him about her father? Even more amazing was that he had never thought to ask. . .' (*NP* 115). Perhaps his silence was due to a suspicion that the answer might be complicated. One day, a school friend blurts out the widespread local belief that the grandfather, also J. J. Liddy, murdered a local priest named Doherty, because the cleric had waged a campaign to abolish traditional dancing, which the family loved but which he saw as an occasion of sin.

The young J.J.'s response is panicky: he wants to change his surname to that of his father, Byrne. He is in most respects a typical Tiger teenager: he goes clubbing with friends, chats with girls and generally feels powerless to affect anything much. Although he is a skilful Irish dancer, his friends find the activity 'nerdy' – Father Doherty has had some influence. Music they are more tolerant of, but would prefer rock lyrics to the old jigs and reels. Nevertheless, the tradition has persisted in the face of clerical and communal disapproval. The 1935 Dance Halls Act had banned private dances in people's homes, as the clergy, ever-growing in power, sought to police public entertainments with a strict supervision of ethical behaviour.[2] The priests feared a sexually provocative element in traditional dances (and some of the itinerant teachers and musicians had indeed left more than slides and polkas in their wake). They were also anxious that a people whose Catholicism was a matter of superficial obedience to mere rules might, when lured by the hypnotic music, return to a more pagan set of practices.[3]

The ambiguities surrounding all this were deep. For every Father Doherty, there was a sympathetic priest who loved the old music and tried to organize a céili, in place of the commercial popular music taking over in dancehalls. Traditional musicians had no sense of 'profit' and played for love; and the dances themselves allowed young people to mingle in a free and open way, quite different from the more furtive and fumbling couplings which occurred outside the dancehalls. One of the effects of the 1935 legislation had been to drive rural couples into the surrounding hills and fields. 'There was not a haystack safe within two miles of each hall', recalled John McGahern, 'and the whole crowd of them seemed to be going off like alarm-clocks'.[4]

Even within the ranks of nationalism, there had long been uncertainty about all these questions. As far back as the days of the

Land League many radicals treasured traditional music, but one of its clerical leaders, Conor McFadden of Donegal, had musicians beaten up and their instruments destroyed. Dances allowed company keeping, which endangered the purity of young men and women. The music left many 'astray in the head' and those who played it might even be fairy folk, who would leave a girl with child and then steal another.

Father Doherty himself has taken the strange precaution of going to live in fairyland, in order to police its borders and combat such vice, but his efforts seem in vain. Yet they may have had some effect, for when J. J. happens upon him in Tír na nÓg, he confides in the priest that nobody sees fairies any more. The holy man did not expect this to happen so soon: but the speech in which he offers J. J. an account of his ideal country sounds (almost) like a vision of a Tiger Ireland, in which over eighty-five per cent of potatoes are imported by a people too busy making money to grow their own food:

> I see a God-fearing Catholic nation peopled by industrious citizens, each one of them determined to put the old, feckless ways behind them. I see an Ireland where every man has a motor-car and spends his time improving his lot and the lot of his family, instead of wasting his days growing potatoes and his nights drinking and dancing. I see an Ireland that has grown wealthy and its place among the great states of Europe... (*NP* 357)

This is in fact a cunning construction on Thompson's part: a counter-version of Éamon de Valera's 1943 radio broadcast, which imagines, less than a decade after the Dance Halls Act, a land of roadside dances and of frugal comfort rather than heedless consumerism:

> The Ireland that we would have, the Ireland that we dreamed of, would be the home of a people who valued material wealth only as a basis of right living, of a people who, satisfied with

frugal comfort, devoted their leisure to the things of the spirit – a land whose countrywide would be bright with the sounds of industry, with the romping of sturdy children, the contest of athletic youths and the laughter of happy maidens, whose firesides would be forums for the wisdom of serene old age. The home, in short, of a people living the life that God desires that men should have.[5]

That speech was initially aimed at the Irish, at home and overseas, in the lead-up to an election – but it has often in later decades been cited as an instance of reactionary pastoral. However, its deep, underlying radicalism shines through in the wider Tiger context of materialist individualism sketched by Thompson.

How does J. J. end up having this conversation in Tír na nÓg? The old music has never fully died, despite the fact that few people now have time for such things; and, in the face of clerical disapproval, musicians have kept coming to the family home to play. Helen Liddy shows her son photographs of the famous old artists, taken in the fateful year of 1935. The fairy faith had by then been largely erased, but not the music that went with it. Father Doherty removed the flute played by grandfather Liddy; and neither it nor the priest was ever seen again. The grandfather, Helen explains at last, was a wild rover who came and went – and then never came back at all. He left her mother big with child (Helen, presumably) and he also left the fiddle which young J. J. plays and which connects him to the fairy folk.

Anne Korff, one of the immigrants from Germany who 'believes' in the tradition, suggests to young J. J. that by placing himself in a souterrain (an underground building), he can gain access to Tír na nÓg – and so he does. Through the charm of his unearthly music on the magic fiddle, he has gained authority, much like his female author who discovers her narrative gift by linking each short chapter to a piece of sheet music. If all art aspires to the condition of music, one way to tell a story is through a sequence of scores, which serve to place music and text on an equal footing (in much the same manner as the Gaelic bards, whose words were recited to the plucked strings of psalteries).[6] In a book about the insufficiency of time in a consumer-driven world, the 'time' of music may be the best way of transcending all time. The use of text may seem to have a vaguely antiquarian ring (would most fiddle players use sheet music at all?) – but the story is cutting-edge postmodern. And Kate Thompson, by telling it, joins a series of previous English artists, radicals and scholars (Robin Flower, George Thompson, Tim Robinson, Mícheál MacLiammóir, Arnold Bax and Derek Hill), who all sought to repair the 'loss of tradition' and to restore Irish culture to itself. While her predecessors might have seemed like Jacobite princes in an *aisling* poem hoping to prod a wan, wilting maiden named Ireland back into life, this rescue mission is quite different: it is done by a woman.

Fairyland is different in J.J.'s perception from contemporary Ireland. Its houses are fewer and farther between, growing naturally out of the earth as if they were organic. The clothes of the people reflect the fashions of successive centuries, as if all times are one time here and everyone partaking in 'some kind of fancy dress party' (*NP* 171). The dances are less drilled and disciplined, more instinctual and individualized. But in other ways Tír na nÓg recalls Tiger Ireland. The only time is the present, for the sense of the past and future is strictly subordinated by a people who insist on living in a perpetual now. Yet already there have been leaks in the membrane and time is starting to overtake the fairy folk. Flies have been found dead. The paucity of the houses suggests that many fairies have been exterminated in a past war. Even more strange to J.J., however, are the socks found everywhere, each marking the spot where a worthless, unnecessary new house has been erected in Tiger Ireland.

Fairyland is not really 'elsewhere', though it takes – as Anne Korff warned J.J. – courage to pass over into it. Each world is a version of the other. The room which J. J. leaves and re-enters in the souterrain is one and the same: the difference lies not in the surroundings so much as in his perception of them. His absence for a while evokes telltale Tiger fears of yet another teenage suicide, another possible victim of child bullies or of inner loneliness. But Tír na nÓg is not perfect either: the injured hound Bran can receive no medical attention and so his wound can in all likelihood neither improve nor get worse. If Tiger Ireland is unhealthily obsessed with 'growth', Tír na nÓg is winding down into a charming but futureless stasis. Fairyland seems less like an alternative to this world than a recognizable version of it, with many compensatory virtues but also some dire flaws.

If Tiger Ireland knows little of its past, Tír na nÓg lacks any sense of a future. If the former has too little time, the latter may have too much. Both states in themselves seem somewhat creepy, even unhealthy – as if one is a necessary condition and creation of the other. The very voyage of various characters between them suggests a half-conscious longing for connection, as if each seeks completion in the other, a zone in which modern state and ancient nation might more finally fuse. Garda Larry O'Dwyer, the new policeman, feels ill at ease administering state law and taking down false names of after-hours revellers in his notebook; but he himself is a split person, who goes by quite another name in fairyland.

The self and shadow in each person cries out for integration. If only the membrane between past and present had not been created, all would be well. In a sense, the leaking of time through the membrane, which discomfits the inhabitants of Tír na nÓg, may be a sign of hope. Yet they are described as trying to hold back leaks everywhere, even in the Bermuda Triangle, as if their mission were the rather Pearsean aim of saving spirituality in the modern world. Even though airplanes and jets fly in the sky, and washing machines permit socks to get disconnected – an image of all the bifurcated, half-people in this tale – there is little sense of contemporary Kinvara being in the grip of technology. (Some younger Irish readers have found this a little stage Irish, but such readers voice no objection to the use of quill pens at J. K. Rowling's Hogwarts.)

It does indeed take audacity to cross between worlds. Genius is the related ability to connect the buried self with the everyday mind. Each zone contains within itself some essential criticisms of the other: but the hope for spiritual recovery lies in those, like J. J., who can hold both codes simultaneously in the head without losing the capacity to function. Garda O'Dwyer finds his new posting such a strain that he attempts to resign it. For related reasons, Anne Korff urges J. J. not to stay too long in Tír na nÓg, lest he know the fate of the legendary Oisín and return, bent and broken, to a wholly different world.

In ancient times people could move more freely between conscious and unconscious worlds, but after the fairies lost the great war with the Danú, their reduced population was permitted to go to Tír na nÓg only on condition that they stay there. Yet some still manage to come and go, and to meet an old acquaintance in the modern world after, say, a lapse of forty years. As in the fairytales of C. S. Lewis's Narnia, one can commute between worlds and each migration reinforces the strangeness of being both 'home' and 'away'. One can spend many years away from the human world and yet find that no time has elapsed at all, because there is plenty of time, a super abundance, in fairyland. But the leaks which have torn the membrane mean that humans never have enough time.

In Tiger Ireland the delivery of children to every event is scheduled by protective parents, who do not allow kids to wander the streets as J. J. wanders through Tír na nÓg. But the fairies' refusal to submit to time means that they have no growth. They are happy to give J. J. something in return for the tune called 'Dowd's Number One', which they have all somehow managed to forget. J. J. offers them a tune of his own composing, but when they hear it, they say that he just thinks he made it. It is really theirs, but they do not regard the inspiration which humans get from them as stealing. In folk tradition all tunes are communally owned.

Angus, king of the fairies, admits that they sometimes stole babies and left one of their own in its place. The possibility that J. J. may himself be such a figure still has not crossed his mind, though his lineage is vague and his musical gifts otherworldly. But that thought may strike the reader. 'It's not so easy these days, of course', says Angus meaningfully, 'what with hospital beds and burglar alarms and baby monitors, and all that malarkey. But we still get the odd few across' (*NP* 250). The socks have a particular use: by marking new houses they warn the fairies where not to come through into someone's kitchen. J. J., as if intuiting something, asks whether the fairies steal back their children, only to be told that they return (when ready, of their own volition, 'usually about your age' (*NP* 267)).

Perhaps that is the very utterance which makes J. J. want to return to Kinvara; but the reason he gives is to find a vet who can cure Bran's wound. Angus says that cannot be done. J. J. is asked instead to play his fiddle for the Dagda, the warrior king who led the lost tribes of Tír na nÓg in their doomed battle. A little later, he loses contact with Bran. In the frenzied search, he stumbles into a chamber where the hound is baying beside a terrified man in black clothes and a dog collar: Father Doherty, still in possession of the fabled flute. A short time later, urged by the priest, J. J. manages to stop the time leak.

This is the precise moment when Tiger Ireland comes to an end. People resume hobbies or discover 'that there was room in their lives for their families as well as their jobs' (*NP* 367). Still in Tír na nÓg himself, J. J. hears how Father Doherty had been commuting between worlds, anxious only to persuade the fairies to stay away from his parish. Angus, who relates all this, is amazed at the discovery of the old flute. When the body of a decomposed priest is found near the souterrain, the village assumes it is that of the murdered cleric. J. J. returns to Kinvara after his month-long unexplained absence, but Bran cannot be helped, turning instantly to dust. J. J. brings with him the flute, like those sacred objects brought back by wanderers from mythic lands to attest to the honesty of their claims. Despite Father Doherty's aversion, the flute also functions as a radiant relic of old Ireland. As with other religious relics, the power it evokes may be waning, so there is a compensatory wistfulness about its production, as if it conveys the hints of a code not yet completely rejected.

The policeman is brought to quiz J. J. about what exactly happened, but some instinct causes the teenager to clam up. Only when the others have left does he speak with him alone, realizing that the Garda is at once the Angus of fairyland and his own grandfather. This is a mind-bender: the idea of 'having parents who are younger than you' (*NP* 423). In primitive religions it was believed that children often 'chose' and begat their own parents, as if setting for themselves in their next incarnation a new set of problems and challenges to be solved. J. J. knows better than to tell these things to his mother, who is in some ways more youthful and bohemian than he but who might not understand.

As for the new policeman, that closing conversation with J. J. seems like his signal to pass over. Neither he nor Anne Korff is seen in Kinvara again. But somehow, whenever J. J. plays his fiddle, he is harmonizing with the music played by Angus, as they share across worlds in a performance of 'Dowd's Number Nine'.

Who is the New Policeman? Thompson's title evokes Flann O'Brien's *The Third Policeman* with its dystopian nightmare world in which every moment is like the next among the undead. Is the policeman Larry O'Dwyer, who hates his job? Or Father Doherty, who patrols his parish in this world and the other one? Or should that name be reserved for J. J., the one who can truly police the borders once O'Dwyer has disappeared, following their last conversation? J. J. is, after all, the central character of the book.

The crises of Tiger Ireland were often narrated through images of an endangered childhood, whether abused, abducted, lost or trafficked. All of those fears shadow *The New Policeman*. Traditional Ireland, in its religious iconography and notions of holy childhood, may have over-invested in the symbol and been then doomed to disappointment and frustration. The rather adolescent qualities of many adults in the Tiger culture meant that some teenagers felt burdened by premature responsibilities. It is hardly surprising that someone like J. J. might seek instruction from a tradition associated with much older generations. The poignancy of the attempt by distinct groups to communicate across a chasm is clear, but there may be something unconvincing about a declaration that the attempt will always be a success.

If childhood's moment of passing is being pushed back by perma-adolescence to eight or nine years of age, adolescence can endure until people are well into their sixties. One result is that genuine adults are disappearing, or decreasing in number, for much the same reason that real children are vaporizing. There is little enough evidence that the adults depicted in *The New Policeman* know who they are. The simplification of the word 'adult' in the wider community, as a warning of explicitly sexual content, is a further sign of this impoverishment. A figure such as J. J., poised between childhood and adolescence, is placed like a litmus paper into the 'solution' of Tiger Ireland, in order to demonstrate how incomplete and immature are many of the standards by which it lives. But the figure, too kind and too sophisticated to judge – because he really is anyway the parent of his own parents – can expose the fact that adults will never control all forms of knowledge. If Kate Thompson has written a Tiger Ireland version of *The Wizard of Oz*, her story suggests that there is no place like home, because home is no place, no where. It is who you are and what you bring. The journey becomes a stage in the growth of its protagonist who, by being confronted with various characters not fully capable of growth or change, is made to understand the meaning of such transformation. In an Ireland apparently enjoying the material fruits of development, while still enduring the after-effects of emotional and economic underdevelopment, that is a telling form of *Bildungsroman.*

In the Tiger years children's literature often expressed ideas which might not have been welcomed in the mature world. The child, still connected with much that the community had buried below the level of consciousness, functioned as a symbol of the despair of intellectuals about all that seemed lost and also as a promise of a more humane future. The music of *The New Policeman*, like stories told to help children sleep, achieves its mesmeric moments in the hours of darkness, when people can explore their shadow side and process the challenges of the workaday, rational world. It used to be said that the spread of electric light put an end to the fairies, but this book suggests that a story told ostensibly for children may have hidden messages for adults too.

29. Conclusion: Going Global?

No movement in painting, said W. B. Yeats, ever outlasts the impulses of its founders. He felt much the same about the Irish nation state. Two of his great poems about the founding acts, 'Easter 1916' and 'Leda and the Swan', are heavy with a sense of loss: the action which marks a birth also leads directly to war and death. If 'the painter's brush consumes his dreams', and 'our love letters wear out our love',[1] then the very expressions of a national idea, once uttered, can never be fully recaptured by their authors. They might, however, be taken up, like baby Moses in his basket rescued by some Pharaoh's daughter, in a different dispensation. Or they might, like the future worlds of Derek Mahon, lie dormant for years in a disused building or an abandoned technology.

In previous phases of Irish culture, a near-death experience had often led to new vitality: the sense of an ending helped to suggest that something else might be beginning. In the cryptic words of Samuel Beckett: 'Imagination dead. Imagine.' Nuala Ní Dhomhnaill's figuring of Irish as the corpse that will not stay dead but sits up to deliver one more final utterance is a recent variation.

But it was Beckett who became the model for a culture that fed on abstinence. The less he had to say, the more wonderfully it was said. The shorter his texts, the richer the commentaries they evoked, like some famished Third World country which was the subject of endless international investigations. He was the author whose imagination was vivified by failure. It was success which he found difficult, as when he fled his home in Paris on the announcement of his Nobel Prize in 1969 with the comment 'quelle catastrophe!'[2] Tiger Ireland evolved only a limited range of forms for coping with affluence – no Gatsby-style allegory; although there was material enough for tragedy, few artists followed the lead of Paul Murray's *The Mark and the Void* (2015). Tiger Ireland, likewise, never fully evolved literary forms for coping with affluence. That reluctance was due to many factors: the difficulty in photographing a still moving object; an unsureness as to whether the prosperity was real and lasting; a desire first of all to look in the rear-view mirror and take the measure of that landscape which people were leaving behind.[3]

It was the more popular forms of romantic fiction and crime novel which engaged with the bright lights and shiny surfaces of Tiger Ireland, as did a small but growing number of films. Strictly literary artists continued to deal mainly with aspects of the recent or remote pasts. The more that international finance broke up old cultures, the more necessary its sponsors in New York and London found it to celebrate writers who could supply vivid accounts of what had been erased. A major play such as *Dancing at Lughnasa* was both analysis and symptom of the underlying process, offering a myth of self-explanation to the diaspora in those cities, but some of Friel's earlier works on such themes had had nothing like the same success on these circuits. The brilliant books of McGahern also remained, outside of Ireland, a rather minority taste. His last great novel, *That They May Face the Rising Sun*, had its title altered by the US publisher to *By the Lake*, lest readers might think it a tour guide to Japan. There were some excellent novels about the social effects of the economic crash, such as Mike McCormack's *The Solar Bones* (2016) and Dónal Ryan's *The Spinning Heart* (2010) (by an author proud to acknowledge a debt to McGahern); just as there have been astute treatments of some of the absurdities of the bling culture in work by Julian Gough, Anne Enright, Claire Kilroy and Kevin Barry. There was also a sense of a new social vision and altered narrative technique emergent post-crash in prose work by Philip Ó Ceallaigh, Paula McGrath, Louise O'Neill, Colum McCann, Belinda McKeon, and Seán O'Reilly; in the poetry of Paula Meehan, Catherine Phil McCarthy, and Theo Dorgan; and in more physical kinds of drama pioneered by Enda Walsh, Marina Carr and Michael Keegan-Dolan. The main poems which Michael D Higgins had time to write after his accession to the Irish presidency offered a moving account of the plight of refugees and of the continuing indebtedness of Europe to a Greek people too often treated as abject debtors themselves.

In so far as versions of national culture triumphed abroad, they tended to offer simplified versions of Irishness. Frank McCourt's *Angela's Ashes*, with its storyline suggestion of a land as desperately interesting and as interestingly desperate as ever, fell on receptive ears. McGahern's inflected narratives never made it anything like as big. Whereas McCourt heightened colours to the point of caricature, McGahern took the view that the artist must tone them down, if only to make them credible.

Yet, through the nineties and noughties, as Ireland became the most globalized economy in Europe, there was much talk of the worlding of Irish writing. More writers were living abroad and writing about 'abroad' than had done so in the 1970s or 1980s. Emerging novelists made a point of setting entire works in New York, Berlin or Central America. The finest of all was, arguably, Joseph O'Neill's *Netherland*, an account of the international members of a cricket team in New York. It would take some straining to read its plot in terms of an occluded 'Irish' narrative, such as might be found in Banville's *Doctor Copernicus*. O'Neill, before it, had written a study of his mingled Irish and Turkish ancestry, *Blood-Dark Track*, but as a long-committed New Yorker has long treated nationality as a sort of postmodern joke: 'for years I was under the impression that Flannery O'Connor was Irish – a Kerryman, perhaps'.[4] Early in *Netherland* the protagonist's wife discusses members of a tribe up the Amazon river who do not know that they live in a country named Colombia: but the same may be true of many of the novelist's fellow New Yorkers.[5] The minds of many Irish writers resident in that city were moving well beyond the national idea, yet most of them, as soon as they featured in a colour supplement, were re-nationalized as fast as any bank: 'the Irish writer X'.

Dozens of poets, as well as novelists, had chosen to set parts of a work in some overseas place, for purposes of comparison and contrast with Ireland. The contrapuntal narrative was all the rage in lyric sequences by Harry Clifton, Derek Mahon, Thomas MacCarthy, Paul Muldoon or Medbh McGuckian, as in novels by Joseph O'Connor or Hugo Hamilton. At the same time, the 1990s was the decade in which it became fashionable to be Irish across the world, as people used the postmodern pub, the spectacle of Riverdance, the music of Enya or the memoirs of McCourt to connect with their inner Paddy. Many overseas authors began to turn to Ireland, as Borges and Pinget had done in the era of high modernism, for setting and for theme. In the subsequent decade, Vargas Llosa wrote a novel about Roger Casement, and Enrique Vila-Matas wrote a Joycean homage in *Dublinesque*.[6]

By 2010, the immigrants who had been arriving in numbers since the affluence of the late 1990s started to appear in novels, plays and films – but most often in rather restricted roles, as examples of what were condescendingly termed 'the new Irish' (i.e., those who had learned enough Hiberno-English to tell customers in pubs and restaurants 'you're grand!'). There was, nonetheless, a sense of expectancy: as if it could only be a matter of time before the fusion food of restaurants would be accompanied by inflections of hybridized poetry or experimental narratives produced by the immigrants themselves.

Ireland, as it approached the millennium, was indeed a multicultural place. Even the *Evening Herald* found it profitable to issue an enclosed newspaper in Polish on Tuesdays. Evangelical churches for Nigerians opened in many places, as did mosques for Muslims (in the rural west as well as in Dublin). The capital city came to a standstill for celebrations of the Chinese New Year. And a granddaughter of one of the Vietnamese boat people took first place in Irish in the country's Leaving Certificate examination.

There were new kinds of writing addressed to the question of hybrid identity in poetry by Seamus Heaney and Medbh McGuckian, in plays by Friel and Doyle, in stories by Maeve Binchy and Claire Keegan; but in the novel, the form in which one might have expected to find subtlest explorations of the encounter with the Other, there was less than might have been expected. Many talented younger novelists had abandoned the attempt to describe a whole society (despite that society still being rather small) and preferred to focus on this or that sub-group: a cluster of graduates from a college class, the workers in a single restaurant, the members of a rock band, and so on. One of the best of these, Keith Ridgway, summed up the technical problem in titling one of his books *The Parts*.[7] It was as if writers now focused novels, as once they had short stories, on outsiders and on the 'submerged population groups' beloved of Frank O'Connor. Within Dublin – with a few honourable exceptions such as Caitriona Lally's *Eggshells* (2015) – authors were reluctant to attempt a contemporary 'Wandering Rocks', let alone a full-blown panoptic portrait of the conurbation now in the style of James Plunkett's *Strumpet City*.[8]

Even more remarkable was the disinclination of novelists to deal with the culture brought to Ireland by the newcomers themselves. The concentration was, rather, on making these people 'more Irish than the Irish themselves' – as happened to the Normans of the 1300s – by offering them crash courses in Irish Studies. Irish novelists who had been educated in the revisionist years after the 1970s, during which so many elements of the national narrative had been erased, were seizing on new arrivals as pretexts for teaching themselves what they should have known anyway. Yet some incomers, such as Daniel Zuchowski, did produce an account of cross-cultural complexities in *The New Dubliners* (2014).

In her book *Strangers to Ourselves*, Julia Kristeva says that we encounter the stranger in others in order to uncover the hidden, untransacted parts of ourselves. In countries like France, she observes, right-wing parties are forever projecting the national culture as the one which newcomers should embrace, whereas leftists care more for the culture which incomers bring with them.[9] Modernity works best, of course, when cultures receive such equal attention from all parties as to permit a genuine possibility of newness and fusion. Something like that process was observable in the early years of the Celtic Tiger from 1996 up to 2002. Many who arrived in Ireland showed a deep interest in traditions still quite new to them, but they also carried the memory of their own pasts and a willingness to share them. After 2002, there was less fusion and less thoughtfulness. The country fell in thrall to a heedless consumerism, while many of the incomers showed little interest in the lore of their ancestors or in the traditions of Ireland. With eyes only for the main chance, many people (in the most repeated phrase of the time) 'lost the run of themselves'.

By 2002, the old currency had made way for the Euro. Banknotes which had once borne images of writers from Scotus Eriugena to Joyce disappeared, to be replaced by featureless bridges and buildings which already had the look of the Lubyanka about them. The loss among many Irish people of a confident sense of who exactly they were made it more difficult for some to deal confidently with the Other. The shyness of novelists to deal directly with the immigrant experience stands in telling contrast with the classic works of the literary tradition: *Gulliver's Travels* (a study in defamiliarization), *Castle Rackrent* and *Ulysses* (which consider the experience of being Jewish in Ireland), Beckett's trilogy and McGahern's stories (both authors constantly exploring alterity).[10] These writers all came out of a monocultural land and yet somehow – perhaps because of that – they managed to explore Otherness. *Ulysses* comes, after all, to a grand climax when a thirty-eight-year-old man of eastern aspect invites a twenty-two-year-old graduate back to his kitchen for cocoa. It is hard to imagine any student accepting such an invitation now. The capital city in Joyce's time allowed people to dice with their own strangeness, but now in the age of *The Parts* it is filled with suburbs and shopping malls, designed to protect people from those very chance encounters which are the lifeblood of most good stories.

By 2000, the sources of that provincializing effect were New York and London, whose editors nonetheless remained ravenous for 'Irish copy'. This had long been the case. Exactly a century earlier, W. B. Yeats had warned writers that they were faced with a choice between expressing Ireland or exploiting it.[11] The expression of a country to its own people could be fraught with excitement and risk, while the exploitation of that material for overseas audiences could bring rapid cash rewards. Yeats, accordingly, sought to bring the centre of gravity back home, by establishing not just a theatre but publishing houses in Dublin. For all his charisma as a cultural leader, his efforts in the area of publishing were not hugely successful. Even in the 1960s, a quarter-century after his death, there were few publishing houses, except for some gathered around coteries of poets; and the work of leading novelists was displayed by Dublin bookshops in alphabetical sequence alongside that of overseas authors – O'Brien next to O'Hara, McLaverty beside Mailer. Although the first chair of Anglo-Irish Literature was founded at University College Dublin in 1964, the booksellers of Dublin for the most part had not yet decided that Irish writing in English was a distinct category.

All that would change in the 1970s and 1980s, as 'Irish Studies' came into their own. But some of the cooler, more hip young writers wanted things both ways: they wished to appeal to a national constituency, even as they questioned its underpinnings. *Paddy No More* was the title of a successful collection of their writings from a Dublin publishing house.[12] Many of the writers included sought an international style. They mocked the Abbey Theatre's annual revival of a play by Synge or O'Casey for the busloads of summer tourists. They wanted to be counted one with Borges, Broch and Benjamin – not Davis, Mangan and Ferguson. Yet, even in their impatience with the national idea, they somehow gave it continuing recognition, density, gravitas. And, of course, their ability to tell a good story won them deserved audiences overseas, as well as at home.

Irish writing remained high fashion in subsequent decades. At one point in 1998, there were seventeen Irish plays being staged in the greater London area. These plays allowed English audiences to address, at a safe remove, their own unresolved national question, and the fear that they were latecomers to the fashion-parade of nations.[13] (Their National Theatre, after all, had opened only in 1978, three-quarters of a century after that of Ireland.) 1998 was also the year in which the Cross of Saint George replaced the Union Jack at many sporting events; and when the Belfast Agreement sketched the prospect of devolved home rule parliaments not just for Northern Ireland, Scotland and Wales but also for England itself.

The lure of national cultures seemed to have been rediscovered after the fall of the Berlin Wall in 1989. The collapse of the communist project led the radical analyst Tom Nairn to remark on how few people, through the twentieth century, had proved willing to die for a social class compared with the millions who had died for country.[14] The richness of Marxian philosophy had come to a dead end. What was needed, Nairn suggested, was a commensurate sophistication in the literature of nationalism, so that its more positive potentials might be explored. Social democrats began to talk up the need for some form of nation state, not only to project identity as a counterweight to globalization, but also to express values of the decolonizing world. They noted rather wistfully that the transnational ideals, which had animated the United Nations upon its foundation in 1945, had not been fully developed, as that organization itself became a mechanism for recognizing newly independent nations. Less than fifty existed in 1945 but by the century's end there were more than 200. Yet all through those intervening decades, while nation states blossomed, languages had continued to die. As had been the case with Ireland, nations were what filled that empty space which lost languages left behind. In an era of rapid globalization, they exercised much less economic and political power than their leaders liked to believe, being often little more than devices for the psychological compensation of dispossessed peoples. Nevertheless, in the eyes of some more radical commentators, the nation state had its uses. In its early days it had assisted peoples in containing and controlling the catastrophic onset of modernity; now, in its venerable age after 1989, liberal social democrats such as Tony Judt hoped that it might act as some sort of brake on the depredations enacted by global capital.[15]

Such hopes soon appeared naive. By the time affluence (of a sort) came to Ireland, the ethical programme of the nation had been all but exhausted. The theory of national revival seventy-five years earlier had been based on the understanding that culture, politics and economics would all work together to promote freedom in conditions of decent self-sufficiency; but these three forces never quite coincided. There was no economic lift-off in the early decades of the state and the weakness of the political elites after the civil war led to a brokerist, clientilist politics, in the conduct of which various sections of society were 'bought off'. The sub-groups so courted did not include intellectuals or artists: rather these were driven out of the public sphere by censorship and belittlement. They never fully re-entered that sphere to create a more thoughtful type of nationalism or a considered lay theology.

The result of this, over time, was a denigration of national tradition by many intellectuals. By 1969, when a tax-holiday was proclaimed for artists, and by 1981, when the government offered artists an annual stipend in Aosdána, the corrosiveness had passed from artists into the mass media. Weak and uncertain politicians now often buckled under pressure from journalists as once they had blanched under the influence of the Catholic Church. The lack of a strong lay theological tradition made it difficult for many to process the liberal doctrines of the Second Vatican Council; and the steady erosion of older religious practices (pilgrimages, pattern days, stations of the cross) led to a privatization of everything from religious practice to consciousness itself. There was no longer an ethical language available for use in the public sphere (other than that employed by artists). Most politicians who talked, as Patrick Pearse had once done, of a patria to be served would have been laughed to scorn by journalists; and the Irish Republican Army helped to discredit the language of 'patriotism' by their casual slaughter of civilians.

In September 1997, it had been announced that there was not a single postulant registered that year to study for the priesthood in the Dublin archdiocese;[16] and a couple of years later it emerged that the number of lawyers in the country now surpassed that of priests for the first time since records began.[17] 'Money is the new Irish religion', proclaimed a feature in the Sunday Times of 2000.[18] The old religion, though hierarchical and repressive in many ways, had provided some of the social glue which held communities together. Although commentators often complained of the state being used by church authorities for their own purposes, the truth was that from its uncertain beginnings an impecunious government had used the Catholic Church as a sort of alternative welfare system in everything from education to health care. The older religion of popular devotionalism had helped people in conditions of adversity 'to preserve an inner detachment from worldly success and from personal tragedy';[19] but in the new state a moralistic Catholicism reduced religion to a civil ethic, stripped of most of its visionary majesty.

That rule-bound Catholicism underwent its final collapse in the years of the Celtic Tiger; but in fact the scandals of clerical child abuse dealt a knockout blow to what were already enfeebled institutions. Vocations to the religious life began to fall in 1967; and between 1971 and 1991 the average number of children in most families dropped from four to two, as the papal teaching on contraception was increasingly flouted. The commitment of even the more conservative sort of Catholic was eroded by the scandals, since the abuse of children for many constituted an ultimate betrayal of trust. The problem for the wider society, however, was that it had evolved no satisfactory liberal humanist code with which to replace that of the exploded religious institutions. One dire consequence was that, as Catholicism weakened, the more predatory kinds of capitalism began to triumph; and there were few voices, apart from those of artists and some independent-minded reporters, to offer any probing criticism of the new materialism.

The financial crisis that beset the global system after 2008 demonstrated just how ill-fitted were the legal frameworks of even the more powerful states to cope with predators. Yet leaders tried as best they could to cope in a national way with a transnational challenge, regulating the degrees of pain experienced by many vulnerable groups. Nobody, however, found a satisfactory way of curbing the ultimate authors of the affliction. Things had not been intended to pan out like this. Those in Ireland who had abandoned nationalist pieties and religious practice in the later years of the twentieth century had believed that they were getting something valuable in return: individual freedom and material well-being.

By 2010, as unemployment rose to almost half a million and the economy was micro-managed by the European Central Bank and International Monetary Fund, these promises rang a little hollow.

Sometimes, when a people are about to surrender a culture, outsiders come to its rescue. It was T. S. Eliot, a young man from St Louis, Missouri, who saved English poetry in the 1920s, abetted by other outsiders such as Ezra Pound and W. B. Yeats. In the previous generation, the English novel had been reconfigured by the American Henry James and the Polish Joseph Conrad, as it would be by Joyce in following years. All cultures which survive well do so because they are open to injections of life from without.

Migrants into a new country often expend their deepest energies on adjusting to the new place; and it used to be left to their children or grandchildren to create an art which explored fusions between the family's older traditions and those of the new country. These days, however, things can happen much faster. It would not be altogether surprising if immigrant writers from Africa or Eastern Europe reopened a dialogue with figures such as Cuchulain or Deirdre. They may well find new meanings in those mythological characters who exist still as buried memories of that landscape in which their people are choosing to live. The model of what Eliot did in 1922 is clear enough: in *The Waste Land* he described a fallen, jaded city, emptied of serious human encounter; but by invoking *The Faerie Queen* and *The Tempest*, the Fisher King and Brahma, he showed how seemingly lost traditions could flow like tributaries back into a resacralized landscape. The fate of the land – with fewer crops being grown every year, but endless ranches being created in a mode of big-farmer pastoralism – suggests a people who no longer feel themselves married to rock and hill. What they desire, at best, is a pleasant view of 'scenery'. Land ownership has become even more important than land use, in ways which would still not be true in France or Italy, whose farmers take pride in bringing homegrown fruits and vegetables to local markets. It is interesting that younger entrepreneurs have drawn a lesson from visits to these countries of continental Europe, setting up successful franchises in artisan foods.

Reviewed against that wider context, Éamon de Valera's radio broadcast of 1943 extolling rural values takes on an insurrectionary intensity. It insisted, in effect, that leaders such as he were not content simply to manage rural decline but were intent on reinvigorating the land. At a time when tens of thousands were leaving every year, and when many who remained showed a disinclination to reproduce themselves, this was a defiant rather than a sentimental speech. Many bishops in their pastoral letters of the 1940s warned communities against selfish bachelors, cautious maids and elderly parents blocking the marital hopes of the young – these were the very images used in de Valera's speech in a more positive key, but they could be employed in more negative mode by bishops as warning rather than vision.[20] Some cultural critics even wondered whether there might be a link between the censorship of creative art (lamented by Beckett) and the growing refusal to procreate (which his art seemed to endorse!). By the 1950s, in a book titled *The Vanishing Irish*, a priest named John O'Brien said that if the decline in population continued, 'the Irish will virtually disappear as a nation and will be found only as an enervated remnant in a land occupied by foreigners'.[21] One bishop predicted that the people would 'vanish like the Mayans, leaving only their monuments behind'.[22] The exclusion of most intellectuals and artists from the national project, under conditions of censorship, robbed de Valera and the bishops of potentially influential allies in this debate.

The state had been established after decades of dire uncertainty, but the cultural domain, in whose name the separatist agitation had been mounted, often seemed marginal. Yet major artwork, as we have seen, continued to lament that most elements of the promised Gaelic revival had never been achieved. *Amongst Women* ends when a man, an apologetic and furtive Fionn after the Fianna, drapes a tricolour over a dead comrade's coffin. *Dancing at Lughnasa* shows just how little the old fire festival now means to ordinary people. By the time these texts were written, the Irish had ceded most of their sovereignty – a subject of central value in Gaelic vision poems long before it became a basis of their wars of independence. Like other European peoples, they were ruled by decrees as often as by traditions or by national codes. The Dáil lost much authority, not only to unelected administrators of the European Union but also to the requirements of multinational companies.

Against that backdrop the vote by ninety-four per cent of the people of the Republic in 1998 to ratify the Belfast Agreement seemed sensible. With so much sovereignty lost in a globalized economy, how much really remained to be surrendered in the Agreement? The old territorial claim on the six counties – which nationalists had once considered a force of nature on an island destined to be one, indivisible place – was now withdrawn. It was recognized that a county such as Antrim could be British or Irish or both at the same time. Clearly the British, in advancing the very notion of Ireland as an administrative unit, had been among the chief inventors of its modern version of nationhood, so it was reasonable to admit that there was a significant British element in the people's identity.

It may well be that the Irish, having confronted their national question for well over a century, can more easily say farewell to the nation state than the English, whose identity has been drained away first by the British and then by the European structures. The vote in June 2016 for Brexit – a departure from the European Union – suggests that the English have a long-suppressed national question and that England may have been, as Oscar Wilde often claimed, the ultimate, most deeply penetrated, British colony. But the English may well be arriving at the fashion parade of nations at just that moment when the show is starting to close down.

Nations will continue to exist for many decades as shells, and in even greater numbers, but they will be divested of real economic or political power. Even the inhabitants of the neglected 'fly-over' states who elected Donald Trump their president in November 2016 will eventually learn a bitter truth: that in an era of instant communication among transnational global elites, it will not be possible to 'make America great again'. These aspirations will increasingly be regarded as anachronisms by people for whom a phrase such as 'After Ireland' may represent an opportunity to move forward rather than the utterance of an adverse judgement. In its day, the national idea created many good things – a welfare state; a belief that virtue is social as well as individual; a conviction that something in us can survive our own deaths. But it also did serious harm, creating over-centralization; bureaucracy; distrust of local culture; and, sometimes, a real hatred of other peoples. The grand renaissance of culture known as the Irish Revival occurred in those decades just *before* the nation was embodied in a new state. There may well be a second cultural flowering in coming years, as the political nation called Ireland dies and culture is once again seen to be the site and stake of all meaningful struggles.

Its prestige is still very high. The community believes that many kinds of leader have betrayed the public trust, but nobody says that about artists. Even in the years before the centenary celebrations of the Easter Rising, as young people left in their thousands and shop fronts were boarded up, there was a willingness to look to artists for pointers. As once again a rather innocent people's trust in a monoculture (this time houses) proved disastrous, they turned to artists for inspiration, figures who might embody the popular longing for form far more successfully than the state had managed to do. Economic collapse, as in the 1890s and the 1980s, had proven one thing – that unemployment in a population educated to relatively high levels can be the very foundation for a revival of the arts. The Dublin of the 1980s had contained a thousand garage bands and the country as a whole nurtured many of the literary talents whose work has been explored in this book.

The children of the 1980s had inherited a strong sense of Ireland, even if many of its elements distressed them mightily. The generation which began to leave after 2008 had a more globalized sense of Ireland; and the prospect of decades spent servicing a debt they did not themselves create led many to opt out: instead of protesting in the streets, like their Greek or French counterparts, they simply emigrated to other parts of the English-speaking world. But, once outside, many learn in a sharpened way what it is to be Irish. They are now part of a worldwide conversation about their country's cultural meaning, much as was the Revival generation of exiles in London, Paris and New York. It may be doubted, however, whether all that many of the current wild geese will choose to 'bring it all back home', as the followers of W. B. Yeats and Augusta Gregory did. More likely they will follow the example of Joyce and Beckett. Yet they still feel an investment in their country: the number of young Irish intellectuals who attended a meeting in New York in autumn 2015 to protest against the commemoration programme of the Abbey Theatre for the following year is proof enough of that.[23]

In Ireland, traditions often appear to die, while in fact being reborn in some new mode. The Irish language never really vaporized, despite O'Faoláin's claim in 1926 that Gaeldom was over; and it is probably stronger now than it was when the Gaelic League was founded in 1893. But it did die out in many places, only to be replaced by that Hiberno-English which, deriving much of its energy from the syntax of the native language, made writers like Synge and Joyce world-famous. In the aftermath of the Belfast Agreement in 1998, nationalism of the old-fashioned kind consented to abolish itself; but it has been reborn for many in subsequent years as civic republicanism. In the same way, what is dying in the spiritual life of the people is not religion but religiosity. The practices of a rule-bound ecclesiocracy are surrendering to the yearnings of ordinary people. Despite legislation permitting divorce, familism is still strong, so much so that sixty-two per cent of the population chose to endorse gay marriage in a referendum on 22 May 2015 of a kind which might not so easily have won such levels of support in other countries of Europe. Ireland remains a place where ancient and modern ideas can often overlap. There is clearly a disconnect between the religious convictions of the people and official church institutions, as there is a disconnect between the population and its political structures (which lag decades behind).

Nature abhors a vacuum. It is likely that entirely new, unimaginable institutions will emerge, just as the Abbey Theatre and Gaelic League (and ultimately a free if flawed state) filled the gap left some decades earlier by the collapse of the old Ireland. The history of a people moves always in cycles. A century ago, a cultural revival led – often against the wishes of its very originators – to economic, political and even military assertions of autonomy.

The commemoration of the Easter Rising was a moment (perhaps passing) when a sense of community was restored in the country's streets, after decades of remorseless privatization. By Easter 2016 commentators were cautiously hailing signs of an economic recovery, at least in Dublin and its dormitory towns, if not yet in rural areas. That recovery may deepen, but if it does, it may establish a pattern predicted by some economists: a return to the era of the city-state, flourishing often at the expense of surrounding regions. All across the world, cities are prospering, often as a result of abandoning any deep sense of obligation to rural communities.

Whatever the underlying trend, an Ireland which had been so recently a poster child for globalization now became a model for 'how to do austerity'. Whether there was any truth in that analysis is a moot point: many critics argue that such recovery as occurred was due to deeper established traditions of modernity geared to export, to an influx of foreign capital (much of it vulture funds), and to a new life in the international economy (consequent upon very low interest rates).[24] The austerity programme imposed by outside institutions to contract state finances was only one element in the slight recovery achieved at the level of national accountancy: but it came at a huge cost to the community (post offices closed, libraries cut back, police stations shut down, teachers dismissed). In the eyes of some, it may well have been an excuse to bring Ireland further into line with that very globalization which gave rise to the crisis, utterly transforming the nature of the state in the process. The results were visible to all in the huge increases in hospital admissions, suicides and mental illness.[25]

As the country in the spring of 2016 celebrated a centenary since the Proclamation of the Republic, many were struck by analogies between the two Irelands. The fear of a lost political and economic sovereignty had troubled Patrick Pearse and Constance Markiewicz. Trepidation about being inundated by publications of the yellow press assailed Douglas Hyde and Maud Gonne, just as global networks of social media seem to overwhelm people today. But the Revival generation turned those challenges into opportunities, offering a confident diagnosis of its situation. Then, as now, people concluded that sovereignty in an era of growing internationalism might be limited, but that it was nonetheless important for Ireland to play a role in building a better, kinder world. Then, as now, culture was at the centre of all human struggles for self-recognition; and the one domain in which an unfettered kind of sovereignty might yet be enjoyed.

Notes

1. Introduction: After Ireland?

1. Michael Lewis, *Boomerang* (New York: Norton, 2011), p. 84.
2. Ibid., p. 114.
3. 'Poblacht na hÉireann: The Provisional Government of the Irish Republic to the People of Ireland', Easter 1916, in Declan Kiberd and P. J. Mathews (eds), *Handbook of the Irish Revival: An Anthology of Irish Cultural and Political Writings 1891–1922* (Dublin: Abbey Theatre Press, 2015), pp. 104–5.
4. See Declan Kiberd, 'What Have We Got That Is Worth So Much?', *Irish Times*, 26 May 1987, p. 10; see also Declan Kiberd, 'Telling the Europeans What We Think of Them', *Irish Times*, 28 April 1987, p. 8.
5. Raymond Crotty, *Ireland in Crisis* (Dingle: Brandon Press, 1986).
6. Anthony Cronin, *Samuel Beckett: The Last Modernist* (London: HarperCollins, 1996), p. 36.
7. Samuel Beckett, *Murphy* (London: Picador Books, 1973), p. 6.
8. Henry James, *The Letters of Henry James, Vol. IV: 1896–1916*, ed. Leon Edel (Cambridge, MA: Belknap Press, 1984), p. 398.
9. Ibid., p. 713.
10. W. B. Yeats, *Collected Poems* (London: Macmillan, 1950), p. 393.
11. The best study of this (including the Irish–Soviet comparison) is Jana Fischerova, 'Literary Censorship in Independent Ireland and Communist Czechoslovakia', unpublished PhD thesis, University College Dublin (2010): but see also Michael Adams, *Censorship: The Irish Experience* (Dublin: Irish University Press, 1968), for an excellent analysis.

12. Robert James Scally, *The End of Hidden Ireland* (Oxford: Oxford University Press, 1995), *passim*.

13. Samuel Beckett, *Waiting for Godot* (London: Faber and Faber, 1965), p. 75. All future references to this text will appear in parentheses with the abbreviation *WG*.

14. Cited by Tomás Ó Fiaich, 'The Language and Political History', in Brian Ó Cuív (ed.), *A View of the Irish Language* (Dublin: Stationery Office, 1969), p. 105.

15. On Sir William Wilde's ideas, see Terence de Vere White, *The Parents of Oscar Wilde: Sir William and Lady Wilde* (London: Hodder and Stoughton, 1967).

16. *Letters of W. B. Yeats*, ed. Allan Wade (London: Macmillan, 1954), p. 31.

17. Samuel Beckett, *Disjecta: Miscellaneous Writings and a Dramatic Fragment*, ed. Ruby Cohn (New York: Grove Press, 1984), p. 70.

18. See extract from Colm Ó Gaora, 'Mise', in Kiberd and Mathews (eds) *Handbook of the Irish Revival*, p. 466.

19. Foundation Scholarship Examination, Irish essay paper, Trinity College Dublin, Spring 1969.

20. The speaker was Michael D. Higgins, who went on to create legislation for the establishment of the successful Irish-language television station TG4 and, in time, to be elected (in 2011) President of Ireland.

2. Beckett's Inner Exile

1. Vivian Mercier, *Beckett/Beckett* (Oxford: Oxford University Press, 1977), p. 46.

2. Samuel Beckett, *Molloy: Malone Dies: The Unnamable* (London: Calder Books, 1959), p. 36.

3. Samuel Beckett, *Endgame* (New York: Grove Press, 1958), p. 49. Future references to this text will appear in parentheses under *E*.

4. Salman Rushdie, *Imaginary Homelands* (London: Granta, 1992), pp. 124ff.

5. Samuel Beckett, *Happy Days* (New York: Grove Press, 1961), p. 47–8.

6. Patrick O'Farrell, *Ireland's English Question: Anglo-Irish Relations 1534–1970* (New York: Schocken Books, 1971), p. 14.

7. W. B. Yeats, *Collected Poems* (London: Macmillan, 1950), p. 271.

8. Samuel Beckett, *Disjecta*, p. 71.

9. Alain Robbe-Grillet, review of *Waiting for Godot*, in Ruby Cohn (ed.), *Casebook on Waiting for Godot* (New York: Grove Press, 1967), p. 16.

10. John Fletcher, 'Roger Blin at Work', in Ruby Cohn (ed.), *Casebook on Waiting for Godot*, p. 25.

11. Søren Kierkegaard, *The Sickness Unto Death*, trans. Alastair Hannay (Harmondsworth: Penguin Books, 1989), p. 43.

12. Cited by Isaiah Berlin, 'Einstein and Israel', in Robert B. Silvers and Barbara Epstein (eds), *Anthology: Selected Essays from the First 30 Years of The New York Review of Books, 1963–1993* (New York: New York Review of Books,1993), p. 162.

13. Anthony Cronin, *Samuel Beckett: The Last Modernist* (London: Harper Collins, 1996), pp. 460ff.

14. Robert Crawford, *Young Eliot: From St Louis to The Waste Land* (London: Jonathan Cape, 2015), pp. 423–4.

15. J. W. von Goethe, *Wilhelm Meister's Apprenticeship*, Book VII, Chapter III, trans. Robyn Smith (New York: Penguin Books, 1977), p. 411.

Interchapter: A Neutral Ireland?

1. Louis MacNeice, *Collected Poems* (London: Faber & Faber, 1966), p. 132.

2. See Phyllis Gaffney, *Healing Amid the Ruins: The Irish Hospital at Saint Lô (1945–46)*, (Dublin: A & A Farmer, 1999), especially pp. 71–81.

3. 'Gaeldom is Over': *The Bell*

1. Sean O'Faoláin, cited by Kelly Matthews, *The Bell Magazine and the Representation of Irish Identity* (Dublin: Four Courts Press, 2012), p. 67.

2. W. B. Yeats, *Autobiographies* (London: Macmillan, 1955).

3. See Donal Ó Drisceoil, *Censorship in Ireland, 1939–45: Neutrality, Politics and Society* (Cork: Cork University Press, 1996).

4. Jonathan Rose, *The Intellectual Life of the British Working Classes* (New Haven: Yale University Press, 2001).

5. Matthews, *The Bell Magazine*, p. 80.

6. Quoted by Gregory A. Schirmer (ed.), in *Reviews and Essays of Austin Clarke* (Gerrards Cross: Colin Smythe, 1995), p. xi.

7. W. B. Yeats, *Collected Poems* (London: Macmillan, 1950), p. 376.

8. Cited by Matthews, *The Bell Magazine*, p. 162.

9. Cited ibid., p. 50.

10. Ibid., p. 30.

11. Cited ibid., p. 39.

12. 'Sean O'Faoláin: Writer in Profile', television interview with Augustine Martin', RTÉ, 2 October 1972.

13. On this syndrome, see J. M. Synge, 'Can We Go Back Into Our Mother's

Womb?', in Declan Kiberd and P. J. Mathews (eds), *Handbook of the Irish Revival: An Anthology of Irish Cultural and Political Writings 1891–1922* (Dublin: Abbey Theatre Press, 2015), p. 128.

14. Cited by Matthews, *The Bell Magazine*, p. 153.
15. Michael Farrell, *Arming the Protestants* (Dingle: Brandon Books, 1983), pp. 89–92.
16. Mathews, *The Bell Magazine*, pp. 131–40.
17. Cited by Mathews, *The Bell Magazine*, p. 134.
18. Cited ibid., p. 135.
19. On this see Terence Brown, 'After the Revival: The Problem of Adequacy and Genre', in Ron Schleifer (ed.), *The Genres of the Irish Literary Revival* (Dublin: Wolfhound Press, 1980), pp. 153–78.
20. For O'Faoláin's thoughts on the modern novel, see his work *The Vanishing Hero: Studies of Novelists of the Twenties* (London: Eyre & Spottiswoode, 1956).
21. See Paul Delaney, *Sean O'Faoláin: Literature, Inheritance and the 1930s* (Dublin: Irish Academic Press, 2014), *passim*.

4. A Talking Corpse? Sáirséal agus Dill

1. Adrian Kelly, *Compulsory Irish: Language and Education in Ireland 1870–1970* (Dublin: Irish Academic Press, 2002), *passim*.
2. See Declan Kiberd, *Inventing Ireland* (London: Jonathan Cape, 1995), pp. 265–6.
3. Máirtín Ó Cadhain, 'Irish Prose in the Twentieth Century', in J. E. Caerwyn Williams (ed.), *Literature in Celtic Countries* (Cardiff: University of Wales Press, 1970), pp. 137–51.
4. Frank O'Connor, *An Only Child* (London: Macmillan, 1988), p. 147.
5. Cian Ó hÉigeartaigh and Aoileann Nic Gearailt, *Sáirséal agus Dill 1947–1981: Scéal Foilsitheora* (Connemara: Cló Iar-Chonnacht, 2014), pp. 115–28.
6. Gilles Deleuze and Felix Guattari, *Kafka: Toward a Minor Literature* (Minneapolis: University of Minnesota Press, 1986), pp. 26ff.
7. In fact, a good version was produced as part of a doctoral dissertation at University of California, Berkeley, by Joan Trodden Keefe (1984); and Alan Titley's 2015 version has been followed by a further translation (with notes) by Liam Mac Con Iomaire and Tim Robinson (both published in the World Republic of Letters series by Yale University Press). Having been declared untranslatable for many years, the book now bids fair to call forth a small army of translators.
8. Máirtín Ó Cadhain, *Páipéir Bhána agus Páipéir Bhreaca* (Dublin: Club Merriman, 1970).

9. Máirtín Ó Cadhain, *Cré na Cille* (Dublin: Sáirséal agus Dill, 1949), p. 49.
10. Samuel Beckett, *Waiting for Godot* (New York: Grove Press, 1954), p. 48.
11. Eamon Duffy, *The Stripping of the Altars* (New Haven: Yale University Press, 1992), p. 475.
12. Nuala Ní Dhomhnaill, *Selected Essays*, ed. Oona Frawley (Dublin: New Island Books, 2005), pp. 14ff.

5. A Parrot in Ringsend: Máire Mhac an tSaoi

1. Máire Mhac an tSaoi, *The Same Age as the State* (Dublin: O'Brien Press, 2003).
2. Oscar Wilde, *The Artist as Critic: Critical Writings of Oscar Wilde*, ed. Richard Ellmann (London: Batsford, 1970), p. 389.
3. Edward M. Stephens, *My Uncle John*, ed. Andrew Carpenter (Oxford: Oxford University Press, 1974), p. 65.
4. Lecture in Department of Irish, Trinity College Dublin, 21 January 1972; see also 'Fireann ar an Uaigneas: Filíocht Sheáin Úí Ríordáin', in *Scríobh* 1, ed. Seán Ó Mórdha (Dublin: An Clóchomhar, 1974), pp. 11–17.
5. See Emer Ní Dhiarmada, 'Fuarchúis Fir agus Crá Chroí Mná', *Irisleabhar Mhá Nuad* (1972), pp. 37–44.
6. Máire Mhac an tSaoi, *An Paróiste Míorúilteach*, ed. Louis de Paor (Dublin: O'Brien Press, 2011), p. 48. All later quotations from this volume will appear in parentheses under the heading *APM*.
7. Translation by Eiléan Ní Chuilleanáin.
8. Translation by Eiléan Ní Chuilleanáin.
9. Translation by Louis de Paor.
10. Translation by Biddy Jenkinson.
11. Translation by Biddy Jenkinson.
12. There is a good range of critical commentaries on these and other issues raised by the poetry in Louis de Paor (ed.), *Míorúilt an Pharóiste: Aistí ar fhilíocht Mháire Mhac an tSaoi* (Conamara: Cló Iarchonnacht, 2014), *passim*.
13. See Declan Kiberd, *Synge and the Irish Language* (London: Macmillan, 1979), pp. 246ff.
14. Máire Mhac an tSaoi, in conversation with Harry Kreisler, University of California at Berkeley, 4 April 2000.
15. Patrick Pearse, in Declan Kiberd and P. J. Mathews (eds), *Handbook of the Irish Revival: An Anthology of Irish Cultural and Political Writings 1891–1922* (Dublin: Abbey Theatre Press, 2015), pp. 224–5.
16. Translation by Biddy Jenkinson.
17. Translation by James Gleasure.
18. Translation by James Gleasure.

19. Translation by James Gleasure.
20. Cited by Louis de Paor, Introduction to *An Paróiste Míorúilteach*, p. 23.

6. Growing Up Absurd: Edna O'Brien and *The Country Girls*

1. See chapters 1 and 2 of this book.
2. Edna O'Brien, *The Country Girls* (Harmondsworth: Penguin Books, 1963), p. 53. Subsequent references to the book will appear in parentheses with the abbreviation *CG*.
3. Quoted by Julia Carlson, *Banned in Ireland: Censorship and the Irish Writer* (London: Routledge, 1990), p. 79.
4. See Declan Kiberd, *Inventing Ireland: The Literature of the Modern Nation* (London: Jonathan Cape, 1995), pp. 101–14.
5. See Grace Eckley, *Edna O'Brien* (New Jersey: Bucknell University Press, 1974), pp. 84ff.
6. On this postcolonial pathology, see Frantz Fanon, *The Wretched of the Earth*, trans. Constance Farrington (Harmondsworth: Penguin Books, 1967), *passim* – but especially the chapter titled 'The Pitfalls of National Consciousness'.
7. See Carlson, *Banned in Ireland*, p. 71.
8. Marina Warner, *From the Beast to the Blonde: On Fairy Tales and Their Tellers* (London: Chatto and Windus, 1994), p. 204.
9. Ibid., p. 201.
10. Ibid., p. 205.
11. Maria Tatar, *Off With Their Heads: Fairy Tales and the Culture of Childhood* (New Jersey: Princeton University Press, 1993), p. 127.
12. Cited by Barbara Bannon, 'Authors and Editors', *Publishers' Weekly*, 197 (1970), pp. 21–2.
13. Edna O'Brien, *James Joyce* (London: Weidenfeld & Nicolson, 1999), p. 170.
14. James Joyce, *Ulysses* (London: Penguin Books, 1992), p. 11.
15. Bruno Bettelheim, *The Uses of Enchantment: The Meaning and Importance of Fairy Tales* (Harmondsworth: Penguin Books, 1978), pp. 68–9.
16. Melanie Klein, *The Psychoanalysis of Children*, trans. Alix Strachey (New York: Grove Press, 1960), *passim*.
17. O'Brien, *James Joyce*, p. 6.
18. Quoted ibid., p. 36.
19. Cited by A. Norman Jeffares in *A Commentary on the Collected Poems of W. B. Yeats* (Stanford: University of California Press, 1968), p. 372.
20. Quoted by Eckley, *Edna O'Brien*, p. 43.
21. Franco Moretti, *The Way of the World : The Bildungsroman in European Culture*, trans. Albert Sbragia (London: Verso Books, 2000), p. 27.

22. Ibid., pp. 185ff.
23. Quoted by Richard Ellmann, *James Joyce* (Oxford: Oxford University Press, 1966), p. 175.
24. O'Brien, *James Joyce*, pp. 74–5.
25. On this see Susan Sontag, *Styles of Radical Will* (New York: Secker & Warburg, 1968); and Angela Carter, *The Sadeian Woman* (London: Virago, 1974), *passim*.
26. The phrase was first used by the mystic poet William Blake and quoted by Joyce – and O'Brien: see her *James Joyce*, p. 89.

7. Frank O'Connor: A Mammy's Boy

1. John Mitchel, 'Introduction', *Poems of James Clarence Mangan* (New York: D & J Sadleir, 1859), p. 14.
2. James Olney, *Metaphors of Self: The Meaning of Autobiography* (Princeton University Press: New Jersey 1972), *passim*.
3. Cited by James Olney in *Autobiography: Essays Theoretical and Critical* (New Jersey: Princeton University Press, 1980), p. 69.
4. Frank O'Connor, *An Only Child* and *My Father's Son* (London: Penguin Modern Classics, 2005), p. 110. Future references to this combined volume will appear in parentheses with the abbreviations *OC* and *MFS*.
5. Walt Whitman, *The Portable Walt Whitman*, ed. Mark van Doren (New York: Viking Books, 1969), p. 56.
6. James Matthews, *Voices: A Life of Frank O'Connor* (New York: Atheneum, 1983), p. 335. See also *My Father's Son*, pp. 251ff.
7. James Joyce, *A Portrait of the Artist as a Young Man* (London: Penguin Modern Classics, 1969), p. 189.
8. Daniel Corkery, *Synge and Anglo-Irish Literature* (Cork: Mercier Books, 1966), p. 14; also V. S. Naipaul, *The Mimic-Men* (Harmondsworth: Penguin Books, 1969), p. 146.
9. Patrick Kavanagh, *Collected Pruse* (London: Martin Brian & O'Keeffe, 1973), p. 13.
10. See especially Conor Cruise O'Brien, *States of Ireland* (London: Hutchinson, 1972), *passim*.
11. Frank O'Connor, *The Lonely Voice* (London: Macmillan, 1962), pp. 13ff.

8. Richard Power and *The Hungry Grass*

1. Richard Power, *The Hungry Grass* (London: Bodley Head, 1969), p. 194.

All subsequent references will appear in parentheses in main text indicated by *HG*.

2. See Peter Connolly, 'Review of *The Hungry Grass*', *The Furrow*, 21:6 (1970).

3. Louise Fuller, *Irish Catholicism Since 1950: The Undoing of a Culture* (Dublin: Gill and Macmillan, 2002): see also Mary Kenny, *Goodbye to Catholic Ireland* (Dublin: New Island Books, 2000); and D. Vincent Twomey, *The End of Irish Catholicism?* (Dublin: Veritas Publications, 2003).

4. He cited this in an address at Yeats International Summer School, Sligo, 8 August 1986.

5. See Fuller, *Irish Catholicism Since 1950*, especially final chapter.

6. On the decline of deference and the reassertion of conservative values, see David Fitzpatrick, *Politics and Irish Life 1913–21* (Dublin: Gill and Macmillan,1977), p. 234; also J.J. Lee, *The Modernisation of Irish Society 1848–1918* (Dublin: Gill and Macmillan,1973).

7. Raymond Crotty, *Ireland in Crisis* (Dingle: Brandon Press, 1986).

8. Antonio Gramsci, 'The Southern Question', cited in Robert Wohl, *The Generation of 1914* (Cambridge, MA: Harvard University Press, 1979), p. 196.

9. James Joyce, *A Portrait of the Artist as a Young Man* (Harmondsworth: Penguin Modern Classics, 1969), p. 158.

10. Flann O'Brien, *At Swim-Two-Birds* (Harmondsworth: Penguin Modern Classics, 1967), p. 9.

11. On this element in Shaw, see in particular the use of the phrase in his play *The Doctor's Dilemma* – but also the more general critique of professional specialists in *Mrs Warren's Profession*.

12. See Connolly, 'Review of *The Hungry Grass*'.

9. Emigration Once Again: Friel's *Philadelphia*

1. Quoted by W. B. Yeats, *Autobiographies* (London: Macmillan, 1955), p. 96.

2. P. H. Pearse, *Plays, Stories, Poems* (Dublin: Phoenix Publishing Co., 1924), p. 333.

3. Patrick Kavanagh, *Collected Poems* (London: Martin Brian & O'Keeffe, 1972), p. 53.

4. Brian Friel, *Philadelphia, Here I Come!* (London: Faber & Faber, 1965), p. 77. All subsequent references to this work appear in parentheses with the abbreviation *PHIC*.

5. Kavanagh, *Collected Poems*, pp. 36–7.

6. Nancy Scheper-Hughes, *Saints, Scholars and Schizophrenics: Mental Illness in Rural Ireland* (California, Berkeley: University of California Press, 1979), pp. 3, 65, 111.

7. Hugh Brody, *Inishkillane: Change and Decline in the West of Ireland* (Harmondsworth: Pelican Books, 1973), *passim*.

10. Seamus Heaney: The Death of Ritual and the Ritual of Death

1. G. K. Chesterton, *The Autobiography of G. K. Chesterton* (New York: Sheed & Ward Inc., 1936), p. 139.
2. Seamus Heaney, 'The Poet as a Christian', *The Furrow*, 29:10 (1978), pp. 604–5.
3. Ibid., p. 606.
4. Seamus Heaney, *Place and Displacement* (Cumbria: Trustees of Dove Cottage, 1984), p. 3.
5. James Randall, 'An Interview with Seamus Heaney', *Ploughshares*, 5:3 (1979), p. 20.
6. Seamus Heaney, 'View', *The Listener*, 31 December 1970, p. 102.
7. Heaney, 'Poet as a Christian', p. 603.
8. Ibid., p. 604.
9. Richard Rose, *Governing Without Consensus: An Irish Perspective* (London: Faber & Faber, 1971).
10. Heaney, *Place and Displacement*, p. 1.
11. Richard Kearney, 'The IRA's Strategy of Failure', in Mark Patrick Hederman and Richard Kearney (eds), *Crane Bag Book of Irish Studies* (Dublin: Blackwater Press, 1982), pp. 699–707; also Richard Kearney, *Myth and Motherland* (Derry: Field Day Publications, 1984).
12. Seamus Heaney, 'Prairies', in *Door into the Dark* (London: Faber & Faber, 1969).
13. Seamus Heaney, *North* (London: Faber & Faber, 1975). Subsequent quotations are from this edition, cited parenthetically by page number in the text with the abbreviation *N*.
14. On this see Elmer Andrews, *The Poetry of Seamus Heaney: All the Realms of Whisper* (London: Macmillan, 1988), pp. 105ff.
15. Seamus Heaney, 'A Tale of Two Islands: Reflections on the Irish Literary Revival', in P. J. Drudy (ed.), *Irish Studies 1* (Cambridge: Cambridge University Press, 1980), p. 9.
16. The phrase was first used of Yeats by W. H. Auden in 'The Public Versus the Late Mr William Butler Yeats'. See William H. Pritchard (ed.), *W. B. Yeats: A Critical Anthology* (Harmondsworth: Penguin Books, 1972), pp. 136–42.
17. W. B. Yeats, *Collected Poems* (London: Macmillan, 1952), p. 232.
18. Auden, 'The People Versus the late Mr William Butler Yeats'.
19. J. M. Synge, 'Preface' to *Poems*, ed. Robin Skelton (London: Oxford University Press, 1962), p. xxxvi.

20. J. M. Synge, *Letters to Molly: John Millington Synge to Maire O'Neill, 1906–1909*, ed. Ann Saddlemyer (Cambridge, MA: Harvard University Press, 1971), *passim*.

21. Synge, 'Preface', p. xxxvi.

22. Walter Benjamin, *One-Way Street and Other Writings*, trans. J. A. Underwood (London: Harcourt Brace, 1979), p. 107.

23. Geoffrey Moore (ed.), *The Penguin Book of American Verse* (London: Penguin Books, 1977), p. 575.

24. Sean O'Casey, *Drums Under the Windows*, vol. 3 of *Autobiography* (London: Macmillan, 1972), p. 164.

25. Yeats, *Collected Poems*, p. 398.

26. For an analysis of 'Punishment', see my *Inventing Ireland: The Literature of a Modern Nation* (London: Jonathan Cape, 1995), pp. 593 ff.

27. Cited in James Clifford, *The Predicament of Culture: Twentieth-Century Ethnography, Literature, and Art* (Cambridge, MA: Harvard University Press, 1988), p. 207.

28. Gerry Fitt, speech to College Historical Society, Trinity College Dublin, 12 February 1973.

29. John Haffenden, *Viewpoints: Poets in Conversation with John Haffenden* (London: Faber & Faber, 1981), p. 61.

30. Seamus Heaney, *Preoccupations: Selected Prose, 1968–1978* (London: Faber & Faber, 1984), p. 57.

31. Helen Vendler, *Seamus Heaney* (Cambridge, MA: Harvard University Press, 1998), p. 45.

32. Blake Morrison, 'Speech and Reticence: Seamus Heaney's *North*', in Peter Jones and Michael Schmidt (eds), *British Poetry since 1970: A Critical Survey* (Manchester: Carcanet Press, 1980), p. 110.

33. For even harsher analyses, see Edna Longley, '*North*: "Inner Émigré" or "Artful Voyeur"?', in Tony Curtis (ed.), *The Art of Seamus Heaney* (Dublin: Wolfhound, 1994), p. 78; and Ciaran Carson, review of *North*, *The Honest Ulsterman*, 50 (1975), pp. 184ff. For a more positive and convincing analysis, see Henry Hart, *Seamus Heaney: Poet of Contrary Progressions* (Syracuse, NY: Syracuse University Press, 1992), pp. 88ff.

34. Heaney, *Preoccupations*, p. 52.

35. Derek Walcott, 'The Muse of History', lecture at South Bank, London, 3 March 1995.

36. Derek Walcott, *The Arkansas Testament* (London: Faber & Faber, 1987).

37. Seamus Heaney, *The Redress of Poetry: Oxford Lectures* (London: Faber & Faber, 1995), pp. 9–10.

38. Ibid., p. 82.

39. Cited by Heaney, *Preoccupations*, p. 34.

11. The Art of Science: Banville's *Doctor Copernicus*

1. Declan Kiberd, unpublished interview with John Banville, 20 September 1986.

2. This opening summary of Banville's aesthetic ideas derives from two sources: the articles he wrote for *Hibernia* magazine's book review section in the years immediately before and after the publication of *Doctor Copernicus* in 1976, and my own interview with the author in Dublin on 20 September 1986.

3. John Banville, 'Out of Focus', *Hibernia*, 20 January 1978.

4. Declan Kiberd, unpublished interview with John Banville, 20 September 1986.

5. Later Banville would greatly alter his view of Joyce, even to the extent of celebrating his stylistic experiments: see Hedvig Schwall, 'An Interview with John Banville', *European English Messenger* (EESE), 6:1 (1997).

6. Rudiger Imhof, 'An Interview with John Banville', *Irish University Review*, 11:1 (1981), Special Issue: John Banville, p. 6.

7. Ibid., p. 5.

8. W. B. Yeats, *A Vision* (London: Macmillan, 1978), p. 25.

9. W. B. Yeats, *Autobiographies* (London: Macmillan, 1955), p. 293.

10. W. B. Yeats, 'Meru', *Collected Poems* (London: Macmillan, 1950), p. 333.

11. Keith Thomas, *Religion and the Decline of Magic* (Harmondsworth: Penguin, 1973).

12. Joseph McMinn, *The Supreme Fictions of John Banville* (Manchester: Manchester University Press, 1999), p. 46.

13. John Banville, *Doctor Copernicus: A Novel* (London: Secker & Warburg, 1976), p. 83. Subsequent references to the book will appear in parentheses with the abbreviation *DC*.

14. For more on this, see McMinn, *The Supreme Fictions*, pp. 4ff.

15. T. S. Eliot, 'Four Quartets', *The Complete Poems and Plays of T. S. Eliot*, (London: Faber & Faber, 1969), p.182.

16. Flann O'Brien, *At Swim-Two-Birds* (Harmondsworth: Penguin, 1967), p. 25.

17. 'Novelists on the Novels: Ronan Sheehan talks to John Banville and Francis Stuart', in *The Crane Bag*, 3:1 (1979), p. 84.

18. In the years just before and after *Doctor Copernicus*, Hayden White initiated a major debate on this very point among historians: see his *Metahistory: The Historical Imagination in Nineteenth-Century Europe* (Baltimore: John Hopkins University Press, 1978).

19. McMinn, *The Supreme Fictions*, p. 6.

20. Imhof, 'Interview with Banville', p. 8.

21. Declan Kiberd, unpublished interview with Banville: the opening sentence of the next paragraph comes from this.

22. See Roland Barthes, 'Fourier', in Susan Sontag (ed.), *A Barthes Reader* (London: Cape, 1982).

23. Sheehan, 'Novelists on the Novel', p. 79.

24. John Banville, 'It's Only a Novel', *Hibernia*, 11 November 1977; and 'It's a Mad, Mad World', 22 July 1977.

25. Sheehan, 'Novelists on the Novel', pp. 83–4.

26. John Banville, 'Enigma Variations', *Hibernia*, 16 February 1978.

27. Ibid.; and 'Saul Bellow's World', *Hibernia*, 18 March 1977. For a much fuller account of Banville's ideas in his *Hibernia* years, see Christine Breen's unpublished master's essay, 'The Magic Circle', University College Dublin, 1980. This essay is much indebted to her work, which has become even more valuable over the years.

28. John Banville, 'In the Monster House', *Hibernia*, 12 April 1974.

29. Thomas Kuhn, *The Copernican Revolution* (Cambridge, MA: Harvard University Press, 1976), p. 136.

30. McMinn, *The Supreme Fictions*, p. 52.

31. See T. S. Eliot, 'Tradition and the Individual Talent', *The Sacred Wood: Essays on Poetry and Criticism* (New York: Alfred A. Knopf, 1921).

32. Derek Hand has explored this interpretation in a number of studies, culminating in *A History of the Irish Novel* (Cambridge: Cambridge University Press, 2014).

33. See Richard Rose, *Governing without Consensus* (London: Faber & Faber, 1971), *passim*.

34. White, *Metahistory*.

35. For Banville's own version of this story, see Stanley van der Ziel, *John McGahern and the Imagination of Tradition* (Cork: Cork University Press 2016), p. 20.

36. Ibid., *passim*.

37. John Banville, *Birchwood* (London: Secker and Warburg, 1973), p. 128.

38. Teilhard de Chardin, *Hymne de l'univers* (Paris: Les Éditions du Seuil, 1961), *passim*.

12. The Double Vision of Michael Hartnett

1. W. B. Yeats, 'Letter to the Editor', *The Leader*, September 1900.

2. The phrase is used by Salman Rushdie, *Imaginary Homelands* (London: Granta, 1992), *passim*.

3. In Irish *bhí sé agat gach bealach*, translated by Ulick O'Connor as 'both ways'.

4. Seosamh Mac Grianna, *Pádraic Ó Conaire agus Aistí Eile* (Dublin: An Gúm, 1969), p. 5.
5. P. H. Pearse, 'Letter to the Editor', *An Claidheamh Soluis*, 20 May 1899, p. 157.
6. Daniel Corkery, *What's this about the Gaelic League?* (Dublin and Cork: Connradh na Gaedhilge, 1941).
7. The poem is titled simply 'Yeats' and is in *The Complete Poems of Patrick Kavanagh* (New York: Peter Kavanagh, 1978).
8. Michael Hartnett, *Collected Poems*, ed. Peter Fallon (Oldcastle, Meath: Gallery Press, 2001), p. 143. Subsequent quotations are from this edition, cited parenthetically by page number in the text with the abbreviation *HCP*.
9. Sean O'Casey, *Drums under the Windows* (London: Macmillan, 1945), p. 73.
10. Máirtín Ó Direáin, *Ár Ré Dhearóil* (Dublin: Clóchomhar, 1963), p. 17.
11. Osborn Bergin, *Irish Bardic Poetry*, ed. F. Kelly (Dublin: Dublin Institute for Advanced Studies, 1970), p. 120.
12. Jacques Derrida, 'Des Tours de Babel', in R. Schutte and J. Biguenet (eds), *Theories of Translation* (Chicago: University of Chicago Press, 1992), p. 28.
13. Bergin, *Bardic Poetry*, p. 127.
14. Ngugi Wa Thiong'o, *Decolonising the Mind: The Politics of Language in African Literature* (London: Currey, 1986), cover blurb.
15. Ibid., p. 11.
16. Ibid., p. 17.
17. Ibid., p. 21.
18. Ibid., p. 21.
19. Ibid., p. 30.
20. Colm Ó Gaora, *Mise*, 2nd ed. (Dublin: An Gum, 1967).
21. Synge manuscripts, TCD, MS 4J84, f. 54.
22. R. W. Emerson, *Selected Essays* (Harmondsworth: Penguin Classics, 1965), p. 12.
23. W. B. Yeats, *Essays and Introductions* (London: Macmillan, 1961), p. 208.
24. Text and translation are in *An Crann Faoi Bhláth: The Flowering Tree: Irish Poetry with Verse Translations*, eds Gabriel Fitzmaurice and Declan Kiberd (Dublin: Woolfhound, 1989), p. 128.
25. Michael Hartnett, 'Why Write in Irish?', *Irish Times*, 26 August 1975. I am grateful to my student Allan Gregory for drawing this valuable essay to my attention.
26. Ibid.
27. Dennis O'Driscoll, interview, *Poetry Ireland Review*, 20 (1987), pp. 16–21; I am again indebted to Allan Gregory for this reference. See, for more, Gregory's unpublished short dissertation, 'Michael Hartnett: Poet and Translator 1941–1999', UCD, 2001.
28. Niklaus Gessner, *Die Unzulanglichkeit der Sprache* (Zurich: Juris Verlag, 1957), p. 32.

29. Michael Hartnett, *Ó Bruadair: Selected Poems of Dáibhí Ó Bruadair*, translated and introduced by Michael Hartnett (Oldcastle, Meath: Gallery Press, 1985), p. 26.

30. Ibid., introduction, p. II.

31. Ibid., p. 48.

32. Renato Poggioli, 'The added artificer', in Reuben A. Brower (ed.), *On Translation* (Cambridge, MA: Harvard University Press, 1959), p. 142.

33. Walter Benjamin, 'The Task of the Translator', *Illuminations*, trans. Harry Zohn (London: Fontana Books, 1970), p. 80 ff.

13. Brian Friel's *Faith Healer*

1. Brian Friel, *Faith Healer* (London: Faber & Faber, 1980), p. 16. Subsequent quotations are from this edition, cited parenthetically by page number in the text with the abbreviation *FH*.

2. J. M. Synge, *Collected Works: Plays Book 2*, ed. Ann Saddlemyer (Oxford: Oxford University Press, 1968), p. 249.

3. Ibid., p. 247.

4. J. M. Synge, *Collected Works* (Vol. 2): *Prose*, ed. Alan Price (Oxford: Oxford University Press, 1966), p. 216.

5. Seamus Heaney, *Wintering Out* (London: Faber & Faber, 1972), p. 48.

6. Seamus Heaney, 'Digging and Divining', talk on BBC Radio 3, 1975.

7. Anthony Bailey, 'A Gift for Being in Touch; Seamus Heaney Builds Houses of Truth', *Quest*, January/February 1978.

8. Heaney, 'Digging and Divining'; see also 'Feeling into Words', *Preoccupations: Selected Prose 1968–78* (London: Faber & Faber, 1980), pp. 41–60.

9. Lawrence Graver and Raymond Federman, *Samuel Beckett; The Critical Heritage* (London: Routledge & Kegan Paul, 1979), p. 173.

10. Harold Bloom, *The Anxiety of Influence* (Oxford: Oxford University Press, 1975).

11. Samuel Beckett, *Murphy* (London: Picador, 1973), p. 5.

12. Hugh Kenner, *Dublin's Joyce* (London: Faber & Faber, 1956), p. 212.

14. Theatre as Opera: *The Gigli Concert*

1. Sean McMahon (ed.), *Rich and Rare: A Book of Ireland* (Dublin: Poolbeg Press, 1984), p. 62.

2. James Joyce, *Ulysses: Annotated Student's Edition*, with notes and introduction by Declan Kiberd (London: Penguin, 1992), pp. 328–76.

3. Ibid., p. 149.
4. Ibid., p. 477.
5. Ibid., p. 482.
6. Ibid., p. 479.
7. Samuel Beckett et al., *Our Exagmination round his Factification for Incamination of Work in Progress* (London: Faber & Faber, 1929), p. 1.
8. Richard Poirier, *The Performing Self: Compositions and Decompositions in the Languages of Contemporary Life* (New York: Oxford University Press, 1971) p. xi.
9. Ibid., p. xiv.
10. A revised and shortened version was published by Methuen, London, in 1991; my reasons for preferring the original are implied later in this commentary, where I argue for the central role of the character Mona.
11. Fintan O'Toole, *The Politics of Magic: The Work and Times of Tom Murphy* (Dublin: Raven Arts Press, 1987), pp. 19–29.
12. Patrick Mason, Interview with Christopher Murray, *Irish University Review*, 17:1 (1987), Special Issue: Tom Murphy, p. 105.
13. Tom Murphy, *The Gigli Concert* (Oldcastle, Co. Meath: Gallery Press, 1984), p. 13. Subsequent quotations are from this edition, cited parenthetically by page number in the text with the abbreviation *GC*.
14. Caroline Spurgeon, *Shakespeare's Imagery and What it Tells Us* (Cambridge: Cambridge University Press, 1934).
15. G. B. Shaw, *An Autobiography 1856–98*, selected from his writing by Stanley Weintraub (London: Max Reinhardt, 1969), p. 284.
16. Ibid., p. 284.
17. W. H. Auden, 'An Improbable Life', in Richard Ellmann (ed.), *Oscar Wilde: Twentieth Century Views* (New Jersey: Prentice-Hall, 1969), p. 136.
18. O'Toole, *Politics of Magic*, p. 169.
19. Richard Kearney, *Transitions: Narratives in Modern Irish Culture* (Dublin: Wolfhound, 1988), p. 161–71.
20. Ibid.
21. Patrick Mason, interview with Declan Kiberd, 'Exhibit A', RTÉ television, 27 September 1983.
22. Kearney, *Transitions*, p. 76.
23. Ernst Bloch, *The Utopian Function of Art and Literature*, trans. Jack Zipes and Frank Mecklenberg (Cambridge, MA: MIT Press, 1988) p. 41.
24. Ibid., p. 39.
25. Cited ibid., p. 41.
26. Erich Stern, 'Review of Otto Rank, *The Double*', *Die Literatur*, xxix (Vienna 1926/7), p. 555.
27. Otto Rank, *The Double: A Psychoanalytical Study*, trans. and ed. Harry Tucker Jr. (Chapel Hill: Beacon Press, 1971), pp. 50ff.

28. Cited by Harry Tucker Jr., Introduction to *The Double* (Chapel Hill: Beacon Press, 1971), p. xvi.
29. Rank, *The Double*, p. 48.
30. Ibid.

15. Frank McGuinness and *Observe the Sons*

1. Kevin Jackson, 'Speaking for the Dead: Playwright Frank McGuinness', *Independent*, 27 September 1989.
2. Myles Dungan, *Irish Voices from the Great War* (Dublin: Irish Academic Press, 1995), p. 105.
3. Frank McGuinness, *Observe the Sons of Ulster Marching towards the Somme* (London: Faber & Faber, 1986), p. 12. All subsequent references in parentheses are to this edition with the abbreviation *OS*.
4. Desmond Fitzgerald, *Memoirs 1913–1916* (London: Routledge, 1968), pp. 142–3.
5. Desmond O'Rawe, 'Encountering Eros: Discourses of Desire in Contemporary Irish Literature', unpublished PhD thesis, Queen's University Belfast (1999), p. 50.
6. Dungan, *Irish Voices*, p. 108.
7. Anthony Roche, *Contemporary Irish Drama* (Dublin: Gill and Macmillan, 1994), p. 267.
8. On this see Hugh Kenner, *A Reader's Guide to Samuel Beckett* (London: Thames & Hudson, 1973), p. 134.
9. Patrick Pearse, *Plays, Stories, Poems* (Dublin: Phoenix, 1924), p. 24.
10. Dungan, *Irish Voices*, p. 126.
11. Robert Wohl, *The Generation of 1914* (Cambridge, MA: Harvard University Press, 1979), p. 115.
12. Ibid., p. 105.
13. Paul Fussell, *The Great War and Modern Memory* (London: Oxford University Press, 1977), p. 191.
14. Ibid., p. 196.
15. Helen Lojek, 'Myth and Bonding in Frank McGuinness's *Observe the Sons*', *Canadian Journal of Irish Studies*, 14:1 (1988), pp. 47–8.
16. Samuel Beckett, *Murphy* (London: Routledge, 1938), p. 65.
17. Fussell, *The Great War*, p. 64.
18. Ibid., p. 86.
19. Ibid., p. 174.
20. David Nowlan, *Irish Times*, 19 February 1985; on this see Christopher Murray, *Twentieth-Century Irish Drama: Mirror up to Nation* (Manchester: Manchester University Press, 1977), p. 204.

21. *Collected Letters of D. H. Lawrence*, ed. Harry T. Moore (London: Heinemann, 1962), p. 456.

22. Fussell, *The Great War*, p. 272.

23. Cited ibid., p. 271.

24. Ibid., p. 299.

25. Jonathan Rutherford, *Forever England: Reflections on Masculinity and Empire* (London: Lawrence & Wishart, 1997), p. 49; excerpted from *Granta*, 5 February 1910.

26. Fussell, *The Great War*, p. 271.

27. Hannah Arendt, *The Origins of Totalitarianism* (London: Deutsch, 1986), p. 217.

28. Dungan, *Irish Voices*, p. 113.

29. Sir Frank Fox, *The Royal Inniskilling Fusiliers in the World War* (London: Constable, 1928), p. 69.

30. *Letters of Henry James*, ed. Percy Lubbock, 10 vols., II (New York: Scribner, 1920), p. 384.

31. Barry Sloan, 'Sectarianism and the Protestant Mind: Some Approaches to a Current Theme in Anglo-Irish Drama', *Études Irlandaises*, 18:2 (1993), p. 40.

32. For a brilliant analysis of the syndrome in terms of English culture see Rutherford, *Forever England*, p. 23.

33. Ibid., p. 14.

34. Ibid., p. 34.

35. Ruth Dudley Edwards, *Patrick Pearse: The Triumph of Failure* (London: Gollancz, 1977), p. 53.

36. Pearse, *Plays, Stories, Poems*, p. 49.

37. See Graham Dawson, *Soldier Heroes: British Adventure, Empire and the Imagining of Masculinities* (London: Routledge, 1994).

38. O'Rawe, 'Encountering Eros', p. 47.

39. Fussell, *The Great War*, p. 27.

40. Cited by Martin Middlebrook, *The First Day on the Somme* (London: Allen Lane, 1971), p. 124.

41. Personal conversation with Mrs Lemass, niece of MacDonagh at the Pearse House, Rathfarnham.

42. Fussell, *The Great War*, p. 51.

43. O'Rawe, 'Encountering Eros', p. 47.

44. Helen Lojek, 'Difference without Indifference: The Drama of Frank McGuinness and Anne Devlin', *Eire-Ireland*, 25:2 (1990), p. 59.

45. The Belfast Agreement, published in Dublin, Belfast, and London by Stationery Offices, 1998, pp. 2–3.

16. Derek Mahon's Lost Worlds

1. Derek Mahon, *New Collected Poems* (Oldcastle, Meath: Gallery Press, 2011), p. 16. All following quotations from this volume are in parentheses in the text with the abbreviation *NCP*.
2. Andrew Marvell, *The Complete Poems*, ed. George Lord (London: Everyman Classics, 1995), p. 23.
3. See, for instance, his poem 'Dover Beach'.
4. E. P. Thompson, *The Making of the English Working Class* (Harmondsworth: Pelican Books: 1968), p. 13.
5. W. B. Yeats, *Autobiographies* (London: Macmillan, 1955), p. 189.
6. Samuel Beckett, *Waiting for Godot* (New York: Grove Press, 1954), p. 40.
7. Anthony Raftery, 'Mise Raiftearaí', in Seán Ó Tuama and Thomas Kinsella (eds), *An Duanaire, 1600–1900: Poems of the Dispossessed* (Mountrath: Dolmen Press, 1981), p. 292.
8. J. M. Synge, *Collected Works: Prose*, ed. Alan Price (Oxford: Oxford University Press, 1966), p. 347.
9. For a reading on these lines, see Hugh Haughton, *The Poetry of Derek Mahon* (Oxford: Oxford University Press, 2007), pp. 114–17.
10. Brendan Kennelly, 'My Dark Fathers', *My Dark Fathers* (Dublin: New Square Publications, 1964).
11. W. B. Yeats, *Collected Poems* (London: Macmillan, 1950), p. 213.
12. See Haughton, *Derek Mahon*, pp. 188–9.

17. Nuala Ní Dhomhnaill: *Pharaoh's Daughter*

1. See Declan Kiberd, *Synge and the Irish Language* (London: Macmillan, 1979); especially the chapter 'Scholar and Translator'.
2. Nuala Ní Dhomhnaill, *Selected Essays*, ed. Oona Frawley (Dublin: New Island, 2005), p. 10.
3. Máirtín Ó Cadhain, *Páipéir Bhána agus Páipéir Bhreaca* (Dublin: Club Merriman, 1969).
4. W. B. Yeats, Letter to the Editor, the *Leader*, September 1900.
5. Ní Dhomhnaill, *Selected Essays*, p. 105.
6. Ibid., p. 41.
7. Edward W. Said, *Culture and Imperialism* (London: Chatto & Windus, 1993), *passim*.
8. Gilles Deleuze and Felix Guattari, *Kafka: Toward a Minor Literature* (Minneapolis: University of Minnesota Press, 1986), pp. 28ff.

9. Patrick Kavanagh, *Collected Pruse* (London: McGibbon & Kee, 1973), p. 19.

10. *Report of the Committee on Irish Language Attitudes and Research* (Dublin: Government Publications, 1975), pp. 24ff.

11. Thomas MacDonagh, *Literature in Ireland: Studies Irish and Anglo-Irish* (Dublin: Talbot Press, 1916).

12. Thomas Kinsella, 'The Divided Mind', in Seán Lucy (ed.), *Irish Poets in English* (Cork: Mercier Press, 1972).

13. Ní Dhomhnaill, *Selected Essays*, p. 14.

14. Nuala Ní Dhomhnaill, *Pharaoh's Daughter* (Oldcastle, Meath: Gallery Books, 1990), p. 154. Subsequent references to poems in Irish or in translation from this volume will appear in parentheses in the text with the abbreviation *PD*.

15. Cited by Ní Dhomhnaill, *Selected Essays*, p. 115: see Ngugi Wa Thiong'o, *Decolonizing the Mind: The Politics of Language in African Art* (London: Lawrence & Wishart, 1986), pp. 97–108.

16. Ní Dhomhnaill, *Selected Essays*, p. 85.

17. 'Mairgne ar an nDíbeart go Cúige Chonnact', *Dánta Árd-Teastais*, p. 56.

18. See Declan Kiberd, 'George Moore agus an Ghaeilge', *Idir Dhá Chultúr* (Dublin: Coiscéim, 1993), pp. 129–30.

19. Walter Benjamin, *Illuminations*, trans. Harry Zohn (London: Fontana Books, 1970), pp. 81ff.

20. Renato Poggioli, 'The added artificer', in Reuben Brower (ed.), *On Translation* (Cambridge, MA: Harvard University Press, 1959), p. 142.

21. Ní Dhomhnaill, *Selected Essays*, p. 55.

22. Ibid., p. 45. For a somewhat more positive take on this Irish tradition, see Declan Kiberd, *Men and Feminism in Modern Literature* (London: Macmillan, 1985), pp. 103–35 and pp. 168–203; and see my additional comments on pp. 372–3 of this volume.

23. See Mary Colum, *Life and the Dream* (New York: Macmillan, 1947), p. 107–8.

24. On this choice confronted by many Irish authors, see Declan Kiberd, 'Writers in Quarantine?', in Kiberd, *The Irish Writer and the World* (Cambridge: Cambridge University Press, 2005) pp. 52–69.

25. Benjamin, *Illuminations*, p. 70.

26. Ní Dhomhnaill, *Selected Essays*, p. 70.

27. F. Scott Fitzgerald, *The Crack-Up and Other Pieces and Stories* (Harmondsworth: Penguin, 1965), p. 39.

28. Máirtín Ó Direáin, *Feamainn Bhealtaine* (Dublin: An Clóchomhar, 1961), pp. 87–8.

29. Ní Dhomhnaill, *Selected Essays*, p. 102.

30. John Bowlby, *Separation: Anxiety and Anger* (New York: Basic Books, 1976), *passim*.

31. See Robert F. Garratt, *Trauma and History in the Irish Novel* (London: Macmillan, 2011), *passim*.

32. Cathal Póirtéir and Caoimhín Mac Giolla Léith have discussed this background to Gaelic culture on RTÉ. See www.rte.ie for archives.

33. Laura O'Connor, *Haunted English: The Celtic Fringe, the British Empire and De-Anglicization* (Baltimore: Johns Hopkins, 2006).

34. Ní Dhomhnaill, *Selected Essays*, p. 87.

35. Adam Phillips, review of *The Fifty-Minute Mermaid*, *Guardian Books*, 27 January 2008.

36. Liam Ó Casaide, interview with Ní Dhomhnaill on Gaelcast, 2 September 2006. See archives at www.gaelcast.com.

37. Ibid.

18. Eavan Boland: *Outside History*

1. This was a term widely used, notably in the *Irish Independent* and the *Irish Times* of the decade.

2. W. B. Yeats, *Autobiographies* (London: Macmillan, 1955), p. 94.

3. Ibid., p. 520.

4. Mícheál MacLiammóir and Eavan Boland, *W. B. Yeats and His World* (London: Thames & Hudson, 1971).

5. See Edna Longley, *The Living Stream: Literature and Revisionism in Ireland* (Newcastle: Bloodaxe Books, 1994), p. 175.

6. Eavan Boland, *New Collected Poems* (Manchester: Carcanet Press, 2012), p. 255. All further quotations of Boland's poetry are from this text, indicated in parentheses by *NCP*.

7. See Richard Wolin, *Walter Benjamin: The Aesthetic of Redemption* (New York: Schocken Books, 1982), pp. 53ff.

8. James Joyce, 'The Day of the Rabblement', in Declan Kiberd and P. J. Mathew (eds), *Handbook of the Irish Revival: An Anthology of Irish Cultural and Political Writings 1891–1922* (Dublin: Abbey Theatre Press, 2015), p. 164.

9. Eavan Boland, cited in *Eavan Boland: A Sourcebook*, ed. Jody Allen-Randolph (Manchester: Carcanet Press: Manchester 2007), p. 139.

10. Kuno Meyer, *Selections from Ancient Irish Poetry* (London: Constable, 1911).

11. Translation by current author: text from Aindrias Ó Muimhneachain, *Dánta Árd-Teastais 1969–70* (Dublin: Folens, 1967), p. 12.

12. Allen-Randolph, *Boland: A Sourcebook*, p. 137.

13. Ibid., p. 60.

14. Ibid., p. 69.

15. Ibid., p. 79.

16. Ibid., p. 108.
17. Speech to Yeats International Summer School, 7 August 1986.
18. Allen-Randolph, *Boland: A Sourcebook*, p. 73.
19. Ibid., p. 125.
20. Virginia Woolf, *A Room of One's Own* (London: Hogarth Press, 1930), *passim*.
21. Jody Allen-Randolph, *Close to the Next Moment: Interviews from a Changing Ireland* (Manchester: Carcanet Press, 2010), pp. 234–6.
22. Ibid., p. 239.
23. Ibid., p. 241.
24. Eavan Boland, *Outside History* (London: Vintage Books, 1996), p. 60.
25. Ibid.

19. John McGahern's *Amongst Women*

1. John McGahern, *Amongst Women* (London: Faber & Faber, 1990). All subsequent references in parentheses are to this edition with the abbreviation *AW*.
2. John McGahern, 'A Revolutionary Mind', *Irish Times*, Weekend Supplement, 11 April 1998, p. 4.
3. I am very indebted to Sampson's excellent chapter on *Amongst Women* in Denis Sampson, *Outstaring Nature's Eye: The Fiction of John McGahern* (Dublin: Lilliput Press, 1993), p. 235.
4. W. B. Yeats, *Autobiographies* (London: Macmillan, 1955), p. 27.
5. John McGahern, '*An tOileánach*', *Irish Review* 6 (1989), p. 56. See also John McGahern, *Love of the World: Essays*, ed. Stanley van der Ziel (London: Faber & Faber, 2009) for a collection of McGahern's prose writings, including a slightly revised edition of this McGahern essay.
6. John McGahern, lecture at University College Dublin, 6 March 1999. The echo of James Joyce (who said that 'the ordinary is the domain of the artist; the extraordinary can safely be left to journalists'; quoted in my introduction to Joyce's *Ulysses* (London: Penguin, 1992), p. xii) is almost certainly deliberate.
7. John McGahern, interview with Gerry Moriarty, *Irish Press*, 6 August 1993, p. 11.
8. John McGahern, 'Dubliners', in Augustine Martin (ed.), *James Joyce: The Artist and the Labyrinth* (London: Ryan Publishing, 1990) pp. 68–9.
9. Quoted in McGahern, '*An tOileánach*', p. 58.
10. John McGahern, lecture at University College Dublin, 24 February 1999.
11. Sampson, *Outstaring*, p. 217.

12. McGahern, '*An tOileánach*', p. 56.

13. Quoted in Brendan Kennelly, 'Patrick Kavanagh', in Sean Lucy (ed.), *Irish Poets in English: The Thomas Davis Lectures on Anglo-Irish Poetry* (Cork: Mercier, 1973), p. 180.

14. W. B. Yeats, *The Poems: A New Edition*, ed. Richard J. Finneran (New York: Macmillan, 1983), p. 181.

15. Maud Gonne pointed this out to Yeats in a letter responding to an early version of the poem; see *The Gonne–Yeats Letters: 1893–1938*, eds Anna MacBride White and Norman A. Jeffares (London: Hutchinson, 1992), pp. 384–5.

16. Yeats, *The Poems*, p. 181.

17. This was first pointed out by Denis Sampson in a brilliant passage in *Outstaring Nature's Eye*, see pp. 220–3.

18. Claude Levi-Strauss, *Le Cru et le Cuit* (Paris: Pion, 1964), p. 20.

19. Quoted in McGahern, '*An tOileánach*', p. 57.

20. Ibid., p. 59.

21. This is, for example, McGahern's reading of the symbolic meaning of Yeats's *Purgatory*, as expressed in his lecture at University College Dublin, 17 February 1999. But the same interpretation might be offered of *On Baile's Strand*.

22. John McGahern, 'Out of the Dark', *Irish Times*, 28 May 1990, p. 10.

23. On this concept see Richard Wolin, *Walter Benjamin: An Aesthetic of Redemption* (New York: Columbia University Press, 1982); for a good summary of the Proustian analysis see Sampson, *Outstaring*, pp. 13–20.

24. McGahern, '*An tOileánach*', p. 56.

25. Quoted ibid., p. 57.

26. Ibid., p. 57.

27. Eileen Kennedy, 'Question and Answer with John McGahern', *Irish Literary Supplement* (1984), p. 40.

20. Between First and Third World: Friel's *Lughnasa*

1. Edward W. Said, *After the Last Sky* (New York: Pantheon Books, 1986), p. 159.

2. Brian Friel, *Dancing at Lughnasa* (London: Faber & Faber, 1990), p. 2. Subsequent quotations are from this edition, cited parenthetically by page number in the text with the abbreviation *DL*.

3. Basil Davidson, *The Black Man's Burden: Africa and the Curse of the Nation-State* (London: James Currey, 1992), p. 191.

4. Ibid., p. 138.

5. See Marshall McLuhan and Quentin Fiore, *The Medium is the Message* (London: Allen Lane, 1968).

6. J. M. Synge, *Collected Works: Plays Book 2*, ed. Ann Saddlemyer (Oxford: Oxford University Press, 1968), p. 95.

7. For further readings of the mirror, see Declan Kiberd, *Inventing Ireland* (London: Jonathan Cape, 1995), pp. 166–88.

8. Kwame Anthony Appiah, *In My Father's House* (London: Methuen, 1994), p. 2.

9. On these debates see Claudia W. Harris, 'The Engendered Space: Performing Friel's Women from Cass Maguire to Molly Sweeney', in William Kerwin (ed.), *Brian Friel: A Casebook* (New York: Garland, 1997), pp. 43–76.

10. See J. J. Lee and Gearóid Ó Tuathaigh, *The Age of de Valera* (Dublin: Ward Riter in association with Radio Telefis Éireann, 1982).

11. Terence Brown, 'Have We a Context? Tradition, Self and Society in the Theatre of Brian Friel', in Elmer Andrews (ed.), *The Achievement of Brian Friel* (Gerrards Cross: Colin Smythe, 1992), p. 201.

12. See Helen Brennan, *The Story of Irish Dance* (Dingle: Brandon, 1999).

13. See Said, *Last Sky* pp. 53–5. He reports a similar pathology in Palestinians.

14. The phrase was used of Field Day by Colm Tóibín.

15. The process began in Algeria during the late 1950s when the resistance movement set up Radio Fighting Algeria: see Frantz Fanon, *A Dying Colonialism* (Harmondsworth: Penguin Books, 1968); by the 1970s a Gaeltacht radio station had been established in the west of Ireland, but only in the 1980s was local radio widely broadcast in most European countries.

16. See McLuhan and Fiore *The Medium is the Message*; also McLuhan's *War and Peace in the Global Village* (New York: McGraw-Hill, 1968).

17. Donnchadh Ó Corráin, 'Women in Early Irish Society', in D. Ó Corráin and M. MacCurtain (eds), *Women in Irish Society: The Historical Dimension* (Dublin: Arlen House, 1978), p. 11.

18. Cited by Appiah, *Father's House*, p. 184.

19. Brian Rothery (Dublin: Institute of Public Administration, 1987).

20. Brian Girvin, *Between Two Worlds: Politics and Economy in Independent Ireland* (Dublin: Gill and MacMillan, 1989).

21. See Peadar Kirby, *Has Ireland a Future?* (Cork: Mercier, 1988); and *Ireland and Latin America* (Dublin: Trócaire and Gill and MacMillan, 1992). See also Therese Caherty (ed.), *Is Ireland a Third World Country?* (Belfast: Beyond the Pale Publications, 1992).

22. Roland Barthes, *Camera Lucida*, trans. Richard Howard (New York: Hill & Wang, 1981), p. 39.

23. James Joyce, *Ulysses* (London, Penguin Modern Classics, 1992), p. 249.

24. Ibid., p. 30.

25. If Friel found Steiner's *After Babel* of service in the writing of *Translations*, or O'Faoláin's *The Great O'Neill* an aid to *Making History*, then the book

which lies behind *Dancing at Lughnasa* could be Victor Turner's *The Ritual Process*. There the beheading of a cock at the close of a ritual represents the suffering of the women, and the slaughterer is the witch doctor (or African priest). Equally, the boy's use of masks enacts his progression from the female-dominated family to the men's house, his removal from the domestic sphere.

26. The monstrous faces on the masks would be explicable as identifications with a terrifying object (a fearful authority figure), a way for the vulnerable child to increase his own power by assimilating himself to that very power which subjugates him.

27. See Harris, 'Engendered Space', pp. 44–9.

28. This is from a letter by Yeats to Olivia Shakespeare in *Letters of W. B. Yeats*, ed. Allan Wade (London: Rupert Hart-Davis, 1954), p. 788.

29. Davidson, *The Black Man's Burden*, p. 47.

30. James T. Clifford, introduction to *The Predicament of Culture* (Cambridge, MA: Harvard University Press, 1988).

31. Davidson, *The Black Man's Burden*, pp. 76–7.

32. For the full exchange, see '*The Silver Tassie*: Letters', in Thomas Kilroy (ed.), *Sean O'Casey: A Collection of Critical Essays* (New Jersey: Princeton Hall, 1975), pp. 113–17.

33. Quoted by Appiah, *Father's House*, p. 36.

34. See J. J. Lee, *Ireland 1912–1985: Politics and Society* (Cambridge: Cambridge University Press, 1989); and Declan Kiberd, 'Fasten Your Seat Belts for the Third World', *Irish Times*, 10 February 1987; and 'Hall-Marks of the Third World', *Irish Times*, 18 August 1987.

35. See Patrick Burke, 'As if Language No Longer Existed: Non-Verbal Theatricality in the Plays of Brian Friel', in William Kerwin (ed.), *Brian Friel: A Casebook*, p. 19.

21. Roddy Doyle: *Paddy Clarke Ha Ha Ha*

1. Roddy Doyle, *Paddy Clarke Ha Ha Ha* (London: Secker & Warburg, 1993), p. 75. Subsequent quotations from this novel appear in parentheses in the text with the abbreviation *PCH*.

2. Conor McPherson, *Plays: Three* (London: Nick Hern Books, 2013), p. 132.

3. See Louise Fuller, *Irish Catholicism Since 1950: The Undoing of a Culture* (Dublin: Gill & Macmillan, 2004), *passim*.

4. James Joyce, *A Portrait of the Artist as a Young Man* (Harmondsworth: Penguin Modern Classics, 1969), pp. 171–2.

22. Seamus Deane: *Reading in the Dark*

1. Cited in Michael Farrell, *Arming the Protestants* (Dingle: Brandon Books, 1983), pp. 89–92; also see pp. 114–15.
2. One of the best accounts of growing up in Derry in the years covered by this novel is Eamonn McCann, *War and an Irish Town* (Harmondsworth: Penguin Special, 1974).
3. On this see Seamus Deane, *Strange Country: Modernity and Nationhood in Irish Writing* (Oxford: Oxford University Press, 1997), *passim*.
4. Liam Harte, *Reading the Contemporary Irish Novel 1989–2007* (Oxford: Blackwell, 2014), pp. 173–96.
5. See his introduction and notes to the Penguin Modern Classics edition published in 1992.
6. Seamus Deane, *Reading in the Dark* (London: Jonathan Cape, 1996), p. 13. All subsequent quotations from this text appear in parentheses indicated with the abbreviation *RD*.
7. Derek Hand, *A History of the Irish Novel* (Cambridge: Cambridge University Press, 2014), pp. 247–53.
8. Michael Farrell, *The Orange State* (London: Pluto Press, 1976), pp. 93–8.
9. Hand, *Irish Novel*, p. 253.

23. Reading Éilís Ní Dhuibhne

1. Gertrude Stein, *Everybody's Autobiography* (New York: Exact Change Books, 1993), p. 289.
2. The Gaeltacht areas were both 'backward' and 'forward' by the 1970s – modernized by the influence of emigrants returning from major cities on holiday, yet economically undeveloped. Anxious officials sought to repair the effects of such uneven development – for example, a Gaeltacht radio station was set up in that decade, as were many local publishing houses, making the place (at least in cultural terms) a crucible of postmodernity.
3. The Belfast Agreement, published in Dublin, Belfast, and London by Stationery Offices, 1998, pp. 2 and 16.
4. Éilís Ní Dhuibhne, *The Dancers Dancing* (Belfast: Blackstaff Press, 1999), *passim*. Future reference to the novel will appear in parentheses with the abbreviation *DD*.
5. The comment was made to journalist Mary Holland, who worked for ITV's Weekend World and who further analysed its meaning in an article in *The Observer*.

6. The unemployment rate among males in Connemara, according to figures releases by Cearta Sibhialta na Gaeltachta hovered around 30% – slightly higher than that recorded among men in Derry by the Northern Ireland Civil Rights Association in 1969.
7. Although the most famous hunger strikes of the period covered in this book occurred in 1980–81 at Long Kesh prison, there were periodic strikes in the earlier 1970s: for instance by Michael Farrell, a leader of People's Democracy.
8. See William Butler Yeats, 'Hiberno-English', *Handbook of the Irish Revival 1891–1922*, pp. 149–51.
9. One of the subtlest analysts of this process is the French writer René Char.

24. Making History: Joseph O'Connor

1. See Terry Eagleton, *Heathcliff and the Great Hunger* (London: Verso Books, 1995), *passim*.
2. Seán de Fréine, *The Great Silence* (Dublin: Foilseacháin Náisiúnta Teoranta, 1966), p. 68.
3. The remark is widely attributed to Henry James; and the accompanying analysis is conducted most fully in his book-length study of Nathaniel Hawthorne.
4. See also Joseph O'Connor, *The Secret World of the Irish Male* (Dublin, New Island: Dublin, 1995), *passim*.
5. Joseph O'Connor, *Star of the Sea* (London: Secker and Warburg, 2002), p. 29. All future page references in the text are to this edition and will appear in parentheses in the main text indicated by *SS*.
6. Amartya Sen, *Poverty and Famines* (Oxford: Oxford University Press, 1982); and Cormac Ó Gráda, *Famine: A Short History* (Princeton: Princeton University Press, 2009).
7. For a sustained examination of many instances, see Walter Benjamin, *Illuminations*, trans. Harry Zohn (London: Fontana Books, 1970), *passim*.
8. Joseph O'Connor, *Redemption Falls* (London: Harvill Secker, 2007) p. 333. All future page references in the text are to this edition and will appear in parentheses in the main text indicated by *RF*.
9. Toni Morrison, *What Moves at the Margin: Selected Nonfiction*, ed. Carolyn C. Denard (University of Mississippi Press, 2008), p. 17.

25. Fallen Nobility: McGahern's *Rising Sun*

1. John McGahern, *That They May Face the Rising Sun* (London: Faber & Faber,

2002), p. 2. Subsequent quotations are from this edition, cited parenthetically by page number in the text with the abbreviation *RS*.

2. I am grateful to Tania Scott for pointing this out in a brilliant seminar paper delivered on 21 February 2005 in University College Dublin.

3. John McGahern, *Amongst Women* (London: Faber & Faber, 1990), p. 172.

4. Ibid., p. 47.

5. J. M. Synge, *Collected Works: Prose*, ed. Alan Price (Oxford: Oxford University Press, 1966), pp. 132–3.

6. I am indebted to P. J. Mathews for pointing this out to me.

7. Michael D. Higgins, 'The Gombeen-Man in Irish Fact and Fiction', *Études Irlandaises* 10 (1985), pp. 31–52.

8. Synge, *Collected Prose*, p. 130.

9. Patrick Kavanagh, *Collected Pruse* (London: Martin, Brian, & O'Keefe, 1973).

10. The reference is to Beckett's Winnie in the play, *Happy Days*.

11. See Samuel Beckett, *Proust* (New York: Calder, 1970), p. 8.

12. Tomás Ó Criomhthain, *An tOileánach* (Baile Átha Cliath: Ó Fallamhain i gcomhair le hOifig an tSoláthair, 1929).

26. Conor McPherson: *The Seafarer*

1. Conor McPherson, *The Seafarer*, in *Plays: Three* (London: Nick Hern Books, 2013), p. 61. All following references to *The Seafarer* in the text will be in parentheses with the abbreviation *S*.

2. Gerald C. Wood, *Conor McPherson: Imagining Mischief* (Dublin: Liffey Press, 2003), p. 139.

3. Conor McPherson, interview, 'McPherson on Beckett', available at www.beckettonfilm.com/plays/endgame/interview_macphearson/ (accessed 21 July 2016).

4. Lillian Chambers and Eamonn Jordan, *The Theatre of Conor McPherson* (Dublin: Carysfort Press, 2012), p. 245.

5. Conor Cruise O'Brien, *Writers and Politics* (London: Chatto & Windus, 1965), p. 104.

6. Samuel Beckett, *Endgame* (Faber & Faber: London, 1964), p. 62.

27. Claire Keegan: *Foster*

1. Bronagh Ní Chonaill, 'Fosterage: Child-rearing in Medieval Ireland', *History Ireland*, 5:1 (1997), pp. 28–31.

2. Conrad Arensberg and Solon T. Kimball, *Family and Community in Ireland* (Cambridge, MA: Harvard University Press, 1940), *passim.*

3. Claire Keegan, *Foster* (London: Faber & Faber, 2010), p. 5. References to subsequent quotations from this text will appear in parentheses with the abbreviation *F*. A somewhat different version of this 'long short story' was published in the *New Yorker*, 15 February 2010, but all references here are to the Faber text.

4. On bad foster parents, see Bruno Bettelheim, *The Uses of Enchantment: The Meaning and Importance of Fairy Tales* (Harmondsworth: Penguin Books, 1978), pp. 68ff. Also Marina Warner, *From the Beast to the Blonde: On Fairy Tales and Their Tellers* (London: Chatto & Windus, 1994), pp. 204ff.

5. Claire Keegan, lecture at University College Dublin, 20 February 2002.

6. See J. M. Synge, *Collected Works: Prose*, ed. Alan Price (Oxford: Oxford University Press 1966), pp. 75ff.

7. Reidar Th. Christiansen, 'The Dead and the Living', *Studia Norvegica*, 2 (1946), p. 15.

8. Alex Leslie, 'The Secret and the Unsaid', unpublished undergraduate essay, University of Notre Dame (2014), p. 4.

9. Padraig O'Malley, *Biting at the Grave* (Belfast: Blackstaff Press, 1991), *passim.*

10. Walter Benjamin, 'The Storyteller', *Illuminations*, trans. Harry Zohn (London: Fontana Books, 1970), pp. 142ff.

11. Frank O'Connor, *The Lonely Voice* (London: Macmillan, 1968), *passim.*

28. Kate Thompson and *The New Policeman*

1. Kate Thompson, *The New Policeman* (London: Bodley Head, 2005), p. 91. All subsequent quotations from this text will be noted in parentheses indicated by *NP*.

2. Helen Brennan, *The Story of Irish Dance* (Kerry: Brandon Press, 1999), *passim.*

3. Louise Fuller, *Irish Catholicism Since 1950: The Undoing of a Culture* (Dublin: Gill & Macmillan, 2004), *passim.*

4. John McGahern, lecture at University College Dublin, 7 February 1999.

5. Éamon de Valera, 'On Language and the Irish Nation', Radio Éireann, 17 March 1943.

6. See Declan Kiberd, *The Irish Writer and the World* (Cambridge: Cambridge University Press, 2005), pp. 79–89.

29. Conclusion: Going Global?

1. W. B. Yeats, *Collected Poems* (London: Macmillan, 1950), p. 240; and *Autobiographies* (London: Macmillan, 1955), p. 315.

2. Anthony Cronin, *Samuel Beckett: The Last Modernist* (London: Harper Collins, 1996), p. 543.

3. See 'The Celtic Tiger: A Cultural History', in Declan Kiberd, *The Irish Writer and the World* (Cambridge: Cambridge University Press, 1995), pp. 269–88.

4. Joseph O'Neill, review of *Flannery* by Brad Goode, *The Atlantic Monthly* (June 2009), p. 88.

5. For a brilliant analysis of the book in this light, see Stanley van der Ziel, 'It's a Long Way to Tipperary', *The Irish Review*, 45 (2012), pp. 60–76.

6. See Enrique Vila-Matas, *Dublinesque*, trans. Rosalind Harvey and Anne McLean (New York: New Directions, 2012).

7. Keith Ridgway, *The Parts* (London: Faber & Faber, 2003).

8. James Plunkett, *Strumpet City* (London: Hutchinson,1969).

9. Julia Kristeva, *Strangers to Ourselves*, trans. Leon S. Roudiez (New York: Columbia University Press, 1991), *passim*.

10. For a caustic and amusing analysis of this contrast see Zeljka Doljanin, 'The Theme of Displacement in John McGahern and Other Contemporary Irish Writers', unpublished PhD thesis, University College Dublin (2011).

11. W. B. Yeats, Letter to the Editor, the *Leader*, September 1900.

12. See William Vorm (ed.), *Paddy No More* (Dublin: Wolfhound Press, 1976); writers included Juanita Casey, John Montague but also Neil Jordan, Dermot Healy and Lucille Redmond.

13. This interpretation was first suggested to me by Harold Fish, who served for some years as Director of the British Council in Dublin.

14. Tom Nairn, *Faces of Nationalism* (London: Verso Books, 1996), pp. 59ff.

15. Tony Judt, *Postwar* (London: Heinemann, 2005), *passim*.

16. D. Vincent Twomey, *The End of Irish Catholicism?* (Dublin: Veritas Publishers, 2003), p. 142.

17. See the *Irish Times*, 2 April 2002, p. 12.

18. Cited by Mary Kenny, *Goodbye to Catholic Ireland* (Dublin: New Island Books, 2000), p. 176.

19. D. Vincent Twomey, *The End of Irish Catholicism?*, p. 176.

20. See Mary Kenny, *Goodbye to Catholic Ireland*, p. 177.

21. Cited by Mary Kenny, *Goodbye to Catholic Ireland*, p. 176.

22. Ibid.

23. The Abbey programme for 2016 was titled 'Waking the Nation' but provoked a counter-movement called 'Waking the Feminists', led by theatre

practitioners who objected to the fact that there was only one work by a woman projected for production in the year.

24. William K. Roche, Philip J. O'Connell, Andrea Prothero (eds), *Austerity and Recovery in Ireland: Europe's Poster Child and the Great Recession* (Oxford: Oxford University Press, 2016.)

25. Colin Coulter and Angela Nagle (eds), *Ireland Under Austerity* (Manchester: Manchester University Press 2015); Gene Kerrigan, *The Big Lie: Who Profits from Ireland's Austerity?* (Dublin: Transworld Ireland, 2012).

Index